2018 WORLD INDUSTRY & MARKET OUTLOOK

WORLD EDITION

The 2018 World Industry & Market Outlook
report is the leading annual publication that describes
over 120 major global industries. Published
each year in January the Outlook report provides the
most current and accurate estimates of the size of the
largest manufacutring, retail, wholesale and services
industries in the World

With over 250 pages, the
2018 World Industry & Market Outlook features:

- 2017 establishments, employment and sales totals for each industry
- 2018 forecast establishments, employment and sales totals
- 45 of the largest countries in the world
- Industry definitions and descriptions

The 2018 World Industry & Market Outlook report
is available for purchase in
either PDF, spreadsheet (Excel) or print format edition.

The 2018 World Industry & Market Outlook report is an
essential reference tool for industry researchers, market
analysts, CEOs and leading industry executives.

2018 WORLD INDUSTRY & MARKET OUTLOOK

TABLE OF CONTENTS

TABLE OF CONTENTS

INDUSTRY	PAGE NUMBER

TABLE OF CONTENTS

TABLE OF CONTENTS

Worldwide Current & Forecast Gross Domestic Product

Barnes Reports predicts that worldwide economic performance will increase by 3.1 percent from 2016 to 2017. Many European countries (Greece, Portugal, Spain, Italy) struggle with high unemployment and poor economic performance. Energy-producing countries were surprised with lower economic performance in 2016 (Qatar, Nigeria, Saudi Arabia, Iraq) when OPEC dramatically increased oil releases in an attempt to destroy the U.S. shale and fracking industries. Oil prices have recovered somewhat so these countries' economies are improving. Countries with low income per capita also have above average GDP (Bangladesh, China, India, Vietnam), benefitting from developing manufacturing industries and large exports to more developed countries.

The worldwide economic should continue to increase from 2017 to 2018 by 3.5 percent. There are risks on the horizon (high inflation, large government and private debt) but a boom/bust is not forecast.

Country	2012 GDP	2013 GDP	2014 GDP	2015 GDP	2014-2015 Pct. Change
Algeria	209.0	209.7	213.5	222.6	4.3%
Argentina	604.4	614.4	537.7	540.7	0.6%
Australia	1,537.5	1,564.0	1,454.7	1,498.5	3.0%
Austria	407.4	428.7	436.9	442.6	1.3%
Bangladesh	133.4	150.0	172.9	184.7	6.8%
Belgium	497.8	521.4	531.5	541.5	1.9%
Brazil	2,413.1	2,392.1	2,346.1	2,319.5	-1.1%
Canada	1,832.7	1,839.0	1,785.4	1,825.6	2.3%
Chile	265.2	276.7	258.1	264.7	2.6%
China	8,461.6	9,490.6	10,354.8	11,141.7	7.6%
Colombia	369.7	380.1	377.7	393.7	4.2%
Czech Republic	206.4	208.3	205.3	214.5	4.5%
Denmark	322.3	335.9	342.4	349.6	2.1%
Egypt	262.8	272.0	286.5	298.4	4.1%
Finland	256.7	269.2	272.2	272.7	0.2%
France	2,681.4	2,810.2	2,829.2	2,871.8	1.5%
Germany	3,539.6	3,745.3	3,868.3	3,958.7	2.3%
Greece	245.7	239.5	235.6	237.3	0.7%
Hong Kong	262.6	275.7	290.9	299.9	3.1%
Hungary	127.2	134.4	138.3	144.3	4.3%
India	1,831.8	1,861.8	2,048.5	2,217.7	8.3%
Indonesia	917.9	910.5	888.5	936.9	5.4%
Iran	587.2	511.6	425.3	434.4	2.1%
Iraq	218.0	232.5	223.5	230.8	3.3%
Ireland	224.7	238.3	250.8	294.6	17.4%
Israel	259.6	292.4	305.7	317.1	3.7%

WORLDWIDE CURRENT & FORECAST GROSS DOMESTIC PRODUCT

Country	2012 GDP	2013 GDP	2014 GDP	2015 GDP	2014-2015 Pct. Change
Italy	2,074.6	2,133.5	2,141.2	2,163.8	1.1%
Japan	5,954.5	4,919.6	4,601.5	4,660.2	1.3%
Kazakhstan	203.5	231.9	217.9	224.8	3.2%
Kuwait	174.1	174.2	163.6	165.3	1.0%
Malaysia	314.4	323.3	338.1	358.4	6.0%
Mexico	1,184.5	1,258.8	1,294.7	1,333.0	3.0%
Netherlands	828.9	864.2	879.3	899.9	2.3%
New Zealand	170.6	174.8	179.9	186.8	3.9%
Nigeria	461.0	515.0	568.5	596.8	5.0%
Norway	509.7	522.3	499.8	512.2	2.5%
Pakistan	224.6	231.1	243.6	256.3	5.2%
Peru	192.7	201.8	202.6	209.3	3.3%
Phillipines	250.1	271.9	284.8	303.6	6.6%
Poland	500.2	524.1	545.0	567.1	4.1%
Portugal	216.4	226.1	230.1	234.4	1.9%
Puerto Rico	101.1	103.1	102.0	102.0	0.0%
Qatar	190.3	201.9	210.1	219.1	4.3%
Romania	172.0	191.6	199.0	207.1	4.0%
Russia	2,016.1	2,079.0	1,860.6	1,850.5	-0.5%
Saudi Arabia	734.0	744.3	746.2	778.9	4.4%
Singapore	289.9	302.2	307.9	317.9	3.3%
South Africa	397.4	366.2	350.1	357.1	2.0%
South Korea	1,222.8	1,305.6	1,410.4	1,460.7	3.6%
Spain	1,339.9	1,369.3	1,381.3	1,421.5	2.9%
Sweden	543.9	578.7	571.1	594.3	4.1%
Switzerland	665.4	684.9	701.0	717.4	2.3%
Taiwan	508.3	519.5	530.8	545.0	2.7%
Thailand	397.5	420.2	404.8	414.7	2.4%
Turkey	788.9	823.2	798.4	847.3	6.1%
Ukraine	175.8	183.3	131.8	121.7	-7.7%
UAE	373.4	387.2	399.5	415.7	4.1%
United Kingdom	2,630.5	2,712.3	2,988.9	3,084.5	3.2%
United States	16,163.2	16,768.1	17,419.0	17,961.8	3.1%
Venezuela	391.8	404.6	414.3	414.5	0.1%
Vietnam	155.8	171.2	186.2	198.9	6.8%

SINGLE-FAMILY HOUSING CONSTRUCTION INDUSTRY (NAICS 236115)

NAICS 236115: Single-Family Housing Construction. This industry comprises establishments primarily responsible for the entire construction (i.e., new work, additions, alterations, and repairs) of single family residential housing units (e.g., single family detached houses, town houses, or row houses where each housing unit is separated by a ground-to-roof wall and where no housing units are constructed above or below). This industry includes establishments responsible for additions and alterations to mobile homes and on-site assembly of modular and prefabricated houses. Establishments identified as single family construction management firms are also included in this industry.

COUNTRY ESTIMATES

Country	Establishments		Employment		Sales ($B)		Local Sales (B)		Currency
	2018	2019	2018	2019	2018	2019	2018	2019	
Algeria	186	187	6,897	7,158	0.7	0.7	81.0	80.4	Dinar
Argentina	129	129	4,782	4,937	1.7	1.6	31.9	31.1	Pesos
Australia	80	81	2,976	3,097	4.2	4.2	5.3	5.3	Dollars
Austria	29	29	1,065	1,093	1.2	1.1	1.0	1.0	Euro
Bangladesh	565	565	20,971	21,664	0.7	0.7	56.7	58.8	Taka
Belgium	36	36	1,334	1,377	1.3	1.3	1.1	1.1	Euro
Brazil	688	693	25,539	26,575	5.1	4.9	16,469.7	15,809.5	Real
Canada	120	121	4,476	4,631	4.8	4.8	6.0	5.9	Dollars
Chile	67	67	2,476	2,574	0.8	0.8	503.8	501.6	Pesos*
China	4,755	4,739	176,642	181,667	42.6	43.7	276.5	283.3	RMB
Colombia	143	143	5,311	5,482	0.9	0.9	2.7	2.7	Pesos*
Czech Republic	34	34	1,273	1,306	0.6	0.6	13.2	13.4	Koruna
Denmark	18	18	670	687	0.9	0.9	5.5	5.5	Kroner
Egypt	304	312	11,300	11,941	1.0	1.0	18.4	18.3	Pounds
Finland	18	18	663	681	0.7	0.7	0.6	0.6	Euro
France	199	199	7,410	7,631	6.9	6.8	5.7	5.6	Euro
Germany	254	251	9,433	9,609	10.5	10.5	8.8	8.7	Euro
Greece	33	33	1,241	1,271	0.5	0.5	0.4	0.4	Euro
Hong Kong	20	20	761	782	0.8	0.8	6,125.1	6,127.5	Dollar
Hungary	30	30	1,119	1,140	0.4	0.4	96.8	97.9	Forint*
India	3,993	4,053	148,335	155,372	6.8	7.0	432.8	446.2	Rupees
Indonesia	993	1,006	36,886	38,550	3.4	3.5	45.4	46.4	Rupiah*

SINGLE-FAMILY HOUSING CONSTRUCTION INDUSTRY (NAICS 236115)

COUNTRY ESTIMATES

Country	Establishments		Employment		Sales ($B)		Local Sales (B)		
	2018	2019	2018	2019	2018	2019	2018	2019	Currency
Iran	272	275	10,102	10,548	1.2	1.2	43.9	42.7	Rial*
Iraq	143	145	5,298	5,551	0.6	0.6	0.8	0.7	Dinar*
Ireland	20	20	743	777	1.6	1.8	1.3	1.5	Euro
Israel	28	29	1,053	1,102	1.0	1.0	3.4	3.4	Shekel
Italy	201	200	7,464	7,666	5.5	5.4	4.6	4.5	Euro
Japan	423	419	15,709	16,044	13.1	12.8	1,473.6	1,448.7	Yen*
Kazakhstan	69	69	2,559	2,654	0.6	0.6	213.5	213.8	Tenge
Kuwait	16	17	598	644	0.4	0.4	0.1	0.1	Dinar
Malaysia	132	134	4,897	5,138	1.2	1.2	4.8	5.0	Ringgit
Mexico	429	434	15,953	16,652	3.5	3.5	68.0	67.9	New pesos
Netherlands	54	53	1,996	2,047	2.3	2.2	1.9	1.9	Euro
New Zealand	14	15	537	557	0.5	0.5	0.7	0.7	Dollar
Nigeria	741	753	27,518	28,870	1.8	1.8	646,289.5	645,939.5	Naira
Norway	20	20	737	763	1.3	1.3	10.9	10.8	Krone
Pakistan	594	606	22,050	23,226	0.8	0.8	88.1	90.0	Rupees
Peru	118	118	4,365	4,509	0.6	0.6	2.1	2.1	Nuevo Sol
Phillipines	320	326	11,885	12,477	1.0	1.0	48.5	50.1	Pesos
Poland	110	108	4,071	4,155	1.6	1.6	5.5	5.6	Zloty
Portugal	35	34	1,287	1,318	0.6	0.6	0.5	0.5	Euro
Puerto Rico	15	15	557	566	0.4	0.3	0.4	0.3	Dollar
Qatar	15	17	561	659	0.6	0.6	2.2	2.2	Riyal
Romania	79	78	2,931	2,976	0.6	0.6	2.5	2.5	New Leu
Russia	490	484	18,203	18,566	4.2	4.0	213.9	206.5	Rubles
Saudi Arabia	137	142	5,107	5,437	2.6	2.5	0.0	0.0	Rials*
Singapore	22	22	815	861	1.0	1.0	1,316.5	1,319.3	Dollar
South Africa	136	137	5,034	5,260	0.9	0.9	11,143.8	11,032.6	Rand
South Korea	192	191	7,116	7,313	4.9	4.9	5,245.0	5,271.6	Won*
Spain	159	160	5,907	6,129	3.8	3.7	3,143.1	3,078.7	Euro
Sweden	33	33	1,210	1,247	1.6	1.6	13,238.6	13,369.1	Krona
Switzerland	30	30	1,107	1,146	2.2	2.2	2,156.7	2,142.2	Swiss franc
Taiwan	119	123	4,435	4,728	1.7	1.7	49,555.0	49,382.3	Dollar
Thailand	289	290	10,719	11,116	1.4	1.4	45,611.0	45,343.7	Baht
Turkey	219	218	8,122	8,342	2.7	2.7	10,128.6	10,234.6	Euro
Ukraine	160	157	5,925	6,022	0.2	0.2	5,901.7	5,181.3	Hryvna
UAE	74	83	2,761	3,190	1.5	1.5	5,384.0	5,333.3	Dirham
United Kingdom	208	207	7,720	7,944	8.7	8.8	6,444.7	6,454.8	Pounds
United States	2,018	2,019	74,962	77,389	106.1	106.1	106,058.5	106,138.5	Dollars
Venezuela	103	104	3,823	4,005	1.4	1.4	14,431.4	13,740.0	Bolivar
Vietnam	362	362	13,452	13,888	0.8	0.8	17,223.6	17,851.7	Dong*

Note: Due to rounding, establishments will vary by + or - one establishment. Therefore, zero establishments may also be one establishment.

* Local Sales are in trillions

NAICS 23821: Electrical Contractors . This industry comprises
establishments primarily engaged in one or more of the following:
(1) performing electrical work at the site (e.g., installing wiring);
(2) servicing electrical equipment at the site; and (3) the combined
activity of selling and installing electrical equipment. The electrical
work performed includes new work, additions, alterations, and
maintenance and repairs.

COUNTRY ESTIMATES

Country	Establishments 2018	2019	Employment 2018	2019	Sales ($B) 2018	2019	Local Sales (B) 2018	2019	Currency
Algeria	371	373	31,081	33,838	1.8	1.8	205.6	207.4	Dinar
Argentina	257	258	21,548	23,338	4.2	4.2	80.9	80.3	Pesos
Australia	160	162	13,408	14,642	10.5	10.7	13.4	13.6	Dollars
Austria	57	57	4,797	5,168	3.0	3.0	2.5	2.5	Euro
Bangladesh	1,129	1,130	94,499	102,417	1.7	1.8	143.9	151.5	Taka
Belgium	72	72	6,013	6,511	3.4	3.4	2.8	2.8	Euro
Brazil	1,375	1,387	115,082	125,636	12.9	12.6	41,781.7	40,767.5	Real
Canada	241	242	20,169	21,893	12.3	12.4	15.2	15.3	Dollars
Chile	133	134	11,158	12,167	2.1	2.1	1,278.1	1,293.4	Pesos*
China	9,511	9,479	795,961	858,842	108.1	112.6	701.5	730.6	RMB
Colombia	286	286	23,933	25,915	2.3	2.4	6.7	6.9	Pesos*
Czech Republic	69	68	5,737	6,176	1.6	1.6	33.5	34.5	Koruna
Denmark	36	36	3,018	3,250	2.3	2.3	14.1	14.2	Kroner
Egypt	608	623	50,917	56,453	2.7	2.7	46.7	47.1	Pounds
Finland	36	36	2,989	3,221	1.7	1.7	1.4	1.4	Euro
France	399	398	33,389	36,075	17.4	17.4	14.5	14.6	Euro
Germany	508	501	42,504	45,428	26.8	27.0	22.3	22.6	Euro
Greece	67	66	5,592	6,010	1.4	1.3	1.1	1.1	Euro
Hong Kong	41	41	3,430	3,696	2.0	2.0	15,538.7	15,800.8	Dollar
Hungary	60	59	5,044	5,391	1.0	1.0	245.5	252.6	Forint*
India	7,986	8,107	668,410	734,534	17.3	18.1	1,098.0	1,150.6	Rupees
Indonesia	1,986	2,011	166,210	182,249	8.6	8.9	115.1	119.7	Rupiah*

ELECTRICAL CONTRACTORS INDUSTRY
NAICS 23821

COUNTRY ESTIMATES

Country	Establishments 2018	Establishments 2019	Employment 2018	Employment 2019	Sales ($B) 2018	Sales ($B) 2019	Local Sales (B) 2018	Local Sales (B) 2019	Currency
Iran	544	550	45,522	49,867	3.1	3.1	111.4	110.1	Rial*
Iraq	285	290	23,873	26,241	1.6	1.6	1.9	1.9	Dinar*
Ireland	40	41	3,350	3,672	4.0	4.5	3.3	3.8	Euro
Israel	57	57	4,747	5,209	2.5	2.6	8.7	8.9	Shekel
Italy	402	400	33,634	36,242	13.9	13.9	11.6	11.6	Euro
Japan	846	837	70,787	75,849	33.1	33.1	3,738.3	3,735.6	Yen*
Kazakhstan	138	138	11,533	12,545	1.6	1.7	541.6	551.4	Tenge
Kuwait	32	34	2,695	3,044	1.0	0.9	0.3	0.3	Dinar
Malaysia	264	268	22,066	24,292	3.1	3.2	12.2	12.8	Ringgit
Mexico	859	869	71,886	78,724	9.0	9.1	172.5	175.2	New pesos
Netherlands	107	107	8,992	9,679	5.7	5.8	4.8	4.8	Euro
New Zealand	29	29	2,418	2,633	1.3	1.3	1.8	1.8	Dollar
Nigeria	1,482	1,506	123,996	136,485	4.6	4.6	1,639,561.0	1,665,663.3	Naira
Norway	40	40	3,322	3,608	3.4	3.4	27.6	27.9	Krone
Pakistan	1,187	1,212	99,360	109,803	2.0	2.1	223.6	232.0	Rupees
Peru	235	235	19,668	21,318	1.6	1.7	5.2	5.3	Nuevo Sol
Phillipines	640	651	53,556	58,986	2.5	2.6	123.0	129.3	Pesos
Poland	219	217	18,346	19,644	4.0	4.1	14.0	14.4	Zloty
Portugal	69	69	5,801	6,229	1.5	1.5	1.3	1.2	Euro
Puerto Rico	30	30	2,510	2,674	0.9	0.9	0.9	0.9	Dollar
Qatar	30	34	2,527	3,116	1.5	1.5	5.6	5.6	Riyal
Romania	158	155	13,205	14,070	1.6	1.7	6.3	6.4	New Leu
Russia	980	969	82,025	87,771	10.6	10.4	542.6	532.5	Rubles
Saudi Arabia	275	284	23,011	25,704	6.5	6.6	0.0	0.0	Rials*
Singapore	44	45	3,673	4,071	2.5	2.6	3,339.9	3,401.9	Dollar
South Africa	271	274	22,685	24,866	2.3	2.3	28,270.6	28,449.4	Rand
South Korea	383	382	32,063	34,573	12.5	12.7	13,305.9	13,593.7	Won*
Spain	318	320	26,615	28,977	9.5	9.5	7,973.7	7,938.9	Euro
Sweden	65	65	5,454	5,896	4.1	4.2	33,584.9	34,474.6	Krona
Switzerland	60	60	4,990	5,416	5.6	5.7	5,471.4	5,524.1	Swiss franc
Taiwan	239	247	19,982	22,350	4.3	4.3	125,715.3	127,340.6	Dollar
Thailand	577	580	48,302	52,550	3.6	3.6	115,709.9	116,926.5	Baht
Turkey	437	435	36,601	39,437	6.9	7.0	25,695.2	26,391.7	Euro
Ukraine	319	314	26,699	28,469	0.5	0.5	14,972.0	13,360.8	Hryvna
UAE	149	166	12,443	15,083	3.7	3.7	13,658.6	13,752.7	Dirham
United Kingdom	416	414	34,788	37,554	22.2	22.6	16,349.4	16,644.7	Pounds
United States	2,018	2,019	168,892	182,932	134.5	136.8	134,529.1	136,848.0	Dollars
Venezuela	206	209	17,228	18,935	3.7	3.6	36,610.9	35,430.9	Bolivar
Vietnam	724	725	60,616	65,657	1.9	2.0	43,694.3	46,033.6	Dong*

Note: Due to rounding, establishments will vary by + or - one establishment. Therefore, zero establishments may also be one establishment.

* Local Sales are in trillions

NAICS 23822: Plumbing & Heating & A/C Contractors. This industry comprises establishments primarily engaged in one or more of the following: (1) installing plumbing, heating, and air-conditioning equipment; (2) servicing plumbing, heating, and air-conditioning equipment; and (3) the combined activity of selling and installing plumbing, heating, and air-conditioning equipment. The plumbing, heating, and air-conditioning work performed includes new work, additions, alterations, and maintenance and repairs.

COUNTRY ESTIMATES

Country	Establishments		Employment		Sales ($B)		Local Sales (B)		Currency
	2018	2019	2018	2019	2018	2019	2018	2019	
Algeria	371	373	38,599	41,870	2.1	2.1	241.7	246.0	Dinar
Argentina	257	258	26,760	28,877	5.0	5.0	95.2	95.3	Pesos
Australia	160	162	16,652	18,118	12.4	12.7	15.7	16.1	Dollars
Austria	57	57	5,958	6,395	3.5	3.5	2.9	2.9	Euro
Bangladesh	1,129	1,130	117,357	126,725	2.0	2.2	169.1	179.7	Taka
Belgium	72	72	7,468	8,056	4.0	4.0	3.3	3.4	Euro
Brazil	1,375	1,387	142,920	155,456	15.2	15.0	49,124.4	48,347.0	Real
Canada	241	242	25,048	27,089	14.4	14.7	17.9	18.2	Dollars
Chile	133	134	13,857	15,055	2.5	2.5	1,502.7	1,533.9	Pesos*
China	9,511	9,479	988,502	1,062,687	127.1	133.5	824.8	866.5	RMB
Colombia	286	286	29,723	32,065	2.7	2.8	7.9	8.2	Pesos*
Czech Republic	69	68	7,124	7,642	1.8	1.9	39.4	41.0	Koruna
Denmark	36	36	3,748	4,021	2.7	2.7	16.6	16.8	Kroner
Egypt	608	623	63,233	69,852	3.1	3.2	54.9	55.8	Pounds
Finland	36	36	3,712	3,986	2.0	2.0	1.7	1.7	Euro
France	399	398	41,465	44,637	20.5	20.7	17.1	17.3	Euro
Germany	508	501	52,786	56,211	31.5	32.0	26.3	26.7	Euro
Greece	67	66	6,945	7,436	1.6	1.6	1.3	1.3	Euro
Hong Kong	41	41	4,259	4,574	2.3	2.4	18,269.5	18,738.5	Dollar
Hungary	60	59	6,264	6,670	1.1	1.2	288.6	299.5	Forint*
India	7,986	8,107	830,096	908,875	20.3	21.5	1,290.9	1,364.5	Rupees
Indonesia	1,986	2,011	206,416	225,505	10.1	10.6	135.4	142.0	Rupiah*

PLUMBING & HEATING & A/C CONTRACTORS
NAICS 23822

COUNTRY ESTIMATES

Country	Establishments 2018	2019	Employment 2018	2019	Sales ($B) 2018	2019	Local Sales (B) 2018	2019	Currency
Iran	544	550	56,533	61,702	3.6	3.6	131.0	130.6	Rial*
Iraq	285	290	29,648	32,469	1.9	1.9	2.3	2.3	Dinar*
Ireland	40	41	4,160	4,544	4.7	5.4	3.9	4.5	Euro
Israel	57	57	5,895	6,446	3.0	3.1	10.2	10.5	Shekel
Italy	402	400	41,770	44,843	16.4	16.5	13.7	13.7	Euro
Japan	846	837	87,910	93,851	38.9	39.2	4,395.3	4,430.2	Yen*
Kazakhstan	138	138	14,323	15,522	1.9	2.0	636.8	653.9	Tenge
Kuwait	32	34	3,348	3,767	1.1	1.1	0.3	0.3	Dinar
Malaysia	264	268	27,403	30,057	3.6	3.8	14.4	15.1	Ringgit
Mexico	859	869	89,275	97,409	10.6	10.8	202.8	207.8	New pesos
Netherlands	107	107	11,167	11,976	6.7	6.9	5.6	5.7	Euro
New Zealand	29	29	3,003	3,259	1.5	1.6	2.1	2.2	Dollar
Nigeria	1,482	1,506	153,990	168,879	5.4	5.5	1,927,695.1	1,975,342.2	Naira
Norway	40	40	4,125	4,464	4.0	4.1	32.4	33.0	Krone
Pakistan	1,187	1,212	123,395	135,865	2.4	2.5	262.9	275.2	Rupees
Peru	235	235	24,426	26,378	1.9	2.0	6.2	6.3	Nuevo Sol
Phillipines	640	651	66,511	72,986	2.9	3.1	144.6	153.3	Pesos
Poland	219	217	22,784	24,307	4.7	4.9	16.5	17.1	Zloty
Portugal	69	69	7,204	7,708	1.8	1.8	1.5	1.5	Euro
Puerto Rico	30	30	3,117	3,309	1.1	1.0	1.1	1.0	Dollar
Qatar	30	34	3,138	3,855	1.8	1.8	6.5	6.7	Riyal
Romania	158	155	16,400	17,409	1.9	2.0	7.4	7.6	New Leu
Russia	980	969	101,866	108,604	12.5	12.4	637.9	631.5	Rubles
Saudi Arabia	275	284	28,577	31,805	7.7	7.8	0.0	0.0	Rials*
Singapore	44	45	4,561	5,038	3.0	3.0	3,926.9	4,034.4	Dollar
South Africa	271	274	28,172	30,768	2.7	2.7	33,238.8	33,738.7	Rand
South Korea	383	382	39,819	42,779	14.7	15.1	15,644.2	16,121.1	Won*
Spain	318	320	33,053	35,855	11.2	11.3	9,374.9	9,414.9	Euro
Sweden	65	65	6,774	7,295	4.8	5.0	39,487.1	40,884.1	Krona
Switzerland	60	60	6,197	6,701	6.6	6.7	6,432.9	6,551.1	Swiss franc
Taiwan	239	247	24,816	27,655	5.0	5.1	147,808.3	151,015.7	Dollar
Thailand	577	580	59,986	65,022	4.2	4.3	136,044.6	138,665.3	Baht
Turkey	437	435	45,454	48,797	8.1	8.3	30,210.8	31,298.5	Euro
Ukraine	319	314	33,158	35,226	0.6	0.6	17,603.2	15,844.8	Hryvna
UAE	149	166	15,453	18,663	4.4	4.4	16,059.0	16,309.6	Dirham
United Kingdom	416	414	43,203	46,468	26.1	26.8	19,222.6	19,739.2	Pounds
United States	2,018	2,019	209,747	226,351	158.2	162.3	158,171.0	162,290.7	Dollars
Venezuela	206	209	21,396	23,429	4.3	4.2	43,044.8	42,018.2	Bolivar
Vietnam	724	725	75,279	81,241	2.3	2.4	51,373.1	54,592.1	Dong*

Note: Due to rounding, establishments will vary by + or - one establishment. Therefore, zero establishments may also be one establishment.

* Local Sales are in trillions

CARPENTRY CONTRACTORS INDUSTRY
NAICS 23835

NAICS 23835: Carpentry Contractors. This industry comprises establishments primarily engaged in framing, carpentry, and finishing work. The carpentry work performed includes new work, additions, alterations, and maintenance and repairs. Activities performed by establishments in this industry range from the installation of doors and windows to paneling, steel framing work, and ship joinery.

COUNTRY ESTIMATES

Country	Establishments 2018	2019	Employment 2018	2019	Sales ($B) 2018	2019	Local Sales (B) 2018	2019	Currency
Algeria	371	373	5,684	6,207	1.1	1.1	129.4	131.5	Dinar
Argentina	257	258	3,940	4,281	2.7	2.7	51.0	50.9	Pesos
Australia	160	162	2,452	2,686	6.6	6.8	8.4	8.6	Dollars
Austria	57	57	877	948	1.9	1.9	1.6	1.6	Euro
Bangladesh	1,129	1,130	17,280	18,787	1.1	1.2	90.6	96.1	Taka
Belgium	72	72	1,100	1,194	2.1	2.2	1.8	1.8	Euro
Brazil	1,375	1,387	21,044	23,046	8.1	8.0	26,309.3	25,848.1	Real
Canada	241	242	3,688	4,016	7.7	7.8	9.6	9.7	Dollars
Chile	133	134	2,040	2,232	1.3	1.4	804.8	820.1	Pesos*
China	9,511	9,479	145,553	157,544	68.1	71.4	441.7	463.3	RMB
Colombia	286	286	4,377	4,754	1.5	1.5	4.2	4.4	Pesos*
Czech Republic	69	68	1,049	1,133	1.0	1.0	21.1	21.9	Koruna
Denmark	36	36	552	596	1.4	1.4	8.9	9.0	Kroner
Egypt	608	623	9,311	10,356	1.7	1.7	29.4	29.8	Pounds
Finland	36	36	547	591	1.1	1.1	0.9	0.9	Euro
France	399	398	6,106	6,618	11.0	11.1	9.2	9.2	Euro
Germany	508	501	7,772	8,333	16.8	17.1	14.1	14.3	Euro
Greece	67	66	1,023	1,102	0.9	0.8	0.7	0.7	Euro
Hong Kong	41	41	627	678	1.3	1.3	9,784.5	10,018.3	Dollar
Hungary	60	59	922	989	0.6	0.6	154.6	160.1	Forint*
India	7,986	8,107	122,228	134,741	10.9	11.5	691.4	729.5	Rupees
Indonesia	1,986	2,011	30,394	33,431	5.4	5.7	72.5	75.9	Rupiah*

CARPENTRY CONTRACTORS INDUSTRY
NAICS 23835

COUNTRY ESTIMATES

Country	Establishments 2018	2019	Employment 2018	2019	Sales ($B) 2018	2019	Local Sales (B) 2018	2019	Currency
Iran	544	550	8,324	9,147	1.9	1.9	70.2	69.8	Rial*
Iraq	285	290	4,366	4,814	1.0	1.0	1.2	1.2	Dinar*
Ireland	40	41	613	674	2.5	2.9	2.1	2.4	Euro
Israel	57	57	868	956	1.6	1.6	5.4	5.6	Shekel
Italy	402	400	6,151	6,648	8.8	8.8	7.3	7.3	Euro
Japan	846	837	12,944	13,913	20.9	21.0	2,354.0	2,368.5	Yen*
Kazakhstan	138	138	2,109	2,301	1.0	1.1	341.0	349.6	Tenge
Kuwait	32	34	493	558	0.6	0.6	0.2	0.2	Dinar
Malaysia	264	268	4,035	4,456	1.9	2.0	7.7	8.1	Ringgit
Mexico	859	869	13,145	14,441	5.7	5.8	108.6	111.1	New pesos
Netherlands	107	107	1,644	1,776	3.6	3.7	3.0	3.1	Euro
New Zealand	29	29	442	483	0.8	0.8	1.1	1.2	Dollar
Nigeria	1,482	1,506	22,674	25,036	2.9	2.9	1,032,407.8	1,056,092.1	Naira
Norway	40	40	607	662	2.1	2.2	17.4	17.7	Krone
Pakistan	1,187	1,212	18,169	20,142	1.3	1.3	140.8	147.1	Rupees
Peru	235	235	3,597	3,911	1.0	1.1	3.3	3.4	Nuevo Sol
Phillipines	640	651	9,793	10,820	1.5	1.6	77.4	82.0	Pesos
Poland	219	217	3,355	3,604	2.5	2.6	8.8	9.1	Zloty
Portugal	69	69	1,061	1,143	1.0	0.9	0.8	0.8	Euro
Puerto Rico	30	30	459	491	0.6	0.6	0.6	0.6	Dollar
Qatar	30	34	462	572	1.0	1.0	3.5	3.6	Riyal
Romania	158	155	2,415	2,581	1.0	1.1	4.0	4.1	New Leu
Russia	980	969	14,999	16,101	6.7	6.6	341.6	337.6	Rubles
Saudi Arabia	275	284	4,208	4,715	4.1	4.2	0.0	0.0	Rials*
Singapore	44	45	672	747	1.6	1.6	2,103.1	2,157.0	Dollar
South Africa	271	274	4,148	4,561	1.4	1.5	17,801.6	18,038.0	Rand
South Korea	383	382	5,863	6,342	7.9	8.1	8,378.5	8,618.9	Won*
Spain	318	320	4,867	5,316	6.0	6.0	5,020.9	5,033.6	Euro
Sweden	65	65	997	1,082	2.6	2.7	21,147.9	21,858.2	Krona
Switzerland	60	60	912	993	3.5	3.6	3,445.3	3,502.5	Swiss franc
Taiwan	239	247	3,654	4,100	2.7	2.7	79,161.1	80,738.7	Dollar
Thailand	577	580	8,833	9,640	2.3	2.3	72,860.8	74,135.7	Baht
Turkey	437	435	6,693	7,234	4.3	4.5	16,179.9	16,733.3	Euro
Ukraine	319	314	4,882	5,222	0.3	0.3	9,427.7	8,471.2	Hryvna
UAE	149	166	2,275	2,767	2.3	2.4	8,600.6	8,719.7	Dirham
United Kingdom	416	414	6,362	6,889	14.0	14.3	10,295.0	10,553.3	Pounds
United States	2,018	2,019	30,884	33,557	84.7	86.8	84,711.0	86,766.7	Dollars
Venezuela	206	209	3,150	3,473	2.3	2.3	23,053.3	22,464.5	Bolivar
Vietnam	724	725	11,084	12,044	1.2	1.3	27,513.7	29,187.0	Dong*

Note: Due to rounding, establishments will vary by + or - one establishment. Therefore, zero establishments may also be one establishment.

* Local Sales are in trillions

BREAKFAST CEREAL MANUFACTURING INDUSTRY
NAICS 31123

NAICS 31123: Breakfast Cereal Manufacturing. This industry comprises establishments primarily responsible for manufacturing cereal breakfast foods and related preparations, except breakfast bars. Establishments primarily engaged in manufacturing granola bars and other types of breakfast bars are classified in 2064.

COUNTRY ESTIMATES

Country	Establishments 2018	Establishments 2019	Employment 2018	Employment 2019	Sales ($B) 2018	Sales ($B) 2019	Local Sales (B) 2018	Local Sales (B) 2019	Currency
Algeria	371	373	2,244	2,415	0.0	0.0	0.1	0.1	Dinar
Argentina	257	258	1,556	1,665	0.0	0.0	0.1	0.1	Pesos
Australia	160	162	968	1,045	0.0	0.0	0.0	0.0	Dollars
Austria	57	57	346	369	0.0	0.0	0.0	0.0	Euro
Bangladesh	1,129	1,130	6,824	7,309	0.0	0.0	0.1	0.1	Taka
Belgium	72	72	434	465	0.0	0.0	0.0	0.0	Euro
Brazil	1,375	1,387	8,311	8,965	0.0	0.0	29.6	29.1	Real
Canada	241	242	1,457	1,562	0.0	0.0	0.0	0.0	Dollars
Chile	133	134	806	868	0.0	0.0	0.9	0.9	Pesos*
China	9,511	9,479	57,480	61,288	0.1	0.1	0.5	0.5	RMB
Colombia	286	286	1,728	1,849	0.0	0.0	0.0	0.0	Pesos*
Czech Republic	69	68	414	441	0.0	0.0	0.0	0.0	Koruna
Denmark	36	36	218	232	0.0	0.0	0.0	0.0	Kroner
Egypt	608	623	3,677	4,029	0.0	0.0	0.0	0.0	Pounds
Finland	36	36	216	230	0.0	0.0	0.0	0.0	Euro
France	399	398	2,411	2,574	0.0	0.0	0.0	0.0	Euro
Germany	508	501	3,069	3,242	0.0	0.0	0.0	0.0	Euro
Greece	67	66	404	429	0.0	0.0	0.0	0.0	Euro
Hong Kong	41	41	248	264	0.0	0.0	11.0	11.3	Dollar
Hungary	60	59	364	385	0.0	0.0	0.2	0.2	Forint*
India	7,986	8,107	48,269	52,417	0.0	0.0	0.8	0.8	Rupees
Indonesia	1,986	2,011	12,003	13,005	0.0	0.0	0.1	0.1	Rupiah*

BREAKFAST CEREAL MANUFACTURING INDUSTRY
NAICS 31123

COUNTRY ESTIMATES

Country	Establishments 2018	2019	Employment 2018	2019	Sales ($B) 2018	2019	Local Sales (B) 2018	2019	Currency
Iran	544	550	3,287	3,559	0.0	0.0	0.1	0.1	Rial*
Iraq	285	290	1,724	1,873	0.0	0.0	0.0	0.0	Dinar*
Ireland	40	41	242	262	0.0	0.0	0.0	0.0	Euro
Israel	57	57	343	372	0.0	0.0	0.0	0.0	Shekel
Italy	402	400	2,429	2,586	0.0	0.0	0.0	0.0	Euro
Japan	846	837	5,112	5,413	0.0	0.0	2.6	2.7	Yen*
Kazakhstan	138	138	833	895	0.0	0.0	0.4	0.4	Tenge
Kuwait	32	34	195	217	0.0	0.0	0.0	0.0	Dinar
Malaysia	264	268	1,593	1,733	0.0	0.0	0.0	0.0	Ringgit
Mexico	859	869	5,191	5,618	0.0	0.0	0.1	0.1	New pesos
Netherlands	107	107	649	691	0.0	0.0	0.0	0.0	Euro
New Zealand	29	29	175	188	0.0	0.0	0.0	0.0	Dollar
Nigeria	1,482	1,506	8,954	9,740	0.0	0.0	1,161.4	1,188.9	Naira
Norway	40	40	240	257	0.0	0.0	0.0	0.0	Krone
Pakistan	1,187	1,212	7,175	7,836	0.0	0.0	0.2	0.2	Rupees
Peru	235	235	1,420	1,521	0.0	0.0	0.0	0.0	Nuevo Sol
Phillipines	640	651	3,868	4,209	0.0	0.0	0.1	0.1	Pesos
Poland	219	217	1,325	1,402	0.0	0.0	0.0	0.0	Zloty
Portugal	69	69	419	445	0.0	0.0	0.0	0.0	Euro
Puerto Rico	30	30	181	191	0.0	0.0	0.0	0.0	Dollar
Qatar	30	34	182	222	0.0	0.0	0.0	0.0	Riyal
Romania	158	155	954	1,004	0.0	0.0	0.0	0.0	New Leu
Russia	980	969	5,923	6,263	0.0	0.0	0.4	0.4	Rubles
Saudi Arabia	275	284	1,662	1,834	0.0	0.0	0.0	0.0	Rials*
Singapore	44	45	265	291	0.0	0.0	2.4	2.4	Dollar
South Africa	271	274	1,638	1,774	0.0	0.0	20.0	20.3	Rand
South Korea	383	382	2,315	2,467	0.0	0.0	9.4	9.7	Won*
Spain	318	320	1,922	2,068	0.0	0.0	5.6	5.7	Euro
Sweden	65	65	394	421	0.0	0.0	23.8	24.6	Krona
Switzerland	60	60	360	386	0.0	0.0	3.9	3.9	Swiss franc
Taiwan	239	247	1,443	1,595	0.0	0.0	89.1	90.9	Dollar
Thailand	577	580	3,488	3,750	0.0	0.0	82.0	83.5	Baht
Turkey	437	435	2,643	2,814	0.0	0.0	18.2	18.8	Euro
Ukraine	319	314	1,928	2,032	0.0	0.0	10.6	9.5	Hryvna
UAE	149	166	899	1,076	0.0	0.0	9.7	9.8	Dirham
United Kingdom	416	414	2,512	2,680	0.0	0.0	11.6	11.9	Pounds
United States	2,018	2,019	12,196	13,054	0.1	0.1	95.3	97.7	Dollars
Venezuela	206	209	1,244	1,351	0.0	0.0	25.9	25.3	Bolivar
Vietnam	724	725	4,377	4,685	0.0	0.0	31.0	32.9	Dong*

Note: Due to rounding, establishments will vary by + or - one establishment. Therefore, zero establishments may also be one establishment.

* Local Sales are in trillions

NAICS 31141: Frozen Food Manufacturing. This industry comprises establishments primarily manufacturing frozen bakery products, except bread and bread-type rolls. Establishments primarily engaged in manufacturing frozen bread and bread-type rolls are classified in 2051.

COUNTRY ESTIMATES

Country	Establishments 2018	Establishments 2019	Employment 2018	Employment 2019	Sales ($B) 2018	Sales ($B) 2019	Local Sales (B) 2018	Local Sales (B) 2019	Currency
Algeria	371	373	6,111	6,428	0.0	0.0	2.2	2.2	Dinar
Argentina	257	258	4,237	4,433	0.0	0.0	0.9	0.9	Pesos
Australia	160	162	2,636	2,781	0.1	0.1	0.1	0.1	Dollars
Austria	57	57	943	982	0.0	0.0	0.0	0.0	Euro
Bangladesh	1,129	1,130	18,581	19,454	0.0	0.0	1.6	1.6	Taka
Belgium	72	72	1,182	1,237	0.0	0.0	0.0	0.0	Euro
Brazil	1,375	1,387	22,628	23,865	0.1	0.1	450.6	437.0	Real
Canada	241	242	3,966	4,159	0.1	0.1	0.2	0.2	Dollars
Chile	133	134	2,194	2,311	0.0	0.0	13.8	13.9	Pesos*
China	9,511	9,479	156,506	163,138	1.2	1.2	7.6	7.8	RMB
Colombia	286	286	4,706	4,922	0.0	0.0	0.1	0.1	Pesos*
Czech Republic	69	68	1,128	1,173	0.0	0.0	0.4	0.4	Koruna
Denmark	36	36	593	617	0.0	0.0	0.2	0.2	Kroner
Egypt	608	623	10,012	10,723	0.0	0.0	0.5	0.5	Pounds
Finland	36	36	588	612	0.0	0.0	0.0	0.0	Euro
France	399	398	6,565	6,852	0.2	0.2	0.2	0.2	Euro
Germany	508	501	8,357	8,629	0.3	0.3	0.2	0.2	Euro
Greece	67	66	1,100	1,142	0.0	0.0	0.0	0.0	Euro
Hong Kong	41	41	674	702	0.0	0.0	167.6	169.4	Dollar
Hungary	60	59	992	1,024	0.0	0.0	2.6	2.7	Forint*
India	7,986	8,107	131,426	139,525	0.2	0.2	11.8	12.3	Rupees
Indonesia	1,986	2,011	32,681	34,618	0.1	0.1	1.2	1.3	Rupiah*

FROZEN FOOD MANUFACTURING INDUSTRY
NAICS 31141

COUNTRY ESTIMATES

Country	Establishments 2018	Establishments 2019	Employment 2018	Employment 2019	Sales ($B) 2018	Sales ($B) 2019	Local Sales (B) 2018	Local Sales (B) 2019	Currency
Iran	544	550	8,951	9,472	0.0	0.0	1.2	1.2	Rial*
Iraq	285	290	4,694	4,984	0.0	0.0	0.0	0.0	Dinar*
Ireland	40	41	659	698	0.0	0.0	0.0	0.0	Euro
Israel	57	57	933	990	0.0	0.0	0.1	0.1	Shekel
Italy	402	400	6,613	6,884	0.2	0.1	0.1	0.1	Euro
Japan	846	837	13,919	14,407	0.4	0.4	40.3	40.0	Yen*
Kazakhstan	138	138	2,268	2,383	0.0	0.0	5.8	5.9	Tenge
Kuwait	32	34	530	578	0.0	0.0	0.0	0.0	Dinar
Malaysia	264	268	4,339	4,614	0.0	0.0	0.1	0.1	Ringgit
Mexico	859	869	14,135	14,954	0.1	0.1	1.9	1.9	New pesos
Netherlands	107	107	1,768	1,839	0.1	0.1	0.1	0.1	Euro
New Zealand	29	29	475	500	0.0	0.0	0.0	0.0	Dollar
Nigeria	1,482	1,506	24,381	25,925	0.0	0.0	17,680.4	17,854.2	Naira
Norway	40	40	653	685	0.0	0.0	0.3	0.3	Krone
Pakistan	1,187	1,212	19,537	20,857	0.0	0.0	2.4	2.5	Rupees
Peru	235	235	3,867	4,049	0.0	0.0	0.1	0.1	Nuevo Sol
Phillipines	640	651	10,530	11,204	0.0	0.0	1.3	1.4	Pesos
Poland	219	217	3,607	3,731	0.0	0.0	0.2	0.2	Zloty
Portugal	69	69	1,141	1,183	0.0	0.0	0.0	0.0	Euro
Puerto Rico	30	30	493	508	0.0	0.0	0.0	0.0	Dollar
Qatar	30	34	497	592	0.0	0.0	0.1	0.1	Riyal
Romania	158	155	2,597	2,673	0.0	0.0	0.1	0.1	New Leu
Russia	980	969	16,128	16,672	0.1	0.1	5.9	5.7	Rubles
Saudi Arabia	275	284	4,525	4,882	0.1	0.1	0.0	0.0	Rials*
Singapore	44	45	722	773	0.0	0.0	36.0	36.5	Dollar
South Africa	271	274	4,460	4,723	0.0	0.0	304.9	304.9	Rand
South Korea	383	382	6,304	6,567	0.1	0.1	143.5	145.7	Won*
Spain	318	320	5,233	5,504	0.1	0.1	86.0	85.1	Euro
Sweden	65	65	1,072	1,120	0.0	0.0	362.2	369.5	Krona
Switzerland	60	60	981	1,029	0.1	0.1	59.0	59.2	Swiss franc
Taiwan	239	247	3,929	4,245	0.0	0.0	1,355.7	1,365.0	Dollar
Thailand	577	580	9,497	9,982	0.0	0.0	1,247.8	1,253.3	Baht
Turkey	437	435	7,197	7,491	0.1	0.1	277.1	282.9	Euro
Ukraine	319	314	5,250	5,408	0.0	0.0	161.5	143.2	Hryvna
UAE	149	166	2,447	2,865	0.0	0.0	147.3	147.4	Dirham
United Kingdom	416	414	6,840	7,133	0.2	0.2	176.3	178.4	Pounds
United States	2,018	2,019	33,208	34,748	1.5	1.5	1,450.7	1,466.9	Dollars
Venezuela	206	209	3,387	3,597	0.0	0.0	394.8	379.8	Bolivar
Vietnam	724	725	11,919	12,472	0.0	0.0	471.2	493.4	Dong*

Note: Due to rounding, establishments will vary by + or - one establishment. Therefore, zero establishments may also be one establishment.

* Local Sales are in trillions

COOKIE CRACKER & PASTA MFG. INDUSTRY
NAICS 31182

NAICS 31182: Cookie Cracker & Pasta Mfg. This industry comprises establishments primarily manufacturing fresh cookies, crackers, pretzels, and similar `dry' bakery products. Establishments primarily engaged in producing other fresh bakery products are classified in 2051.

COUNTRY ESTIMATES

Country	Establishments 2018	2019	Employment 2018	2019	Sales ($B) 2018	2019	Local Sales (B) 2018	2019	Currency
Algeria	371	373	4,890	5,221	0.0	0.0	2.5	2.5	Dinar
Argentina	257	258	3,390	3,601	0.1	0.1	1.0	1.0	Pesos
Australia	160	162	2,109	2,259	0.1	0.1	0.2	0.2	Dollars
Austria	57	57	755	797	0.0	0.0	0.0	0.0	Euro
Bangladesh	1,129	1,130	14,867	15,804	0.0	0.0	1.7	1.8	Taka
Belgium	72	72	946	1,005	0.0	0.0	0.0	0.0	Euro
Brazil	1,375	1,387	18,106	19,386	0.2	0.2	507.4	493.9	Real
Canada	241	242	3,173	3,378	0.1	0.1	0.2	0.2	Dollars
Chile	133	134	1,755	1,877	0.0	0.0	15.5	15.7	Pesos*
China	9,511	9,479	125,227	132,525	1.3	1.4	8.5	8.9	RMB
Colombia	286	286	3,765	3,999	0.0	0.0	0.1	0.1	Pesos*
Czech Republic	69	68	903	953	0.0	0.0	0.4	0.4	Koruna
Denmark	36	36	475	501	0.0	0.0	0.2	0.2	Kroner
Egypt	608	623	8,011	8,711	0.0	0.0	0.6	0.6	Pounds
Finland	36	36	470	497	0.0	0.0	0.0	0.0	Euro
France	399	398	5,253	5,567	0.2	0.2	0.2	0.2	Euro
Germany	508	501	6,687	7,010	0.3	0.3	0.3	0.3	Euro
Greece	67	66	880	927	0.0	0.0	0.0	0.0	Euro
Hong Kong	41	41	540	570	0.0	0.0	188.7	191.4	Dollar
Hungary	60	59	794	832	0.0	0.0	3.0	3.1	Forint*
India	7,986	8,107	105,160	113,343	0.2	0.2	13.3	13.9	Rupees
Indonesia	1,986	2,011	26,150	28,122	0.1	0.1	1.4	1.5	Rupiah*

COOKIE CRACKER & PASTA MFG. INDUSTRY
NAICS 31182

COUNTRY ESTIMATES

Country	Establishments 2018	Establishments 2019	Employment 2018	Employment 2019	Sales ($B) 2018	Sales ($B) 2019	Local Sales (B) 2018	Local Sales (B) 2019	Currency
Iran	544	550	7,162	7,695	0.0	0.0	1.4	1.3	Rial*
Iraq	285	290	3,756	4,049	0.0	0.0	0.0	0.0	Dinar*
Ireland	40	41	527	567	0.0	0.1	0.0	0.0	Euro
Israel	57	57	747	804	0.0	0.0	0.1	0.1	Shekel
Italy	402	400	5,292	5,592	0.2	0.2	0.1	0.1	Euro
Japan	846	837	11,137	11,704	0.4	0.4	45.4	45.3	Yen*
Kazakhstan	138	138	1,814	1,936	0.0	0.0	6.6	6.7	Tenge
Kuwait	32	34	424	470	0.0	0.0	0.0	0.0	Dinar
Malaysia	264	268	3,472	3,748	0.0	0.0	0.1	0.2	Ringgit
Mexico	859	869	11,310	12,148	0.1	0.1	2.1	2.1	New pesos
Netherlands	107	107	1,415	1,494	0.1	0.1	0.1	0.1	Euro
New Zealand	29	29	380	406	0.0	0.0	0.0	0.0	Dollar
Nigeria	1,482	1,506	19,508	21,060	0.1	0.1	19,911.6	20,178.6	Naira
Norway	40	40	523	557	0.0	0.0	0.3	0.3	Krone
Pakistan	1,187	1,212	15,632	16,943	0.0	0.0	2.7	2.8	Rupees
Peru	235	235	3,094	3,290	0.0	0.0	0.1	0.1	Nuevo Sol
Phillipines	640	651	8,426	9,102	0.0	0.0	1.5	1.6	Pesos
Poland	219	217	2,886	3,031	0.0	0.1	0.2	0.2	Zloty
Portugal	69	69	913	961	0.0	0.0	0.0	0.0	Euro
Puerto Rico	30	30	395	413	0.0	0.0	0.0	0.0	Dollar
Qatar	30	34	398	481	0.0	0.0	0.1	0.1	Riyal
Romania	158	155	2,078	2,171	0.0	0.0	0.1	0.1	New Leu
Russia	980	969	12,905	13,544	0.1	0.1	6.6	6.5	Rubles
Saudi Arabia	275	284	3,620	3,966	0.1	0.1	0.0	0.0	Rials*
Singapore	44	45	578	628	0.0	0.0	40.6	41.2	Dollar
South Africa	271	274	3,569	3,837	0.0	0.0	343.3	344.7	Rand
South Korea	383	382	5,044	5,335	0.2	0.2	161.6	164.7	Won*
Spain	318	320	4,187	4,471	0.1	0.1	96.8	96.2	Euro
Sweden	65	65	858	910	0.0	0.1	407.9	417.6	Krona
Switzerland	60	60	785	836	0.1	0.1	66.4	66.9	Swiss franc
Taiwan	239	247	3,144	3,449	0.1	0.1	1,526.7	1,542.7	Dollar
Thailand	577	580	7,599	8,109	0.0	0.0	1,405.2	1,416.5	Baht
Turkey	437	435	5,758	6,085	0.1	0.1	312.1	319.7	Euro
Ukraine	319	314	4,201	4,393	0.0	0.0	181.8	161.9	Hryvna
UAE	149	166	1,958	2,327	0.0	0.0	165.9	166.6	Dirham
United Kingdom	416	414	5,473	5,795	0.3	0.3	198.6	201.6	Pounds
United States	2,018	2,019	26,572	28,228	1.6	1.7	1,633.8	1,657.8	Dollars
Venezuela	206	209	2,710	2,922	0.0	0.0	444.6	429.2	Bolivar
Vietnam	724	725	9,537	10,131	0.0	0.0	530.6	557.7	Dong*

Note: Due to rounding, establishments will vary by + or - one establishment. Therefore, zero establishments may also be one establishment.

* Local Sales are in trillions

SNACK FOOD MANUFACTURING INDUSTRY
NAICS 31191

NAICS 31191: Snack Food Manufacturing. This industry comprises establishments primarily responsible for manufacturing potato chips, corn chips, and similar snacks. Pretzels and crackers are classified in 2052; candy covered popcorn is classified in 2064; salted, roasted, cooked or canned nuts and seeds are classified in 2068; and packaged unpopped popcorn is classified in 2099.

COUNTRY ESTIMATES

Country	Establishments 2018	Establishments 2019	Employment 2018	Employment 2019	Sales ($B) 2018	Sales ($B) 2019	Local Sales (B) 2018	Local Sales (B) 2019	Currency
Algeria	371	373	7,528	8,074	0.1	0.1	10.4	10.5	Dinar
Argentina	257	258	5,219	5,569	0.2	0.2	4.1	4.1	Pesos
Australia	160	162	3,247	3,494	0.5	0.5	0.7	0.7	Dollars
Austria	57	57	1,162	1,233	0.1	0.1	0.1	0.1	Euro
Bangladesh	1,129	1,130	22,888	24,439	0.1	0.1	7.3	7.7	Taka
Belgium	72	72	1,456	1,554	0.2	0.2	0.1	0.1	Euro
Brazil	1,375	1,387	27,873	29,979	0.7	0.6	2,112.9	2,065.8	Real
Canada	241	242	4,885	5,224	0.6	0.6	0.8	0.8	Dollars
Chile	133	134	2,702	2,903	0.1	0.1	64.6	65.5	Pesos*
China	9,511	9,479	192,782	204,936	5.5	5.7	35.5	37.0	RMB
Colombia	286	286	5,797	6,184	0.1	0.1	0.3	0.4	Pesos*
Czech Republic	69	68	1,389	1,474	0.1	0.1	1.7	1.8	Koruna
Denmark	36	36	731	775	0.1	0.1	0.7	0.7	Kroner
Egypt	608	623	12,332	13,471	0.1	0.1	2.4	2.4	Pounds
Finland	36	36	724	769	0.1	0.1	0.1	0.1	Euro
France	399	398	8,087	8,608	0.9	0.9	0.7	0.7	Euro
Germany	508	501	10,294	10,840	1.4	1.4	1.1	1.1	Euro
Greece	67	66	1,354	1,434	0.1	0.1	0.1	0.1	Euro
Hong Kong	41	41	831	882	0.1	0.1	785.8	800.7	Dollar
Hungary	60	59	1,222	1,286	0.0	0.0	12.4	12.8	Forint*
India	7,986	8,107	161,889	175,274	0.9	0.9	55.5	58.3	Rupees
Indonesia	1,986	2,011	40,256	43,488	0.4	0.5	5.8	6.1	Rupiah*

COUNTRY ESTIMATES

Country	Establishments 2018	2019	Employment 2018	2019	Sales ($B) 2018	2019	Local Sales (B) 2018	2019	Currency
Iran	544	550	11,025	11,899	0.2	0.2	5.6	5.6	Rial*
Iraq	285	290	5,782	6,262	0.1	0.1	0.1	0.1	Dinar*
Ireland	40	41	811	876	0.2	0.2	0.2	0.2	Euro
Israel	57	57	1,150	1,243	0.1	0.1	0.4	0.4	Shekel
Italy	402	400	8,146	8,648	0.7	0.7	0.6	0.6	Euro
Japan	846	837	17,145	18,099	1.7	1.7	189.0	189.3	Yen*
Kazakhstan	138	138	2,793	2,993	0.1	0.1	27.4	27.9	Tenge
Kuwait	32	34	653	726	0.0	0.0	0.0	0.0	Dinar
Malaysia	264	268	5,344	5,796	0.2	0.2	0.6	0.6	Ringgit
Mexico	859	869	17,411	18,785	0.5	0.5	8.7	8.9	New pesos
Netherlands	107	107	2,178	2,310	0.3	0.3	0.2	0.2	Euro
New Zealand	29	29	586	628	0.1	0.1	0.1	0.1	Dollar
Nigeria	1,482	1,506	30,032	32,568	0.2	0.2	82,912.0	84,401.7	Naira
Norway	40	40	805	861	0.2	0.2	1.4	1.4	Krone
Pakistan	1,187	1,212	24,065	26,201	0.1	0.1	11.3	11.8	Rupees
Peru	235	235	4,764	5,087	0.1	0.1	0.3	0.3	Nuevo Sol
Phillipines	640	651	12,971	14,075	0.1	0.1	6.2	6.6	Pesos
Poland	219	217	4,444	4,688	0.2	0.2	0.7	0.7	Zloty
Portugal	69	69	1,405	1,486	0.1	0.1	0.1	0.1	Euro
Puerto Rico	30	30	608	638	0.0	0.0	0.0	0.0	Dollar
Qatar	30	34	612	743	0.1	0.1	0.3	0.3	Riyal
Romania	158	155	3,198	3,357	0.1	0.1	0.3	0.3	New Leu
Russia	980	969	19,866	20,944	0.5	0.5	27.4	27.0	Rubles
Saudi Arabia	275	284	5,573	6,133	0.3	0.3	0.0	0.0	Rials*
Singapore	44	45	890	972	0.1	0.1	168.9	172.4	Dollar
South Africa	271	274	5,494	5,933	0.1	0.1	1,429.6	1,441.6	Rand
South Korea	383	382	7,766	8,250	0.6	0.6	672.9	688.8	Won*
Spain	318	320	6,446	6,915	0.5	0.5	403.2	402.3	Euro
Sweden	65	65	1,321	1,407	0.2	0.2	1,698.4	1,746.9	Krona
Switzerland	60	60	1,209	1,292	0.3	0.3	276.7	279.9	Swiss franc
Taiwan	239	247	4,840	5,333	0.2	0.2	6,357.4	6,452.5	Dollar
Thailand	577	580	11,699	12,539	0.2	0.2	5,851.4	5,924.8	Baht
Turkey	437	435	8,865	9,410	0.3	0.4	1,299.4	1,337.3	Euro
Ukraine	319	314	6,467	6,793	0.0	0.0	757.1	677.0	Hryvna
UAE	149	166	3,014	3,599	0.2	0.2	690.7	696.9	Dirham
United Kingdom	416	414	8,426	8,961	1.1	1.1	826.8	843.4	Pounds
United States	2,018	2,019	40,906	43,651	6.8	6.9	6,803.1	6,934.3	Dollars
Venezuela	206	209	4,173	4,518	0.2	0.2	1,851.4	1,795.3	Bolivar
Vietnam	724	725	14,681	15,667	0.1	0.1	2,209.6	2,332.6	Dong*

Note: Due to rounding, establishments will vary by + or - one establishment. Therefore, zero establishments may also be one establishment.

* Local Sales are in trillions

NAICS 312111: Soft Drink Manufacturing
This U.S. industry comprises establishments primarily engaged in establishments primarily engaged in manufacturing soft drinks and carbonated waters. Fruit and vegetable juices are classified in 2032-2038; fruit syrups for flavoring are classified in 2087; and nonalcoholic cider is classified in 2099. Bottling natural spring waters is classified in 5149.

COUNTRY ESTIMATES

Country	Establishments		Employment		Sales ($B)		Local Sales (B)		Currency
	2018	2019	2018	2019	2018	2019	2018	2019	
Algeria	371	373	7,248	7,520	0.0	0.0	0.8	0.8	Dinar
Argentina	257	258	5,025	5,186	0.0	0.0	0.3	0.3	Pesos
Australia	160	162	3,127	3,254	0.0	0.0	0.1	0.1	Dollars
Austria	57	57	1,119	1,149	0.0	0.0	0.0	0.0	Euro
Bangladesh	1,129	1,130	22,036	22,760	0.0	0.0	0.6	0.6	Taka
Belgium	72	72	1,402	1,447	0.0	0.0	0.0	0.0	Euro
Brazil	1,375	1,387	26,836	27,919	0.1	0.0	164.5	151.4	Real
Canada	241	242	4,703	4,865	0.0	0.0	0.1	0.1	Dollars
Chile	133	134	2,602	2,704	0.0	0.0	5.0	4.8	Pesos*
China	9,511	9,479	185,611	190,856	0.4	0.4	2.8	2.7	RMB
Colombia	286	286	5,581	5,759	0.0	0.0	0.0	0.0	Pesos*
Czech Republic	69	68	1,338	1,372	0.0	0.0	0.1	0.1	Koruna
Denmark	36	36	704	722	0.0	0.0	0.1	0.1	Kroner
Egypt	608	623	11,873	12,545	0.0	0.0	0.2	0.2	Pounds
Finland	36	36	697	716	0.0	0.0	0.0	0.0	Euro
France	399	398	7,786	8,017	0.1	0.1	0.1	0.1	Euro
Germany	508	501	9,912	10,095	0.1	0.1	0.1	0.1	Euro
Greece	67	66	1,304	1,336	0.0	0.0	0.0	0.0	Euro
Hong Kong	41	41	800	821	0.0	0.0	61.2	58.7	Dollar
Hungary	60	59	1,176	1,198	0.0	0.0	1.0	0.9	Forint*
India	7,986	8,107	155,867	163,232	0.1	0.1	4.3	4.3	Rupees
Indonesia	1,986	2,011	38,759	40,500	0.0	0.0	0.5	0.4	Rupiah*

Soft Drink Mfg.
(NAICS 312111)

Country Estimates

Country	Establishments 2018	Establishments 2019	Employment 2018	Employment 2019	Sales ($B) 2018	Sales ($B) 2019	Local Sales (B) 2018	Local Sales (B) 2019	Currency
Iran	544	550	10,615	11,082	0.0	0.0	0.4	0.4	Rial*
Iraq	285	290	5,567	5,831	0.0	0.0	0.0	0.0	Dinar*
Ireland	40	41	781	816	0.0	0.0	0.0	0.0	Euro
Israel	57	57	1,107	1,158	0.0	0.0	0.0	0.0	Shekel
Italy	402	400	7,843	8,054	0.1	0.1	0.0	0.0	Euro
Japan	846	837	16,507	16,855	0.1	0.1	14.7	13.9	Yen*
Kazakhstan	138	138	2,689	2,788	0.0	0.0	2.1	2.0	Tenge
Kuwait	32	34	629	676	0.0	0.0	0.0	0.0	Dinar
Malaysia	264	268	5,145	5,398	0.0	0.0	0.0	0.0	Ringgit
Mexico	859	869	16,763	17,494	0.0	0.0	0.7	0.7	New pesos
Netherlands	107	107	2,097	2,151	0.0	0.0	0.0	0.0	Euro
New Zealand	29	29	564	585	0.0	0.0	0.0	0.0	Dollar
Nigeria	1,482	1,506	28,915	30,330	0.0	0.0	6,455.0	6,187.3	Naira
Norway	40	40	775	802	0.0	0.0	0.1	0.1	Krone
Pakistan	1,187	1,212	23,170	24,401	0.0	0.0	0.9	0.9	Rupees
Peru	235	235	4,586	4,737	0.0	0.0	0.0	0.0	Nuevo Sol
Phillipines	640	651	12,489	13,108	0.0	0.0	0.5	0.5	Pesos
Poland	219	217	4,278	4,365	0.0	0.0	0.1	0.1	Zloty
Portugal	69	69	1,353	1,384	0.0	0.0	0.0	0.0	Euro
Puerto Rico	30	30	585	594	0.0	0.0	0.0	0.0	Dollar
Qatar	30	34	589	692	0.0	0.0	0.0	0.0	Riyal
Romania	158	155	3,079	3,127	0.0	0.0	0.0	0.0	New Leu
Russia	980	969	19,127	19,505	0.0	0.0	2.1	2.0	Rubles
Saudi Arabia	275	284	5,366	5,712	0.0	0.0	0.0	0.0	Rials*
Singapore	44	45	857	905	0.0	0.0	13.1	12.6	Dollar
South Africa	271	274	5,290	5,526	0.0	0.0	111.3	105.7	Rand
South Korea	383	382	7,477	7,683	0.0	0.0	52.4	50.5	Won*
Spain	318	320	6,206	6,439	0.0	0.0	31.4	29.5	Euro
Sweden	65	65	1,272	1,310	0.0	0.0	132.2	128.1	Krona
Switzerland	60	60	1,164	1,204	0.0	0.0	21.5	20.5	Swiss franc
Taiwan	239	247	4,660	4,967	0.0	0.0	494.9	473.0	Dollar
Thailand	577	580	11,263	11,678	0.0	0.0	455.6	434.3	Baht
Turkey	437	435	8,535	8,764	0.0	0.0	101.2	98.0	Euro
Ukraine	319	314	6,226	6,326	0.0	0.0	58.9	49.6	Hryvna
UAE	149	166	2,902	3,352	0.0	0.0	53.8	51.1	Dirham
United Kingdom	416	414	8,112	8,345	0.1	0.1	64.4	61.8	Pounds
United States	2,018	2,019	39,384	40,652	0.5	0.5	529.6	508.3	Dollars
Venezuela	206	209	4,017	4,208	0.0	0.0	144.1	131.6	Bolivar
Vietnam	724	725	14,135	14,591	0.0	0.0	172.0	171.0	Dong*

Note: Due to rounding, establishments will vary by + or - one establishment. Therefore, zero establishments may also be one establishment.

* Local Sales are in trillions

BREWERIES & BEER-MAKING INDUSTRY
NAICS 31212

NAICS 31212: Breweries. This industry comprises establishments primarily engaged in brewing beer, ale, malt liquors, and nonalcoholic beer.

COUNTRY ESTIMATES

Country	Establishments 2018	Establishments 2019	Employment 2018	Employment 2019	Sales ($B) 2018	Sales ($B) 2019	Local Sales (B) 2018	Local Sales (B) 2019	Currency
Algeria	-	-	-	-	-	-	0.0	0.0	Dinar
Argentina	257	258	4,765	5,137	0.1	0.1	2.0	2.0	Pesos
Australia	160	162	2,965	3,223	0.3	0.3	0.3	0.3	Dollars
Austria	57	57	1,061	1,138	0.1	0.1	0.1	0.1	Euro
Bangladesh	1,129	1,130	20,899	22,543	0.0	0.0	3.5	3.8	Taka
Belgium	72	72	1,330	1,433	0.1	0.1	0.1	0.1	Euro
Brazil	1,375	1,387	25,451	27,654	0.3	0.3	1,015.5	1,025.2	Real
Canada	241	242	4,461	4,819	0.3	0.3	0.4	0.4	Dollars
Chile	133	134	2,468	2,678	0.1	0.1	31.1	32.5	Pesos*
China	9,511	9,479	176,032	189,040	2.6	2.8	17.1	18.4	RMB
Colombia	286	286	5,293	5,704	0.1	0.1	0.2	0.2	Pesos*
Czech Republic	69	68	1,269	1,359	0.0	0.0	0.8	0.9	Koruna
Denmark	36	36	667	715	0.1	0.1	0.3	0.4	Kroner
Egypt	-	-	-	-	-	-	0.0	0.0	Pounds
Finland	36	36	661	709	0.0	0.0	0.0	0.0	Euro
France	399	398	7,384	7,940	0.4	0.4	0.4	0.4	Euro
Germany	508	501	9,400	9,999	0.7	0.7	0.5	0.6	Euro
Greece	67	66	1,237	1,323	0.0	0.0	0.0	0.0	Euro
Hong Kong	41	41	758	814	0.0	0.1	377.7	397.4	Dollar
Hungary	60	59	1,115	1,187	0.0	0.0	6.0	6.4	Forint*
India	7,986	8,107	147,823	161,679	0.4	0.5	26.7	28.9	Rupees
Indonesia	-	-	-	-	-	-	0.0	0.0	Rupiah*

BREWERIES & BEER-MAKING INDUSTRY
NAICS 31212

COUNTRY ESTIMATES

Country	Establishments 2018	Establishments 2019	Employment 2018	Employment 2019	Sales ($B) 2018	Sales ($B) 2019	Local Sales (B) 2018	Local Sales (B) 2019	Currency
Iran	-	-	-	-	-	-	0.0	0.0	Rial*
Iraq	-	-	-	-	-	-	0.0	0.0	Dinar*
Ireland	40	41	741	808	0.1	0.1	0.1	0.1	Euro
Israel	57	57	1,050	1,147	0.1	0.1	0.2	0.2	Shekel
Italy	402	400	7,438	7,977	0.3	0.3	0.3	0.3	Euro
Japan	846	837	15,655	16,695	0.8	0.8	90.9	93.9	Yen*
Kazakhstan	138	138	2,551	2,761	0.0	0.0	13.2	13.9	Tenge
Kuwait	-	-	-	-	-	-	0.0	0.0	Dinar
Malaysia	-	-	-	-	-	-	0.0	0.0	Ringgit
Mexico	859	869	15,898	17,328	0.2	0.2	4.2	4.4	New pesos
Netherlands	107	107	1,989	2,130	0.1	0.1	0.1	0.1	Euro
New Zealand	29	29	535	580	0.0	0.0	0.0	0.0	Dollar
Nigeria	1,482	1,506	27,423	30,042	0.1	0.1	39,848.6	41,887.5	Naira
Norway	40	40	735	794	0.1	0.1	0.7	0.7	Krone
Pakistan	-	-	-	-	-	-	0.0	0.0	Rupees
Peru	235	235	4,350	4,692	0.0	0.0	0.1	0.1	Nuevo Sol
Phillipines	640	651	11,844	12,983	0.1	0.1	3.0	3.3	Pesos
Poland	219	217	4,057	4,324	0.1	0.1	0.3	0.4	Zloty
Portugal	69	69	1,283	1,371	0.0	0.0	0.0	0.0	Euro
Puerto Rico	30	30	555	589	0.0	0.0	0.0	0.0	Dollar
Qatar	-	-	-	-	-	-	0.0	0.0	Riyal
Romania	158	155	2,920	3,097	0.0	0.0	0.2	0.2	New Leu
Russia	980	969	18,140	19,319	0.3	0.3	13.2	13.4	Rubles
Saudi Arabia	-	-	-	-	-	-	0.0	0.0	Rials*
Singapore	44	45	812	896	0.1	0.1	81.2	85.6	Dollar
South Africa	271	274	5,017	5,473	0.1	0.1	687.1	715.4	Rand
South Korea	383	382	7,091	7,610	0.3	0.3	323.4	341.8	Won*
Spain	318	320	5,886	6,378	0.2	0.2	193.8	199.6	Euro
Sweden	65	65	1,206	1,298	0.1	0.1	816.3	867.0	Krona
Switzerland	60	60	1,104	1,192	0.1	0.1	133.0	138.9	Swiss franc
Taiwan	239	247	4,419	4,919	0.1	0.1	3,055.4	3,202.3	Dollar
Thailand	577	580	10,682	11,567	0.1	0.1	2,812.3	2,940.4	Baht
Turkey	-	-	-	-	-	-	0.0	0.0	Euro
Ukraine	319	314	5,905	6,266	0.0	0.0	363.9	336.0	Hryvna
UAE	-	-	-	-	-	-	0.0	0.0	Dirham
United Kingdom	416	414	7,694	8,266	0.5	0.6	397.4	418.6	Pounds
United States	2,018	2,019	37,352	40,265	3.3	3.4	3,269.7	3,441.4	Dollars
Venezuela	206	209	3,810	4,168	0.1	0.1	889.8	891.0	Bolivar
Vietnam	724	725	13,406	14,452	0.0	0.1	1,062.0	1,157.6	Dong*

Note: Due to rounding, establishments will vary by + or - one establishment. Therefore, zero establishments may also be one establishment.

* Local Sales are in trillions

WINERIES & WINE-MAKING INDUSTRY
NAICS 31213

NAICS 31213: Wineries. This industry comprises establishments primarily engaged in one or more of the following: (1) growing grapes and manufacturing wine and brandies; (2) manufacturing wine and brandies from grapes and other fruits grown elsewhere; and (3) blending wines and brandies.

COUNTRY ESTIMATES

Country	Establishments 2018	2019	Employment 2018	2019	Sales ($B) 2018	2019	Local Sales (B) 2018	2019	Currency
Algeria	371	373	2,701	2,781	0.1	0.1	7.0	7.1	Dinar
Argentina	257	258	1,872	1,918	0.1	0.1	2.8	2.7	Pesos
Australia	160	162	1,165	1,204	0.4	0.4	0.5	0.5	Dollars
Austria	57	57	417	425	0.1	0.1	0.1	0.1	Euro
Bangladesh	1,129	1,130	8,211	8,418	0.1	0.1	4.9	5.2	Taka
Belgium	72	72	522	535	0.1	0.1	0.1	0.1	Euro
Brazil	1,375	1,387	10,000	10,327	0.4	0.4	1,422.5	1,391.5	Real
Canada	241	242	1,753	1,800	0.4	0.4	0.5	0.5	Dollars
Chile	133	134	970	1,000	0.1	0.1	43.5	44.1	Pesos*
China	9,511	9,479	69,161	70,595	3.7	3.8	23.9	24.9	RMB
Colombia	286	286	2,080	2,130	0.1	0.1	0.2	0.2	Pesos*
Czech Republic	69	68	498	508	0.1	0.1	1.1	1.2	Koruna
Denmark	36	36	262	267	0.1	0.1	0.5	0.5	Kroner
Egypt	608	623	4,424	4,640	0.1	0.1	1.6	1.6	Pounds
Finland	36	36	260	265	0.1	0.1	0.0	0.0	Euro
France	399	398	2,901	2,965	0.6	0.6	0.5	0.5	Euro
Germany	508	501	3,693	3,734	0.9	0.9	0.8	0.8	Euro
Greece	67	66	486	494	0.0	0.0	0.0	0.0	Euro
Hong Kong	41	41	298	304	0.1	0.1	529.0	539.3	Dollar
Hungary	60	59	438	443	0.0	0.0	8.4	8.6	Forint*
India	7,986	8,107	58,078	60,377	0.6	0.6	37.4	39.3	Rupees
Indonesia	1,986	2,011	14,442	14,981	0.3	0.3	3.9	4.1	Rupiah*

WINERIES & WINE-MAKING INDUSTRY
NAICS 31213

COUNTRY ESTIMATES

Country	Establishments 2018	Establishments 2019	Employment 2018	Employment 2019	Sales ($B) 2018	Sales ($B) 2019	Local Sales (B) 2018	Local Sales (B) 2019	Currency
Iran	-	-	-	-	-	-	0.0	0.0	Rial*
Iraq	-	-	-	-	-	-	0.0	0.0	Dinar*
Ireland	20	20	146	151	0.1	0.1	0.1	0.1	Euro
Israel	57	57	412	428	0.1	0.1	0.3	0.3	Shekel
Italy	402	400	2,923	2,979	0.5	0.5	0.4	0.4	Euro
Japan	846	837	6,151	6,235	1.1	1.1	127.3	127.5	Yen*
Kazakhstan	138	138	1,002	1,031	0.1	0.1	18.4	18.8	Tenge
Kuwait	-	-	-	-	-	-	0.0	0.0	Dinar
Malaysia	-	-	-	-	-	-	0.0	0.0	Ringgit
Mexico	859	869	6,246	6,471	0.3	0.3	5.9	6.0	New pesos
Netherlands	54	53	391	398	0.1	0.1	0.1	0.1	Euro
New Zealand	29	29	210	216	0.0	0.0	0.1	0.1	Dollar
Nigeria	1,482	1,506	10,774	11,219	0.2	0.2	55,822.2	56,852.1	Naira
Norway	40	40	289	297	0.1	0.1	0.9	1.0	Krone
Pakistan	-	-	-	-	-	-	0.0	0.0	Rupees
Peru	235	235	1,709	1,752	0.1	0.1	0.2	0.2	Nuevo Sol
Phillipines	640	651	4,654	4,849	0.1	0.1	4.2	4.4	Pesos
Poland	219	217	1,594	1,615	0.1	0.1	0.5	0.5	Zloty
Portugal	69	69	504	512	0.1	0.1	0.0	0.0	Euro
Puerto Rico	30	30	218	220	0.0	0.0	0.0	0.0	Dollar
Qatar	-	-	-	-	-	-	0.0	0.0	Riyal
Romania	158	155	1,147	1,157	0.1	0.1	0.2	0.2	New Leu
Russia	980	969	7,127	7,215	0.4	0.4	18.5	18.2	Rubles
Saudi Arabia	-	-	-	-	-	-	0.0	0.0	Rials*
Singapore	44	45	319	335	0.1	0.1	113.7	116.1	Dollar
South Africa	271	274	1,971	2,044	0.1	0.1	962.5	971.0	Rand
South Korea	383	382	2,786	2,842	0.4	0.4	453.0	464.0	Won*
Spain	318	320	2,313	2,382	0.3	0.3	271.5	271.0	Euro
Sweden	33	33	237	242	0.1	0.1	571.7	588.3	Krona
Switzerland	60	60	434	445	0.2	0.2	186.3	188.5	Swiss franc
Taiwan	239	247	1,736	1,837	0.1	0.1	4,280.2	4,346.4	Dollar
Thailand	577	580	4,197	4,319	0.1	0.1	3,939.6	3,990.9	Baht
Turkey	-	-	-	-	-	-	0.0	0.0	Euro
Ukraine	319	314	2,320	2,340	0.0	0.0	509.8	456.0	Hryvna
UAE	-	-	-	-	-	-	0.0	0.0	Dirham
United Kingdom	416	414	3,023	3,087	0.8	0.8	556.6	568.1	Pounds
United States	2,018	2,019	14,675	15,037	4.6	4.7	4,580.3	4,670.9	Dollars
Venezuela	206	209	1,497	1,556	0.1	0.1	1,246.5	1,209.3	Bolivar
Vietnam	724	725	5,267	5,397	0.1	0.1	1,487.7	1,571.2	Dong*

Note: Due to rounding, establishments will vary by + or - one establishment. Therefore, zero establishments may also be one establishment.

* Local Sales are in trillions

DISTILLERIES & ALCOHOL-MAKING INDUSTRY
NAICS 31214

NAICS 31214: Distilleries. This industry comprises establishments primarily engaged in one or more of the following: (1) distilling potable liquors (except brandies); (2) distilling and blending liquors; and (3) blending and mixing liquors and other ingredients.

COUNTRY ESTIMATES

Country	Establishments 2018	2019	Employment 2018	2019	Sales ($B) 2018	2019	Local Sales (B) 2018	2019	Currency
Algeria	-	-	-	-	-	-	0.0	0.0	Dinar
Argentina	257	258	1,845	2,100	0.0	0.0	0.6	0.6	Pesos
Australia	160	162	1,148	1,318	0.1	0.1	0.1	0.1	Dollars
Austria	57	57	411	465	0.0	0.0	0.0	0.0	Euro
Bangladesh	1,129	1,130	8,090	9,218	0.0	0.0	1.1	1.2	Taka
Belgium	72	72	515	586	0.0	0.0	0.0	0.0	Euro
Brazil	1,375	1,387	9,852	11,308	0.1	0.1	315.3	323.7	Real
Canada	241	242	1,727	1,970	0.1	0.1	0.1	0.1	Dollars
Chile	133	134	955	1,095	0.0	0.0	9.6	10.3	Pesos*
China	9,511	9,479	68,141	77,298	0.8	0.9	5.3	5.8	RMB
Colombia	286	286	2,049	2,332	0.0	0.0	0.1	0.1	Pesos*
Czech Republic	69	68	491	556	0.0	0.0	0.3	0.3	Koruna
Denmark	36	36	258	292	0.0	0.0	0.1	0.1	Kroner
Egypt	-	-	-	-	-	-	0.0	0.0	Pounds
Finland	36	36	256	290	0.0	0.0	0.0	0.0	Euro
France	399	398	2,858	3,247	0.1	0.1	0.1	0.1	Euro
Germany	508	501	3,639	4,089	0.2	0.2	0.2	0.2	Euro
Greece	67	66	479	541	0.0	0.0	0.0	0.0	Euro
Hong Kong	41	41	294	333	0.0	0.0	117.3	125.5	Dollar
Hungary	60	59	432	485	0.0	0.0	1.9	2.0	Forint*
India	7,986	8,107	57,222	66,110	0.1	0.1	8.3	9.1	Rupees
Indonesia	-	-	-	-	-	-	0.0	0.0	Rupiah*

DISTILLERIES & ALCOHOL-MAKING INDUSTRY
NAICS 31214

COUNTRY ESTIMATES

Country	Establishments 2018	Establishments 2019	Employment 2018	Employment 2019	Sales ($B) 2018	Sales ($B) 2019	Local Sales (B) 2018	Local Sales (B) 2019	Currency
Iran	-	-	-	-	-	-	0.0	0.0	Rial*
Iraq	-	-	-	-	-	-	0.0	0.0	Dinar*
Ireland	40	41	287	330	0.0	0.0	0.0	0.0	Euro
Israel	57	57	406	469	0.0	0.0	0.1	0.1	Shekel
Italy	402	400	2,879	3,262	0.1	0.1	0.1	0.1	Euro
Japan	846	837	6,060	6,827	0.2	0.3	28.2	29.7	Yen*
Kazakhstan	138	138	987	1,129	0.0	0.0	4.1	4.4	Tenge
Kuwait	-	-	-	-	-	-	0.0	0.0	Dinar
Malaysia	-	-	-	-	-	-	0.0	0.0	Ringgit
Mexico	859	869	6,154	7,085	0.1	0.1	1.3	1.4	New pesos
Netherlands	107	107	770	871	0.0	0.0	0.0	0.0	Euro
New Zealand	29	29	207	237	0.0	0.0	0.0	0.0	Dollar
Nigeria	1,482	1,506	10,615	12,284	0.0	0.0	12,373.0	13,225.8	Naira
Norway	40	40	284	325	0.0	0.0	0.2	0.2	Krone
Pakistan	-	-	-	-	-	-	0.0	0.0	Rupees
Peru	235	235	1,684	1,919	0.0	0.0	0.0	0.0	Nuevo Sol
Phillipines	640	651	4,585	5,309	0.0	0.0	0.9	1.0	Pesos
Poland	438	434	3,141	3,536	0.1	0.1	0.2	0.2	Zloty
Portugal	69	69	497	561	0.0	0.0	0.0	0.0	Euro
Puerto Rico	30	30	215	241	0.0	0.0	0.0	0.0	Dollar
Qatar	-	-	-	-	-	-	0.0	0.0	Riyal
Romania	158	155	1,130	1,266	0.0	0.0	0.0	0.1	New Leu
Russia	1,960	1,937	14,044	15,799	0.2	0.2	8.2	8.5	Rubles
Saudi Arabia	-	-	-	-	-	-	0.0	0.0	Rials*
Singapore	44	45	314	366	0.0	0.0	25.2	27.0	Dollar
South Africa	271	274	1,942	2,238	0.0	0.0	213.3	225.9	Rand
South Korea	383	382	2,745	3,112	0.1	0.1	100.4	107.9	Won*
Spain	318	320	2,278	2,608	0.1	0.1	60.2	63.0	Euro
Sweden	65	65	467	531	0.0	0.0	253.4	273.7	Krona
Switzerland	60	60	427	487	0.0	0.0	41.3	43.9	Swiss franc
Taiwan	239	247	1,711	2,012	0.0	0.0	948.7	1,011.1	Dollar
Thailand	577	580	4,135	4,730	0.0	0.0	873.2	928.4	Baht
Turkey	-	-	-	-	-	-	0.0	0.0	Euro
Ukraine	638	628	4,571	5,125	0.0	0.0	226.0	212.2	Hryvna
UAE	-	-	-	-	-	-	0.0	0.0	Dirham
United Kingdom	831	829	5,956	6,760	0.3	0.4	246.8	264.3	Pounds
United States	2,018	2,019	14,459	16,464	1.0	1.1	1,015.2	1,086.6	Dollars
Venezuela	206	209	1,475	1,704	0.0	0.0	276.3	281.3	Bolivar
Vietnam	724	725	5,189	5,909	0.0	0.0	329.7	365.5	Dong*

Note: Due to rounding, establishments will vary by + or - one establishment. Therefore, zero establishments may also be one establishment.

* Local Sales are in trillions

NAICS 31522: Men's & Boys' Apparel Manufacturing. This industry comprises establishments primarily engaged in manufacturing men's and boys' cut and sew apparel from purchased fabric. Men's and boys' clothing jobbers, who perform entrepreneurial functions involved in apparel manufacture, including buying raw materials, designing and preparing samples, arranging for apparel to be made from their materials, and marketing finished apparel, are included.

COUNTRY ESTIMATES

Country	Establishments 2018	2019	Employment 2018	2019	Sales ($B) 2018	2019	Local Sales (B) 2018	2019	Currency
Algeria	371	373	521	467	0.0	0.0	1.8	1.7	Dinar
Argentina	257	258	361	322	0.0	0.0	0.7	0.6	Pesos
Australia	160	162	225	202	0.1	0.1	0.1	0.1	Dollars
Austria	57	57	80	71	0.0	0.0	0.0	0.0	Euro
Bangladesh	2,710	2,826	3,801	3,531	0.0	0.0	3.0	3.0	Taka
Belgium	72	72	101	90	0.0	0.0	0.0	0.0	Euro
Brazil	1,375	1,387	1,929	1,733	0.1	0.1	360.5	326.8	Real
Canada	241	242	338	302	0.1	0.1	0.1	0.1	Dollars
Chile	133	134	187	168	0.0	0.0	11.0	10.4	Pesos*
China	22,825	23,697	32,018	29,610	2.2	2.3	14.5	14.6	RMB
Colombia	286	286	401	357	0.0	0.0	0.1	0.1	Pesos*
Czech Republic	69	68	96	85	0.0	0.0	0.3	0.3	Koruna
Denmark	36	36	51	45	0.0	0.0	0.1	0.1	Kroner
Egypt	608	623	853	779	0.0	0.0	0.4	0.4	Pounds
Finland	36	36	50	44	0.0	0.0	0.0	0.0	Euro
France	399	398	560	498	0.2	0.1	0.1	0.1	Euro
Germany	508	501	712	626	0.2	0.2	0.2	0.2	Euro
Greece	67	66	94	83	0.0	0.0	0.0	0.0	Euro
Hong Kong	41	41	57	51	0.0	0.0	134.1	126.7	Dollar
Hungary	60	59	85	74	0.0	0.0	2.1	2.0	Forint*
India	19,168	20,267	26,887	25,324	0.4	0.4	22.7	23.1	Rupees
Indonesia	4,766	5,029	6,686	6,283	0.2	0.2	2.4	2.4	Rupiah*

COUNTRY ESTIMATES

Country	Establishments 2018	2019	Employment 2018	2019	Sales ($B) 2018	2019	Local Sales (B) 2018	2019	Currency
Iran	544	550	763	688	0.0	0.0	1.0	0.9	Rial*
Iraq	285	290	400	362	0.0	0.0	0.0	0.0	Dinar*
Ireland	40	41	56	51	0.0	0.0	0.0	0.0	Euro
Israel	57	57	80	72	0.0	0.0	0.1	0.1	Shekel
Italy	402	400	564	500	0.1	0.1	0.1	0.1	Euro
Japan	846	837	1,186	1,046	0.3	0.3	32.3	29.9	Yen*
Kazakhstan	138	138	193	173	0.0	0.0	4.7	4.4	Tenge
Kuwait	32	34	45	42	0.0	0.0	0.0	0.0	Dinar
Malaysia	633	670	888	837	0.1	0.1	0.3	0.3	Ringgit
Mexico	2,061	2,172	2,892	2,714	0.2	0.2	3.6	3.5	New pesos
Netherlands	107	107	151	133	0.0	0.0	0.0	0.0	Euro
New Zealand	29	29	41	36	0.0	0.0	0.0	0.0	Dollar
Nigeria	1,482	1,506	2,078	1,882	0.0	0.0	14,146.9	13,351.0	Naira
Norway	40	40	56	50	0.0	0.0	0.2	0.2	Krone
Pakistan	1,187	1,212	1,665	1,514	0.0	0.0	1.9	1.9	Rupees
Peru	235	235	330	294	0.0	0.0	0.0	0.0	Nuevo Sol
Phillipines	640	651	898	813	0.0	0.0	1.1	1.0	Pesos
Poland	219	217	307	271	0.0	0.0	0.1	0.1	Zloty
Portugal	69	69	97	86	0.0	0.0	0.0	0.0	Euro
Puerto Rico	30	30	42	37	0.0	0.0	0.0	0.0	Dollar
Qatar	30	34	42	43	0.0	0.0	0.0	0.0	Riyal
Romania	158	155	221	194	0.0	0.0	0.1	0.1	New Leu
Russia	980	969	1,375	1,210	0.1	0.1	4.7	4.3	Rubles
Saudi Arabia	275	284	386	354	0.1	0.1	0.0	0.0	Rials*
Singapore	105	112	148	140	0.1	0.1	69.2	68.2	Dollar
South Africa	271	274	380	343	0.0	0.0	243.9	228.0	Rand
South Korea	383	382	537	477	0.1	0.1	114.8	109.0	Won*
Spain	318	320	446	400	0.1	0.1	68.8	63.6	Euro
Sweden	65	65	91	81	0.0	0.0	289.8	276.3	Krona
Switzerland	60	60	84	75	0.0	0.0	47.2	44.3	Swiss franc
Taiwan	239	247	335	308	0.0	0.0	1,084.7	1,020.7	Dollar
Thailand	1,385	1,450	1,943	1,812	0.1	0.1	2,396.2	2,343.0	Baht
Turkey	437	435	613	544	0.1	0.1	221.7	211.5	Euro
Ukraine	319	314	447	393	0.0	0.0	129.2	107.1	Hryvna
UAE	149	166	209	208	0.0	0.0	117.9	110.2	Dirham
United Kingdom	416	414	583	518	0.2	0.2	141.1	133.4	Pounds
United States	2,018	2,019	2,831	2,523	1.2	1.1	1,160.8	1,096.9	Dollars
Venezuela	206	209	289	261	0.0	0.0	315.9	284.0	Bolivar
Vietnam	1,738	1,812	2,438	2,264	0.0	0.0	904.8	922.4	Dong*

Note: Due to rounding, establishments will vary by + or - one establishment. Therefore, zero establishments may also be one establishment.

* Local Sales are in trillions

Women's & Girls' Apparel Mfg. Industry
NAICS 31524

NAICS 31524: Women's & Girls' Apparel Manufacturing Industry. This industry comprises establishments primarily engaged in manufacturing women's and girls' apparel from purchased fabric. Women's and girls' clothing jobbers, who perform entrepreneurial functions involved in apparel manufacture, including buying raw materials, designing and preparing samples, arranging for apparel to be made from their materials, and marketing finished apparel, are included.

COUNTRY ESTIMATES

Country	Establishments 2018	2019	Employment 2018	2019	Sales ($B) 2018	2019	Local Sales (B) 2018	2019	Currency
Algeria	371	373	596	580	0.0	0.0	4.5	4.3	Dinar
Argentina	257	258	414	400	0.1	0.1	1.8	1.7	Pesos
Australia	160	162	257	251	0.2	0.2	0.3	0.3	Dollars
Austria	57	57	92	89	0.1	0.1	0.1	0.1	Euro
Bangladesh	2,710	2,826	4,352	4,386	0.1	0.1	7.5	7.9	Taka
Belgium	72	72	115	112	0.1	0.1	0.1	0.1	Euro
Brazil	1,375	1,387	2,208	2,152	0.3	0.3	911.8	845.4	Real
Canada	241	242	387	375	0.3	0.3	0.3	0.3	Dollars
Chile	133	134	214	208	0.0	0.0	27.9	26.8	Pesos*
China	22,825	23,697	36,659	36,782	5.7	5.8	36.7	37.9	RMB
Colombia	286	286	459	444	0.1	0.0	0.1	0.1	Pesos*
Czech Republic	69	68	110	106	0.0	0.0	0.7	0.7	Koruna
Denmark	36	36	58	56	0.0	0.0	0.3	0.3	Kroner
Egypt	608	623	977	967	0.1	0.1	1.0	1.0	Pounds
Finland	36	36	57	55	0.0	0.0	0.0	0.0	Euro
France	399	398	641	618	0.4	0.4	0.3	0.3	Euro
Germany	508	501	816	778	0.6	0.6	0.5	0.5	Euro
Greece	67	66	107	103	0.0	0.0	0.0	0.0	Euro
Hong Kong	41	41	66	63	0.0	0.0	339.1	327.7	Dollar
Hungary	60	59	97	92	0.0	0.0	5.4	5.2	Forint*
India	19,168	20,267	30,784	31,458	0.9	0.9	57.5	59.6	Rupees
Indonesia	4,766	5,029	7,655	7,805	0.4	0.5	6.0	6.2	Rupiah*

WOMEN'S & GIRLS' APPAREL MFG. INDUSTRY
NAICS 31524

COUNTRY ESTIMATES

Country	Establishments 2018	2019	Employment 2018	2019	Sales ($B) 2018	2019	Local Sales (B) 2018	2019	Currency
Iran	544	550	874	854	0.1	0.1	2.4	2.3	Rial*
Iraq	285	290	458	450	0.0	0.0	0.0	0.0	Dinar*
Ireland	40	41	64	63	0.1	0.1	0.1	0.1	Euro
Israel	57	57	91	89	0.1	0.1	0.2	0.2	Shekel
Italy	402	400	645	621	0.3	0.3	0.3	0.2	Euro
Japan	846	837	1,358	1,299	0.7	0.7	81.6	77.5	Yen*
Kazakhstan	138	138	221	215	0.0	0.0	11.8	11.4	Tenge
Kuwait	32	34	52	52	0.0	0.0	0.0	0.0	Dinar
Malaysia	633	670	1,016	1,040	0.2	0.2	0.6	0.7	Ringgit
Mexico	2,061	2,172	3,311	3,372	0.5	0.5	9.0	9.1	New pesos
Netherlands	107	107	173	166	0.1	0.1	0.1	0.1	Euro
New Zealand	29	29	46	45	0.0	0.0	0.0	0.0	Dollar
Nigeria	1,482	1,506	2,380	2,338	0.1	0.1	35,778.3	34,539.8	Naira
Norway	40	40	64	62	0.1	0.1	0.6	0.6	Krone
Pakistan	1,187	1,212	1,907	1,881	0.0	0.0	4.9	4.8	Rupees
Peru	235	235	377	365	0.0	0.0	0.1	0.1	Nuevo Sol
Phillipines	640	651	1,028	1,010	0.1	0.1	2.7	2.7	Pesos
Poland	219	217	352	337	0.1	0.1	0.3	0.3	Zloty
Portugal	69	69	111	107	0.0	0.0	0.0	0.0	Euro
Puerto Rico	30	30	48	46	0.0	0.0	0.0	0.0	Dollar
Qatar	30	34	48	53	0.0	0.0	0.1	0.1	Riyal
Romania	158	155	253	241	0.0	0.0	0.1	0.1	New Leu
Russia	980	969	1,574	1,504	0.2	0.2	11.8	11.0	Rubles
Saudi Arabia	275	284	442	440	0.1	0.1	0.0	0.0	Rials*
Singapore	105	112	169	174	0.1	0.1	174.9	176.4	Dollar
South Africa	271	274	435	426	0.0	0.0	616.9	589.9	Rand
South Korea	383	382	615	592	0.3	0.3	290.4	281.9	Won*
Spain	318	320	511	496	0.2	0.2	174.0	164.6	Euro
Sweden	65	65	105	101	0.1	0.1	732.9	714.9	Krona
Switzerland	60	60	96	93	0.1	0.1	119.4	114.6	Swiss franc
Taiwan	239	247	383	383	0.1	0.1	2,743.3	2,640.6	Dollar
Thailand	1,385	1,450	2,225	2,251	0.2	0.2	6,060.0	6,061.6	Baht
Turkey	437	435	702	676	0.1	0.1	560.7	547.3	Euro
Ukraine	319	314	512	488	0.0	0.0	326.7	277.1	Hryvna
UAE	149	166	239	258	0.1	0.1	298.1	285.2	Dirham
United Kingdom	416	414	668	643	0.5	0.5	356.8	345.2	Pounds
United States	2,018	2,019	3,241	3,134	2.9	2.8	2,935.7	2,837.7	Dollars
Venezuela	206	209	331	324	0.1	0.1	798.9	734.7	Bolivar
Vietnam	1,738	1,812	2,792	2,812	0.1	0.1	2,288.4	2,386.4	Dong*

Note: Due to rounding, establishments will vary by + or - one establishment. Therefore, zero establishments may also be one establishment.

* Local Sales are in trillions

PAPER MILLS INDUSTRY
NAICS 32212

NAICS 32212: Paper Mills Industry. This industry comprises establishments primarily engaged in manufacturing paper from pulp. These establishments may manufacture or purchase pulp. In addition, the establishments may convert the paper they make. The activity of making paper classifies an establishment into this industry regardless of the output.

COUNTRY ESTIMATES

Country	Establishments 2018	Establishments 2019	Employment 2018	Employment 2019	Sales ($B) 2018	Sales ($B) 2019	Local Sales (B) 2018	Local Sales (B) 2019	Currency
Algeria	186	187	3,821	3,976	0.0	0.0	0.2	0.2	Dinar
Argentina	129	129	2,649	2,742	0.0	0.0	0.1	0.1	Pesos
Australia	80	81	1,649	1,720	0.0	0.0	0.0	0.0	Dollars
Austria	29	29	590	607	0.0	0.0	0.0	0.0	Euro
Bangladesh	565	565	11,618	12,033	0.0	0.0	0.1	0.1	Taka
Belgium	36	36	739	765	0.0	0.0	0.0	0.0	Euro
Brazil	688	693	14,149	14,761	0.0	0.0	37.2	34.4	Real
Canada	241	242	4,960	5,144	0.0	0.0	0.0	0.0	Dollars
Chile	67	67	1,372	1,430	0.0	0.0	1.1	1.1	Pesos*
China	4,755	4,739	97,862	100,905	0.1	0.1	0.6	0.6	RMB
Colombia	143	143	2,943	3,045	0.0	0.0	0.0	0.0	Pesos*
Czech Republic	34	34	705	726	0.0	0.0	0.0	0.0	Koruna
Denmark	18	18	371	382	0.0	0.0	0.0	0.0	Kroner
Egypt	304	312	6,260	6,633	0.0	0.0	0.0	0.0	Pounds
Finland	36	36	735	757	0.0	0.0	0.0	0.0	Euro
France	199	199	4,105	4,238	0.0	0.0	0.0	0.0	Euro
Germany	254	251	5,226	5,337	0.0	0.0	0.0	0.0	Euro
Greece	33	33	688	706	0.0	0.0	0.0	0.0	Euro
Hong Kong	20	20	422	434	0.0	0.0	13.8	13.3	Dollar
Hungary	30	30	620	633	0.0	0.0	0.2	0.2	Forint*
India	3,993	4,053	82,180	86,300	0.0	0.0	1.0	1.0	Rupees
Indonesia	993	1,006	20,435	21,412	0.0	0.0	0.1	0.1	Rupiah*

PAPER MILLS INDUSTRY
NAICS 32212

COUNTRY ESTIMATES

Country	Establishments 2018	Establishments 2019	Employment 2018	Employment 2019	Sales ($B) 2018	Sales ($B) 2019	Local Sales (B) 2018	Local Sales (B) 2019	Currency
Iran	272	275	5,597	5,859	0.0	0.0	0.1	0.1	Rial*
Iraq	143	145	2,935	3,083	0.0	0.0	0.0	0.0	Dinar*
Ireland	20	20	412	431	0.0	0.0	0.0	0.0	Euro
Israel	28	29	584	612	0.0	0.0	0.0	0.0	Shekel
Italy	201	200	4,135	4,258	0.0	0.0	0.0	0.0	Euro
Japan	423	419	8,703	8,911	0.0	0.0	3.3	3.2	Yen*
Kazakhstan	69	69	1,418	1,474	0.0	0.0	0.5	0.5	Tenge
Kuwait	16	17	331	358	0.0	0.0	0.0	0.0	Dinar
Malaysia	132	134	2,713	2,854	0.0	0.0	0.0	0.0	Ringgit
Mexico	429	434	8,838	9,249	0.0	0.0	0.2	0.1	New pesos
Netherlands	54	53	1,106	1,137	0.0	0.0	0.0	0.0	Euro
New Zealand	14	15	297	309	0.0	0.0	0.0	0.0	Dollar
Nigeria	1,482	1,506	30,490	32,071	0.0	0.0	2,917.3	2,810.4	Naira
Norway	40	40	817	848	0.0	0.0	0.0	0.0	Krone
Pakistan	594	606	12,216	12,901	0.0	0.0	0.2	0.2	Rupees
Peru	118	118	2,418	2,505	0.0	0.0	0.0	0.0	Nuevo Sol
Phillipines	320	326	6,585	6,930	0.0	0.0	0.1	0.1	Pesos
Poland	110	108	2,256	2,308	0.0	0.0	0.0	0.0	Zloty
Portugal	35	34	713	732	0.0	0.0	0.0	0.0	Euro
Puerto Rico	15	15	309	314	0.0	0.0	0.0	0.0	Dollar
Qatar	15	17	311	366	0.0	0.0	0.0	0.0	Riyal
Romania	79	78	1,624	1,653	0.0	0.0	0.0	0.0	New Leu
Russia	490	484	10,085	10,312	0.0	0.0	0.5	0.4	Rubles
Saudi Arabia	137	142	2,829	3,020	0.0	0.0	0.0	0.0	Rials*
Singapore	22	22	452	478	0.0	0.0	3.0	2.9	Dollar
South Africa	136	137	2,789	2,921	0.0	0.0	25.2	24.0	Rand
South Korea	192	191	3,942	4,062	0.0	0.0	11.8	11.5	Won*
Spain	159	160	3,272	3,405	0.0	0.0	7.1	6.7	Euro
Sweden	65	65	1,341	1,385	0.0	0.0	59.8	58.2	Krona
Switzerland	30	30	614	636	0.0	0.0	4.9	4.7	Swiss franc
Taiwan	119	123	2,457	2,626	0.0	0.0	111.8	107.4	Dollar
Thailand	289	290	5,939	6,174	0.0	0.0	102.9	98.6	Baht
Turkey	219	218	4,500	4,633	0.0	0.0	22.9	22.3	Euro
Ukraine	160	157	3,283	3,345	0.0	0.0	13.3	11.3	Hryvna
UAE	74	83	1,530	1,772	0.0	0.0	12.2	11.6	Dirham
United Kingdom	208	207	4,277	4,412	0.0	0.0	14.5	14.0	Pounds
United States	2,018	2,019	41,530	42,985	0.2	0.2	239.4	230.9	Dollars
Venezuela	103	104	2,118	2,225	0.0	0.0	32.6	29.9	Bolivar
Vietnam	362	362	7,453	7,714	0.0	0.0	38.9	38.8	Dong*

Note: Due to rounding, establishments will vary by + or - one establishment. Therefore, zero establishments may also be one establishment.

* Local Sales are in trillions

NAICS 32311: Printing Industry. This industry comprises establishments primarily engaged in printing on apparel and textile products, paper, metal, glass, plastics, and other materials, except fabric (grey goods). The printing processes employed include, but are not limited to, lithographic, gravure, screen, flexographic, digital, and letterpress. Establishments in this industry do not manufacture the stock that they print but may perform postprinting activities, such as bending, cutting, or laminating the materials they print, and mailing.

COUNTRY ESTIMATES

Country	Establishments 2018	2019	Employment 2018	2019	Sales ($B) 2018	2019	Local Sales (B) 2018	2019	Currency
Algeria	371	373	14,438	14,655	0.4	0.4	48.5	46.7	Dinar
Argentina	257	258	10,010	10,107	1.0	0.9	19.1	18.1	Pesos
Australia	160	162	6,229	6,341	2.5	2.4	3.2	3.1	Dollars
Austria	57	57	2,228	2,238	0.7	0.7	0.6	0.6	Euro
Bangladesh	1,129	1,130	43,898	44,355	0.4	0.4	33.9	34.1	Taka
Belgium	72	72	2,793	2,820	0.8	0.8	0.7	0.6	Euro
Brazil	1,375	1,387	53,460	54,411	3.1	2.8	9,851.8	9,184.6	Real
Canada	241	242	9,369	9,482	2.9	2.8	3.6	3.5	Dollars
Chile	133	134	5,183	5,270	0.5	0.5	301.4	291.4	Pesos*
China	9,511	9,479	369,752	371,954	25.5	25.4	165.4	164.6	RMB
Colombia	286	286	11,118	11,223	0.5	0.5	1.6	1.6	Pesos*
Czech Republic	69	68	2,665	2,675	0.4	0.4	7.9	7.8	Koruna
Denmark	36	36	1,402	1,407	0.5	0.5	3.3	3.2	Kroner
Egypt	608	623	23,653	24,449	0.6	0.6	11.0	10.6	Pounds
Finland	36	36	1,389	1,395	0.4	0.4	0.3	0.3	Euro
France	399	398	15,510	15,624	4.1	3.9	3.4	3.3	Euro
Germany	508	501	19,745	19,674	6.3	6.1	5.3	5.1	Euro
Greece	67	66	2,598	2,603	0.3	0.3	0.3	0.2	Euro
Hong Kong	41	41	1,593	1,601	0.5	0.5	3,663.9	3,559.8	Dollar
Hungary	60	59	2,343	2,335	0.2	0.2	57.9	56.9	Forint*
India	7,986	8,107	310,500	318,118	4.1	4.1	258.9	259.2	Rupees
Indonesia	1,986	2,011	77,211	78,930	2.0	2.0	27.1	27.0	Rupiah*

PRINTING INDUSTRY
NAICS 32311

COUNTRY ESTIMATES

Country	Establishments 2018	Establishments 2019	Employment 2018	Employment 2019	Sales ($B) 2018	Sales ($B) 2019	Local Sales (B) 2018	Local Sales (B) 2019	Currency
Iran	544	550	21,146	21,597	0.7	0.7	26.3	24.8	Rial*
Iraq	285	290	11,090	11,365	0.4	0.4	0.5	0.4	Dinar*
Ireland	40	41	1,556	1,590	0.9	1.0	0.8	0.8	Euro
Israel	57	57	2,205	2,256	0.6	0.6	2.0	2.0	Shekel
Italy	402	400	15,624	15,696	3.3	3.1	2.7	2.6	Euro
Japan	846	837	32,883	32,849	7.8	7.5	881.5	841.6	Yen*
Kazakhstan	138	138	5,358	5,433	0.4	0.4	127.7	124.2	Tenge
Kuwait	32	34	1,252	1,318	0.2	0.2	0.1	0.1	Dinar
Malaysia	264	268	10,250	10,520	0.7	0.7	2.9	2.9	Ringgit
Mexico	859	869	33,393	34,095	2.1	2.1	40.7	39.5	New pesos
Netherlands	107	107	4,177	4,192	1.3	1.3	1.1	1.1	Euro
New Zealand	29	29	1,123	1,141	0.3	0.3	0.4	0.4	Dollar
Nigeria	1,482	1,506	57,601	59,110	1.1	1.0	386,595.8	375,259.6	Naira
Norway	40	40	1,543	1,562	0.8	0.8	6.5	6.3	Krone
Pakistan	1,187	1,212	46,156	47,555	0.5	0.5	52.7	52.3	Rupees
Peru	235	235	9,137	9,233	0.4	0.4	1.2	1.2	Nuevo Sol
Phillipines	640	651	24,879	25,546	0.6	0.6	29.0	29.1	Pesos
Poland	219	217	8,523	8,508	1.0	0.9	3.3	3.2	Zloty
Portugal	69	69	2,695	2,698	0.4	0.3	0.3	0.3	Euro
Puerto Rico	30	30	1,166	1,158	0.2	0.2	0.2	0.2	Dollar
Qatar	30	34	1,174	1,349	0.4	0.3	1.3	1.3	Riyal
Romania	158	155	6,134	6,093	0.4	0.4	1.5	1.5	New Leu
Russia	980	969	38,103	38,013	2.5	2.3	127.9	120.0	Rubles
Saudi Arabia	275	284	10,689	11,132	1.5	1.5	0.0	0.0	Rials*
Singapore	44	45	1,706	1,763	0.6	0.6	787.5	766.4	Dollar
South Africa	271	274	10,538	10,769	0.5	0.5	6,666.0	6,409.4	Rand
South Korea	383	382	14,895	14,973	2.9	2.9	3,137.4	3,062.5	Won*
Spain	318	320	12,364	12,550	2.3	2.1	1,880.1	1,788.6	Euro
Sweden	65	65	2,534	2,553	1.0	0.9	7,919.1	7,766.8	Krona
Switzerland	60	60	2,318	2,345	1.3	1.3	1,290.1	1,244.5	Swiss franc
Taiwan	239	247	9,283	9,679	1.0	1.0	29,642.7	28,688.7	Dollar
Thailand	577	580	22,438	22,759	0.8	0.8	27,283.5	26,342.5	Baht
Turkey	437	435	17,002	17,080	1.6	1.6	6,058.7	5,945.8	Euro
Ukraine	319	314	12,403	12,330	0.1	0.1	3,530.3	3,010.1	Hryvna
UAE	149	166	5,780	6,532	0.9	0.8	3,220.6	3,098.4	Dirham
United Kingdom	416	414	16,160	16,264	5.2	5.1	3,855.1	3,749.9	Pounds
United States	2,018	2,019	78,456	79,226	31.7	30.8	31,720.9	30,830.7	Dollars
Venezuela	206	209	8,003	8,200	0.9	0.8	8,632.6	7,982.3	Bolivar
Vietnam	724	725	28,158	28,435	0.5	0.5	10,302.8	10,371.0	Dong*

Note: Due to rounding, establishments will vary by + or - one establishment. Therefore, zero establishments may also be one establishment.

* Local Sales are in trillions

PETROLEUM REFINERIES INDUSTRY
NAICS 32411

NAICS 32411: Petroleum Refineries. Establishments primarily engaged in producing gasoline, kerosene, distillate fuel oils, residual fuel oils, and lubricants, through fractionation or straight distillation of crude oil, redistillation of unfinished petroleum derivatives, cracking or other processes. Establishments of this business also produce aliphatic and aromatic chemicals as byproducts. Natural gasoline from natural gas is classified in mining.

COUNTRY ESTIMATES

Country	Establishments 2018	Establishments 2019	Employment 2018	Employment 2019	Sales ($B) 2018	Sales ($B) 2019	Local Sales (B) 2018	Local Sales (B) 2019	Currency
Algeria	186	187	75,176	82,773	0.0	0.0	0.2	0.2	Dinar
Argentina	129	129	52,118	57,088	0.0	0.0	0.1	0.1	Pesos
Australia	80	81	32,431	35,818	0.0	0.0	0.0	0.0	Dollars
Austria	29	29	11,603	12,642	0.0	0.0	0.0	0.0	Euro
Bangladesh	565	565	228,568	250,525	0.0	0.0	0.2	0.2	Taka
Belgium	36	36	14,545	15,927	0.0	0.0	0.0	0.0	Euro
Brazil	688	693	278,354	307,323	0.0	0.0	44.8	44.7	Real
Canada	120	121	48,784	53,554	0.0	0.0	0.0	0.0	Dollars
Chile	67	67	26,989	29,763	0.0	0.0	1.4	1.4	Pesos*
China	4,755	4,739	1,925,227	2,100,845	0.1	0.1	0.8	0.8	RMB
Colombia	143	143	57,888	63,391	0.0	0.0	0.0	0.0	Pesos*
Czech Republic	34	34	13,875	15,107	0.0	0.0	0.0	0.0	Koruna
Denmark	18	18	7,300	7,950	0.0	0.0	0.0	0.0	Kroner
Egypt	304	312	123,154	138,091	0.0	0.0	0.1	0.1	Pounds
Finland	18	18	7,230	7,879	0.0	0.0	0.0	0.0	Euro
France	199	199	80,759	88,244	0.0	0.0	0.0	0.0	Euro
Germany	254	251	102,806	111,124	0.0	0.0	0.0	0.0	Euro
Greece	33	33	13,526	14,701	0.0	0.0	0.0	0.0	Euro
Hong Kong	20	20	8,296	9,042	0.0	0.0	16.7	17.3	Dollar
Hungary	30	30	12,199	13,187	0.0	0.0	0.3	0.3	Forint*
India	3,993	4,053	1,616,712	1,796,771	0.0	0.0	1.2	1.3	Rupees
Indonesia	993	1,006	402,020	445,806	0.0	0.0	0.1	0.1	Rupiah*

PETROLEUM REFINERIES INDUSTRY
NAICS 32411

COUNTRY ESTIMATES

Country	Establishments 2018	2019	Employment 2018	2019	Sales ($B) 2018	2019	Local Sales (B) 2018	2019	Currency
Iran	544	550	220,211	243,961	0.0	0.0	0.2	0.2	Rial*
Iraq	285	290	115,488	128,377	0.0	0.0	0.0	0.0	Dinar*
Ireland	20	20	8,102	8,982	0.0	0.0	0.0	0.0	Euro
Israel	28	29	11,481	12,743	0.0	0.0	0.0	0.0	Shekel
Italy	201	200	81,353	88,652	0.0	0.0	0.0	0.0	Euro
Japan	423	419	171,216	185,536	0.0	0.0	4.0	4.1	Yen*
Kazakhstan	69	69	27,896	30,686	0.0	0.0	0.6	0.6	Tenge
Kuwait	149	166	60,194	73,790	0.0	0.0	0.0	0.0	Dinar
Malaysia	132	134	53,371	59,421	0.0	0.0	0.0	0.0	Ringgit
Mexico	859	869	347,746	385,141	0.0	0.0	0.4	0.4	New pesos
Netherlands	54	53	21,750	23,676	0.0	0.0	0.0	0.0	Euro
New Zealand	14	15	5,849	6,442	0.0	0.0	0.0	0.0	Dollar
Nigeria	741	753	299,915	333,861	0.0	0.0	1,757.2	1,825.1	Naira
Norway	20	20	8,035	8,825	0.0	0.0	0.0	0.0	Krone
Pakistan	594	606	240,327	268,594	0.0	0.0	0.2	0.3	Rupees
Peru	118	118	47,573	52,148	0.0	0.0	0.0	0.0	Nuevo Sol
Phillipines	320	326	129,538	144,288	0.0	0.0	0.1	0.1	Pesos
Poland	110	108	44,375	48,053	0.0	0.0	0.0	0.0	Zloty
Portugal	35	34	14,030	15,238	0.0	0.0	0.0	0.0	Euro
Puerto Rico	15	15	6,070	6,541	0.0	0.0	0.0	0.0	Dollar
Qatar	30	34	12,223	15,242	0.0	0.0	0.0	0.0	Riyal
Romania	79	78	31,941	34,417	0.0	0.0	0.0	0.0	New Leu
Russia	490	484	198,397	214,701	0.0	0.0	0.6	0.6	Rubles
Saudi Arabia	275	284	111,316	125,751	0.0	0.0	0.0	0.0	Rials*
Singapore	22	22	8,884	9,959	0.0	0.0	3.6	3.7	Dollar
South Africa	136	137	54,868	60,825	0.0	0.0	30.3	31.2	Rand
South Korea	192	191	77,553	84,571	0.0	0.0	14.3	14.9	Won*
Spain	159	160	64,376	70,882	0.0	0.0	8.5	8.7	Euro
Sweden	33	33	13,193	14,422	0.0	0.0	36.0	37.8	Krona
Switzerland	30	30	12,069	13,248	0.0	0.0	5.9	6.1	Swiss franc
Taiwan	119	123	48,332	54,671	0.0	0.0	134.7	139.5	Dollar
Thailand	289	290	116,829	128,544	0.0	0.0	124.0	128.1	Baht
Turkey	219	218	88,527	96,468	0.0	0.0	27.5	28.9	Euro
Ukraine	160	157	64,579	69,639	0.0	0.0	16.0	14.6	Hryvna
UAE	149	166	60,194	73,790	0.0	0.0	29.3	30.1	Dirham
United Kingdom	208	207	84,144	91,863	0.0	0.0	17.5	18.2	Pounds
United States	2,018	2,019	817,014	894,954	0.3	0.3	288.4	299.9	Dollars
Venezuela	206	209	83,341	92,635	0.0	0.0	78.5	77.6	Bolivar
Vietnam	362	362	146,614	160,607	0.0	0.0	46.8	50.4	Dong*

Note: Due to rounding, establishments will vary by + or - one establishment. Therefore, zero establishments may also be one establishment.

* Local Sales are in trillions

PETROCHEMICAL MANUFACTURING INDUSTRY
NAICS 32511

NAICS 32511: Petrochemical Manufacturing Industry. This industry comprises establishments primarily engaged in (1) manufacturing acyclic (i.e., aliphatic) hydrocarbons such as ethylene, propylene, and butylene made from refined petroleum or liquid hydrocarbon and/or (2) manufacturing cyclic aromatic hydrocarbons such as benzene, toluene, styrene, xylene, ethyl benzene, and cumene made from refined petroleum or liquid hydrocarbons.

COUNTRY ESTIMATES

Country	Establishments		Employment		Sales ($B)		Local Sales (B)		Currency
	2018	2019	2018	2019	2018	2019	2018	2019	
Algeria	371	373	9,325	10,495	0.0	0.0	0.1	0.1	Dinar
Argentina	257	258	6,465	7,238	0.0	0.0	0.0	0.0	Pesos
Australia	160	162	4,023	4,541	0.0	0.0	0.0	0.0	Dollars
Austria	57	57	1,439	1,603	0.0	0.0	0.0	0.0	Euro
Bangladesh	1,129	1,130	28,352	31,764	0.0	0.0	0.1	0.1	Taka
Belgium	72	72	1,804	2,019	0.0	0.0	0.0	0.0	Euro
Brazil	1,375	1,387	34,527	38,966	0.0	0.0	22.9	22.7	Real
Canada	241	242	6,051	6,790	0.0	0.0	0.0	0.0	Dollars
Chile	133	134	3,348	3,774	0.0	0.0	0.7	0.7	Pesos*
China	9,511	9,479	238,806	266,369	0.1	0.1	0.4	0.4	RMB
Colombia	286	286	7,181	8,037	0.0	0.0	0.0	0.0	Pesos*
Czech Republic	69	68	1,721	1,915	0.0	0.0	0.0	0.0	Koruna
Denmark	36	36	905	1,008	0.0	0.0	0.0	0.0	Kroner
Egypt	608	623	15,276	17,509	0.0	0.0	0.0	0.0	Pounds
Finland	36	36	897	999	0.0	0.0	0.0	0.0	Euro
France	399	398	10,017	11,189	0.0	0.0	0.0	0.0	Euro
Germany	508	501	12,752	14,090	0.0	0.0	0.0	0.0	Euro
Greece	67	66	1,678	1,864	0.0	0.0	0.0	0.0	Euro
Hong Kong	41	41	1,029	1,146	0.0	0.0	8.5	8.8	Dollar
Hungary	60	59	1,513	1,672	0.0	0.0	0.1	0.1	Forint*
India	7,986	8,107	200,538	227,815	0.0	0.0	0.6	0.6	Rupees
Indonesia	1,986	2,011	49,867	56,524	0.0	0.0	0.1	0.1	Rupiah*

PETROCHEMICAL MANUFACTURING INDUSTRY
NAICS 32511

COUNTRY ESTIMATES

Country	Establishments 2018	Establishments 2019	Employment 2018	Employment 2019	Sales ($B) 2018	Sales ($B) 2019	Local Sales (B) 2018	Local Sales (B) 2019	Currency
Iran	544	550	13,658	15,466	0.0	0.0	0.1	0.1	Rial*
Iraq	285	290	7,163	8,139	0.0	0.0	0.0	0.0	Dinar*
Ireland	40	41	1,005	1,139	0.0	0.0	0.0	0.0	Euro
Israel	57	57	1,424	1,616	0.0	0.0	0.0	0.0	Shekel
Italy	402	400	10,091	11,240	0.0	0.0	0.0	0.0	Euro
Japan	846	837	21,238	23,524	0.0	0.0	2.0	2.1	Yen*
Kazakhstan	138	138	3,460	3,891	0.0	0.0	0.3	0.3	Tenge
Kuwait	32	34	809	944	0.0	0.0	0.0	0.0	Dinar
Malaysia	264	268	6,620	7,534	0.0	0.0	0.0	0.0	Ringgit
Mexico	859	869	21,567	24,416	0.0	0.0	0.1	0.1	New pesos
Netherlands	107	107	2,698	3,002	0.0	0.0	0.0	0.0	Euro
New Zealand	29	29	725	817	0.0	0.0	0.0	0.0	Dollar
Nigeria	1,482	1,506	37,202	42,331	0.0	0.0	897.2	926.2	Naira
Norway	40	40	997	1,119	0.0	0.0	0.0	0.0	Krone
Pakistan	1,187	1,212	29,810	34,055	0.0	0.0	0.1	0.1	Rupees
Peru	235	235	5,901	6,612	0.0	0.0	0.0	0.0	Nuevo Sol
Phillipines	640	651	16,068	18,294	0.0	0.0	0.1	0.1	Pesos
Poland	219	217	5,504	6,093	0.0	0.0	0.0	0.0	Zloty
Portugal	69	69	1,740	1,932	0.0	0.0	0.0	0.0	Euro
Puerto Rico	30	30	753	829	0.0	0.0	0.0	0.0	Dollar
Qatar	30	34	758	966	0.0	0.0	0.0	0.0	Riyal
Romania	158	155	3,962	4,364	0.0	0.0	0.0	0.0	New Leu
Russia	980	969	24,609	27,222	0.0	0.0	0.3	0.3	Rubles
Saudi Arabia	275	284	6,904	7,972	0.0	0.0	0.0	0.0	Rials*
Singapore	44	45	1,102	1,263	0.0	0.0	1.8	1.9	Dollar
South Africa	271	274	6,806	7,712	0.0	0.0	15.5	15.8	Rand
South Korea	383	382	9,620	10,723	0.0	0.0	7.3	7.6	Won*
Spain	318	320	7,985	8,987	0.0	0.0	4.4	4.4	Euro
Sweden	65	65	1,636	1,829	0.0	0.0	18.4	19.2	Krona
Switzerland	60	60	1,497	1,680	0.0	0.0	3.0	3.1	Swiss franc
Taiwan	239	247	5,995	6,932	0.0	0.0	68.8	70.8	Dollar
Thailand	577	580	14,492	16,298	0.0	0.0	63.3	65.0	Baht
Turkey	437	435	10,981	12,231	0.0	0.0	14.1	14.7	Euro
Ukraine	319	314	8,010	8,830	0.0	0.0	8.2	7.4	Hryvna
UAE	149	166	3,733	4,678	0.0	0.0	7.5	7.6	Dirham
United Kingdom	416	414	10,437	11,647	0.0	0.0	8.9	9.3	Pounds
United States	2,018	2,019	50,671	56,736	0.1	0.1	73.6	76.1	Dollars
Venezuela	206	209	5,169	5,873	0.0	0.0	20.0	19.7	Bolivar
Vietnam	724	725	18,186	20,364	0.0	0.0	23.9	25.6	Dong*

Note: Due to rounding, establishments will vary by + or - one establishment. Therefore, zero establishments may also be one establishment.

* Local Sales are in trillions

PHARMACEUTICAL PREPARATION MFG. INDUSTRY (NAICS 325412)

NAICS 325412: Pharmaceutical Preparation Manufacturing . This U.S. industry comprises establishments primarily engaged in manufacturing in-vivo diagnostic substances and pharmaceutical preparations (except biological) intended for internal and external consumption in dose forms, such as ampoules, tablets, capsules, vials, ointments, powders, solutions, and suspensions.

COUNTRY ESTIMATES

Country	Establishments 2018	2019	Employment 2018	2019	Sales ($B) 2018	2019	Local Sales (B) 2018	2019	Currency
Algeria	186	187	16,518	17,782	0.0	0.0	1.4	1.4	Dinar
Argentina	129	129	11,452	12,264	0.0	0.0	0.5	0.5	Pesos
Australia	80	81	7,126	7,694	0.1	0.1	0.1	0.1	Dollars
Austria	29	29	2,550	2,716	0.0	0.0	0.0	0.0	Euro
Bangladesh	565	565	50,223	53,818	0.0	0.0	1.0	1.0	Taka
Belgium	36	36	3,196	3,421	0.0	0.0	0.0	0.0	Euro
Brazil	688	693	61,163	66,020	0.1	0.1	276.5	277.5	Real
Canada	120	121	10,719	11,504	0.1	0.1	0.1	0.1	Dollars
Chile	67	67	5,930	6,394	0.0	0.0	8.5	8.8	Pesos*
China	4,755	4,739	423,032	451,308	0.7	0.8	4.6	5.0	RMB
Colombia	143	143	12,720	13,618	0.0	0.0	0.0	0.0	Pesos*
Czech Republic	34	34	3,049	3,245	0.0	0.0	0.2	0.2	Koruna
Denmark	18	18	1,604	1,708	0.0	0.0	0.1	0.1	Kroner
Egypt	304	312	27,061	29,665	0.0	0.0	0.3	0.3	Pounds
Finland	18	18	1,589	1,693	0.0	0.0	0.0	0.0	Euro
France	199	199	17,745	18,957	0.1	0.1	0.1	0.1	Euro
Germany	254	251	22,590	23,872	0.2	0.2	0.1	0.2	Euro
Greece	33	33	2,972	3,158	0.0	0.0	0.0	0.0	Euro
Hong Kong	20	20	1,823	1,942	0.0	0.0	102.8	107.6	Dollar
Hungary	30	30	2,681	2,833	0.0	0.0	1.6	1.7	Forint*
India	3,993	4,053	355,242	385,986	0.1	0.1	7.3	7.8	Rupees
Indonesia	993	1,006	88,336	95,769	0.1	0.1	0.8	0.8	Rupiah*

COUNTRY ESTIMATES

Country	Establishments 2018	Establishments 2019	Employment 2018	Employment 2019	Sales ($B) 2018	Sales ($B) 2019	Local Sales (B) 2018	Local Sales (B) 2019	Currency
Iran	272	275	24,194	26,204	0.0	0.0	0.7	0.7	Rial*
Iraq	143	145	12,688	13,789	0.0	0.0	0.0	0.0	Dinar*
Ireland	20	20	1,780	1,930	0.0	0.0	0.0	0.0	Euro
Israel	28	29	2,523	2,738	0.0	0.0	0.1	0.1	Shekel
Italy	201	200	17,876	19,044	0.1	0.1	0.1	0.1	Euro
Japan	423	419	37,621	39,857	0.2	0.2	24.7	25.4	Yen*
Kazakhstan	69	69	6,130	6,592	0.0	0.0	3.6	3.8	Tenge
Kuwait	16	17	1,433	1,600	0.0	0.0	0.0	0.0	Dinar
Malaysia	132	134	11,727	12,765	0.0	0.0	0.1	0.1	Ringgit
Mexico	429	434	38,205	41,368	0.1	0.1	1.1	1.2	New pesos
Netherlands	54	53	4,779	5,086	0.0	0.0	0.0	0.0	Euro
New Zealand	14	15	1,285	1,384	0.0	0.0	0.0	0.0	Dollar
Nigeria	741	753	65,901	71,721	0.0	0.0	10,849.5	11,339.6	Naira
Norway	20	20	1,765	1,896	0.0	0.0	0.2	0.2	Krone
Pakistan	594	606	52,807	57,700	0.0	0.0	1.5	1.6	Rupees
Peru	118	118	10,453	11,202	0.0	0.0	0.0	0.0	Nuevo Sol
Phillipines	320	326	28,464	30,996	0.0	0.0	0.8	0.9	Pesos
Poland	110	108	9,751	10,323	0.0	0.0	0.1	0.1	Zloty
Portugal	35	34	3,083	3,273	0.0	0.0	0.0	0.0	Euro
Puerto Rico	15	15	1,334	1,405	0.0	0.0	0.0	0.0	Dollar
Qatar	15	17	1,343	1,637	0.0	0.0	0.0	0.0	Riyal
Romania	79	78	7,018	7,393	0.0	0.0	0.0	0.0	New Leu
Russia	490	484	43,594	46,123	0.1	0.1	3.6	3.6	Rubles
Saudi Arabia	137	142	12,230	13,507	0.0	0.0	0.0	0.0	Rials*
Singapore	22	22	1,952	2,139	0.0	0.0	22.1	23.2	Dollar
South Africa	136	137	12,056	13,067	0.0	0.0	187.1	193.7	Rand
South Korea	192	191	17,041	18,168	0.1	0.1	88.0	92.5	Won*
Spain	159	160	14,145	15,227	0.1	0.1	52.8	54.0	Euro
Sweden	33	33	2,899	3,098	0.0	0.0	222.2	234.7	Krona
Switzerland	30	30	2,652	2,846	0.0	0.0	36.2	37.6	Swiss franc
Taiwan	119	123	10,620	11,745	0.0	0.0	831.9	866.9	Dollar
Thailand	289	290	25,671	27,614	0.0	0.0	765.7	796.0	Baht
Turkey	219	218	19,452	20,724	0.0	0.0	170.0	179.7	Euro
Ukraine	160	157	14,190	14,960	0.0	0.0	99.1	91.0	Hryvna
UAE	74	83	6,613	7,926	0.0	0.0	90.4	93.6	Dirham
United Kingdom	208	207	18,489	19,734	0.1	0.2	108.2	113.3	Pounds
United States	2,018	2,019	179,523	192,256	1.8	1.9	1,780.4	1,863.3	Dollars
Venezuela	103	104	9,156	9,950	0.0	0.0	242.3	241.2	Bolivar
Vietnam	362	362	32,216	34,502	0.0	0.0	289.1	313.4	Dong*

Note: Due to rounding, establishments will vary by + or - one establishment. Therefore, zero establishments may also be one establishment.

* Local Sales are in trillions

ELECTRONIC COMPUTER MANUFACTURING INDUSTRY (NAICS 334111)

NAICS 334111: Electronic Computer Manufacturing . This U.S. industry comprises establishments primarily engaged in manufacturing and/or assembling electronic computers, such as mainframes, personal computers, workstations, laptops, and computer servers. Computers can be analog, digital, or hybrid. Digital computers, the most common type, are devices that do all of the following: (1) store the processing program or programs and the data immediately necessary for the execution of the program; (2) can be freely programmed in accordance with the requirements of the user; (3) perform arithmetical computations specified by the user.

COUNTRY ESTIMATES

Country	Establishments		Employment		Sales ($B)		Local Sales (B)		Currency
	2018	2019	2018	2019	2018	2019	2018	2019	
Algeria	371	373	3,892	3,949	0.0	0.0	0.7	0.7	Dinar
Argentina	257	258	2,698	2,723	0.0	0.0	0.3	0.3	Pesos
Australia	160	162	1,679	1,709	0.0	0.0	0.0	0.0	Dollars
Austria	57	57	601	603	0.0	0.0	0.0	0.0	Euro
Bangladesh	1,129	1,130	11,833	11,951	0.0	0.0	0.5	0.5	Taka
Belgium	72	72	753	760	0.0	0.0	0.0	0.0	Euro
Brazil	1,375	1,387	14,410	14,661	0.0	0.0	140.0	133.0	Real
Canada	241	242	2,525	2,555	0.0	0.0	0.1	0.0	Dollars
Chile	133	134	1,397	1,420	0.0	0.0	4.3	4.2	Pesos*
China	9,511	9,479	99,666	100,219	0.4	0.4	2.4	2.4	RMB
Colombia	286	286	2,997	3,024	0.0	0.0	0.0	0.0	Pesos*
Czech Republic	69	68	718	721	0.0	0.0	0.1	0.1	Koruna
Denmark	36	36	378	379	0.0	0.0	0.0	0.0	Kroner
Egypt	608	623	6,375	6,588	0.0	0.0	0.2	0.2	Pounds
Finland	36	36	374	376	0.0	0.0	0.0	0.0	Euro
France	399	398	4,181	4,210	0.1	0.1	0.0	0.0	Euro
Germany	508	501	5,322	5,301	0.1	0.1	0.1	0.1	Euro
Greece	67	66	700	701	0.0	0.0	0.0	0.0	Euro
Hong Kong	41	41	429	431	0.0	0.0	52.1	51.5	Dollar
Hungary	60	59	632	629	0.0	0.0	0.8	0.8	Forint*
India	7,986	8,107	83,694	85,713	0.1	0.1	3.7	3.8	Rupees
Indonesia	1,986	2,011	20,812	21,267	0.0	0.0	0.4	0.4	Rupiah*

Electronic Computer Manufacturing Industry (NAICS 334111)

Country Estimates

Country	Establishments 2018	2019	Employment 2018	2019	Sales ($B) 2018	2019	Local Sales (B) 2018	2019	Currency
Iran	544	550	5,700	5,819	0.0	0.0	0.4	0.4	Rial*
Iraq	285	290	2,989	3,062	0.0	0.0	0.0	0.0	Dinar*
Ireland	40	41	419	428	0.0	0.0	0.0	0.0	Euro
Israel	57	57	594	608	0.0	0.0	0.0	0.0	Shekel
Italy	402	400	4,211	4,229	0.0	0.0	0.0	0.0	Euro
Japan	846	837	8,864	8,851	0.1	0.1	12.5	12.2	Yen*
Kazakhstan	138	138	1,444	1,464	0.0	0.0	1.8	1.8	Tenge
Kuwait	32	34	338	355	0.0	0.0	0.0	0.0	Dinar
Malaysia	264	268	2,763	2,835	0.0	0.0	0.0	0.0	Ringgit
Mexico	859	869	9,001	9,186	0.0	0.0	0.6	0.6	New pesos
Netherlands	107	107	1,126	1,129	0.0	0.0	0.0	0.0	Euro
New Zealand	29	29	303	307	0.0	0.0	0.0	0.0	Dollar
Nigeria	1,482	1,506	15,526	15,927	0.0	0.0	5,494.9	5,432.4	Naira
Norway	40	40	416	421	0.0	0.0	0.1	0.1	Krone
Pakistan	1,187	1,212	12,441	12,813	0.0	0.0	0.7	0.8	Rupees
Peru	235	235	2,463	2,488	0.0	0.0	0.0	0.0	Nuevo Sol
Phillipines	640	651	6,706	6,883	0.0	0.0	0.4	0.4	Pesos
Poland	219	217	2,297	2,292	0.0	0.0	0.0	0.0	Zloty
Portugal	69	69	726	727	0.0	0.0	0.0	0.0	Euro
Puerto Rico	30	30	314	312	0.0	0.0	0.0	0.0	Dollar
Qatar	30	34	316	364	0.0	0.0	0.0	0.0	Riyal
Romania	158	155	1,654	1,642	0.0	0.0	0.0	0.0	New Leu
Russia	980	969	10,271	10,242	0.0	0.0	1.8	1.7	Rubles
Saudi Arabia	275	284	2,881	2,999	0.0	0.0	0.0	0.0	Rials*
Singapore	44	45	460	475	0.0	0.0	11.2	11.1	Dollar
South Africa	271	274	2,840	2,902	0.0	0.0	94.7	92.8	Rand
South Korea	383	382	4,015	4,034	0.0	0.0	44.6	44.3	Won*
Spain	318	320	3,333	3,381	0.0	0.0	26.7	25.9	Euro
Sweden	65	65	683	688	0.0	0.0	112.6	112.4	Krona
Switzerland	60	60	625	632	0.0	0.0	18.3	18.0	Swiss franc
Taiwan	239	247	2,502	2,608	0.0	0.0	421.3	415.3	Dollar
Thailand	577	580	6,048	6,132	0.0	0.0	387.8	381.3	Baht
Turkey	437	435	4,583	4,602	0.0	0.0	86.1	86.1	Euro
Ukraine	319	314	3,343	3,322	0.0	0.0	50.2	43.6	Hryvna
UAE	149	166	1,558	1,760	0.0	0.0	45.8	44.9	Dirham
United Kingdom	416	414	4,356	4,382	0.1	0.1	54.8	54.3	Pounds
United States	2,018	2,019	21,148	21,347	0.5	0.4	450.9	446.3	Dollars
Venezuela	206	209	2,157	2,210	0.0	0.0	122.7	115.6	Bolivar
Vietnam	724	725	7,590	7,662	0.0	0.0	146.4	150.1	Dong*

Note: Due to rounding, establishments will vary by + or - one establishment. Therefore, zero establishments may also be one establishment.

* Local Sales are in trillions

NAICS 33421: Telephone Apparatus Manufacturing This industry comprises establishments primarily engaged in manufacturing wire telephone and data communications equipment. These products may be standalone or board-level components of a larger system. Examples of products made by these establishments are central office switching equipment, cordless telephones (except cellular), PBX equipment, telephones, telephone answering machines, and data communications equipment, such as bridges, routers, and gateways.

COUNTRY ESTIMATES

Country	Establishments 2018	2019	Employment 2018	2019	Sales ($B) 2018	2019	Local Sales (B) 2018	2019	Currency
Algeria	371	373	1,283	1,272	0.0	0.0	0.5	0.4	Dinar
Argentina	257	258	890	877	0.0	0.0	0.2	0.2	Pesos
Australia	160	162	554	551	0.0	0.0	0.0	0.0	Dollars
Austria	57	57	198	194	0.0	0.0	0.0	0.0	Euro
Bangladesh	1,129	1,130	3,902	3,851	0.0	0.0	0.3	0.3	Taka
Belgium	72	72	248	245	0.0	0.0	0.0	0.0	Euro
Brazil	1,375	1,387	4,752	4,724	0.0	0.0	92.4	87.9	Real
Canada	241	242	833	823	0.0	0.0	0.0	0.0	Dollars
Chile	133	134	461	457	0.0	0.0	2.8	2.8	Pesos*
China	9,511	9,479	32,868	32,292	0.2	0.2	1.6	1.6	RMB
Colombia	286	286	988	974	0.0	0.0	0.0	0.0	Pesos*
Czech Republic	69	68	237	232	0.0	0.0	0.1	0.1	Koruna
Denmark	36	36	125	122	0.0	0.0	0.0	0.0	Kroner
Egypt	608	623	2,103	2,123	0.0	0.0	0.1	0.1	Pounds
Finland	36	36	123	121	0.0	0.0	0.0	0.0	Euro
France	399	398	1,379	1,356	0.0	0.0	0.0	0.0	Euro
Germany	508	501	1,755	1,708	0.1	0.1	0.0	0.0	Euro
Greece	67	66	231	226	0.0	0.0	0.0	0.0	Euro
Hong Kong	41	41	142	139	0.0	0.0	34.4	34.1	Dollar
Hungary	60	59	208	203	0.0	0.0	0.5	0.5	Forint*
India	7,986	8,107	27,601	27,618	0.0	0.0	2.4	2.5	Rupees
Indonesia	1,986	2,011	6,863	6,852	0.0	0.0	0.3	0.3	Rupiah*

TELEPHONE EQUIPMENT MFG. INDUSTRY
NAICS 33421

COUNTRY ESTIMATES

Country	Establishments 2018	2019	Employment 2018	2019	Sales ($B) 2018	2019	Local Sales (B) 2018	2019	Currency
Iran	544	550	1,880	1,875	0.0	0.0	0.2	0.2	Rial*
Iraq	285	290	986	987	0.0	0.0	0.0	0.0	Dinar*
Ireland	40	41	138	138	0.0	0.0	0.0	0.0	Euro
Israel	57	57	196	196	0.0	0.0	0.0	0.0	Shekel
Italy	402	400	1,389	1,363	0.0	0.0	0.0	0.0	Euro
Japan	846	837	2,923	2,852	0.1	0.1	8.3	8.1	Yen*
Kazakhstan	138	138	476	472	0.0	0.0	1.2	1.2	Tenge
Kuwait	32	34	111	114	0.0	0.0	0.0	0.0	Dinar
Malaysia	264	268	911	913	0.0	0.0	0.0	0.0	Ringgit
Mexico	859	869	2,968	2,960	0.0	0.0	0.4	0.4	New pesos
Netherlands	107	107	371	364	0.0	0.0	0.0	0.0	Euro
New Zealand	29	29	100	99	0.0	0.0	0.0	0.0	Dollar
Nigeria	1,482	1,506	5,120	5,132	0.0	0.0	3,626.1	3,591.4	Naira
Norway	40	40	137	136	0.0	0.0	0.1	0.1	Krone
Pakistan	1,187	1,212	4,103	4,128	0.0	0.0	0.5	0.5	Rupees
Peru	235	235	812	802	0.0	0.0	0.0	0.0	Nuevo Sol
Phillipines	640	651	2,212	2,218	0.0	0.0	0.3	0.3	Pesos
Poland	219	217	758	739	0.0	0.0	0.0	0.0	Zloty
Portugal	69	69	240	234	0.0	0.0	0.0	0.0	Euro
Puerto Rico	30	30	104	101	0.0	0.0	0.0	0.0	Dollar
Qatar	30	34	104	117	0.0	0.0	0.0	0.0	Riyal
Romania	158	155	545	529	0.0	0.0	0.0	0.0	New Leu
Russia	980	969	3,387	3,300	0.0	0.0	1.2	1.1	Rubles
Saudi Arabia	275	284	950	966	0.0	0.0	0.0	0.0	Rials*
Singapore	44	45	152	153	0.0	0.0	7.4	7.3	Dollar
South Africa	271	274	937	935	0.0	0.0	62.5	61.3	Rand
South Korea	383	382	1,324	1,300	0.0	0.0	29.4	29.3	Won*
Spain	318	320	1,099	1,090	0.0	0.0	17.6	17.1	Euro
Sweden	65	65	225	222	0.0	0.0	74.3	74.3	Krona
Switzerland	60	60	206	204	0.0	0.0	12.1	11.9	Swiss franc
Taiwan	239	247	825	840	0.0	0.0	278.0	274.6	Dollar
Thailand	577	580	1,995	1,976	0.0	0.0	255.9	252.1	Baht
Turkey	437	435	1,511	1,483	0.0	0.0	56.8	56.9	Euro
Ukraine	319	314	1,103	1,070	0.0	0.0	33.1	28.8	Hryvna
UAE	149	166	514	567	0.0	0.0	30.2	29.7	Dirham
United Kingdom	416	414	1,437	1,412	0.0	0.0	36.2	35.9	Pounds
United States	2,018	2,019	6,974	6,878	0.3	0.3	297.5	295.1	Dollars
Venezuela	206	209	711	712	0.0	0.0	81.0	76.4	Bolivar
Vietnam	724	725	2,503	2,469	0.0	0.0	96.6	99.3	Dong*

Note: Due to rounding, establishments will vary by + or - one establishment. Therefore, zero establishments may also be one establishment.

* Local Sales are in trillions

RADIO/TV BROADCAST EQUIPMENT INDUSTRY
NAICS 33422

NAICS 33422: Radio/TV Broadcast Equipment. Establishments primarily engaged in manufacturing radio and television broadcasting and communications equipment. Includes closed-circuit and cable television equipment; studio equipment; light communications equipment; transmitters, transceivers and receivers (except household and automotive); cellular radio telephones; communication antennas; receivers; RF power amplifiers; and fixed and mobile radio systems.

COUNTRY ESTIMATES

Country	Establishments 2018	Establishments 2019	Employment 2018	Employment 2019	Sales ($B) 2018	Sales ($B) 2019	Local Sales (B) 2018	Local Sales (B) 2019	Currency
Algeria	371	373	5,255	5,210	0.0	0.0	1.4	1.3	Dinar
Argentina	257	258	3,643	3,593	0.0	0.0	0.5	0.5	Pesos
Australia	160	162	2,267	2,254	0.1	0.1	0.1	0.1	Dollars
Austria	57	57	811	796	0.0	0.0	0.0	0.0	Euro
Bangladesh	1,129	1,130	15,977	15,769	0.0	0.0	1.0	1.0	Taka
Belgium	72	72	1,017	1,002	0.0	0.0	0.0	0.0	Euro
Brazil	1,375	1,387	19,457	19,344	0.1	0.1	277.3	263.6	Real
Canada	241	242	3,410	3,371	0.1	0.1	0.1	0.1	Dollars
Chile	133	134	1,887	1,873	0.0	0.0	8.5	8.4	Pesos*
China	9,511	9,479	134,574	132,231	0.7	0.7	4.7	4.7	RMB
Colombia	286	286	4,046	3,990	0.0	0.0	0.0	0.0	Pesos*
Czech Republic	69	68	970	951	0.0	0.0	0.2	0.2	Koruna
Denmark	36	36	510	500	0.0	0.0	0.1	0.1	Kroner
Egypt	608	623	8,609	8,692	0.0	0.0	0.3	0.3	Pounds
Finland	36	36	505	496	0.0	0.0	0.0	0.0	Euro
France	399	398	5,645	5,554	0.1	0.1	0.1	0.1	Euro
Germany	508	501	7,186	6,994	0.2	0.2	0.1	0.1	Euro
Greece	67	66	945	925	0.0	0.0	0.0	0.0	Euro
Hong Kong	41	41	580	569	0.0	0.0	103.1	102.2	Dollar
Hungary	60	59	853	830	0.0	0.0	1.6	1.6	Forint*
India	7,986	8,107	113,009	113,092	0.1	0.1	7.3	7.4	Rupees
Indonesia	1,986	2,011	28,101	28,060	0.1	0.1	0.8	0.8	Rupiah*

Radio/TV Broadcast Equipment Industry
NAICS 33422

Country Estimates

Country	Establishments 2018	2019	Employment 2018	2019	Sales ($B) 2018	2019	Local Sales (B) 2018	2019	Currency
Iran	544	550	7,696	7,678	0.0	0.0	0.7	0.7	Rial*
Iraq	285	290	4,036	4,040	0.0	0.0	0.0	0.0	Dinar*
Ireland	40	41	566	565	0.0	0.0	0.0	0.0	Euro
Israel	57	57	803	802	0.0	0.0	0.1	0.1	Shekel
Italy	402	400	5,687	5,580	0.1	0.1	0.1	0.1	Euro
Japan	846	837	11,968	11,678	0.2	0.2	24.8	24.2	Yen*
Kazakhstan	138	138	1,950	1,931	0.0	0.0	3.6	3.6	Tenge
Kuwait	32	34	456	469	0.0	0.0	0.0	0.0	Dinar
Malaysia	264	268	3,731	3,740	0.0	0.0	0.1	0.1	Ringgit
Mexico	859	869	12,154	12,121	0.1	0.1	1.1	1.1	New pesos
Netherlands	107	107	1,520	1,490	0.0	0.0	0.0	0.0	Euro
New Zealand	29	29	409	405	0.0	0.0	0.0	0.0	Dollar
Nigeria	1,482	1,506	20,964	21,014	0.0	0.0	10,882.9	10,768.7	Naira
Norway	40	40	562	555	0.0	0.0	0.2	0.2	Krone
Pakistan	1,187	1,212	16,799	16,906	0.0	0.0	1.5	1.5	Rupees
Peru	235	235	3,325	3,282	0.0	0.0	0.0	0.0	Nuevo Sol
Phillipines	640	651	9,055	9,082	0.0	0.0	0.8	0.8	Pesos
Poland	219	217	3,102	3,025	0.0	0.0	0.1	0.1	Zloty
Portugal	69	69	981	959	0.0	0.0	0.0	0.0	Euro
Puerto Rico	30	30	424	412	0.0	0.0	0.0	0.0	Dollar
Qatar	30	34	427	480	0.0	0.0	0.0	0.0	Riyal
Romania	158	155	2,233	2,166	0.0	0.0	0.0	0.0	New Leu
Russia	980	969	13,868	13,514	0.1	0.1	3.6	3.4	Rubles
Saudi Arabia	275	284	3,891	3,957	0.0	0.0	0.0	0.0	Rials*
Singapore	44	45	621	627	0.0	0.0	22.2	22.0	Dollar
South Africa	271	274	3,835	3,828	0.0	0.0	187.7	183.9	Rand
South Korea	383	382	5,421	5,323	0.1	0.1	88.3	87.9	Won*
Spain	318	320	4,500	4,461	0.1	0.1	52.9	51.3	Euro
Sweden	65	65	922	908	0.0	0.0	222.9	222.9	Krona
Switzerland	60	60	844	834	0.0	0.0	36.3	35.7	Swiss franc
Taiwan	239	247	3,378	3,441	0.0	0.0	834.5	823.3	Dollar
Thailand	577	580	8,166	8,091	0.0	0.0	768.0	755.9	Baht
Turkey	437	435	6,188	6,072	0.0	0.0	170.6	170.6	Euro
Ukraine	319	314	4,514	4,383	0.0	0.0	99.4	86.4	Hryvna
UAE	149	166	2,104	2,322	0.0	0.0	90.7	88.9	Dirham
United Kingdom	416	414	5,882	5,782	0.1	0.1	108.5	107.6	Pounds
United States	2,018	2,019	28,555	28,165	0.9	0.9	893.0	884.7	Dollars
Venezuela	206	209	2,913	2,915	0.0	0.0	243.0	229.1	Bolivar
Vietnam	724	725	10,248	10,109	0.0	0.0	290.0	297.6	Dong*

Note: Due to rounding, establishments will vary by + or - one establishment. Therefore, zero establishments may also be one establishment.

* Local Sales are in trillions

NAICS 33431: Audio & Video Equipment Manufacturing Industry.
This industry comprises establishments primarily engaged in manufacturing electronic audio and video equipment for home entertainment, motor vehicle, public address and musical instrument amplifications. Examples of products made by these establishments are video cassette recorders, televisions, stereo equipment, speaker systems, household-type video cameras, jukeboxes, and amplifiers for musical instruments and public address systems.

COUNTRY ESTIMATES

Country	Establishments 2018	2019	Employment 2018	2019	Sales ($B) 2018	2019	Local Sales (B) 2018	2019	Currency
Algeria	371	373	437	443	0.0	0.0	0.9	0.9	Dinar
Argentina	257	258	303	305	0.0	0.0	0.3	0.3	Pesos
Australia	160	162	189	192	0.0	0.0	0.1	0.1	Dollars
Austria	57	57	67	68	0.0	0.0	0.0	0.0	Euro
Bangladesh	1,129	1,130	1,329	1,340	0.0	0.0	0.6	0.6	Taka
Belgium	72	72	85	85	0.0	0.0	0.0	0.0	Euro
Brazil	1,375	1,387	1,619	1,643	0.1	0.1	177.9	171.1	Real
Canada	241	242	284	286	0.1	0.1	0.1	0.1	Dollars
Chile	133	134	157	159	0.0	0.0	5.4	5.4	Pesos*
China	9,511	9,479	11,196	11,234	0.5	0.5	3.0	3.1	RMB
Colombia	286	286	337	339	0.0	0.0	0.0	0.0	Pesos*
Czech Republic	69	68	81	81	0.0	0.0	0.1	0.1	Koruna
Denmark	36	36	42	43	0.0	0.0	0.1	0.1	Kroner
Egypt	608	623	716	738	0.0	0.0	0.2	0.2	Pounds
Finland	36	36	42	42	0.0	0.0	0.0	0.0	Euro
France	399	398	470	472	0.1	0.1	0.1	0.1	Euro
Germany	508	501	598	594	0.1	0.1	0.1	0.1	Euro
Greece	67	66	79	79	0.0	0.0	0.0	0.0	Euro
Hong Kong	41	41	48	48	0.0	0.0	66.2	66.3	Dollar
Hungary	60	59	71	71	0.0	0.0	1.0	1.1	Forint*
India	7,986	8,107	9,402	9,608	0.1	0.1	4.7	4.8	Rupees
Indonesia	1,986	2,011	2,338	2,384	0.0	0.0	0.5	0.5	Rupiah*

Audio & Visual Equipment Mfg. Industry
NAICS 33431

Country Estimates

Country	Establishments 2018	Establishments 2019	Employment 2018	Employment 2019	Sales ($B) 2018	Sales ($B) 2019	Local Sales (B) 2018	Local Sales (B) 2019	Currency
Iran	544	550	640	652	0.0	0.0	0.5	0.5	Rial*
Iraq	285	290	336	343	0.0	0.0	0.0	0.0	Dinar*
Ireland	40	41	47	48	0.0	0.0	0.0	0.0	Euro
Israel	57	57	67	68	0.0	0.0	0.0	0.0	Shekel
Italy	402	400	473	474	0.1	0.1	0.0	0.0	Euro
Japan	846	837	996	992	0.1	0.1	15.9	15.7	Yen*
Kazakhstan	138	138	162	164	0.0	0.0	2.3	2.3	Tenge
Kuwait	32	34	38	40	0.0	0.0	0.0	0.0	Dinar
Malaysia	264	268	310	318	0.0	0.0	0.1	0.1	Ringgit
Mexico	859	869	1,011	1,030	0.0	0.0	0.7	0.7	New pesos
Netherlands	107	107	126	127	0.0	0.0	0.0	0.0	Euro
New Zealand	29	29	34	34	0.0	0.0	0.0	0.0	Dollar
Nigeria	1,482	1,506	1,744	1,785	0.0	0.0	6,981.1	6,989.4	Naira
Norway	40	40	47	47	0.0	0.0	0.1	0.1	Krone
Pakistan	1,187	1,212	1,398	1,436	0.0	0.0	1.0	1.0	Rupees
Peru	235	235	277	279	0.0	0.0	0.0	0.0	Nuevo Sol
Phillipines	640	651	753	772	0.0	0.0	0.5	0.5	Pesos
Poland	219	217	258	257	0.0	0.0	0.1	0.1	Zloty
Portugal	69	69	82	81	0.0	0.0	0.0	0.0	Euro
Puerto Rico	30	30	35	35	0.0	0.0	0.0	0.0	Dollar
Qatar	30	34	36	41	0.0	0.0	0.0	0.0	Riyal
Romania	158	155	186	184	0.0	0.0	0.0	0.0	New Leu
Russia	980	969	1,154	1,148	0.0	0.0	2.3	2.2	Rubles
Saudi Arabia	275	284	324	336	0.0	0.0	0.0	0.0	Rials*
Singapore	44	45	52	53	0.0	0.0	14.2	14.3	Dollar
South Africa	271	274	319	325	0.0	0.0	120.4	119.4	Rand
South Korea	383	382	451	452	0.1	0.1	56.7	57.0	Won*
Spain	318	320	374	379	0.0	0.0	34.0	33.3	Euro
Sweden	65	65	77	77	0.0	0.0	143.0	144.7	Krona
Switzerland	60	60	70	71	0.0	0.0	23.3	23.2	Swiss franc
Taiwan	239	247	281	292	0.0	0.0	535.3	534.3	Dollar
Thailand	577	580	679	687	0.0	0.0	492.7	490.6	Baht
Turkey	437	435	515	516	0.0	0.0	109.4	110.7	Euro
Ukraine	319	314	376	372	0.0	0.0	63.7	56.1	Hryvna
UAE	149	166	175	197	0.0	0.0	58.2	57.7	Dirham
United Kingdom	416	414	489	491	0.1	0.1	69.6	69.8	Pounds
United States	2,018	2,019	2,376	2,393	0.6	0.6	572.8	574.2	Dollars
Venezuela	206	209	242	248	0.0	0.0	155.9	148.7	Bolivar
Vietnam	724	725	853	859	0.0	0.0	186.0	193.2	Dong*

Note: Due to rounding, establishments will vary by + or - one establishment. Therefore, zero establishments may also be one establishment.

* Local Sales are in trillions

NAICS 33441: Semiconductor and Other Electronic Component Manufacturing This industry comprises establishments primarily engaged in manufacturing semiconductors and other components for electronic applications. Examples of products made by these establishments are capacitors, resistors, microprocessors, bare and loaded printed circuit boards, electron tubes, electronic connectors, and computer modems.

COUNTRY ESTIMATES

Country	Establishments 2018	2019	Employment 2018	2019	Sales ($B) 2018	2019	Local Sales (B) 2018	2019	Currency
Algeria	371	373	27,975	29,151	0.1	0.1	7.3	7.2	Dinar
Argentina	257	258	19,395	20,105	0.2	0.1	2.9	2.8	Pesos
Australia	160	162	12,069	12,614	0.4	0.4	0.5	0.5	Dollars
Austria	57	57	4,318	4,452	0.1	0.1	0.1	0.1	Euro
Bangladesh	1,129	1,130	85,058	88,230	0.1	0.1	5.1	5.2	Taka
Belgium	72	72	5,413	5,609	0.1	0.1	0.1	0.1	Euro
Brazil	1,375	1,387	103,585	108,234	0.5	0.4	1,479.8	1,405.9	Real
Canada	241	242	18,154	18,861	0.4	0.4	0.5	0.5	Dollars
Chile	133	134	10,043	10,482	0.1	0.1	45.3	44.6	Pesos*
China	9,511	9,479	716,442	739,880	3.8	3.9	24.8	25.2	RMB
Colombia	286	286	21,542	22,325	0.1	0.1	0.2	0.2	Pesos*
Czech Republic	69	68	5,163	5,320	0.1	0.1	1.2	1.2	Koruna
Denmark	36	36	2,716	2,800	0.1	0.1	0.5	0.5	Kroner
Egypt	608	623	45,830	48,633	0.1	0.1	1.7	1.6	Pounds
Finland	36	36	2,691	2,775	0.1	0.1	0.1	0.0	Euro
France	399	398	30,053	31,078	0.6	0.6	0.5	0.5	Euro
Germany	508	501	38,258	39,136	0.9	0.9	0.8	0.8	Euro
Greece	67	66	5,033	5,177	0.0	0.0	0.0	0.0	Euro
Hong Kong	41	41	3,087	3,184	0.1	0.1	550.3	544.9	Dollar
Hungary	60	59	4,540	4,644	0.0	0.0	8.7	8.7	Forint*
India	7,986	8,107	601,633	632,791	0.6	0.6	38.9	39.7	Rupees
Indonesia	1,986	2,011	149,605	157,005	0.3	0.3	4.1	4.1	Rupiah*

SEMI-CONDUCTOR & ELECTRONIC COMPONENTS MFG.
NAICS 33441

COUNTRY ESTIMATES

Country	Establishments 2018	Establishments 2019	Employment 2018	Employment 2019	Sales ($B) 2018	Sales ($B) 2019	Local Sales (B) 2018	Local Sales (B) 2019	Currency
Iran	544	550	40,974	42,959	0.1	0.1	3.9	3.8	Rial*
Iraq	285	290	21,488	22,606	0.1	0.1	0.1	0.1	Dinar*
Ireland	40	41	3,015	3,163	0.1	0.2	0.1	0.1	Euro
Israel	57	57	4,272	4,488	0.1	0.1	0.3	0.3	Shekel
Italy	402	400	30,274	31,222	0.5	0.5	0.4	0.4	Euro
Japan	846	837	63,715	65,342	1.2	1.1	132.4	128.8	Yen*
Kazakhstan	138	138	10,381	10,807	0.1	0.1	19.2	19.0	Tenge
Kuwait	32	34	2,426	2,622	0.0	0.0	0.0	0.0	Dinar
Malaysia	264	268	19,861	20,927	0.1	0.1	0.4	0.4	Ringgit
Mexico	859	869	64,704	67,820	0.3	0.3	6.1	6.0	New pesos
Netherlands	107	107	8,094	8,338	0.2	0.2	0.2	0.2	Euro
New Zealand	29	29	2,176	2,269	0.0	0.0	0.1	0.1	Dollar
Nigeria	1,482	1,506	111,608	117,580	0.2	0.2	58,068.6	57,440.6	Naira
Norway	40	40	2,990	3,108	0.1	0.1	1.0	1.0	Krone
Pakistan	1,187	1,212	89,434	94,594	0.1	0.1	7.9	8.0	Rupees
Peru	235	235	17,703	18,365	0.1	0.1	0.2	0.2	Nuevo Sol
Phillipines	640	651	48,206	50,816	0.1	0.1	4.4	4.5	Pesos
Poland	219	217	16,514	16,923	0.1	0.1	0.5	0.5	Zloty
Portugal	69	69	5,221	5,367	0.1	0.1	0.0	0.0	Euro
Puerto Rico	30	30	2,259	2,304	0.0	0.0	0.0	0.0	Dollar
Qatar	30	34	2,274	2,684	0.1	0.1	0.2	0.2	Riyal
Romania	158	155	11,886	12,121	0.1	0.1	0.2	0.2	New Leu
Russia	980	969	73,830	75,614	0.4	0.4	19.2	18.4	Rubles
Saudi Arabia	275	284	20,712	22,144	0.2	0.2	0.0	0.0	Rials*
Singapore	44	45	3,306	3,507	0.1	0.1	118.3	117.3	Dollar
South Africa	271	274	20,418	21,422	0.1	0.1	1,001.3	981.1	Rand
South Korea	383	382	28,860	29,784	0.4	0.4	471.3	468.8	Won*
Spain	318	320	23,956	24,963	0.3	0.3	282.4	273.8	Euro
Sweden	65	65	4,909	5,079	0.1	0.1	1,189.5	1,188.9	Krona
Switzerland	60	60	4,491	4,666	0.2	0.2	193.8	190.5	Swiss franc
Taiwan	239	247	17,986	19,254	0.2	0.1	4,452.5	4,391.4	Dollar
Thailand	577	580	43,476	45,271	0.1	0.1	4,098.1	4,032.2	Baht
Turkey	437	435	32,944	33,974	0.2	0.2	910.1	910.1	Euro
Ukraine	319	314	24,032	24,526	0.0	0.0	530.3	460.7	Hryvna
UAE	149	166	11,200	12,994	0.1	0.1	483.7	474.3	Dirham
United Kingdom	416	414	31,313	32,352	0.8	0.8	579.0	574.0	Pounds
United States	2,018	2,019	152,019	157,593	4.8	4.7	4,764.6	4,719.2	Dollars
Venezuela	206	209	15,507	16,312	0.1	0.1	1,296.7	1,221.8	Bolivar
Vietnam	724	725	54,560	56,563	0.1	0.1	1,547.5	1,587.5	Dong*

Note: Due to rounding, establishments will vary by + or - one establishment. Therefore, zero establishments may also be one establishment.

* Local Sales are in trillions

NAICS 33522: Appliance Manufacturing Industry. This industry comprises establishments primarily engaged in manufacturing household-type cooking appliances, household-type laundry equipment, household-type refrigerators, upright and chest freezers, and other electrical and nonelectrical major household-type appliances, such as dishwashers, water heaters, and garbage disposal units.

COUNTRY ESTIMATES

Country	Establishments		Employment		Sales ($B)		Local Sales (B)		Currency
	2018	2019	2018	2019	2018	2019	2018	2019	
Algeria	371	373	2,372	2,353	0.0	0.0	0.3	0.3	Dinar
Argentina	257	258	1,644	1,623	0.0	0.0	0.1	0.1	Pesos
Australia	160	162	1,023	1,018	0.0	0.0	0.0	0.0	Dollars
Austria	57	57	366	359	0.0	0.0	0.0	0.0	Euro
Bangladesh	1,129	1,130	7,211	7,121	0.0	0.0	0.2	0.2	Taka
Belgium	72	72	459	453	0.0	0.0	0.0	0.0	Euro
Brazil	1,375	1,387	8,781	8,735	0.0	0.0	60.7	56.3	Real
Canada	241	242	1,539	1,522	0.0	0.0	0.0	0.0	Dollars
Chile	133	134	851	846	0.0	0.0	1.9	1.8	Pesos*
China	9,511	9,479	60,734	59,715	0.2	0.2	1.0	1.0	RMB
Colombia	286	286	1,826	1,802	0.0	0.0	0.0	0.0	Pesos*
Czech Republic	69	68	438	429	0.0	0.0	0.0	0.0	Koruna
Denmark	36	36	230	226	0.0	0.0	0.0	0.0	Kroner
Egypt	608	623	3,885	3,925	0.0	0.0	0.1	0.1	Pounds
Finland	36	36	228	224	0.0	0.0	0.0	0.0	Euro
France	399	398	2,548	2,508	0.0	0.0	0.0	0.0	Euro
Germany	508	501	3,243	3,159	0.0	0.0	0.0	0.0	Euro
Greece	67	66	427	418	0.0	0.0	0.0	0.0	Euro
Hong Kong	41	41	262	257	0.0	0.0	22.6	21.8	Dollar
Hungary	60	59	385	375	0.0	0.0	0.4	0.3	Forint*
India	7,986	8,107	51,002	51,072	0.0	0.0	1.6	1.6	Rupees
Indonesia	1,986	2,011	12,682	12,672	0.0	0.0	0.2	0.2	Rupiah*

Major Appliance Manufacturing Industry
NAICS 33522

Country Estimates

Country	Establishments 2018	2019	Employment 2018	2019	Sales ($B) 2018	2019	Local Sales (B) 2018	2019	Currency
Iran	544	550	3,473	3,467	0.0	0.0	0.2	0.2	Rial*
Iraq	285	290	1,822	1,825	0.0	0.0	0.0	0.0	Dinar*
Ireland	40	41	256	255	0.0	0.0	0.0	0.0	Euro
Israel	57	57	362	362	0.0	0.0	0.0	0.0	Shekel
Italy	402	400	2,566	2,520	0.0	0.0	0.0	0.0	Euro
Japan	846	837	5,401	5,274	0.0	0.0	5.4	5.2	Yen*
Kazakhstan	138	138	880	872	0.0	0.0	0.8	0.8	Tenge
Kuwait	32	34	206	212	0.0	0.0	0.0	0.0	Dinar
Malaysia	264	268	1,684	1,689	0.0	0.0	0.0	0.0	Ringgit
Mexico	859	869	5,485	5,474	0.0	0.0	0.3	0.2	New pesos
Netherlands	107	107	686	673	0.0	0.0	0.0	0.0	Euro
New Zealand	29	29	185	183	0.0	0.0	0.0	0.0	Dollar
Nigeria	1,482	1,506	9,461	9,490	0.0	0.0	2,383.1	2,299.2	Naira
Norway	40	40	253	251	0.0	0.0	0.0	0.0	Krone
Pakistan	1,187	1,212	7,582	7,635	0.0	0.0	0.3	0.3	Rupees
Peru	235	235	1,501	1,482	0.0	0.0	0.0	0.0	Nuevo Sol
Phillipines	640	651	4,086	4,101	0.0	0.0	0.2	0.2	Pesos
Poland	219	217	1,400	1,366	0.0	0.0	0.0	0.0	Zloty
Portugal	69	69	443	433	0.0	0.0	0.0	0.0	Euro
Puerto Rico	30	30	191	186	0.0	0.0	0.0	0.0	Dollar
Qatar	30	34	193	217	0.0	0.0	0.0	0.0	Riyal
Romania	158	155	1,008	978	0.0	0.0	0.0	0.0	New Leu
Russia	980	969	6,259	6,103	0.0	0.0	0.8	0.7	Rubles
Saudi Arabia	275	284	1,756	1,787	0.0	0.0	0.0	0.0	Rials*
Singapore	44	45	280	283	0.0	0.0	4.9	4.7	Dollar
South Africa	271	274	1,731	1,729	0.0	0.0	41.1	39.3	Rand
South Korea	383	382	2,447	2,404	0.0	0.0	19.3	18.8	Won*
Spain	318	320	2,031	2,015	0.0	0.0	11.6	11.0	Euro
Sweden	65	65	416	410	0.0	0.0	48.8	47.6	Krona
Switzerland	60	60	381	377	0.0	0.0	8.0	7.6	Swiss franc
Taiwan	239	247	1,525	1,554	0.0	0.0	182.7	175.8	Dollar
Thailand	577	580	3,686	3,654	0.0	0.0	168.2	161.4	Baht
Turkey	437	435	2,793	2,742	0.0	0.0	37.3	36.4	Euro
Ukraine	319	314	2,037	1,979	0.0	0.0	21.8	18.4	Hryvna
UAE	149	166	949	1,049	0.0	0.0	19.9	19.0	Dirham
United Kingdom	416	414	2,654	2,611	0.0	0.0	23.8	23.0	Pounds
United States	2,018	2,019	12,887	12,719	0.2	0.2	195.5	188.9	Dollars
Venezuela	206	209	1,315	1,317	0.0	0.0	53.2	48.9	Bolivar
Vietnam	724	725	4,625	4,565	0.0	0.0	63.5	63.5	Dong*

Note: Due to rounding, establishments will vary by + or - one establishment. Therefore, zero establishments may also be one establishment.

* Local Sales are in trillions

Automobile & Motor Vehicle Mfg. Industry NAICS 33611

NAICS 33611: Automobile & Light Motor Vehicle Manufacturing .
This industry comprises establishments primarily engaged in (1)
manufacturing complete automobile and light duty motor vehicles (i.e.,
body and chassis or unibody) or (2) manufacturing chassis only.

COUNTRY ESTIMATES

Country	Establishments 2018	2019	Employment 2018	2019	Sales ($B) 2018	2019	Local Sales (B) 2018	2019	Currency
Algeria	186	187	18,611	18,912	0.0	0.0	0.2	0.2	Dinar
Argentina	129	129	12,902	13,044	0.0	0.0	0.1	0.1	Pesos
Australia	80	81	8,029	8,184	0.0	0.0	0.0	0.0	Dollars
Austria	29	29	2,872	2,889	0.0	0.0	0.0	0.0	Euro
Bangladesh	565	565	56,585	57,241	0.0	0.0	0.2	0.2	Taka
Belgium	36	36	3,601	3,639	0.0	0.0	0.0	0.0	Euro
Brazil	688	693	68,910	70,218	0.0	0.0	45.9	43.6	Real
Canada	120	121	12,077	12,236	0.0	0.0	0.0	0.0	Dollars
Chile	67	67	6,681	6,800	0.0	0.0	1.4	1.4	Pesos*
China	4,755	4,739	476,614	480,007	0.1	0.1	0.8	0.8	RMB
Colombia	143	143	14,331	14,484	0.0	0.0	0.0	0.0	Pesos*
Czech Republic	34	34	3,435	3,452	0.0	0.0	0.0	0.0	Koruna
Denmark	18	18	1,807	1,816	0.0	0.0	0.0	0.0	Kroner
Egypt	304	312	30,488	31,552	0.0	0.0	0.1	0.1	Pounds
Finland	18	18	1,790	1,800	0.0	0.0	0.0	0.0	Euro
France	199	199	19,993	20,162	0.0	0.0	0.0	0.0	Euro
Germany	508	501	50,902	50,780	0.1	0.1	0.0	0.0	Euro
Greece	33	33	3,348	3,359	0.0	0.0	0.0	0.0	Euro
Hong Kong	20	20	2,054	2,066	0.0	0.0	17.1	16.9	Dollar
Hungary	30	30	3,020	3,013	0.0	0.0	0.3	0.3	Forint*
India	3,993	4,053	400,237	410,532	0.0	0.0	1.2	1.2	Rupees
Indonesia	993	1,006	99,525	101,859	0.0	0.0	0.1	0.1	Rupiah*

Automobile & Motor Vehicle Mfg. Industry
NAICS 33611

Country Estimates

Country	Establishments 2018	Establishments 2019	Employment 2018	Employment 2019	Sales ($B) 2018	Sales ($B) 2019	Local Sales (B) 2018	Local Sales (B) 2019	Currency
Iran	272	275	27,258	27,870	0.0	0.0	0.1	0.1	Rial*
Iraq	143	145	14,295	14,666	0.0	0.0	0.0	0.0	Dinar*
Ireland	20	20	2,006	2,052	0.0	0.0	0.0	0.0	Euro
Israel	28	29	2,842	2,912	0.0	0.0	0.0	0.0	Shekel
Italy	201	200	20,140	20,255	0.0	0.0	0.0	0.0	Euro
Japan	846	837	84,773	84,784	0.1	0.1	8.2	8.0	Yen*
Kazakhstan	69	69	6,906	7,011	0.0	0.0	0.6	0.6	Tenge
Kuwait	16	17	1,614	1,701	0.0	0.0	0.0	0.0	Dinar
Malaysia	132	134	13,213	13,577	0.0	0.0	0.0	0.0	Ringgit
Mexico	429	434	43,044	43,999	0.0	0.0	0.2	0.2	New pesos
Netherlands	54	53	5,384	5,410	0.0	0.0	0.0	0.0	Euro
New Zealand	14	15	1,448	1,472	0.0	0.0	0.0	0.0	Dollar
Nigeria	741	753	74,248	76,281	0.0	0.0	1,800.0	1,783.1	Naira
Norway	20	20	1,989	2,016	0.0	0.0	0.0	0.0	Krone
Pakistan	594	606	59,496	61,369	0.0	0.0	0.2	0.2	Rupees
Peru	118	118	11,777	11,915	0.0	0.0	0.0	0.0	Nuevo Sol
Phillipines	320	326	32,069	32,967	0.0	0.0	0.1	0.1	Pesos
Poland	110	108	10,986	10,979	0.0	0.0	0.0	0.0	Zloty
Portugal	35	34	3,473	3,482	0.0	0.0	0.0	0.0	Euro
Puerto Rico	15	15	1,503	1,494	0.0	0.0	0.0	0.0	Dollar
Qatar	15	17	1,513	1,741	0.0	0.0	0.0	0.0	Riyal
Romania	79	78	7,907	7,864	0.0	0.0	0.0	0.0	New Leu
Russia	490	484	49,116	49,056	0.0	0.0	0.6	0.6	Rubles
Saudi Arabia	137	142	13,779	14,366	0.0	0.0	0.0	0.0	Rials*
Singapore	22	22	2,199	2,275	0.0	0.0	3.7	3.6	Dollar
South Africa	136	137	13,583	13,898	0.0	0.0	31.0	30.5	Rand
South Korea	383	382	38,398	38,646	0.0	0.0	29.2	29.1	Won*
Spain	159	160	15,937	16,195	0.0	0.0	8.8	8.5	Euro
Sweden	33	33	3,266	3,295	0.0	0.0	36.9	36.9	Krona
Switzerland	30	30	2,988	3,027	0.0	0.0	6.0	5.9	Swiss franc
Taiwan	119	123	11,965	12,491	0.0	0.0	138.0	136.3	Dollar
Thailand	289	290	28,922	29,370	0.0	0.0	127.0	125.2	Baht
Turkey	219	218	21,916	22,041	0.0	0.0	28.2	28.3	Euro
Ukraine	160	157	15,987	15,911	0.0	0.0	16.4	14.3	Hryvna
UAE	74	83	7,451	8,430	0.0	0.0	15.0	14.7	Dirham
United Kingdom	208	207	20,831	20,989	0.0	0.0	17.9	17.8	Pounds
United States	2,018	2,019	202,262	204,482	0.3	0.3	295.4	293.0	Dollars
Venezuela	103	104	10,316	10,583	0.0	0.0	40.2	37.9	Bolivar
Vietnam	362	362	36,296	36,696	0.0	0.0	48.0	49.3	Dong*

Note: Due to rounding, establishments will vary by + or - one establishment. Therefore, zero establishments may also be one establishment.

* Local Sales are in trillions

HEAVY DUTY TRUCK MANUFACTURING INDUSTRY
NAICS 33612

NAICS 33612: Heavy Duty Truck Manufacturing Industry
This industry comprises establishments primarily engaged in (1) manufacturing heavy duty truck chassis and assembling complete heavy duty trucks, buses, heavy duty motor homes, and other special purpose heavy duty motor vehicles for highway use or (2) manufacturing heavy duty truck chassis only.

COUNTRY ESTIMATES

Country	Establishments 2018	Establishments 2019	Employment 2018	Employment 2019	Sales ($B) 2018	Sales ($B) 2019	Local Sales (B) 2018	Local Sales (B) 2019	Currency
Algeria	186	187	1,850	1,867	0.0	0.0	0.1	0.1	Dinar
Argentina	129	129	1,283	1,288	0.0	0.0	0.0	0.0	Pesos
Australia	80	81	798	808	0.0	0.0	0.0	0.0	Dollars
Austria	29	29	286	285	0.0	0.0	0.0	0.0	Euro
Bangladesh	565	565	5,625	5,652	0.0	0.0	0.0	0.0	Taka
Belgium	36	36	358	359	0.0	0.0	0.0	0.0	Euro
Brazil	688	693	6,850	6,934	0.0	0.0	13.9	13.1	Real
Canada	120	121	1,201	1,208	0.0	0.0	0.0	0.0	Dollars
Chile	67	67	664	671	0.0	0.0	0.4	0.4	Pesos*
China	4,755	4,739	47,379	47,398	0.0	0.0	0.2	0.2	RMB
Colombia	143	143	1,425	1,430	0.0	0.0	0.0	0.0	Pesos*
Czech Republic	34	34	341	341	0.0	0.0	0.0	0.0	Koruna
Denmark	18	18	180	179	0.0	0.0	0.0	0.0	Kroner
Egypt	304	312	3,031	3,116	0.0	0.0	0.0	0.0	Pounds
Finland	18	18	178	178	0.0	0.0	0.0	0.0	Euro
France	199	199	1,987	1,991	0.0	0.0	0.0	0.0	Euro
Germany	508	501	5,060	5,014	0.0	0.0	0.0	0.0	Euro
Greece	33	33	333	332	0.0	0.0	0.0	0.0	Euro
Hong Kong	20	20	204	204	0.0	0.0	5.2	5.1	Dollar
Hungary	30	30	300	298	0.0	0.0	0.1	0.1	Forint*
India	3,993	4,053	39,787	40,537	0.0	0.0	0.4	0.4	Rupees
Indonesia	993	1,006	9,894	10,058	0.0	0.0	0.0	0.0	Rupiah*

Heavy Duty Truck Manufacturing Industry
NAICS 33612

Country Estimates

Country	Establishments 2018	2019	Employment 2018	2019	Sales ($B) 2018	2019	Local Sales (B) 2018	2019	Currency
Iran	272	275	2,710	2,752	0.0	0.0	0.0	0.0	Rial*
Iraq	143	145	1,421	1,448	0.0	0.0	0.0	0.0	Dinar*
Ireland	20	20	199	203	0.0	0.0	0.0	0.0	Euro
Israel	28	29	283	288	0.0	0.0	0.0	0.0	Shekel
Italy	201	200	2,002	2,000	0.0	0.0	0.0	0.0	Euro
Japan	846	837	8,427	8,372	0.0	0.0	2.5	2.4	Yen*
Kazakhstan	69	69	686	692	0.0	0.0	0.2	0.2	Tenge
Kuwait	16	17	160	168	0.0	0.0	0.0	0.0	Dinar
Malaysia	132	134	1,313	1,341	0.0	0.0	0.0	0.0	Ringgit
Mexico	429	434	4,279	4,345	0.0	0.0	0.1	0.1	New pesos
Netherlands	54	53	535	534	0.0	0.0	0.0	0.0	Euro
New Zealand	14	15	144	145	0.0	0.0	0.0	0.0	Dollar
Nigeria	741	753	7,381	7,532	0.0	0.0	546.4	533.6	Naira
Norway	20	20	198	199	0.0	0.0	0.0	0.0	Krone
Pakistan	594	606	5,914	6,060	0.0	0.0	0.1	0.1	Rupees
Peru	118	118	1,171	1,177	0.0	0.0	0.0	0.0	Nuevo Sol
Phillipines	320	326	3,188	3,255	0.0	0.0	0.0	0.0	Pesos
Poland	110	108	1,092	1,084	0.0	0.0	0.0	0.0	Zloty
Portugal	35	34	345	344	0.0	0.0	0.0	0.0	Euro
Puerto Rico	15	15	149	148	0.0	0.0	0.0	0.0	Dollar
Qatar	15	17	150	172	0.0	0.0	0.0	0.0	Riyal
Romania	79	78	786	776	0.0	0.0	0.0	0.0	New Leu
Russia	490	484	4,882	4,844	0.0	0.0	0.2	0.2	Rubles
Saudi Arabia	137	142	1,370	1,419	0.0	0.0	0.0	0.0	Rials*
Singapore	22	22	219	225	0.0	0.0	1.1	1.1	Dollar
South Africa	136	137	1,350	1,372	0.0	0.0	9.4	9.1	Rand
South Korea	383	382	3,817	3,816	0.0	0.0	8.9	8.7	Won*
Spain	159	160	1,584	1,599	0.0	0.0	2.7	2.5	Euro
Sweden	33	33	325	325	0.0	0.0	11.2	11.0	Krona
Switzerland	30	30	297	299	0.0	0.0	1.8	1.8	Swiss franc
Taiwan	119	123	1,189	1,233	0.0	0.0	41.9	40.8	Dollar
Thailand	289	290	2,875	2,900	0.0	0.0	38.6	37.5	Baht
Turkey	219	218	2,179	2,176	0.0	0.0	8.6	8.5	Euro
Ukraine	160	157	1,589	1,571	0.0	0.0	5.0	4.3	Hryvna
UAE	74	83	741	832	0.0	0.0	4.6	4.4	Dirham
United Kingdom	208	207	2,071	2,073	0.0	0.0	5.4	5.3	Pounds
United States	2,018	2,019	20,106	20,191	0.1	0.1	89.7	87.7	Dollars
Venezuela	103	104	1,025	1,045	0.0	0.0	12.2	11.4	Bolivar
Vietnam	362	362	3,608	3,623	0.0	0.0	14.6	14.7	Dong*

Note: Due to rounding, establishments will vary by + or - one establishment. Therefore, zero establishments may also be one establishment.

* Local Sales are in trillions

NAICS 33631: Motor Vehicle Gas Engine & Engine Parts Manufacturing Industry. This industry comprises establishments primarily engaged in manufacturing and/or rebuilding motor vehicle gasoline engines, and engine parts, whether or not for vehicular use.

COUNTRY ESTIMATES

Country	Establishments 2018	2019	Employment 2018	2019	Sales ($B) 2018	2019	Local Sales (B) 2018	2019	Currency
Algeria	186	187	1,905	1,839	0.0	0.0	0.7	0.7	Dinar
Argentina	129	129	1,321	1,268	0.0	0.0	0.3	0.3	Pesos
Australia	80	81	822	796	0.0	0.0	0.0	0.0	Dollars
Austria	29	29	294	281	0.0	0.0	0.0	0.0	Euro
Bangladesh	565	565	5,792	5,566	0.0	0.0	0.5	0.5	Taka
Belgium	36	36	369	354	0.0	0.0	0.0	0.0	Euro
Brazil	688	693	7,054	6,828	0.0	0.0	146.9	138.7	Real
Canada	120	121	1,236	1,190	0.0	0.0	0.1	0.1	Dollars
Chile	67	67	684	661	0.0	0.0	4.5	4.4	Pesos*
China	4,755	4,739	48,787	46,676	0.4	0.4	2.5	2.5	RMB
Colombia	143	143	1,467	1,408	0.0	0.0	0.0	0.0	Pesos*
Czech Republic	34	34	352	336	0.0	0.0	0.1	0.1	Koruna
Denmark	18	18	185	177	0.0	0.0	0.0	0.0	Kroner
Egypt	304	312	3,121	3,068	0.0	0.0	0.2	0.2	Pounds
Finland	18	18	183	175	0.0	0.0	0.0	0.0	Euro
France	199	199	2,047	1,961	0.1	0.1	0.1	0.0	Euro
Germany	508	501	5,210	4,938	0.2	0.2	0.2	0.2	Euro
Greece	33	33	343	327	0.0	0.0	0.0	0.0	Euro
Hong Kong	20	20	210	201	0.0	0.0	54.6	53.8	Dollar
Hungary	30	30	309	293	0.0	0.0	0.9	0.9	Forint*
India	3,993	4,053	40,969	39,920	0.1	0.1	3.9	3.9	Rupees
Indonesia	993	1,006	10,188	9,905	0.0	0.0	0.4	0.4	Rupiah*

AUTOMOBILE GAS ENGINE & ENGINE PARTS MFG.
NAICS 33631

COUNTRY ESTIMATES

Country	Establishments 2018	Establishments 2019	Employment 2018	Employment 2019	Sales ($B) 2018	Sales ($B) 2019	Local Sales (B) 2018	Local Sales (B) 2019	Currency
Iran	272	275	2,790	2,710	0.0	0.0	0.4	0.4	Rial*
Iraq	143	145	1,463	1,426	0.0	0.0	0.0	0.0	Dinar*
Ireland	20	20	205	200	0.0	0.0	0.0	0.0	Euro
Israel	28	29	291	283	0.0	0.0	0.0	0.0	Shekel
Italy	201	200	2,062	1,970	0.0	0.0	0.0	0.0	Euro
Japan	846	837	8,678	8,244	0.2	0.2	26.3	25.4	Yen*
Kazakhstan	69	69	707	682	0.0	0.0	1.9	1.9	Tenge
Kuwait	16	17	165	165	0.0	0.0	0.0	0.0	Dinar
Malaysia	132	134	1,352	1,320	0.0	0.0	0.0	0.0	Ringgit
Mexico	429	434	4,406	4,278	0.0	0.0	0.6	0.6	New pesos
Netherlands	54	53	551	526	0.0	0.0	0.0	0.0	Euro
New Zealand	14	15	148	143	0.0	0.0	0.0	0.0	Dollar
Nigeria	741	753	7,600	7,418	0.0	0.0	5,764.8	5,667.9	Naira
Norway	20	20	204	196	0.0	0.0	0.1	0.1	Krone
Pakistan	594	606	6,090	5,967	0.0	0.0	0.8	0.8	Rupees
Peru	118	118	1,206	1,159	0.0	0.0	0.0	0.0	Nuevo Sol
Phillipines	320	326	3,283	3,206	0.0	0.0	0.4	0.4	Pesos
Poland	110	108	1,125	1,068	0.0	0.0	0.0	0.0	Zloty
Portugal	35	34	356	339	0.0	0.0	0.0	0.0	Euro
Puerto Rico	15	15	154	145	0.0	0.0	0.0	0.0	Dollar
Qatar	15	17	155	169	0.0	0.0	0.0	0.0	Riyal
Romania	79	78	809	765	0.0	0.0	0.0	0.0	New Leu
Russia	490	484	5,028	4,770	0.0	0.0	1.9	1.8	Rubles
Saudi Arabia	137	142	1,410	1,397	0.0	0.0	0.0	0.0	Rials*
Singapore	22	22	225	221	0.0	0.0	11.7	11.6	Dollar
South Africa	136	137	1,390	1,351	0.0	0.0	99.4	96.8	Rand
South Korea	383	382	3,931	3,758	0.1	0.1	93.6	92.5	Won*
Spain	159	160	1,631	1,575	0.0	0.0	28.0	27.0	Euro
Sweden	33	33	334	320	0.0	0.0	118.1	117.3	Krona
Switzerland	30	30	306	294	0.0	0.0	19.2	18.8	Swiss franc
Taiwan	119	123	1,225	1,215	0.0	0.0	442.0	433.3	Dollar
Thailand	289	290	2,961	2,856	0.0	0.0	406.8	397.9	Baht
Turkey	219	218	2,243	2,143	0.0	0.0	90.3	89.8	Euro
Ukraine	160	157	1,636	1,547	0.0	0.0	52.6	45.5	Hryvna
UAE	74	83	763	820	0.0	0.0	48.0	46.8	Dirham
United Kingdom	208	207	2,132	2,041	0.1	0.1	57.5	56.6	Pounds
United States	2,018	2,019	20,704	19,884	0.9	0.9	946.0	931.3	Dollars
Venezuela	103	104	1,056	1,029	0.0	0.0	128.7	120.6	Bolivar
Vietnam	362	362	3,715	3,568	0.0	0.0	153.6	156.6	Dong*

Note: Due to rounding, establishments will vary by + or - one establishment. Therefore, zero establishments may also be one establishment.

* Local Sales are in trillions

Aircraft Manufacturing Industry (NAICS 336411)

NAICS 336411: Aircraft Manufacturing . This U.S. industry comprises establishments primarily engaged in one or more of the following: (1) manufacturing or assembling complete aircraft; (2) developing and making aircraft prototypes; (3) aircraft conversion (i.e., major modifications to systems); and (4) complete aircraft overhaul and rebuilding (i.e., periodic restoration of aircraft to original design specifications).

Country Estimates

Country	Establishments 2018	Establishments 2019	Employment 2018	Employment 2019	Sales ($B) 2018	Sales ($B) 2019	Local Sales (B) 2018	Local Sales (B) 2019	Currency
Algeria	186	187	9,957	10,391	0.0	0.0	0.3	0.3	Dinar
Argentina	129	129	6,903	7,167	0.0	0.0	0.1	0.1	Pesos
Australia	80	81	4,295	4,496	0.0	0.0	0.0	0.0	Dollars
Austria	29	29	1,537	1,587	0.0	0.0	0.0	0.0	Euro
Bangladesh	565	565	30,273	31,450	0.0	0.0	0.2	0.2	Taka
Belgium	36	36	1,926	1,999	0.0	0.0	0.0	0.0	Euro
Brazil	688	693	36,866	38,581	0.0	0.0	59.7	57.8	Real
Canada	120	121	6,461	6,723	0.0	0.0	0.0	0.0	Dollars
Chile	67	67	3,574	3,736	0.0	0.0	1.8	1.8	Pesos*
China	4,755	4,739	254,986	263,735	0.2	0.2	1.0	1.0	RMB
Colombia	143	143	7,667	7,958	0.0	0.0	0.0	0.0	Pesos*
Czech Republic	34	34	1,838	1,896	0.0	0.0	0.0	0.0	Koruna
Denmark	18	18	967	998	0.0	0.0	0.0	0.0	Kroner
Egypt	304	312	16,311	17,336	0.0	0.0	0.1	0.1	Pounds
Finland	18	18	958	989	0.0	0.0	0.0	0.0	Euro
France	199	199	10,696	11,078	0.0	0.0	0.0	0.0	Euro
Germany	254	251	13,616	13,950	0.0	0.0	0.0	0.0	Euro
Greece	33	33	1,791	1,846	0.0	0.0	0.0	0.0	Euro
Hong Kong	20	20	1,099	1,135	0.0	0.0	22.2	22.4	Dollar
Hungary	30	30	1,616	1,655	0.0	0.0	0.4	0.4	Forint*
India	3,993	4,053	214,125	225,562	0.0	0.0	1.6	1.6	Rupees
Indonesia	993	1,006	53,245	55,965	0.0	0.0	0.2	0.2	Rupiah*

AIRCRAFT MANUFACTURING INDUSTRY
(NAICS 336411)

COUNTRY ESTIMATES

Country	Establishments 2018	Establishments 2019	Employment 2018	Employment 2019	Sales ($B) 2018	Sales ($B) 2019	Local Sales (B) 2018	Local Sales (B) 2019	Currency
Iran	272	275	14,583	15,313	0.0	0.0	0.2	0.2	Rial*
Iraq	143	145	7,648	8,058	0.0	0.0	0.0	0.0	Dinar*
Ireland	20	20	1,073	1,128	0.0	0.0	0.0	0.0	Euro
Israel	28	29	1,521	1,600	0.0	0.0	0.0	0.0	Shekel
Italy	201	200	10,775	11,129	0.0	0.0	0.0	0.0	Euro
Japan	423	419	22,677	23,292	0.0	0.0	5.3	5.3	Yen*
Kazakhstan	69	69	3,695	3,852	0.0	0.0	0.8	0.8	Tenge
Kuwait	16	17	863	935	0.0	0.0	0.0	0.0	Dinar
Malaysia	132	134	7,069	7,460	0.0	0.0	0.0	0.0	Ringgit
Mexico	429	434	23,029	24,175	0.0	0.0	0.2	0.2	New pesos
Netherlands	54	53	2,881	2,972	0.0	0.0	0.0	0.0	Euro
New Zealand	14	15	775	809	0.0	0.0	0.0	0.0	Dollar
Nigeria	741	753	39,722	41,912	0.0	0.0	2,344.0	2,361.7	Naira
Norway	20	20	1,064	1,108	0.0	0.0	0.0	0.0	Krone
Pakistan	594	606	31,830	33,719	0.0	0.0	0.3	0.3	Rupees
Peru	118	118	6,301	6,546	0.0	0.0	0.0	0.0	Nuevo Sol
Phillipines	320	326	17,157	18,114	0.0	0.0	0.2	0.2	Pesos
Poland	110	108	5,877	6,032	0.0	0.0	0.0	0.0	Zloty
Portugal	35	34	1,858	1,913	0.0	0.0	0.0	0.0	Euro
Puerto Rico	15	15	804	821	0.0	0.0	0.0	0.0	Dollar
Qatar	15	17	809	957	0.0	0.0	0.0	0.0	Riyal
Romania	79	78	4,230	4,321	0.0	0.0	0.0	0.0	New Leu
Russia	490	484	26,277	26,953	0.0	0.0	0.8	0.8	Rubles
Saudi Arabia	137	142	7,372	7,893	0.0	0.0	0.0	0.0	Rials*
Singapore	22	22	1,177	1,250	0.0	0.0	4.8	4.8	Dollar
South Africa	136	137	7,267	7,636	0.0	0.0	40.4	40.3	Rand
South Korea	192	191	10,271	10,617	0.0	0.0	19.0	19.3	Won*
Spain	159	160	8,526	8,898	0.0	0.0	11.4	11.3	Euro
Sweden	33	33	1,747	1,811	0.0	0.0	48.0	48.9	Krona
Switzerland	30	30	1,599	1,663	0.0	0.0	7.8	7.8	Swiss franc
Taiwan	119	123	6,401	6,863	0.0	0.0	179.7	180.5	Dollar
Thailand	289	290	15,473	16,137	0.0	0.0	165.4	165.8	Baht
Turkey	219	218	11,725	12,110	0.0	0.0	36.7	37.4	Euro
Ukraine	160	157	8,553	8,742	0.0	0.0	21.4	18.9	Hryvna
UAE	74	83	3,986	4,632	0.0	0.0	19.5	19.5	Dirham
United Kingdom	208	207	11,144	11,532	0.0	0.0	23.4	23.6	Pounds
United States	2,018	2,019	108,209	112,350	0.4	0.4	384.7	388.1	Dollars
Venezuela	103	104	5,519	5,815	0.0	0.0	52.3	50.2	Bolivar
Vietnam	362	362	19,418	20,162	0.0	0.0	62.5	65.3	Dong*

Note: Due to rounding, establishments will vary by + or - one establishment. Therefore, zero establishments may also be one establishment.

* Local Sales are in trillions

NAICS 33711: Kitchen Cabinet & Countertop Mfg Industry. This industry comprises establishments primarily engaged in manufacturing wood or plastics laminated on wood kitchen cabinets, bathroom vanities, and countertops (except freestanding). The cabinets and counters may be made on a stock or custom basis.

COUNTRY ESTIMATES

Country	Establishments 2018	2019	Employment 2018	2019	Sales ($B) 2018	2019	Local Sales (B) 2018	2019	Currency
Algeria	371	373	2,405	2,470	0.1	0.1	11.8	11.2	Dinar
Argentina	257	258	1,667	1,704	0.2	0.2	4.6	4.4	Pesos
Australia	160	162	1,038	1,069	0.6	0.6	0.8	0.7	Dollars
Austria	57	57	371	377	0.2	0.2	0.1	0.1	Euro
Bangladesh	1,129	1,130	7,313	7,477	0.1	0.1	8.2	8.2	Taka
Belgium	72	72	465	475	0.2	0.2	0.2	0.2	Euro
Brazil	1,375	1,387	8,905	9,172	0.7	0.7	2,388.4	2,208.1	Real
Canada	241	242	1,561	1,598	0.7	0.7	0.9	0.8	Dollars
Chile	133	134	863	888	0.1	0.1	73.1	70.1	Pesos*
China	9,511	9,479	61,594	62,700	6.2	6.1	40.1	39.6	RMB
Colombia	286	286	1,852	1,892	0.1	0.1	0.4	0.4	Pesos*
Czech Republic	69	68	444	451	0.1	0.1	1.9	1.9	Koruna
Denmark	36	36	234	237	0.1	0.1	0.8	0.8	Kroner
Egypt	608	623	3,940	4,121	0.2	0.1	2.7	2.5	Pounds
Finland	36	36	231	235	0.1	0.1	0.1	0.1	Euro
France	399	398	2,584	2,634	1.0	0.9	0.8	0.8	Euro
Germany	508	501	3,289	3,317	1.5	1.5	1.3	1.2	Euro
Greece	67	66	433	439	0.1	0.1	0.1	0.1	Euro
Hong Kong	41	41	265	270	0.1	0.1	888.3	855.8	Dollar
Hungary	60	59	390	394	0.1	0.1	14.0	13.7	Forint*
India	7,986	8,107	51,723	53,625	1.0	1.0	62.8	62.3	Rupees
Indonesia	1,986	2,011	12,862	13,305	0.5	0.5	6.6	6.5	Rupiah*

KITCHEN CABINET & COUNTERTOP MFG. INDUSTRY
NAICS 33711

COUNTRY ESTIMATES

Country	Establishments 2018	2019	Employment 2018	2019	Sales ($B) 2018	2019	Local Sales (B) 2018	2019	Currency
Iran	544	550	3,523	3,641	0.2	0.2	6.4	6.0	Rial*
Iraq	285	290	1,847	1,916	0.1	0.1	0.1	0.1	Dinar*
Ireland	40	41	259	268	0.2	0.2	0.2	0.2	Euro
Israel	57	57	367	380	0.1	0.1	0.5	0.5	Shekel
Italy	402	400	2,603	2,646	0.8	0.8	0.7	0.6	Euro
Japan	846	837	5,478	5,537	1.9	1.8	213.7	202.3	Yen*
Kazakhstan	138	138	892	916	0.1	0.1	31.0	29.9	Tenge
Kuwait	32	34	209	222	0.1	0.1	0.0	0.0	Dinar
Malaysia	264	268	1,707	1,773	0.2	0.2	0.7	0.7	Ringgit
Mexico	859	869	5,563	5,747	0.5	0.5	9.9	9.5	New pesos
Netherlands	107	107	696	707	0.3	0.3	0.3	0.3	Euro
New Zealand	29	29	187	192	0.1	0.1	0.1	0.1	Dollar
Nigeria	1,482	1,506	9,595	9,964	0.3	0.3	93,724.8	90,217.2	Naira
Norway	40	40	257	263	0.2	0.2	1.6	1.5	Krone
Pakistan	1,187	1,212	7,689	8,016	0.1	0.1	12.8	12.6	Rupees
Peru	235	235	1,522	1,556	0.1	0.1	0.3	0.3	Nuevo Sol
Phillipines	640	651	4,144	4,306	0.1	0.1	7.0	7.0	Pesos
Poland	219	217	1,420	1,434	0.2	0.2	0.8	0.8	Zloty
Portugal	69	69	449	455	0.1	0.1	0.1	0.1	Euro
Puerto Rico	30	30	194	195	0.1	0.0	0.1	0.0	Dollar
Qatar	30	34	196	227	0.1	0.1	0.3	0.3	Riyal
Romania	158	155	1,022	1,027	0.1	0.1	0.4	0.3	New Leu
Russia	980	969	6,347	6,408	0.6	0.6	31.0	28.8	Rubles
Saudi Arabia	275	284	1,781	1,877	0.4	0.4	0.0	0.0	Rials*
Singapore	44	45	284	297	0.1	0.1	190.9	184.3	Dollar
South Africa	271	274	1,755	1,815	0.1	0.1	1,616.1	1,540.9	Rand
South Korea	383	382	2,481	2,524	0.7	0.7	760.6	736.3	Won*
Spain	318	320	2,060	2,115	0.5	0.5	455.8	430.0	Euro
Sweden	65	65	422	430	0.2	0.2	1,919.9	1,867.2	Krona
Switzerland	60	60	386	395	0.3	0.3	312.8	299.2	Swiss franc
Taiwan	239	247	1,546	1,632	0.2	0.2	7,186.5	6,897.1	Dollar
Thailand	577	580	3,738	3,836	0.2	0.2	6,614.5	6,333.1	Baht
Turkey	437	435	2,832	2,879	0.4	0.4	1,468.9	1,429.5	Euro
Ukraine	319	314	2,066	2,078	0.0	0.0	855.9	723.7	Hryvna
UAE	149	166	963	1,101	0.2	0.2	780.8	744.9	Dirham
United Kingdom	416	414	2,692	2,742	1.3	1.2	934.6	901.5	Pounds
United States	2,018	2,019	13,069	13,355	7.7	7.4	7,690.3	7,412.1	Dollars
Venezuela	206	209	1,333	1,382	0.2	0.2	2,092.8	1,919.0	Bolivar
Vietnam	724	725	4,691	4,793	0.1	0.1	2,497.8	2,493.3	Dong*

Note: Due to rounding, establishments will vary by + or - one establishment. Therefore, zero establishments may also be one establishment.

* Local Sales are in trillions

NAICS 33712: Household and Institutional Furniture Manufacturing
This industry comprises establishments primarily engaged in manufacturing household-type and public building furniture (i.e., library, school, theater, and church furniture). The furniture may be made on a stock or custom basis and may be assembled or unassembled (i.e., knockdown).

COUNTRY ESTIMATES

Country	Establishments 2018	2019	Employment 2018	2019	Sales ($B) 2018	2019	Local Sales (B) 2018	2019	Currency
Algeria	371	373	3,525	3,511	0.1	0.1	8.2	7.9	Dinar
Argentina	257	258	2,444	2,422	0.2	0.2	3.2	3.1	Pesos
Australia	160	162	1,521	1,519	0.4	0.4	0.5	0.5	Dollars
Austria	57	57	544	536	0.1	0.1	0.1	0.1	Euro
Bangladesh	1,129	1,130	10,717	10,627	0.1	0.1	5.8	5.8	Taka
Belgium	72	72	682	676	0.1	0.1	0.1	0.1	Euro
Brazil	1,375	1,387	13,051	13,036	0.5	0.5	1,675.9	1,551.5	Real
Canada	241	242	2,287	2,272	0.5	0.5	0.6	0.6	Dollars
Chile	133	134	1,265	1,263	0.1	0.1	51.3	49.2	Pesos*
China	9,511	9,479	90,267	89,116	4.3	4.3	28.1	27.8	RMB
Colombia	286	286	2,714	2,689	0.1	0.1	0.3	0.3	Pesos*
Czech Republic	69	68	651	641	0.1	0.1	1.3	1.3	Koruna
Denmark	36	36	342	337	0.1	0.1	0.6	0.5	Kroner
Egypt	608	623	5,774	5,858	0.1	0.1	1.9	1.8	Pounds
Finland	36	36	339	334	0.1	0.1	0.1	0.1	Euro
France	399	398	3,786	3,743	0.7	0.7	0.6	0.6	Euro
Germany	508	501	4,820	4,714	1.1	1.0	0.9	0.9	Euro
Greece	67	66	634	624	0.1	0.1	0.0	0.0	Euro
Hong Kong	41	41	389	384	0.1	0.1	623.3	601.3	Dollar
Hungary	60	59	572	559	0.0	0.0	9.8	9.6	Forint*
India	7,986	8,107	75,802	76,217	0.7	0.7	44.0	43.8	Rupees
Indonesia	1,986	2,011	18,849	18,911	0.3	0.3	4.6	4.6	Rupiah*

HOUSEHOLD & INSTITUTIONAL FURNITURE MFG.
NAICS 33712

COUNTRY ESTIMATES

Country	Establishments 2018	2019	Employment 2018	2019	Sales ($B) 2018	2019	Local Sales (B) 2018	2019	Currency
Iran	544	550	5,162	5,174	0.1	0.1	4.5	4.2	Rial*
Iraq	285	290	2,707	2,723	0.1	0.1	0.1	0.1	Dinar*
Ireland	40	41	380	381	0.2	0.2	0.1	0.1	Euro
Israel	57	57	538	541	0.1	0.1	0.3	0.3	Shekel
Italy	402	400	3,814	3,761	0.6	0.5	0.5	0.4	Euro
Japan	846	837	8,028	7,870	1.3	1.3	150.0	142.2	Yen*
Kazakhstan	138	138	1,308	1,302	0.1	0.1	21.7	21.0	Tenge
Kuwait	32	34	306	316	0.0	0.0	0.0	0.0	Dinar
Malaysia	264	268	2,502	2,521	0.1	0.1	0.5	0.5	Ringgit
Mexico	859	869	8,152	8,169	0.4	0.3	6.9	6.7	New pesos
Netherlands	107	107	1,020	1,004	0.2	0.2	0.2	0.2	Euro
New Zealand	29	29	274	273	0.1	0.1	0.1	0.1	Dollar
Nigeria	1,482	1,506	14,062	14,162	0.2	0.2	65,766.1	63,388.8	Naira
Norway	40	40	377	374	0.1	0.1	1.1	1.1	Krone
Pakistan	1,187	1,212	11,268	11,394	0.1	0.1	9.0	8.8	Rupees
Peru	235	235	2,231	2,212	0.1	0.1	0.2	0.2	Nuevo Sol
Phillipines	640	651	6,074	6,121	0.1	0.1	4.9	4.9	Pesos
Poland	219	217	2,081	2,038	0.2	0.2	0.6	0.5	Zloty
Portugal	69	69	658	646	0.1	0.1	0.1	0.0	Euro
Puerto Rico	30	30	285	277	0.0	0.0	0.0	0.0	Dollar
Qatar	30	34	287	323	0.1	0.1	0.2	0.2	Riyal
Romania	158	155	1,498	1,460	0.1	0.1	0.3	0.2	New Leu
Russia	980	969	9,302	9,107	0.4	0.4	21.8	20.3	Rubles
Saudi Arabia	275	284	2,610	2,667	0.3	0.3	0.0	0.0	Rials*
Singapore	44	45	417	422	0.1	0.1	134.0	129.5	Dollar
South Africa	271	274	2,573	2,580	0.1	0.1	1,134.0	1,082.7	Rand
South Korea	383	382	3,636	3,587	0.5	0.5	533.7	517.3	Won*
Spain	318	320	3,018	3,007	0.4	0.4	319.8	302.1	Euro
Sweden	65	65	619	612	0.2	0.2	1,347.2	1,312.0	Krona
Switzerland	60	60	566	562	0.2	0.2	219.5	210.2	Swiss franc
Taiwan	239	247	2,266	2,319	0.2	0.2	5,042.7	4,846.1	Dollar
Thailand	577	580	5,478	5,453	0.1	0.1	4,641.4	4,449.8	Baht
Turkey	437	435	4,151	4,092	0.3	0.3	1,030.7	1,004.4	Euro
Ukraine	319	314	3,028	2,954	0.0	0.0	600.6	508.5	Hryvna
UAE	149	166	1,411	1,565	0.1	0.1	547.9	523.4	Dirham
United Kingdom	416	414	3,945	3,897	0.9	0.9	655.8	633.4	Pounds
United States	2,018	2,019	19,153	18,982	5.4	5.2	5,396.2	5,207.9	Dollars
Venezuela	206	209	1,954	1,965	0.1	0.1	1,468.5	1,348.4	Bolivar
Vietnam	724	725	6,874	6,813	0.1	0.1	1,752.7	1,751.9	Dong*

Note: Due to rounding, establishments will vary by + or - one establishment. Therefore, zero establishments may also be one establishment.

* Local Sales are in trillions

OFFICE FURNITURE MANUFACTURING INDUSTRY
NAICS 33721

NAICS 33721: Office Furniture Manufacturing Industry. This industry comprises establishments primarily engaged in manufacturing office furniture and/or office and store fixtures. The furniture may be made on a stock or custom basis and may be assembled or unassembled (i.e., knockdown).

COUNTRY ESTIMATES

Country	Establishments		Employment		Sales ($B)		Local Sales (B)		
	2018	2019	2018	2019	2018	2019	2018	2019	Currency
Algeria	371	373	4,172	4,276	0.1	0.1	7.2	7.0	Dinar
Argentina	257	258	2,892	2,949	0.1	0.1	2.8	2.7	Pesos
Australia	160	162	1,800	1,850	0.4	0.4	0.5	0.5	Dollars
Austria	57	57	644	653	0.1	0.1	0.1	0.1	Euro
Bangladesh	1,129	1,130	12,684	12,943	0.1	0.1	5.0	5.1	Taka
Belgium	72	72	807	823	0.1	0.1	0.1	0.1	Euro
Brazil	1,375	1,387	15,447	15,877	0.5	0.4	1,463.3	1,384.3	Real
Canada	241	242	2,707	2,767	0.4	0.4	0.5	0.5	Dollars
Chile	133	134	1,498	1,538	0.1	0.1	44.8	43.9	Pesos*
China	9,511	9,479	106,838	108,534	3.8	3.8	24.6	24.8	RMB
Colombia	286	286	3,212	3,275	0.1	0.1	0.2	0.2	Pesos*
Czech Republic	69	68	770	780	0.1	0.1	1.2	1.2	Koruna
Denmark	36	36	405	411	0.1	0.1	0.5	0.5	Kroner
Egypt	608	623	6,834	7,134	0.1	0.1	1.6	1.6	Pounds
Finland	36	36	401	407	0.1	0.1	0.1	0.0	Euro
France	399	398	4,482	4,559	0.6	0.6	0.5	0.5	Euro
Germany	508	501	5,705	5,741	0.9	0.9	0.8	0.8	Euro
Greece	67	66	751	759	0.0	0.0	0.0	0.0	Euro
Hong Kong	41	41	460	467	0.1	0.1	544.2	536.5	Dollar
Hungary	60	59	677	681	0.0	0.0	8.6	8.6	Forint*
India	7,986	8,107	89,717	92,825	0.6	0.6	38.5	39.1	Rupees
Indonesia	1,986	2,011	22,310	23,031	0.3	0.3	4.0	4.1	Rupiah*

OFFICE FURNITURE MANUFACTURING INDUSTRY
NAICS 33721

COUNTRY ESTIMATES

Country	Establishments		Employment		Sales ($B)		Local Sales (B)		
	2018	2019	2018	2019	2018	2019	2018	2019	Currency
Iran	544	550	6,110	6,302	0.1	0.1	3.9	3.7	Rial*
Iraq	285	290	3,204	3,316	0.1	0.1	0.1	0.1	Dinar*
Ireland	40	41	450	464	0.1	0.2	0.1	0.1	Euro
Israel	57	57	637	658	0.1	0.1	0.3	0.3	Shekel
Italy	402	400	4,515	4,580	0.5	0.5	0.4	0.4	Euro
Japan	846	837	9,501	9,585	1.2	1.1	130.9	126.8	Yen*
Kazakhstan	138	138	1,548	1,585	0.1	0.1	19.0	18.7	Tenge
Kuwait	32	34	362	385	0.0	0.0	0.0	0.0	Dinar
Malaysia	264	268	2,962	3,070	0.1	0.1	0.4	0.4	Ringgit
Mexico	859	869	9,649	9,949	0.3	0.3	6.0	5.9	New pesos
Netherlands	107	107	1,207	1,223	0.2	0.2	0.2	0.2	Euro
New Zealand	29	29	325	333	0.0	0.0	0.1	0.1	Dollar
Nigeria	1,482	1,506	16,643	17,248	0.2	0.2	57,420.0	56,558.2	Naira
Norway	40	40	446	456	0.1	0.1	1.0	0.9	Krone
Pakistan	1,187	1,212	13,337	13,876	0.1	0.1	7.8	7.9	Rupees
Peru	235	235	2,640	2,694	0.1	0.1	0.2	0.2	Nuevo Sol
Phillipines	640	651	7,189	7,454	0.1	0.1	4.3	4.4	Pesos
Poland	219	217	2,463	2,483	0.1	0.1	0.5	0.5	Zloty
Portugal	69	69	779	787	0.1	0.1	0.0	0.0	Euro
Puerto Rico	30	30	337	338	0.0	0.0	0.0	0.0	Dollar
Qatar	30	34	339	394	0.1	0.1	0.2	0.2	Riyal
Romania	158	155	1,772	1,778	0.1	0.1	0.2	0.2	New Leu
Russia	980	969	11,010	11,092	0.4	0.4	19.0	18.1	Rubles
Saudi Arabia	275	284	3,089	3,248	0.2	0.2	0.0	0.0	Rials*
Singapore	44	45	493	515	0.1	0.1	117.0	115.5	Dollar
South Africa	271	274	3,045	3,142	0.1	0.1	990.1	966.0	Rand
South Korea	383	382	4,304	4,369	0.4	0.4	466.0	461.6	Won*
Spain	318	320	3,572	3,662	0.3	0.3	279.2	269.6	Euro
Sweden	65	65	732	745	0.1	0.1	1,176.2	1,170.6	Krona
Switzerland	60	60	670	684	0.2	0.2	191.6	187.6	Swiss franc
Taiwan	239	247	2,682	2,824	0.1	0.1	4,402.7	4,323.9	Dollar
Thailand	577	580	6,483	6,641	0.1	0.1	4,052.3	3,970.3	Baht
Turkey	437	435	4,913	4,984	0.2	0.2	899.9	896.1	Euro
Ukraine	319	314	3,584	3,598	0.0	0.0	524.3	453.7	Hryvna
UAE	149	166	1,670	1,906	0.1	0.1	478.3	467.0	Dirham
United Kingdom	416	414	4,669	4,746	0.8	0.8	572.6	565.2	Pounds
United States	2,018	2,019	22,669	23,118	4.7	4.6	4,711.4	4,646.7	Dollars
Venezuela	206	209	2,312	2,393	0.1	0.1	1,282.2	1,203.1	Bolivar
Vietnam	724	725	8,136	8,297	0.1	0.1	1,530.2	1,563.1	Dong*

Note: Due to rounding, establishments will vary by + or - one establishment. Therefore, zero establishments may also be one establishment.

* Local Sales are in trillions

MEDICAL EQUIPMENT & SUPPLIES MFG. INDUSTRY
NAICS 33911

NAICS 33911: Medical Equipment and Supplies Manufacturing This industry comprises establishments primarily engaged in manufacturing medical equipment and supplies. Examples of products made by these establishments are laboratory apparatus and furniture, surgical and medical instruments, surgical appliances and supplies, dental equipment and supplies, orthodontic goods, dentures, and orthodontic appliances.

COUNTRY ESTIMATES

Country	Establishments		Employment		Sales ($B)		Local Sales (B)		
	2018	2019	2018	2019	2018	2019	2018	2019	Currency
Algeria	371	373	16,537	17,385	0.2	0.2	19.6	19.1	Dinar
Argentina	257	258	11,464	11,990	0.4	0.4	7.7	7.4	Pesos
Australia	160	162	7,134	7,523	1.0	1.0	1.3	1.3	Dollars
Austria	57	57	2,552	2,655	0.3	0.3	0.2	0.2	Euro
Bangladesh	1,129	1,130	50,278	52,617	0.2	0.2	13.7	13.9	Taka
Belgium	72	72	3,199	3,345	0.3	0.3	0.3	0.3	Euro
Brazil	1,375	1,387	61,230	64,546	1.2	1.2	3,980.2	3,751.5	Real
Canada	241	242	10,731	11,248	1.2	1.1	1.4	1.4	Dollars
Chile	133	134	5,937	6,251	0.2	0.2	121.7	119.0	Pesos*
China	9,511	9,479	423,496	441,236	10.3	10.4	66.8	67.2	RMB
Colombia	286	286	12,734	13,314	0.2	0.2	0.6	0.6	Pesos*
Czech Republic	69	68	3,052	3,173	0.1	0.1	3.2	3.2	Koruna
Denmark	36	36	1,606	1,670	0.2	0.2	1.3	1.3	Kroner
Egypt	608	623	27,091	29,003	0.3	0.2	4.4	4.3	Pounds
Finland	36	36	1,590	1,655	0.2	0.2	0.1	0.1	Euro
France	399	398	17,765	18,534	1.7	1.6	1.4	1.3	Euro
Germany	508	501	22,614	23,339	2.5	2.5	2.1	2.1	Euro
Greece	67	66	2,975	3,088	0.1	0.1	0.1	0.1	Euro
Hong Kong	41	41	1,825	1,899	0.2	0.2	1,480.2	1,454.0	Dollar
Hungary	60	59	2,684	2,770	0.1	0.1	23.4	23.2	Forint*
India	7,986	8,107	355,631	377,372	1.6	1.7	104.6	105.9	Rupees
Indonesia	1,986	2,011	88,433	93,632	0.8	0.8	11.0	11.0	Rupiah*

MEDICAL EQUIPMENT & SUPPLIES MFG. INDUSTRY
NAICS 33911

COUNTRY ESTIMATES

Country	Establishments		Employment		Sales ($B)		Local Sales (B)		Currency
	2018	2019	2018	2019	2018	2019	2018	2019	
Iran	544	550	24,220	25,619	0.3	0.3	10.6	10.1	Rial*
Iraq	285	290	12,702	13,481	0.2	0.1	0.2	0.2	Dinar*
Ireland	40	41	1,782	1,887	0.4	0.4	0.3	0.3	Euro
Israel	57	57	2,525	2,676	0.2	0.2	0.8	0.8	Shekel
Italy	402	400	17,895	18,619	1.3	1.3	1.1	1.1	Euro
Japan	846	837	37,663	38,968	3.2	3.0	356.1	343.8	Yen*
Kazakhstan	138	138	6,136	6,445	0.2	0.2	51.6	50.7	Tenge
Kuwait	32	34	1,434	1,564	0.1	0.1	0.0	0.0	Dinar
Malaysia	264	268	11,740	12,480	0.3	0.3	1.2	1.2	Ringgit
Mexico	859	869	38,247	40,445	0.9	0.8	16.4	16.1	New pesos
Netherlands	107	107	4,784	4,973	0.5	0.5	0.5	0.4	Euro
New Zealand	29	29	1,287	1,353	0.1	0.1	0.2	0.2	Dollar
Nigeria	1,482	1,506	65,973	70,120	0.4	0.4	156,186.9	153,276.1	Naira
Norway	40	40	1,767	1,853	0.3	0.3	2.6	2.6	Krone
Pakistan	1,187	1,212	52,865	56,412	0.2	0.2	21.3	21.4	Rupees
Peru	235	235	10,465	10,952	0.2	0.2	0.5	0.5	Nuevo Sol
Phillipines	640	651	28,495	30,305	0.2	0.2	11.7	11.9	Pesos
Poland	219	217	9,761	10,092	0.4	0.4	1.3	1.3	Zloty
Portugal	69	69	3,086	3,200	0.1	0.1	0.1	0.1	Euro
Puerto Rico	30	30	1,335	1,374	0.1	0.1	0.1	0.1	Dollar
Qatar	30	34	1,344	1,601	0.1	0.1	0.5	0.5	Riyal
Romania	158	155	7,026	7,228	0.2	0.2	0.6	0.6	New Leu
Russia	980	969	43,642	45,093	1.0	1.0	51.7	49.0	Rubles
Saudi Arabia	275	284	12,243	13,206	0.6	0.6	0.0	0.0	Rials*
Singapore	44	45	1,954	2,092	0.2	0.2	318.2	313.0	Dollar
South Africa	271	274	12,069	12,775	0.2	0.2	2,693.1	2,617.9	Rand
South Korea	383	382	17,059	17,762	1.2	1.2	1,267.5	1,250.9	Won*
Spain	318	320	14,161	14,887	0.9	0.9	759.6	730.5	Euro
Sweden	65	65	2,902	3,029	0.4	0.4	3,199.3	3,172.4	Krona
Switzerland	60	60	2,655	2,782	0.5	0.5	521.2	508.3	Swiss franc
Taiwan	239	247	10,632	11,482	0.4	0.4	11,975.8	11,718.0	Dollar
Thailand	577	580	25,699	26,998	0.3	0.3	11,022.7	10,759.7	Baht
Turkey	437	435	19,474	20,261	0.7	0.6	2,447.8	2,428.6	Euro
Ukraine	319	314	14,206	14,626	0.1	0.0	1,426.3	1,229.5	Hryvna
UAE	149	166	6,621	7,749	0.4	0.3	1,301.1	1,265.5	Dirham
United Kingdom	416	414	18,509	19,294	2.1	2.1	1,557.5	1,531.7	Pounds
United States	2,018	2,019	89,860	93,983	12.8	12.6	12,815.4	12,592.9	Dollars
Venezuela	206	209	9,166	9,728	0.3	0.3	3,487.6	3,260.4	Bolivar
Vietnam	724	725	32,251	33,732	0.2	0.2	4,162.4	4,236.1	Dong*

Note: Due to rounding, establishments will vary by + or - one establishment. Therefore, zero establishments may also be one establishment.

* Local Sales are in trillions

SIGN MANUFACTURING
NAICS 33995

NAICS 33995: Sign Manufacturing Industry. This industry comprises establishments primarily engaged in manufacturing signs and related displays of all materials (except printing paper and paperboard signs, notices, displays).

COUNTRY ESTIMATES

Country	Establishments 2018	2019	Employment 2018	2019	Sales ($B) 2018	2019	Local Sales (B) 2018	2019	Currency
Algeria	371	373	2,540	2,627	0.2	0.2	22.9	22.1	Dinar
Argentina	257	258	1,761	1,812	0.5	0.4	9.0	8.5	Pesos
Australia	160	162	1,096	1,137	1.2	1.1	1.5	1.4	Dollars
Austria	57	57	392	401	0.3	0.3	0.3	0.3	Euro
Bangladesh	1,129	1,130	7,722	7,952	0.2	0.2	16.0	16.1	Taka
Belgium	72	72	491	506	0.4	0.4	0.3	0.3	Euro
Brazil	1,375	1,387	9,404	9,754	1.4	1.3	4,644.6	4,338.7	Real
Canada	241	242	1,648	1,700	1.4	1.3	1.7	1.6	Dollars
Chile	133	134	912	945	0.2	0.2	142.1	137.7	Pesos*
China	9,511	9,479	65,044	66,680	12.0	12.0	78.0	77.8	RMB
Colombia	286	286	1,956	2,012	0.3	0.3	0.7	0.7	Pesos*
Czech Republic	69	68	469	479	0.2	0.2	3.7	3.7	Koruna
Denmark	36	36	247	252	0.3	0.2	1.6	1.5	Kroner
Egypt	608	623	4,161	4,383	0.3	0.3	5.2	5.0	Pounds
Finland	36	36	244	250	0.2	0.2	0.2	0.2	Euro
France	399	398	2,728	2,801	1.9	1.9	1.6	1.5	Euro
Germany	508	501	3,473	3,527	3.0	2.9	2.5	2.4	Euro
Greece	67	66	457	467	0.2	0.1	0.1	0.1	Euro
Hong Kong	41	41	280	287	0.2	0.2	1,727.4	1,681.6	Dollar
Hungary	60	59	412	419	0.1	0.1	27.3	26.9	Forint*
India	7,986	8,107	54,621	57,028	1.9	1.9	122.1	122.5	Rupees
Indonesia	1,986	2,011	13,582	14,150	1.0	0.9	12.8	12.7	Rupiah*

SIGN MANUFACTURING
NAICS 33995

COUNTRY ESTIMATES

Country	Establishments 2018	Establishments 2019	Employment 2018	Employment 2019	Sales ($B) 2018	Sales ($B) 2019	Local Sales (B) 2018	Local Sales (B) 2019	Currency
Iran	544	550	3,720	3,872	0.3	0.3	12.4	11.7	Rial*
Iraq	285	290	1,951	2,037	0.2	0.2	0.2	0.2	Dinar*
Ireland	40	41	274	285	0.4	0.5	0.4	0.4	Euro
Israel	57	57	388	404	0.3	0.3	1.0	0.9	Shekel
Italy	402	400	2,749	2,814	1.5	1.5	1.3	1.2	Euro
Japan	846	837	5,785	5,889	3.7	3.5	415.6	397.6	Yen*
Kazakhstan	138	138	942	974	0.2	0.2	60.2	58.7	Tenge
Kuwait	32	34	220	236	0.1	0.1	0.0	0.0	Dinar
Malaysia	264	268	1,803	1,886	0.3	0.3	1.4	1.4	Ringgit
Mexico	859	869	5,874	6,112	1.0	1.0	19.2	18.6	New pesos
Netherlands	107	107	735	751	0.6	0.6	0.5	0.5	Euro
New Zealand	29	29	198	204	0.1	0.1	0.2	0.2	Dollar
Nigeria	1,482	1,506	10,133	10,597	0.5	0.5	182,260.9	177,267.6	Naira
Norway	40	40	271	280	0.4	0.4	3.1	3.0	Krone
Pakistan	1,187	1,212	8,119	8,525	0.2	0.2	24.9	24.7	Rupees
Peru	235	235	1,607	1,655	0.2	0.2	0.6	0.6	Nuevo Sol
Phillipines	640	651	4,376	4,580	0.3	0.3	13.7	13.8	Pesos
Poland	219	217	1,499	1,525	0.4	0.4	1.6	1.5	Zloty
Portugal	69	69	474	484	0.2	0.2	0.1	0.1	Euro
Puerto Rico	30	30	205	208	0.1	0.1	0.1	0.1	Dollar
Qatar	30	34	206	242	0.2	0.2	0.6	0.6	Riyal
Romania	158	155	1,079	1,092	0.2	0.2	0.7	0.7	New Leu
Russia	980	969	6,703	6,814	1.2	1.1	60.3	56.7	Rubles
Saudi Arabia	275	284	1,880	1,996	0.7	0.7	0.0	0.0	Rials*
Singapore	44	45	300	316	0.3	0.3	371.3	362.0	Dollar
South Africa	271	274	1,854	1,931	0.3	0.2	3,142.7	3,027.7	Rand
South Korea	383	382	2,620	2,684	1.4	1.4	1,479.1	1,446.7	Won*
Spain	318	320	2,175	2,250	1.1	1.0	886.4	844.9	Euro
Sweden	65	65	446	458	0.5	0.4	3,733.4	3,668.9	Krona
Switzerland	60	60	408	420	0.6	0.6	608.2	587.9	Swiss franc
Taiwan	239	247	1,633	1,735	0.5	0.5	13,975.1	13,552.2	Dollar
Thailand	577	580	3,947	4,080	0.4	0.4	12,862.8	12,443.9	Baht
Turkey	437	435	2,991	3,062	0.8	0.7	2,856.4	2,808.7	Euro
Ukraine	319	314	2,182	2,210	0.1	0.1	1,664.4	1,421.9	Hryvna
UAE	149	166	1,017	1,171	0.4	0.4	1,518.4	1,463.6	Dirham
United Kingdom	416	414	2,843	2,916	2.5	2.4	1,817.5	1,771.4	Pounds
United States	2,018	2,019	13,801	14,203	15.0	14.6	14,954.8	14,564.0	Dollars
Venezuela	206	209	1,408	1,470	0.4	0.4	4,069.8	3,770.7	Bolivar
Vietnam	724	725	4,953	5,098	0.2	0.2	4,857.3	4,899.1	Dong*

Note: Due to rounding, establishments will vary by + or - one establishment. Therefore, zero establishments may also be one establishment.

* Local Sales are in trillions

AUTOMOBILE & OTHER VEHICLES WHOLESALE (NAICS 42311)

NAICS 42311: Automobile & Other Vehicle Wholesale. This industry comprises establishments primarily engaged in wholesaling new and used passenger automobiles, trucks, trailers, and other motor vehicles, such as motorcycles, motor homes, and snowmobiles.

COUNTRY ESTIMATES

Country	Establishments 2018	2019	Employment 2018	2019	Sales ($B) 2018	2019	Local Sales (B) 2018	2019	Currency
Algeria	186	187	36,578	36,623	0.0	0.0	5.7	5.7	Dinar
Argentina	129	129	25,359	25,258	0.1	0.1	2.2	2.2	Pesos
Australia	80	81	15,780	15,847	0.3	0.3	0.4	0.4	Dollars
Austria	29	29	5,646	5,593	0.1	0.1	0.1	0.1	Euro
Bangladesh	565	565	111,212	110,844	0.0	0.1	4.0	4.2	Taka
Belgium	36	36	7,077	7,047	0.1	0.1	0.1	0.1	Euro
Brazil	688	693	135,435	135,974	0.4	0.3	1,161.2	1,124.5	Real
Canada	120	121	23,736	23,695	0.3	0.3	0.4	0.4	Dollars
Chile	67	67	13,132	13,169	0.1	0.1	35.5	35.7	Pesos*
China	4,755	4,739	936,737	929,514	3.0	3.1	19.5	20.2	RMB
Colombia	143	143	28,166	28,047	0.1	0.1	0.2	0.2	Pesos*
Czech Republic	34	34	6,751	6,684	0.0	0.0	0.9	1.0	Koruna
Denmark	18	18	3,552	3,517	0.1	0.1	0.4	0.4	Kroner
Egypt	304	312	59,922	61,098	0.1	0.1	1.3	1.3	Pounds
Finland	18	18	3,518	3,486	0.0	0.0	0.0	0.0	Euro
France	199	199	39,294	39,044	0.5	0.5	0.4	0.4	Euro
Germany	508	501	100,043	98,333	1.5	1.5	1.2	1.2	Euro
Greece	33	33	6,581	6,504	0.0	0.0	0.0	0.0	Euro
Hong Kong	20	20	4,036	4,000	0.1	0.1	431.8	435.8	Dollar
Hungary	30	30	5,936	5,834	0.0	0.0	6.8	7.0	Forint*
India	3,993	4,053	786,626	794,977	0.5	0.5	30.5	31.7	Rupees
Indonesia	993	1,006	195,607	197,246	0.2	0.2	3.2	3.3	Rupiah*

Automobile & Other Vehicles Wholesale (NAICS 42311)

Country Estimates

Country	Establishments		Employment		Sales ($B)		Local Sales (B)		
	2018	2019	2018	2019	2018	2019	2018	2019	Currency
Iran	272	275	53,573	53,970	0.1	0.1	3.1	3.0	Rial*
Iraq	143	145	28,096	28,400	0.0	0.0	0.1	0.1	Dinar*
Ireland	20	20	3,942	3,974	0.1	0.1	0.1	0.1	Euro
Israel	28	29	5,586	5,638	0.1	0.1	0.2	0.2	Shekel
Italy	201	200	39,583	39,224	0.4	0.4	0.3	0.3	Euro
Japan	846	837	166,614	164,180	1.8	1.8	207.8	206.1	Yen*
Kazakhstan	69	69	13,573	13,577	0.0	0.0	15.1	15.2	Tenge
Kuwait	16	17	3,172	3,295	0.0	0.0	0.0	0.0	Dinar
Malaysia	132	134	25,968	26,291	0.1	0.1	0.3	0.4	Ringgit
Mexico	429	434	84,600	85,202	0.2	0.3	4.8	4.8	New pesos
Netherlands	54	53	10,583	10,475	0.2	0.2	0.1	0.1	Euro
New Zealand	14	15	2,846	2,850	0.0	0.0	0.0	0.1	Dollar
Nigeria	741	753	145,926	147,716	0.1	0.1	45,565.7	45,943.3	Naira
Norway	20	20	3,909	3,904	0.1	0.1	0.8	0.8	Krone
Pakistan	594	606	116,934	118,839	0.1	0.1	6.2	6.4	Rupees
Peru	118	118	23,147	23,073	0.0	0.0	0.1	0.1	Nuevo Sol
Phillipines	320	326	63,028	63,840	0.1	0.1	3.4	3.6	Pesos
Poland	110	108	21,591	21,261	0.1	0.1	0.4	0.4	Zloty
Portugal	35	34	6,826	6,742	0.0	0.0	0.0	0.0	Euro
Puerto Rico	15	15	2,953	2,894	0.0	0.0	0.0	0.0	Dollar
Qatar	15	17	2,974	3,372	0.0	0.0	0.2	0.2	Riyal
Romania	79	78	15,541	15,227	0.0	0.0	0.2	0.2	New Leu
Russia	490	484	96,532	94,994	0.3	0.3	15.1	14.7	Rubles
Saudi Arabia	137	142	27,081	27,819	0.2	0.2	0.0	0.0	Rials*
Singapore	22	22	4,323	4,406	0.1	0.1	92.8	93.8	Dollar
South Africa	136	137	26,697	26,912	0.1	0.1	785.7	784.7	Rand
South Korea	383	382	75,468	74,837	0.7	0.7	739.6	749.9	Won*
Spain	159	160	31,323	31,362	0.3	0.3	221.6	219.0	Euro
Sweden	33	33	6,419	6,381	0.1	0.1	933.4	950.9	Krona
Switzerland	30	30	5,872	5,861	0.2	0.2	152.1	152.4	Swiss franc
Taiwan	119	123	23,517	24,189	0.1	0.1	3,493.8	3,512.4	Dollar
Thailand	289	290	56,844	56,874	0.1	0.1	3,215.7	3,225.1	Baht
Turkey	219	218	43,074	42,682	0.2	0.2	714.1	728.0	Euro
Ukraine	160	157	31,422	30,812	0.0	0.0	416.1	368.5	Hryvna
UAE	74	83	14,644	16,324	0.1	0.1	379.6	379.3	Dirham
United Kingdom	208	207	40,941	40,644	0.6	0.6	454.4	459.1	Pounds
United States	2,018	2,019	397,526	395,970	7.5	7.5	7,477.5	7,549.3	Dollars
Venezuela	103	104	20,275	20,493	0.1	0.1	1,017.5	977.3	Bolivar
Vietnam	362	362	71,336	71,060	0.1	0.1	1,214.3	1,269.7	Dong*

Note: Due to rounding, establishments will vary by + or - one establishment. Therefore, zero establishments may also be one establishment.

* Local Sales are in trillions

MOTOR VEHICLE PARTS & SUPPLIES WHOLESALES (NAICS 42312)

NAICS 42312: Motor Vehicle Parts & Supplies Wholesale. Establishments primarily engaged in the wholesale distribution of new and used passenger automobiles, trucks, trailers, and other motor vehicles, including motorcycles, motor homes, and snowmobiles. Automotive distributors primarily engaged in selling at retail to individual consumers for personal use, and also selling a limited amount of new and used passenger automobiles and trucks at wholesale, are classified in SIC 5511.

COUNTRY ESTIMATES

Country	Establishments 2018	2019	Employment 2018	2019	Sales ($B) 2018	2019	Local Sales (B) 2018	2019	Currency
Algeria	186	187	20,205	21,715	0.1	0.1	12.2	12.2	Dinar
Argentina	129	129	14,008	14,977	0.3	0.2	4.8	4.7	Pesos
Australia	80	81	8,717	9,397	0.6	0.6	0.8	0.8	Dollars
Austria	29	29	3,119	3,317	0.2	0.2	0.1	0.1	Euro
Bangladesh	565	565	61,433	65,724	0.1	0.1	8.5	8.9	Taka
Belgium	36	36	3,909	4,178	0.2	0.2	0.2	0.2	Euro
Brazil	688	693	74,814	80,625	0.8	0.7	2,478.2	2,400.5	Real
Canada	120	121	13,112	14,050	0.7	0.7	0.9	0.9	Dollars
Chile	67	67	7,254	7,808	0.1	0.1	75.8	76.2	Pesos*
China	4,755	4,739	517,447	551,149	6.4	6.6	41.6	43.0	RMB
Colombia	143	143	15,559	16,630	0.1	0.1	0.4	0.4	Pesos*
Czech Republic	34	34	3,729	3,963	0.1	0.1	2.0	2.0	Koruna
Denmark	18	18	1,962	2,086	0.1	0.1	0.8	0.8	Kroner
Egypt	304	312	33,100	36,228	0.2	0.2	2.8	2.8	Pounds
Finland	18	18	1,943	2,067	0.1	0.1	0.1	0.1	Euro
France	199	199	21,706	23,151	1.0	1.0	0.9	0.9	Euro
Germany	508	501	55,263	58,306	3.2	3.2	2.6	2.7	Euro
Greece	33	33	3,635	3,857	0.1	0.1	0.1	0.1	Euro
Hong Kong	20	20	2,230	2,372	0.1	0.1	921.7	930.4	Dollar
Hungary	30	30	3,279	3,459	0.1	0.1	14.6	14.9	Forint*
India	3,993	4,053	434,527	471,376	1.0	1.1	65.1	67.7	Rupees
Indonesia	993	1,006	108,052	116,955	0.5	0.5	6.8	7.1	Rupiah*

MOTOR VEHICLE PARTS & SUPPLIES WHOLESALES (NAICS 42312)

COUNTRY ESTIMATES

Country	Establishments 2018	Establishments 2019	Employment 2018	Employment 2019	Sales ($B) 2018	Sales ($B) 2019	Local Sales (B) 2018	Local Sales (B) 2019	Currency
Iran	272	275	29,593	32,001	0.2	0.2	6.6	6.5	Rial*
Iraq	143	145	15,520	16,840	0.1	0.1	0.1	0.1	Dinar*
Ireland	20	20	2,178	2,356	0.2	0.3	0.2	0.2	Euro
Israel	28	29	3,086	3,343	0.1	0.2	0.5	0.5	Shekel
Italy	201	200	21,865	23,258	0.8	0.8	0.7	0.7	Euro
Japan	846	837	92,036	97,349	3.9	3.9	443.5	439.9	Yen*
Kazakhstan	69	69	7,498	8,050	0.1	0.1	32.1	32.5	Tenge
Kuwait	16	17	1,752	1,954	0.1	0.1	0.0	0.0	Dinar
Malaysia	132	134	14,345	15,589	0.2	0.2	0.7	0.8	Ringgit
Mexico	429	434	46,732	50,520	0.5	0.5	10.2	10.3	New pesos
Netherlands	54	53	5,846	6,211	0.3	0.3	0.3	0.3	Euro
New Zealand	14	15	1,572	1,690	0.1	0.1	0.1	0.1	Dollar
Nigeria	741	753	80,609	87,587	0.3	0.3	97,249.3	98,076.9	Naira
Norway	20	20	2,160	2,315	0.2	0.2	1.6	1.6	Krone
Pakistan	594	606	64,593	70,465	0.1	0.1	13.3	13.7	Rupees
Peru	118	118	12,786	13,681	0.1	0.1	0.3	0.3	Nuevo Sol
Phillipines	320	326	34,816	37,853	0.1	0.2	7.3	7.6	Pesos
Poland	110	108	11,927	12,606	0.2	0.2	0.8	0.8	Zloty
Portugal	35	34	3,771	3,998	0.1	0.1	0.1	0.1	Euro
Puerto Rico	15	15	1,631	1,716	0.1	0.1	0.1	0.1	Dollar
Qatar	15	17	1,643	1,999	0.1	0.1	0.3	0.3	Riyal
Romania	79	78	8,585	9,029	0.1	0.1	0.4	0.4	New Leu
Russia	490	484	53,323	56,326	0.6	0.6	32.2	31.4	Rubles
Saudi Arabia	137	142	14,959	16,495	0.4	0.4	0.0	0.0	Rials*
Singapore	22	22	2,388	2,613	0.1	0.2	198.1	200.3	Dollar
South Africa	136	137	14,747	15,957	0.1	0.1	1,676.8	1,675.1	Rand
South Korea	383	382	41,688	44,374	1.5	1.5	1,578.5	1,600.8	Won*
Spain	159	160	17,302	18,596	0.6	0.6	473.0	467.5	Euro
Sweden	33	33	3,546	3,784	0.2	0.2	1,992.1	2,029.9	Krona
Switzerland	30	30	3,244	3,475	0.3	0.3	324.5	325.3	Swiss franc
Taiwan	119	123	12,990	14,343	0.3	0.3	7,456.7	7,498.0	Dollar
Thailand	289	290	31,400	33,723	0.2	0.2	6,863.2	6,884.8	Baht
Turkey	219	218	23,794	25,308	0.4	0.4	1,524.1	1,554.0	Euro
Ukraine	160	157	17,357	18,269	0.0	0.0	888.1	786.7	Hryvna
UAE	74	83	8,089	9,679	0.2	0.2	810.2	809.8	Dirham
United Kingdom	208	207	22,616	24,100	1.3	1.3	969.8	980.1	Pounds
United States	2,018	2,019	219,590	234,788	16.0	16.1	15,959.0	16,115.7	Dollars
Venezuela	103	104	11,200	12,151	0.2	0.2	2,171.5	2,086.2	Bolivar
Vietnam	362	362	39,406	42,135	0.1	0.1	2,591.7	2,710.5	Dong*

Note: Due to rounding, establishments will vary by + or - one establishment. Therefore, zero establishments may also be one establishment.

* Local Sales are in trillions

FURNITURE WHOLESALE INDUSTRY (NAICS 42321)

NAICS 42321: Furniture Wholesale. Establishments primarily engaged in the wholesale distribution of furniture, including bedsprings, mattresses, and other household furniture; office furniture; and furniture for public parks and buildings. Establishments primarily engaged in the wholesale distribution of partitions, shelving, lockers, and store fixtures are classified in SIC 5046.

COUNTRY ESTIMATES

Country	Establishments 2018	2019	Employment 2018	2019	Sales ($B) 2018	2019	Local Sales (B) 2018	2019	Currency
Algeria	371	373	9,257	9,872	0.1	0.1	11.3	11.3	Dinar
Argentina	257	258	6,418	6,808	0.2	0.2	4.5	4.4	Pesos
Australia	160	162	3,993	4,272	0.6	0.6	0.7	0.7	Dollars
Austria	57	57	1,429	1,508	0.2	0.2	0.1	0.1	Euro
Bangladesh	1,129	1,130	28,145	29,878	0.1	0.1	7.9	8.3	Taka
Belgium	72	72	1,791	1,899	0.2	0.2	0.2	0.2	Euro
Brazil	1,375	1,387	34,276	36,652	0.7	0.7	2,297.2	2,229.4	Real
Canada	241	242	6,007	6,387	0.7	0.7	0.8	0.8	Dollars
Chile	133	134	3,323	3,550	0.1	0.1	70.3	70.7	Pesos*
China	9,511	9,479	237,068	250,553	5.9	6.2	38.6	40.0	RMB
Colombia	286	286	7,128	7,560	0.1	0.1	0.4	0.4	Pesos*
Czech Republic	69	68	1,709	1,802	0.1	0.1	1.8	1.9	Koruna
Denmark	36	36	899	948	0.1	0.1	0.8	0.8	Kroner
Egypt	608	623	15,165	16,469	0.1	0.1	2.6	2.6	Pounds
Finland	36	36	890	940	0.1	0.1	0.1	0.1	Euro
France	399	398	9,944	10,524	1.0	1.0	0.8	0.8	Euro
Germany	508	501	12,659	13,253	1.5	1.5	1.2	1.2	Euro
Greece	67	66	1,666	1,753	0.1	0.1	0.1	0.1	Euro
Hong Kong	41	41	1,021	1,078	0.1	0.1	854.3	864.1	Dollar
Hungary	60	59	1,502	1,573	0.1	0.1	13.5	13.8	Forint*
India	7,986	8,107	199,078	214,288	1.0	1.0	60.4	62.9	Rupees
Indonesia	1,986	2,011	49,504	53,168	0.5	0.5	6.3	6.5	Rupiah*

Furniture Wholesale Industry
(NAICS 42321)

Country Estimates

Country	Establishments		Employment		Sales ($B)		Local Sales (B)		Currency
	2018	2019	2018	2019	2018	2019	2018	2019	
Iran	544	550	13,558	14,548	0.2	0.2	6.1	6.0	Rial*
Iraq	285	290	7,110	7,655	0.1	0.1	0.1	0.1	Dinar*
Ireland	40	41	998	1,071	0.2	0.2	0.2	0.2	Euro
Israel	57	57	1,414	1,520	0.1	0.1	0.5	0.5	Shekel
Italy	402	400	10,018	10,573	0.8	0.8	0.6	0.6	Euro
Japan	846	837	21,083	22,128	1.8	1.8	205.5	204.3	Yen*
Kazakhstan	138	138	3,435	3,660	0.1	0.1	29.8	30.2	Tenge
Kuwait	32	34	803	888	0.1	0.1	0.0	0.0	Dinar
Malaysia	264	268	6,572	7,087	0.2	0.2	0.7	0.7	Ringgit
Mexico	859	869	21,410	22,967	0.5	0.5	9.5	9.6	New pesos
Netherlands	107	107	2,678	2,824	0.3	0.3	0.3	0.3	Euro
New Zealand	29	29	720	768	0.1	0.1	0.1	0.1	Dollar
Nigeria	1,482	1,506	36,931	39,817	0.3	0.3	90,143.8	91,087.0	Naira
Norway	40	40	989	1,052	0.2	0.2	1.5	1.5	Krone
Pakistan	1,187	1,212	29,593	32,033	0.1	0.1	12.3	12.7	Rupees
Peru	235	235	5,858	6,219	0.1	0.1	0.3	0.3	Nuevo Sol
Phillipines	640	651	15,951	17,208	0.1	0.1	6.8	7.1	Pesos
Poland	219	217	5,464	5,731	0.2	0.2	0.8	0.8	Zloty
Portugal	69	69	1,728	1,817	0.1	0.1	0.1	0.1	Euro
Puerto Rico	30	30	747	780	0.1	0.0	0.1	0.0	Dollar
Qatar	30	34	753	909	0.1	0.1	0.3	0.3	Riyal
Romania	158	155	3,933	4,105	0.1	0.1	0.3	0.4	New Leu
Russia	980	969	24,430	25,606	0.6	0.6	29.8	29.1	Rubles
Saudi Arabia	275	284	6,854	7,499	0.4	0.4	0.0	0.0	Rials*
Singapore	44	45	1,094	1,188	0.1	0.1	183.6	186.0	Dollar
South Africa	271	274	6,756	7,254	0.1	0.1	1,554.3	1,555.8	Rand
South Korea	383	382	9,550	10,086	0.7	0.7	731.6	743.4	Won*
Spain	318	320	7,927	8,454	0.5	0.5	438.4	434.1	Euro
Sweden	65	65	1,625	1,720	0.2	0.2	1,846.5	1,885.2	Krona
Switzerland	60	60	1,486	1,580	0.3	0.3	300.8	302.1	Swiss franc
Taiwan	239	247	5,952	6,520	0.2	0.2	6,911.9	6,963.6	Dollar
Thailand	577	580	14,386	15,331	0.2	0.2	6,361.8	6,394.1	Baht
Turkey	437	435	10,901	11,505	0.4	0.4	1,412.7	1,443.2	Euro
Ukraine	319	314	7,952	8,305	0.0	0.0	823.2	730.6	Hryvna
UAE	149	166	3,706	4,400	0.2	0.2	751.0	752.1	Dirham
United Kingdom	416	414	10,361	10,956	1.2	1.2	898.9	910.2	Pounds
United States	2,018	2,019	50,303	53,367	7.4	7.5	7,396.5	7,483.6	Dollars
Venezuela	206	209	5,131	5,524	0.2	0.2	2,012.9	1,937.5	Bolivar
Vietnam	724	725	18,054	19,154	0.1	0.1	2,402.3	2,517.4	Dong*

Note: Due to rounding, establishments will vary by + or - one establishment. Therefore, zero establishments may also be one establishment.

* Local Sales are in trillions

HOME FURNISHINGS WHOLESALE INDUSTRY (NAICS 42322)

NAICS 42322: Home Furnishings Wholesales. Establishments primarily engaged in the wholesale distribution of homefurnishings and housewares, including antiques; china; glassware and earthenware; lamps (including electric); curtains and draperies; linens and towels; and carpets, linoleum, and all other types of hard and soft surface floor coverings. Wholesale distribution of other electrical household goods is classified in SIC 5064; precious metal flatware in SIC 5094.

COUNTRY ESTIMATES

Country	Establishments 2018	2019	Employment 2018	2019	Sales ($B) 2018	2019	Local Sales (B) 2018	2019	Currency
Algeria	371	373	9,624	10,227	0.1	0.1	12.8	12.8	Dinar
Argentina	257	258	6,672	7,053	0.3	0.3	5.1	4.9	Pesos
Australia	160	162	4,152	4,425	0.7	0.7	0.8	0.8	Dollars
Austria	57	57	1,485	1,562	0.2	0.2	0.2	0.2	Euro
Bangladesh	1,129	1,130	29,260	30,952	0.1	0.1	9.0	9.3	Taka
Belgium	72	72	1,862	1,968	0.2	0.2	0.2	0.2	Euro
Brazil	1,375	1,387	35,633	37,969	0.8	0.8	2,609.1	2,508.7	Real
Canada	241	242	6,245	6,616	0.8	0.8	0.9	0.9	Dollars
Chile	133	134	3,455	3,677	0.1	0.1	79.8	79.6	Pesos*
China	9,511	9,479	246,457	259,557	6.8	6.9	43.8	45.0	RMB
Colombia	286	286	7,411	7,832	0.1	0.1	0.4	0.4	Pesos*
Czech Republic	69	68	1,776	1,866	0.1	0.1	2.1	2.1	Koruna
Denmark	36	36	934	982	0.1	0.1	0.9	0.9	Kroner
Egypt	608	623	15,766	17,061	0.2	0.2	2.9	2.9	Pounds
Finland	36	36	926	973	0.1	0.1	0.1	0.1	Euro
France	399	398	10,338	10,902	1.1	1.1	0.9	0.9	Euro
Germany	508	501	13,161	13,729	1.7	1.7	1.4	1.4	Euro
Greece	67	66	1,731	1,816	0.1	0.1	0.1	0.1	Euro
Hong Kong	41	41	1,062	1,117	0.1	0.1	970.3	972.3	Dollar
Hungary	60	59	1,562	1,629	0.1	0.1	15.3	15.5	Forint*
India	7,986	8,107	206,963	221,989	1.1	1.1	68.6	70.8	Rupees
Indonesia	1,986	2,011	51,464	55,079	0.5	0.5	7.2	7.4	Rupiah*

HOME FURNISHINGS WHOLESALE INDUSTRY
(NAICS 42322)

COUNTRY ESTIMATES

Country	Establishments 2018	Establishments 2019	Employment 2018	Employment 2019	Sales ($B) 2018	Sales ($B) 2019	Local Sales (B) 2018	Local Sales (B) 2019	Currency
Iran	544	550	14,095	15,071	0.2	0.2	7.0	6.8	Rial*
Iraq	285	290	7,392	7,930	0.1	0.1	0.1	0.1	Dinar*
Ireland	40	41	1,037	1,110	0.2	0.3	0.2	0.2	Euro
Israel	57	57	1,470	1,574	0.2	0.2	0.5	0.5	Shekel
Italy	402	400	10,414	10,953	0.9	0.9	0.7	0.7	Euro
Japan	846	837	21,918	22,923	2.1	2.0	233.4	229.9	Yen*
Kazakhstan	138	138	3,571	3,791	0.1	0.1	33.8	33.9	Tenge
Kuwait	32	34	835	920	0.1	0.1	0.0	0.0	Dinar
Malaysia	264	268	6,832	7,341	0.2	0.2	0.8	0.8	Ringgit
Mexico	859	869	22,258	23,792	0.6	0.6	10.8	10.8	New pesos
Netherlands	107	107	2,784	2,925	0.4	0.4	0.3	0.3	Euro
New Zealand	29	29	749	796	0.1	0.1	0.1	0.1	Dollar
Nigeria	1,482	1,506	38,393	41,248	0.3	0.3	102,383.0	102,497.7	Naira
Norway	40	40	1,029	1,090	0.2	0.2	1.7	1.7	Krone
Pakistan	1,187	1,212	30,765	33,185	0.1	0.1	14.0	14.3	Rupees
Peru	235	235	6,090	6,443	0.1	0.1	0.3	0.3	Nuevo Sol
Phillipines	640	651	16,583	17,827	0.2	0.2	7.7	8.0	Pesos
Poland	219	217	5,681	5,937	0.3	0.3	0.9	0.9	Zloty
Portugal	69	69	1,796	1,883	0.1	0.1	0.1	0.1	Euro
Puerto Rico	30	30	777	808	0.1	0.1	0.1	0.1	Dollar
Qatar	30	34	782	942	0.1	0.1	0.3	0.3	Riyal
Romania	158	155	4,089	4,252	0.1	0.1	0.4	0.4	New Leu
Russia	980	969	25,398	26,526	0.7	0.6	33.9	32.8	Rubles
Saudi Arabia	275	284	7,125	7,768	0.4	0.4	0.0	0.0	Rials*
Singapore	44	45	1,137	1,230	0.2	0.2	208.6	209.3	Dollar
South Africa	271	274	7,024	7,515	0.1	0.1	1,765.4	1,750.7	Rand
South Korea	383	382	9,928	10,449	0.8	0.8	830.9	836.5	Won*
Spain	318	320	8,241	8,757	0.6	0.6	497.9	488.5	Euro
Sweden	65	65	1,689	1,782	0.3	0.3	2,097.2	2,121.4	Krona
Switzerland	60	60	1,545	1,637	0.3	0.3	341.7	339.9	Swiss franc
Taiwan	239	247	6,187	6,755	0.3	0.3	7,850.3	7,836.0	Dollar
Thailand	577	580	14,956	15,881	0.2	0.2	7,225.5	7,195.1	Baht
Turkey	437	435	11,333	11,919	0.4	0.4	1,604.5	1,624.0	Euro
Ukraine	319	314	8,267	8,604	0.0	0.0	934.9	822.2	Hryvna
UAE	149	166	3,853	4,558	0.2	0.2	852.9	846.3	Dirham
United Kingdom	416	414	10,772	11,350	1.4	1.4	1,020.9	1,024.2	Pounds
United States	2,018	2,019	52,295	55,285	8.4	8.4	8,400.7	8,421.0	Dollars
Venezuela	206	209	5,334	5,722	0.2	0.2	2,286.2	2,180.3	Bolivar
Vietnam	724	725	18,769	19,843	0.1	0.1	2,728.5	2,832.7	Dong*

Note: Due to rounding, establishments will vary by + or - one establishment. Therefore, zero establishments may also be one establishment.

* Local Sales are in trillions

OFFICE EQUIPMENT WHOLESALES INDUSTRY (NAICS 42342)

NAICS 42342: Office Equipment Wholesales. Establishments primarily engaged in the wholesale distribution of office machines and related equipment, including photocopy and microfilm equipment and safes and vaults. These establishments frequently also sell office supplies, but wholesaling most office supplies is classified in SIC 5111-5113. Wholesaling office furniture is classified in SIC 5021, and wholesaling computers and peripheral equipment is classified in SIC 5045.

COUNTRY ESTIMATES

Country	Establishments 2018	2019	Employment 2018	2019	Sales ($B) 2018	2019	Local Sales (B) 2018	2019	Currency
Algeria	371	373	6,157	6,365	0.1	0.1	12.2	12.5	Dinar
Argentina	257	258	4,269	4,390	0.3	0.3	4.8	4.8	Pesos
Australia	160	162	2,656	2,754	0.6	0.6	0.8	0.8	Dollars
Austria	57	57	950	972	0.2	0.2	0.1	0.1	Euro
Bangladesh	1,129	1,130	18,721	19,263	0.1	0.1	8.6	9.1	Taka
Belgium	72	72	1,191	1,225	0.2	0.2	0.2	0.2	Euro
Brazil	1,375	1,387	22,799	23,631	0.8	0.8	2,488.2	2,455.3	Real
Canada	241	242	3,996	4,118	0.7	0.7	0.9	0.9	Dollars
Chile	133	134	2,211	2,289	0.1	0.1	76.1	77.9	Pesos*
China	9,511	9,479	157,691	161,539	6.4	6.8	41.8	44.0	RMB
Colombia	286	286	4,741	4,874	0.1	0.1	0.4	0.4	Pesos*
Czech Republic	69	68	1,136	1,162	0.1	0.1	2.0	2.1	Koruna
Denmark	36	36	598	611	0.1	0.1	0.8	0.9	Kroner
Egypt	608	623	10,087	10,618	0.2	0.2	2.8	2.8	Pounds
Finland	36	36	592	606	0.1	0.1	0.1	0.1	Euro
France	399	398	6,615	6,785	1.0	1.0	0.9	0.9	Euro
Germany	508	501	8,421	8,545	1.6	1.6	1.3	1.4	Euro
Greece	67	66	1,108	1,130	0.1	0.1	0.1	0.1	Euro
Hong Kong	41	41	679	695	0.1	0.1	925.4	951.6	Dollar
Hungary	60	59	999	1,014	0.1	0.1	14.6	15.2	Forint*
India	7,986	8,107	132,421	138,158	1.0	1.1	65.4	69.3	Rupees
Indonesia	1,986	2,011	32,929	34,279	0.5	0.5	6.9	7.2	Rupiah*

OFFICE EQUIPMENT WHOLESALES INDUSTRY
(NAICS 42342)

COUNTRY ESTIMATES

Country	Establishments 2018	2019	Employment 2018	2019	Sales ($B) 2018	2019	Local Sales (B) 2018	2019	Currency
Iran	544	550	9,018	9,379	0.2	0.2	6.6	6.6	Rial*
Iraq	285	290	4,730	4,936	0.1	0.1	0.1	0.1	Dinar*
Ireland	40	41	664	691	0.2	0.3	0.2	0.2	Euro
Israel	57	57	940	980	0.1	0.2	0.5	0.5	Shekel
Italy	402	400	6,663	6,817	0.8	0.8	0.7	0.7	Euro
Japan	846	837	14,024	14,266	2.0	2.0	222.6	225.0	Yen*
Kazakhstan	138	138	2,285	2,360	0.1	0.1	32.3	33.2	Tenge
Kuwait	32	34	534	573	0.1	0.1	0.0	0.0	Dinar
Malaysia	264	268	4,371	4,569	0.2	0.2	0.7	0.8	Ringgit
Mexico	859	869	14,242	14,807	0.5	0.5	10.3	10.6	New pesos
Netherlands	107	107	1,781	1,821	0.3	0.3	0.3	0.3	Euro
New Zealand	29	29	479	495	0.1	0.1	0.1	0.1	Dollar
Nigeria	1,482	1,506	24,565	25,671	0.3	0.3	97,641.3	100,318.4	Naira
Norway	40	40	658	679	0.2	0.2	1.6	1.7	Krone
Pakistan	1,187	1,212	19,685	20,653	0.1	0.1	13.3	14.0	Rupees
Peru	235	235	3,897	4,010	0.1	0.1	0.3	0.3	Nuevo Sol
Phillipines	640	651	10,610	11,095	0.1	0.2	7.3	7.8	Pesos
Poland	219	217	3,635	3,695	0.2	0.2	0.8	0.9	Zloty
Portugal	69	69	1,149	1,172	0.1	0.1	0.1	0.1	Euro
Puerto Rico	30	30	497	503	0.1	0.1	0.1	0.1	Dollar
Qatar	30	34	501	586	0.1	0.1	0.3	0.3	Riyal
Romania	158	155	2,616	2,646	0.1	0.1	0.4	0.4	New Leu
Russia	980	969	16,250	16,509	0.6	0.6	32.3	32.1	Rubles
Saudi Arabia	275	284	4,559	4,835	0.4	0.4	0.0	0.0	Rials*
Singapore	44	45	728	766	0.1	0.2	198.9	204.9	Dollar
South Africa	271	274	4,494	4,677	0.1	0.1	1,683.6	1,713.4	Rand
South Korea	383	382	6,352	6,503	0.7	0.8	792.4	818.7	Won*
Spain	318	320	5,273	5,450	0.6	0.6	474.9	478.1	Euro
Sweden	65	65	1,081	1,109	0.2	0.3	2,000.1	2,076.3	Krona
Switzerland	60	60	989	1,019	0.3	0.3	325.8	332.7	Swiss franc
Taiwan	239	247	3,959	4,204	0.3	0.3	7,486.8	7,669.4	Dollar
Thailand	577	580	9,569	9,884	0.2	0.2	6,890.9	7,042.2	Baht
Turkey	437	435	7,251	7,418	0.4	0.4	1,530.2	1,589.5	Euro
Ukraine	319	314	5,290	5,355	0.0	0.0	891.6	804.7	Hryvna
UAE	149	166	2,465	2,837	0.2	0.2	813.4	828.3	Dirham
United Kingdom	416	414	6,892	7,064	1.3	1.4	973.7	1,002.5	Pounds
United States	2,018	2,019	33,460	34,408	8.0	8.2	8,011.7	8,242.0	Dollars
Venezuela	206	209	3,413	3,561	0.2	0.2	2,180.3	2,133.9	Bolivar
Vietnam	724	725	12,009	12,349	0.1	0.1	2,602.1	2,772.5	Dong*

Note: Due to rounding, establishments will vary by + or - one establishment. Therefore, zero establishments may also be one establishment.

* Local Sales are in trillions

COMPUTER & EQUIPMENT WHOLESALE INDUSTRY (NAICS 42343)

NAICS 42343: Computer & Peripheral Equipment and Software Wholesalers. This U.S. industry comprises establishments primarily engaged in wholesaling computers, computer peripheral equipment, loaded computer boards, and/or computer software.

COUNTRY ESTIMATES

Country	Establishments		Employment		Sales ($B)		Local Sales (B)		
Country	2018	2019	2018	2019	2018	2019	2018	2019	Currency
Algeria	371	373	33,570	34,608	0.1	0.1	13.2	12.8	Dinar
Argentina	257	258	23,273	23,869	0.3	0.3	5.2	5.0	Pesos
Australia	160	162	14,482	14,976	0.7	0.7	0.9	0.8	Dollars
Austria	57	57	5,181	5,286	0.2	0.2	0.2	0.2	Euro
Bangladesh	1,129	1,130	102,067	104,747	0.1	0.1	9.3	9.4	Taka
Belgium	72	72	6,495	6,659	0.2	0.2	0.2	0.2	Euro
Brazil	1,375	1,387	124,298	128,495	0.8	0.8	2,687.5	2,525.5	Real
Canada	241	242	21,784	22,391	0.8	0.8	1.0	0.9	Dollars
Chile	133	134	12,052	12,444	0.1	0.1	82.2	80.1	Pesos*
China	9,511	9,479	859,707	878,384	7.0	7.0	45.1	45.3	RMB
Colombia	286	286	25,850	26,504	0.1	0.1	0.4	0.4	Pesos*
Czech Republic	69	68	6,196	6,316	0.1	0.1	2.2	2.1	Koruna
Denmark	36	36	3,260	3,324	0.1	0.1	0.9	0.9	Kroner
Egypt	608	623	54,994	57,737	0.2	0.2	3.0	2.9	Pounds
Finland	36	36	3,229	3,294	0.1	0.1	0.1	0.1	Euro
France	399	398	36,063	36,896	1.1	1.1	0.9	0.9	Euro
Germany	508	501	45,908	46,462	1.7	1.7	1.4	1.4	Euro
Greece	67	66	6,040	6,147	0.1	0.1	0.1	0.1	Euro
Hong Kong	41	41	3,704	3,780	0.1	0.1	999.5	978.8	Dollar
Hungary	60	59	5,448	5,513	0.1	0.1	15.8	15.6	Forint*
India	7,986	8,107	721,940	751,247	1.1	1.1	70.6	71.3	Rupees
Indonesia	1,986	2,011	179,521	186,396	0.6	0.6	7.4	7.4	Rupiah*

COMPUTER & EQUIPMENT WHOLESALE INDUSTRY (NAICS 42343)

COUNTRY ESTIMATES

Country	Establishments 2018	Establishments 2019	Employment 2018	Employment 2019	Sales ($B) 2018	Sales ($B) 2019	Local Sales (B) 2018	Local Sales (B) 2019	Currency
Iran	544	550	49,167	51,001	0.2	0.2	7.2	6.8	Rial*
Iraq	285	290	25,785	26,838	0.1	0.1	0.1	0.1	Dinar*
Ireland	40	41	3,618	3,756	0.3	0.3	0.2	0.2	Euro
Israel	57	57	5,127	5,328	0.2	0.2	0.6	0.5	Shekel
Italy	402	400	36,328	37,066	0.9	0.9	0.7	0.7	Euro
Japan	846	837	76,456	77,574	2.1	2.0	240.5	231.4	Yen*
Kazakhstan	138	138	12,457	12,830	0.1	0.1	34.8	34.2	Tenge
Kuwait	32	34	2,911	3,113	0.1	0.1	0.0	0.0	Dinar
Malaysia	264	268	23,833	24,844	0.2	0.2	0.8	0.8	Ringgit
Mexico	859	869	77,643	80,515	0.6	0.6	11.1	10.9	New pesos
Netherlands	107	107	9,712	9,899	0.4	0.4	0.3	0.3	Euro
New Zealand	29	29	2,612	2,693	0.1	0.1	0.1	0.1	Dollar
Nigeria	1,482	1,506	133,926	139,590	0.3	0.3	105,462.4	103,184.0	Naira
Norway	40	40	3,588	3,690	0.2	0.2	1.8	1.7	Krone
Pakistan	1,187	1,212	107,318	112,302	0.1	0.1	14.4	14.4	Rupees
Peru	235	235	21,243	21,803	0.1	0.1	0.3	0.3	Nuevo Sol
Phillipines	640	651	57,845	60,328	0.2	0.2	7.9	8.0	Pesos
Poland	219	217	19,816	20,091	0.3	0.3	0.9	0.9	Zloty
Portugal	69	69	6,265	6,371	0.1	0.1	0.1	0.1	Euro
Puerto Rico	30	30	2,711	2,735	0.1	0.1	0.1	0.1	Dollar
Qatar	30	34	2,729	3,186	0.1	0.1	0.4	0.3	Riyal
Romania	158	155	14,263	14,390	0.1	0.1	0.4	0.4	New Leu
Russia	980	969	88,594	89,769	0.7	0.6	34.9	33.0	Rubles
Saudi Arabia	275	284	24,854	26,289	0.4	0.4	0.0	0.0	Rials*
Singapore	44	45	3,967	4,164	0.2	0.2	214.8	210.7	Dollar
South Africa	271	274	24,501	25,432	0.1	0.1	1,818.5	1,762.4	Rand
South Korea	383	382	34,631	35,360	0.8	0.8	855.9	842.1	Won*
Spain	318	320	28,747	29,637	0.6	0.6	512.9	491.8	Euro
Sweden	65	65	5,891	6,030	0.3	0.3	2,160.3	2,135.6	Krona
Switzerland	60	60	5,390	5,539	0.4	0.4	351.9	342.2	Swiss franc
Taiwan	239	247	21,583	22,858	0.3	0.3	8,086.5	7,888.5	Dollar
Thailand	577	580	52,170	53,745	0.2	0.2	7,442.9	7,243.3	Baht
Turkey	437	435	39,532	40,334	0.4	0.4	1,652.8	1,634.9	Euro
Ukraine	319	314	28,838	29,117	0.0	0.0	963.1	827.7	Hryvna
UAE	149	166	13,440	15,426	0.2	0.2	878.6	852.0	Dirham
United Kingdom	416	414	37,574	38,409	1.4	1.4	1,051.7	1,031.1	Pounds
United States	2,018	2,019	182,418	187,094	8.7	8.5	8,653.4	8,477.4	Dollars
Venezuela	206	209	18,608	19,366	0.2	0.2	2,354.9	2,194.9	Bolivar
Vietnam	724	725	65,470	67,151	0.1	0.1	2,810.6	2,851.7	Dong*

Note: Due to rounding, establishments will vary by + or - one establishment. Therefore, zero establishments may also be one establishment.

* Local Sales are in trillions

HARDWARE WHOLESALE INDUSTRY (NAICS 42371)

NAICS 42371: Hardware Wholesales. Establishments primarily engaged in the wholesale distribution of cutlery and general hardware, including handsaws; saw blades; brads, staples, and tacks; and bolts, nuts, rivets, and screws. Establishments primarily engaged in the wholesale distribution of nails, noninsulated wire, and screening are classified in SIC 5051.

COUNTRY ESTIMATES

Country	Establishments		Employment		Sales ($B)		Local Sales (B)		
	2018	2019	2018	2019	2018	2019	2018	2019	Currency
Algeria	371	373	10,440	10,973	0.1	0.1	9.7	9.6	Dinar
Argentina	257	258	7,238	7,568	0.2	0.2	3.8	3.7	Pesos
Australia	160	162	4,504	4,748	0.5	0.5	0.6	0.6	Dollars
Austria	57	57	1,611	1,676	0.1	0.1	0.1	0.1	Euro
Bangladesh	1,129	1,130	31,743	33,212	0.1	0.1	6.8	7.0	Taka
Belgium	72	72	2,020	2,111	0.2	0.2	0.1	0.1	Euro
Brazil	1,375	1,387	38,657	40,742	0.6	0.6	1,969.3	1,888.3	Real
Canada	241	242	6,775	7,100	0.6	0.6	0.7	0.7	Dollars
Chile	133	134	3,748	3,946	0.1	0.1	60.2	59.9	Pesos*
China	9,511	9,479	267,369	278,511	5.1	5.2	33.1	33.8	RMB
Colombia	286	286	8,039	8,404	0.1	0.1	0.3	0.3	Pesos*
Czech Republic	69	68	1,927	2,003	0.1	0.1	1.6	1.6	Koruna
Denmark	36	36	1,014	1,054	0.1	0.1	0.7	0.7	Kroner
Egypt	608	623	17,103	18,307	0.1	0.1	2.2	2.2	Pounds
Finland	36	36	1,004	1,045	0.1	0.1	0.1	0.1	Euro
France	399	398	11,215	11,699	0.8	0.8	0.7	0.7	Euro
Germany	508	501	14,277	14,732	1.3	1.3	1.1	1.0	Euro
Greece	67	66	1,878	1,949	0.1	0.1	0.1	0.1	Euro
Hong Kong	41	41	1,152	1,199	0.1	0.1	732.4	731.9	Dollar
Hungary	60	59	1,694	1,748	0.0	0.0	11.6	11.7	Forint*
India	7,986	8,107	224,524	238,200	0.8	0.8	51.8	53.3	Rupees
Indonesia	1,986	2,011	55,831	59,101	0.4	0.4	5.4	5.5	Rupiah*

Hardware Wholesale Industry
(NAICS 42371)

Country Estimates

Country	Establishments		Employment		Sales ($B)		Local Sales (B)		
	2018	2019	2018	2019	2018	2019	2018	2019	Currency
Iran	544	550	15,291	16,171	0.1	0.1	5.3	5.1	Rial*
Iraq	285	290	8,019	8,510	0.1	0.1	0.1	0.1	Dinar*
Ireland	40	41	1,125	1,191	0.2	0.2	0.2	0.2	Euro
Israel	57	57	1,594	1,689	0.1	0.1	0.4	0.4	Shekel
Italy	402	400	11,298	11,753	0.7	0.6	0.5	0.5	Euro
Japan	846	837	23,778	24,597	1.6	1.5	176.2	173.0	Yen*
Kazakhstan	138	138	3,874	4,068	0.1	0.1	25.5	25.5	Tenge
Kuwait	32	34	905	987	0.0	0.0	0.0	0.0	Dinar
Malaysia	264	268	7,412	7,877	0.1	0.1	0.6	0.6	Ringgit
Mexico	859	869	24,147	25,529	0.4	0.4	8.1	8.1	New pesos
Netherlands	107	107	3,021	3,139	0.3	0.3	0.2	0.2	Euro
New Zealand	29	29	812	854	0.1	0.1	0.1	0.1	Dollar
Nigeria	1,482	1,506	41,651	44,260	0.2	0.2	77,277.9	77,149.7	Naira
Norway	40	40	1,116	1,170	0.2	0.2	1.3	1.3	Krone
Pakistan	1,187	1,212	33,376	35,608	0.1	0.1	10.5	10.7	Rupees
Peru	235	235	6,607	6,913	0.1	0.1	0.2	0.2	Nuevo Sol
Phillipines	640	651	17,990	19,128	0.1	0.1	5.8	6.0	Pesos
Poland	219	217	6,163	6,370	0.2	0.2	0.7	0.7	Zloty
Portugal	69	69	1,948	2,020	0.1	0.1	0.1	0.1	Euro
Puerto Rico	30	30	843	867	0.0	0.0	0.0	0.0	Dollar
Qatar	30	34	849	1,010	0.1	0.1	0.3	0.3	Riyal
Romania	158	155	4,436	4,563	0.1	0.1	0.3	0.3	New Leu
Russia	980	969	27,553	28,463	0.5	0.5	25.6	24.7	Rubles
Saudi Arabia	275	284	7,730	8,335	0.3	0.3	0.0	0.0	Rials*
Singapore	44	45	1,234	1,320	0.1	0.1	157.4	157.6	Dollar
South Africa	271	274	7,620	8,064	0.1	0.1	1,332.5	1,317.7	Rand
South Korea	383	382	10,770	11,212	0.6	0.6	627.1	629.6	Won*
Spain	318	320	8,940	9,397	0.5	0.4	375.8	367.7	Euro
Sweden	65	65	1,832	1,912	0.2	0.2	1,583.0	1,596.8	Krona
Switzerland	60	60	1,676	1,756	0.3	0.3	257.9	255.9	Swiss franc
Taiwan	239	247	6,712	7,248	0.2	0.2	5,925.4	5,898.1	Dollar
Thailand	577	580	16,225	17,041	0.2	0.2	5,453.8	5,415.8	Baht
Turkey	437	435	12,294	12,789	0.3	0.3	1,211.1	1,222.4	Euro
Ukraine	319	314	8,969	9,232	0.0	0.0	705.7	618.8	Hryvna
UAE	149	166	4,180	4,891	0.2	0.2	643.8	637.0	Dirham
United Kingdom	416	414	11,686	12,178	1.0	1.0	770.6	770.9	Pounds
United States	2,018	2,019	56,732	59,322	6.3	6.3	6,340.8	6,338.5	Dollars
Venezuela	206	209	5,787	6,140	0.2	0.2	1,725.6	1,641.1	Bolivar
Vietnam	724	725	20,361	21,292	0.1	0.1	2,059.5	2,132.2	Dong*

Note: Due to rounding, establishments will vary by + or - one establishment. Therefore, zero establishments may also be one establishment.

* Local Sales are in trillions

Printing & Writing Paper Wholesales (NAICS 42411)

NAICS 42411: Printing & Writing Paper Wholesales. Establishments primarily engaged in the wholesale distribution of printing and writing paper, including envelope paper; fine paper; and groundwood paper.

Country Estimates

Country	Establishments 2018	Establishments 2019	Employment 2018	Employment 2019	Sales ($B) 2018	Sales ($B) 2019	Local Sales (B) 2018	Local Sales (B) 2019	Currency
Algeria	371	373	3,692	3,889	0.0	0.0	1.7	1.7	Dinar
Argentina	257	258	2,559	2,682	0.0	0.0	0.7	0.6	Pesos
Australia	160	162	1,593	1,683	0.1	0.1	0.1	0.1	Dollars
Austria	57	57	570	594	0.0	0.0	0.0	0.0	Euro
Bangladesh	1,129	1,130	11,225	11,772	0.0	0.0	1.2	1.2	Taka
Belgium	72	72	714	748	0.0	0.0	0.0	0.0	Euro
Brazil	1,375	1,387	13,670	14,441	0.1	0.1	345.0	328.7	Real
Canada	241	242	2,396	2,516	0.1	0.1	0.1	0.1	Dollars
Chile	133	134	1,325	1,399	0.0	0.0	10.6	10.4	Pesos*
China	9,511	9,479	94,547	98,716	0.9	0.9	5.8	5.9	RMB
Colombia	286	286	2,843	2,979	0.0	0.0	0.1	0.1	Pesos*
Czech Republic	69	68	681	710	0.0	0.0	0.3	0.3	Koruna
Denmark	36	36	358	374	0.0	0.0	0.1	0.1	Kroner
Egypt	608	623	6,048	6,489	0.0	0.0	0.4	0.4	Pounds
Finland	36	36	355	370	0.0	0.0	0.0	0.0	Euro
France	399	398	3,966	4,146	0.1	0.1	0.1	0.1	Euro
Germany	508	501	5,049	5,222	0.2	0.2	0.2	0.2	Euro
Greece	67	66	664	691	0.0	0.0	0.0	0.0	Euro
Hong Kong	41	41	407	425	0.0	0.0	128.3	127.4	Dollar
Hungary	60	59	599	620	0.0	0.0	2.0	2.0	Forint*
India	7,986	8,107	79,396	84,428	0.1	0.1	9.1	9.3	Rupees
Indonesia	1,986	2,011	19,743	20,948	0.1	0.1	1.0	1.0	Rupiah*

PRINTING & WRITING PAPER WHOLESALES (NAICS 42411)

COUNTRY ESTIMATES

Country	Establishments 2018	2019	Employment 2018	2019	Sales ($B) 2018	2019	Local Sales (B) 2018	2019	Currency
Iran	544	550	5,407	5,732	0.0	0.0	0.9	0.9	Rial*
Iraq	285	290	2,836	3,016	0.0	0.0	0.0	0.0	Dinar*
Ireland	40	41	398	422	0.0	0.0	0.0	0.0	Euro
Israel	57	57	564	599	0.0	0.0	0.1	0.1	Shekel
Italy	402	400	3,995	4,166	0.1	0.1	0.1	0.1	Euro
Japan	846	837	8,408	8,718	0.3	0.3	30.9	30.1	Yen*
Kazakhstan	138	138	1,370	1,442	0.0	0.0	4.5	4.4	Tenge
Kuwait	32	34	320	350	0.0	0.0	0.0	0.0	Dinar
Malaysia	264	268	2,621	2,792	0.0	0.0	0.1	0.1	Ringgit
Mexico	859	869	8,539	9,049	0.1	0.1	1.4	1.4	New pesos
Netherlands	107	107	1,068	1,113	0.0	0.0	0.0	0.0	Euro
New Zealand	29	29	287	303	0.0	0.0	0.0	0.0	Dollar
Nigeria	1,482	1,506	14,729	15,688	0.0	0.0	13,539.6	13,429.0	Naira
Norway	40	40	395	415	0.0	0.0	0.2	0.2	Krone
Pakistan	1,187	1,212	11,802	12,621	0.0	0.0	1.8	1.9	Rupees
Peru	235	235	2,336	2,450	0.0	0.0	0.0	0.0	Nuevo Sol
Phillipines	640	651	6,362	6,780	0.0	0.0	1.0	1.0	Pesos
Poland	219	217	2,179	2,258	0.0	0.0	0.1	0.1	Zloty
Portugal	69	69	689	716	0.0	0.0	0.0	0.0	Euro
Puerto Rico	30	30	298	307	0.0	0.0	0.0	0.0	Dollar
Qatar	30	34	300	358	0.0	0.0	0.0	0.0	Riyal
Romania	158	155	1,569	1,617	0.0	0.0	0.1	0.1	New Leu
Russia	980	969	9,743	10,089	0.1	0.1	4.5	4.3	Rubles
Saudi Arabia	275	284	2,733	2,954	0.1	0.1	0.0	0.0	Rials*
Singapore	44	45	436	468	0.0	0.0	27.6	27.4	Dollar
South Africa	271	274	2,695	2,858	0.0	0.0	233.5	229.4	Rand
South Korea	383	382	3,809	3,974	0.1	0.1	109.9	109.6	Won*
Spain	318	320	3,161	3,331	0.1	0.1	65.8	64.0	Euro
Sweden	65	65	648	678	0.0	0.0	277.3	277.9	Krona
Switzerland	60	60	593	622	0.0	0.0	45.2	44.5	Swiss franc
Taiwan	239	247	2,374	2,569	0.0	0.0	1,038.2	1,026.6	Dollar
Thailand	577	580	5,737	6,040	0.0	0.0	955.5	942.7	Baht
Turkey	437	435	4,348	4,533	0.1	0.1	212.2	212.8	Euro
Ukraine	319	314	3,171	3,272	0.0	0.0	123.6	107.7	Hryvna
UAE	149	166	1,478	1,734	0.0	0.0	112.8	110.9	Dirham
United Kingdom	416	414	4,132	4,317	0.2	0.2	135.0	134.2	Pounds
United States	2,018	2,019	20,061	21,026	1.1	1.1	1,111.0	1,103.3	Dollars
Venezuela	206	209	2,046	2,176	0.0	0.0	302.3	285.7	Bolivar
Vietnam	724	725	7,200	7,547	0.0	0.0	360.8	371.1	Dong*

Note: Due to rounding, establishments will vary by + or - one establishment. Therefore, zero establishments may also be one establishment.

* Local Sales are in trillions

Men's & Boys' Clothing Wholesales Industry (NAICS 42432)

NAICS 42432: Men's & Boys' Clothing Wholesales. Establishments primarily engaged in the wholesale distribution of men's and boys' apparel and furnishings, sportswear, hosiery, underwear, nightwear, and work clothing.

Country Estimates

Country	Establishments		Employment		Sales ($B)		Local Sales (B)		
	2018	2019	2018	2019	2018	2019	2018	2019	Currency
Algeria	371	373	10,325	11,022	0.1	0.1	8.9	8.9	Dinar
Argentina	257	258	7,158	7,602	0.2	0.2	3.5	3.4	Pesos
Australia	160	162	4,454	4,769	0.5	0.5	0.6	0.6	Dollars
Austria	57	57	1,594	1,683	0.1	0.1	0.1	0.1	Euro
Bangladesh	1,129	1,130	31,394	33,359	0.1	0.1	6.2	6.5	Taka
Belgium	72	72	1,998	2,121	0.1	0.1	0.1	0.1	Euro
Brazil	1,375	1,387	38,232	40,922	0.6	0.5	1,805.1	1,746.5	Real
Canada	241	242	6,700	7,131	0.5	0.5	0.7	0.7	Dollars
Chile	133	134	3,707	3,963	0.1	0.1	55.2	55.4	Pesos*
China	9,511	9,479	264,428	279,740	4.7	4.8	30.3	31.3	RMB
Colombia	286	286	7,951	8,441	0.1	0.1	0.3	0.3	Pesos*
Czech Republic	69	68	1,906	2,012	0.1	0.1	1.4	1.5	Koruna
Denmark	36	36	1,003	1,059	0.1	0.1	0.6	0.6	Kroner
Egypt	608	623	16,915	18,388	0.1	0.1	2.0	2.0	Pounds
Finland	36	36	993	1,049	0.1	0.1	0.1	0.1	Euro
France	399	398	11,092	11,750	0.8	0.7	0.6	0.6	Euro
Germany	508	501	14,120	14,797	1.2	1.2	1.0	1.0	Euro
Greece	67	66	1,858	1,958	0.1	0.1	0.0	0.0	Euro
Hong Kong	41	41	1,139	1,204	0.1	0.1	671.3	676.9	Dollar
Hungary	60	59	1,676	1,756	0.0	0.0	10.6	10.8	Forint*
India	7,986	8,107	222,054	239,251	0.7	0.8	47.4	49.3	Rupees
Indonesia	1,986	2,011	55,217	59,362	0.4	0.4	5.0	5.1	Rupiah*

MEN'S & BOYS' CLOTHING WHOLESALES INDUSTRY (NAICS 42432)

COUNTRY ESTIMATES

Country	Establishments		Employment		Sales ($B)		Local Sales (B)		Currency
	2018	2019	2018	2019	2018	2019	2018	2019	
Iran	544	550	15,123	16,242	0.1	0.1	4.8	4.7	Rial*
Iraq	285	290	7,931	8,547	0.1	0.1	0.1	0.1	Dinar*
Ireland	40	41	1,113	1,196	0.2	0.2	0.1	0.2	Euro
Israel	57	57	1,577	1,697	0.1	0.1	0.4	0.4	Shekel
Italy	402	400	11,174	11,805	0.6	0.6	0.5	0.5	Euro
Japan	846	837	23,516	24,705	1.4	1.4	161.5	160.0	Yen*
Kazakhstan	138	138	3,831	4,086	0.1	0.1	23.4	23.6	Tenge
Kuwait	32	34	895	992	0.0	0.0	0.0	0.0	Dinar
Malaysia	264	268	7,330	7,912	0.1	0.1	0.5	0.5	Ringgit
Mexico	859	869	23,881	25,642	0.4	0.4	7.5	7.5	New pesos
Netherlands	107	107	2,987	3,153	0.2	0.2	0.2	0.2	Euro
New Zealand	29	29	803	858	0.1	0.1	0.1	0.1	Dollar
Nigeria	1,482	1,506	41,193	44,456	0.2	0.2	70,833.9	71,357.6	Naira
Norway	40	40	1,104	1,175	0.1	0.1	1.2	1.2	Krone
Pakistan	1,187	1,212	33,009	35,765	0.1	0.1	9.7	9.9	Rupees
Peru	235	235	6,534	6,944	0.1	0.1	0.2	0.2	Nuevo Sol
Phillipines	640	651	17,792	19,213	0.1	0.1	5.3	5.5	Pesos
Poland	219	217	6,095	6,399	0.2	0.2	0.6	0.6	Zloty
Portugal	69	69	1,927	2,029	0.1	0.1	0.1	0.1	Euro
Puerto Rico	30	30	834	871	0.0	0.0	0.0	0.0	Dollar
Qatar	30	34	839	1,015	0.1	0.1	0.2	0.2	Riyal
Romania	158	155	4,387	4,583	0.1	0.1	0.3	0.3	New Leu
Russia	980	969	27,250	28,589	0.5	0.4	23.4	22.8	Rubles
Saudi Arabia	275	284	7,645	8,372	0.3	0.3	0.0	0.0	Rials*
Singapore	44	45	1,220	1,326	0.1	0.1	144.3	145.7	Dollar
South Africa	271	274	7,536	8,099	0.1	0.1	1,221.4	1,218.8	Rand
South Korea	383	382	10,652	11,261	0.5	0.5	574.9	582.4	Won*
Spain	318	320	8,842	9,438	0.4	0.4	344.5	340.1	Euro
Sweden	65	65	1,812	1,920	0.2	0.2	1,451.0	1,476.9	Krona
Switzerland	60	60	1,658	1,764	0.2	0.2	236.4	236.7	Swiss franc
Taiwan	239	247	6,638	7,280	0.2	0.2	5,431.3	5,455.3	Dollar
Thailand	577	580	16,046	17,116	0.2	0.2	4,999.0	5,009.2	Baht
Turkey	437	435	12,159	12,845	0.3	0.3	1,110.1	1,130.6	Euro
Ukraine	319	314	8,870	9,273	0.0	0.0	646.8	572.4	Hryvna
UAE	149	166	4,134	4,913	0.2	0.2	590.1	589.2	Dirham
United Kingdom	416	414	11,557	12,232	1.0	1.0	706.3	713.1	Pounds
United States	2,018	2,019	56,108	59,584	5.8	5.9	5,812.1	5,862.6	Dollars
Venezuela	206	209	5,723	6,167	0.2	0.2	1,581.7	1,517.9	Bolivar
Vietnam	724	725	20,137	21,386	0.1	0.1	1,887.7	1,972.1	Dong*

Note: Due to rounding, establishments will vary by + or - one establishment. Therefore, zero establishments may also be one establishment.

* Local Sales are in trillions

WOMEN'S & CHILDREN'S CLOTHING WHOLESALE (NAICS 42433)

NAICS 42433: Women's & Children's Clothing Wholesales.
Establishments primarily engaged in the wholesale distribution of women's, children's, and infants' clothing and accessories, including hosiery, lingerie, millinery, and furs.

COUNTRY ESTIMATES

Country	Establishments		Employment		Sales ($B)		Local Sales (B)		Currency
	2018	2019	2018	2019	2018	2019	2018	2019	
Algeria	371	373	14,369	15,360	0.2	0.2	20.4	20.9	Dinar
Argentina	257	258	9,961	10,594	0.4	0.4	8.0	8.1	Pesos
Australia	160	162	6,199	6,647	1.0	1.1	1.3	1.4	Dollars
Austria	57	57	2,218	2,346	0.3	0.3	0.2	0.2	Euro
Bangladesh	1,129	1,130	43,687	46,490	0.2	0.2	14.3	15.2	Taka
Belgium	72	72	2,780	2,956	0.3	0.3	0.3	0.3	Euro
Brazil	1,375	1,387	53,202	57,031	1.3	1.3	4,155.4	4,102.6	Real
Canada	241	242	9,324	9,938	1.2	1.2	1.5	1.5	Dollars
Chile	133	134	5,158	5,523	0.2	0.2	127.1	130.2	Pesos*
China	9,511	9,479	367,974	389,858	10.8	11.3	69.8	73.5	RMB
Colombia	286	286	11,064	11,764	0.2	0.2	0.7	0.7	Pesos*
Czech Republic	69	68	2,652	2,803	0.2	0.2	3.3	3.5	Koruna
Denmark	36	36	1,395	1,475	0.2	0.2	1.4	1.4	Kroner
Egypt	608	623	23,539	25,626	0.3	0.3	4.6	4.7	Pounds
Finland	36	36	1,382	1,462	0.2	0.2	0.1	0.1	Euro
France	399	398	15,436	16,376	1.7	1.8	1.4	1.5	Euro
Germany	508	501	19,650	20,621	2.7	2.7	2.2	2.3	Euro
Greece	67	66	2,585	2,728	0.1	0.1	0.1	0.1	Euro
Hong Kong	41	41	1,586	1,678	0.2	0.2	1,545.4	1,590.1	Dollar
Hungary	60	59	2,332	2,447	0.1	0.1	24.4	25.4	Forint*
India	7,986	8,107	309,007	333,430	1.7	1.8	109.2	115.8	Rupees
Indonesia	1,986	2,011	76,839	82,729	0.9	0.9	11.5	12.0	Rupiah*

WOMEN'S & CHILDREN'S CLOTHING WHOLESALE
(NAICS 42433)

COUNTRY ESTIMATES

Country	Establishments 2018	Establishments 2019	Employment 2018	Employment 2019	Sales ($B) 2018	Sales ($B) 2019	Local Sales (B) 2018	Local Sales (B) 2019	Currency
Iran	544	550	21,045	22,636	0.3	0.3	11.1	11.1	Rial*
Iraq	285	290	11,037	11,912	0.2	0.2	0.2	0.2	Dinar*
Ireland	40	41	1,549	1,667	0.4	0.5	0.3	0.4	Euro
Israel	57	57	2,194	2,365	0.3	0.3	0.9	0.9	Shekel
Italy	402	400	15,549	16,451	1.4	1.4	1.2	1.2	Euro
Japan	846	837	32,725	34,430	3.3	3.3	371.8	375.9	Yen*
Kazakhstan	138	138	5,332	5,694	0.2	0.2	53.9	55.5	Tenge
Kuwait	32	34	1,246	1,382	0.1	0.1	0.0	0.0	Dinar
Malaysia	264	268	10,201	11,027	0.3	0.3	1.2	1.3	Ringgit
Mexico	859	869	33,233	35,736	0.9	0.9	17.2	17.6	New pesos
Netherlands	107	107	4,157	4,394	0.6	0.6	0.5	0.5	Euro
New Zealand	29	29	1,118	1,195	0.1	0.1	0.2	0.2	Dollar
Nigeria	1,482	1,506	57,324	61,955	0.5	0.5	163,061.5	167,624.1	Naira
Norway	40	40	1,536	1,638	0.3	0.3	2.7	2.8	Krone
Pakistan	1,187	1,212	45,934	49,844	0.2	0.2	22.2	23.4	Rupees
Peru	235	235	9,093	9,677	0.2	0.2	0.5	0.5	Nuevo Sol
Phillipines	640	651	24,759	26,776	0.2	0.3	12.2	13.0	Pesos
Poland	219	217	8,482	8,917	0.4	0.4	1.4	1.4	Zloty
Portugal	69	69	2,682	2,828	0.2	0.1	0.1	0.1	Euro
Puerto Rico	30	30	1,160	1,214	0.1	0.1	0.1	0.1	Dollar
Qatar	30	34	1,168	1,414	0.2	0.2	0.6	0.6	Riyal
Romania	158	155	6,105	6,387	0.2	0.2	0.6	0.6	New Leu
Russia	980	969	37,920	39,843	1.1	1.0	54.0	53.6	Rubles
Saudi Arabia	275	284	10,638	11,668	0.6	0.7	0.0	0.0	Rials*
Singapore	44	45	1,698	1,848	0.2	0.3	332.2	342.4	Dollar
South Africa	271	274	10,487	11,287	0.2	0.2	2,811.6	2,863.0	Rand
South Korea	383	382	14,823	15,694	1.2	1.3	1,323.3	1,368.0	Won*
Spain	318	320	12,304	13,154	0.9	1.0	793.0	798.9	Euro
Sweden	65	65	2,522	2,676	0.4	0.4	3,340.2	3,469.4	Krona
Switzerland	60	60	2,307	2,458	0.6	0.6	544.2	555.9	Swiss franc
Taiwan	239	247	9,238	10,145	0.4	0.4	12,502.9	12,814.9	Dollar
Thailand	577	580	22,330	23,854	0.4	0.4	11,507.8	11,766.9	Baht
Turkey	437	435	16,920	17,902	0.7	0.7	2,555.5	2,655.9	Euro
Ukraine	319	314	12,343	12,923	0.1	0.0	1,489.0	1,344.6	Hryvna
UAE	149	166	5,753	6,847	0.4	0.4	1,358.4	1,384.0	Dirham
United Kingdom	416	414	16,083	17,047	2.2	2.3	1,626.0	1,675.0	Pounds
United States	2,018	2,019	78,079	83,039	13.4	13.8	13,379.5	13,771.7	Dollars
Venezuela	206	209	7,965	8,595	0.4	0.4	3,641.1	3,565.6	Bolivar
Vietnam	724	725	28,023	29,804	0.2	0.2	4,345.6	4,632.6	Dong*

Note: Due to rounding, establishments will vary by + or - one establishment. Therefore, zero establishments may also be one establishment.

* Local Sales are in trillions

General-Line Grocery Wholesale Industry (NAICS 42441)

NAICS 42441: General-Line Grocery Wholesale. Establishments primarily engaged in the wholesale distribution of a general line of groceries. Establishments primarily engaged in roasting coffee, blending tea, or grinding and packaging spices are classified under food processing.

COUNTRY ESTIMATES

Country	Establishments 2018	2019	Employment 2018	2019	Sales ($B) 2018	2019	Local Sales (B) 2018	2019	Currency
Algeria	371	373	27,128	28,688	0.0	0.0	5.0	5.1	Dinar
Argentina	257	258	18,808	19,785	0.1	0.1	2.0	2.0	Pesos
Australia	160	162	11,703	12,414	0.3	0.3	0.3	0.3	Dollars
Austria	57	57	4,187	4,382	0.1	0.1	0.1	0.1	Euro
Bangladesh	1,129	1,130	82,482	86,827	0.0	0.0	3.5	3.7	Taka
Belgium	72	72	5,249	5,520	0.1	0.1	0.1	0.1	Euro
Brazil	1,375	1,387	100,448	106,512	0.3	0.3	1,025.3	993.0	Real
Canada	241	242	17,604	18,561	0.3	0.3	0.4	0.4	Dollars
Chile	133	134	9,739	10,315	0.1	0.1	31.4	31.5	Pesos*
China	9,511	9,479	694,746	728,111	2.7	2.7	17.2	17.8	RMB
Colombia	286	286	20,890	21,970	0.1	0.1	0.2	0.2	Pesos*
Czech Republic	69	68	5,007	5,236	0.0	0.0	0.8	0.8	Koruna
Denmark	36	36	2,634	2,755	0.1	0.1	0.3	0.3	Kroner
Egypt	608	623	44,442	47,860	0.1	0.1	1.1	1.1	Pounds
Finland	36	36	2,609	2,731	0.0	0.0	0.0	0.0	Euro
France	399	398	29,143	30,584	0.4	0.4	0.4	0.4	Euro
Germany	508	501	37,099	38,513	0.7	0.7	0.5	0.5	Euro
Greece	67	66	4,881	5,095	0.0	0.0	0.0	0.0	Euro
Hong Kong	41	41	2,994	3,134	0.0	0.0	381.3	384.9	Dollar
Hungary	60	59	4,402	4,570	0.0	0.0	6.0	6.2	Forint*
India	7,986	8,107	583,414	622,725	0.4	0.4	26.9	28.0	Rupees
Indonesia	1,986	2,011	145,075	154,507	0.2	0.2	2.8	2.9	Rupiah*

GENERAL-LINE GROCERY WHOLESALE INDUSTRY
(NAICS 42441)

COUNTRY ESTIMATES

Country	Establishments 2018	2019	Employment 2018	2019	Sales ($B) 2018	2019	Local Sales (B) 2018	2019	Currency
Iran	544	550	39,733	42,276	0.1	0.1	2.7	2.7	Rial*
Iraq	285	290	20,838	22,246	0.0	0.0	0.0	0.0	Dinar*
Ireland	40	41	2,924	3,113	0.1	0.1	0.1	0.1	Euro
Israel	57	57	4,143	4,417	0.1	0.1	0.2	0.2	Shekel
Italy	402	400	29,357	30,725	0.3	0.3	0.3	0.3	Euro
Japan	846	837	61,786	64,303	0.8	0.8	91.7	91.0	Yen*
Kazakhstan	138	138	10,067	10,635	0.0	0.0	13.3	13.4	Tenge
Kuwait	32	34	2,353	2,581	0.0	0.0	0.0	0.0	Dinar
Malaysia	264	268	19,260	20,594	0.1	0.1	0.3	0.3	Ringgit
Mexico	859	869	62,745	66,741	0.2	0.2	4.2	4.3	New pesos
Netherlands	107	107	7,849	8,206	0.1	0.1	0.1	0.1	Euro
New Zealand	29	29	2,111	2,233	0.0	0.0	0.0	0.0	Dollar
Nigeria	1,482	1,506	108,229	115,709	0.1	0.1	40,232.4	40,570.6	Naira
Norway	40	40	2,899	3,058	0.1	0.1	0.7	0.7	Krone
Pakistan	1,187	1,212	86,726	93,089	0.0	0.1	5.5	5.7	Rupees
Peru	235	235	17,167	18,073	0.0	0.0	0.1	0.1	Nuevo Sol
Phillipines	640	651	46,746	50,007	0.1	0.1	3.0	3.1	Pesos
Poland	219	217	16,013	16,654	0.1	0.1	0.3	0.4	Zloty
Portugal	69	69	5,063	5,281	0.0	0.0	0.0	0.0	Euro
Puerto Rico	30	30	2,190	2,267	0.0	0.0	0.0	0.0	Dollar
Qatar	30	34	2,205	2,641	0.0	0.0	0.1	0.1	Riyal
Romania	158	155	11,526	11,928	0.0	0.0	0.2	0.2	New Leu
Russia	980	969	71,594	74,411	0.3	0.3	13.3	13.0	Rubles
Saudi Arabia	275	284	20,085	21,791	0.2	0.2	0.0	0.0	Rials*
Singapore	44	45	3,206	3,452	0.1	0.1	82.0	82.9	Dollar
South Africa	271	274	19,800	21,081	0.1	0.1	693.7	692.9	Rand
South Korea	383	382	27,986	29,311	0.3	0.3	326.5	331.1	Won*
Spain	318	320	23,231	24,566	0.2	0.2	195.7	193.4	Euro
Sweden	65	65	4,761	4,998	0.1	0.1	824.1	839.7	Krona
Switzerland	60	60	4,355	4,591	0.1	0.1	134.3	134.6	Swiss franc
Taiwan	239	247	17,441	18,948	0.1	0.1	3,084.9	3,101.6	Dollar
Thailand	577	580	42,159	44,551	0.1	0.1	2,839.3	2,848.0	Baht
Turkey	437	435	31,946	33,434	0.2	0.2	630.5	642.8	Euro
Ukraine	319	314	23,304	24,135	0.0	0.0	367.4	325.4	Hryvna
UAE	149	166	10,861	12,787	0.1	0.1	335.2	335.0	Dirham
United Kingdom	416	414	30,365	31,838	0.5	0.6	401.2	405.4	Pounds
United States	2,018	2,019	147,416	155,087	3.3	3.3	3,301.1	3,333.2	Dollars
Venezuela	206	209	15,037	16,053	0.1	0.1	898.4	863.0	Bolivar
Vietnam	724	725	52,908	55,663	0.0	0.0	1,072.2	1,121.2	Dong*

Note: Due to rounding, establishments will vary by + or - one establishment. Therefore, zero establishments may also be one establishment.

* Local Sales are in trillions

NAICS 42481: Beer & Ale Wholesale. Establishments primarily engaged in the wholesale distribution of beer, ale, porter, and other fermented malt beverages.

COUNTRY ESTIMATES

Country	Establishments 2018	Establishments 2019	Employment 2018	Employment 2019	Sales ($B) 2018	Sales ($B) 2019	Local Sales (B) 2018	Local Sales (B) 2019	Currency
Algeria	-	-	-	-	-	-	0.0	0.0	Dinar
Argentina	257	258	8,305	8,702	0.1	0.1	1.5	1.5	Pesos
Australia	160	162	5,168	5,460	0.2	0.2	0.2	0.2	Dollars
Austria	57	57	1,849	1,927	0.1	0.1	0.0	0.0	Euro
Bangladesh	1,129	1,130	36,421	38,189	0.0	0.0	2.7	2.7	Taka
Belgium	72	72	2,318	2,428	0.1	0.1	0.1	0.1	Euro
Brazil	1,375	1,387	44,355	46,847	0.2	0.2	771.5	737.6	Real
Canada	241	242	7,774	8,164	0.2	0.2	0.3	0.3	Dollars
Chile	133	134	4,301	4,537	0.0	0.0	23.6	23.4	Pesos*
China	9,511	9,479	306,778	320,247	2.0	2.0	13.0	13.2	RMB
Colombia	286	286	9,224	9,663	0.0	0.0	0.1	0.1	Pesos*
Czech Republic	69	68	2,211	2,303	0.0	0.0	0.6	0.6	Koruna
Denmark	36	36	1,163	1,212	0.0	0.0	0.3	0.3	Kroner
Egypt	-	-	-	-	-	-	0.0	0.0	Pounds
Finland	36	36	1,152	1,201	0.0	0.0	0.0	0.0	Euro
France	399	398	12,869	13,452	0.3	0.3	0.3	0.3	Euro
Germany	508	501	16,382	16,939	0.5	0.5	0.4	0.4	Euro
Greece	67	66	2,155	2,241	0.0	0.0	0.0	0.0	Euro
Hong Kong	41	41	1,322	1,378	0.0	0.0	286.9	285.9	Dollar
Hungary	60	59	1,944	2,010	0.0	0.0	4.5	4.6	Forint*
India	7,986	8,107	257,617	273,895	0.3	0.3	20.3	20.8	Rupees
Indonesia	-	-	-	-	-	-	0.0	0.0	Rupiah*

Beer & Ale Wholesale Industry
(NAICS 42481)

Country Estimates

Country	Establishments 2018	Establishments 2019	Employment 2018	Employment 2019	Sales ($B) 2018	Sales ($B) 2019	Local Sales (B) 2018	Local Sales (B) 2019	Currency
Iran	-	-	-	-	-	-	0.0	0.0	Rial*
Iraq	-	-	-	-	-	-	0.0	0.0	Dinar*
Ireland	40	41	1,291	1,369	0.1	0.1	0.1	0.1	Euro
Israel	57	57	1,829	1,943	0.0	0.0	0.2	0.2	Shekel
Italy	402	400	12,963	13,514	0.3	0.3	0.2	0.2	Euro
Japan	846	837	27,283	28,283	0.6	0.6	69.0	67.6	Yen*
Kazakhstan	138	138	4,445	4,678	0.0	0.0	10.0	10.0	Tenge
Kuwait	-	-	-	-	-	-	0.0	0.0	Dinar
Malaysia	-	-	-	-	-	-	0.0	0.0	Ringgit
Mexico	859	869	27,706	29,355	0.2	0.2	3.2	3.2	New pesos
Netherlands	107	107	3,466	3,609	0.1	0.1	0.1	0.1	Euro
New Zealand	29	29	932	982	0.0	0.0	0.0	0.0	Dollar
Nigeria	1,482	1,506	47,790	50,893	0.1	0.1	30,274.2	30,135.9	Naira
Norway	40	40	1,280	1,345	0.1	0.1	0.5	0.5	Krone
Pakistan	-	-	-	-	-	-	0.0	0.0	Rupees
Peru	235	235	7,581	7,949	0.0	0.0	0.1	0.1	Nuevo Sol
Phillipines	640	651	20,641	21,995	0.0	0.0	2.3	2.3	Pesos
Poland	219	217	7,071	7,325	0.1	0.1	0.3	0.3	Zloty
Portugal	69	69	2,236	2,323	0.0	0.0	0.0	0.0	Euro
Puerto Rico	30	30	967	997	0.0	0.0	0.0	0.0	Dollar
Qatar	-	-	-	-	-	-	0.0	0.0	Riyal
Romania	158	155	5,090	5,246	0.0	0.0	0.1	0.1	New Leu
Russia	980	969	31,614	32,728	0.2	0.2	10.0	9.6	Rubles
Saudi Arabia	-	-	-	-	-	-	0.0	0.0	Rials*
Singapore	44	45	1,416	1,518	0.0	0.0	61.7	61.5	Dollar
South Africa	271	274	8,743	9,272	0.0	0.0	522.0	514.7	Rand
South Korea	383	382	12,358	12,892	0.2	0.2	245.7	245.9	Won*
Spain	318	320	10,258	10,805	0.2	0.2	147.2	143.6	Euro
Sweden	65	65	2,102	2,198	0.1	0.1	620.1	623.7	Krona
Switzerland	60	60	1,923	2,019	0.1	0.1	101.0	99.9	Swiss franc
Taiwan	239	247	7,702	8,334	0.1	0.1	2,321.3	2,303.9	Dollar
Thailand	577	580	18,616	19,595	0.1	0.1	2,136.6	2,115.5	Baht
Turkey	-	-	-	-	-	-	0.0	0.0	Euro
Ukraine	319	314	10,290	10,616	0.0	0.0	276.5	241.7	Hryvna
UAE	-	-	-	-	-	-	0.0	0.0	Dirham
United Kingdom	416	414	13,408	14,003	0.4	0.4	301.9	301.1	Pounds
United States	2,018	2,019	65,094	68,212	2.5	2.5	2,484.1	2,475.9	Dollars
Venezuela	206	209	6,640	7,061	0.1	0.1	676.0	641.0	Bolivar
Vietnam	724	725	23,362	24,482	0.0	0.0	806.8	832.9	Dong*

Note: Due to rounding, establishments will vary by + or - one establishment. Therefore, zero establishments may also be one establishment.

* Local Sales are in trillions

WINE & ALCOHOLIC BEVERAGES WHOLESALES (NAICS 42482)

NAICS 42482: Wine & Alcoholic Beverages Wholesales. Establishments primarily engaged in the wholesale distribution of distilled spirits, including neutral spirits and ethyl alcohol used in blended wines and distilled liquors.

COUNTRY ESTIMATES

Country	Establishments 2018	Establishments 2019	Employment 2018	Employment 2019	Sales ($B) 2018	Sales ($B) 2019	Local Sales (B) 2018	Local Sales (B) 2019	Currency
Algeria	-	-	-	-	-	-	0.0	0.0	Dinar
Argentina	257	258	12,503	13,679	0.1	0.1	2.4	2.5	Pesos
Australia	160	162	7,780	8,582	0.3	0.3	0.4	0.4	Dollars
Austria	57	57	2,784	3,029	0.1	0.1	0.1	0.1	Euro
Bangladesh	1,129	1,130	54,833	60,030	0.1	0.1	4.3	4.7	Taka
Belgium	72	72	3,489	3,816	0.1	0.1	0.1	0.1	Euro
Brazil	1,375	1,387	66,776	73,640	0.4	0.4	1,248.7	1,256.1	Real
Canada	241	242	11,703	12,832	0.4	0.4	0.5	0.5	Dollars
Chile	133	134	6,475	7,132	0.1	0.1	38.2	39.9	Pesos*
China	9,511	9,479	461,858	503,398	3.2	3.5	21.0	22.5	RMB
Colombia	286	286	13,887	15,189	0.1	0.1	0.2	0.2	Pesos*
Czech Republic	69	68	3,329	3,620	0.0	0.0	1.0	1.1	Koruna
Denmark	36	36	1,751	1,905	0.1	0.1	0.4	0.4	Kroner
Egypt	-	-	-	-	-	-	0.0	0.0	Pounds
Finland	36	36	1,734	1,888	0.1	0.1	0.0	0.0	Euro
France	399	398	19,374	21,145	0.5	0.5	0.4	0.4	Euro
Germany	508	501	24,663	26,627	0.8	0.8	0.7	0.7	Euro
Greece	67	66	3,245	3,523	0.0	0.0	0.0	0.0	Euro
Hong Kong	41	41	1,990	2,167	0.1	0.1	464.4	486.8	Dollar
Hungary	60	59	2,927	3,160	0.0	0.0	7.3	7.8	Forint*
India	7,986	8,107	387,846	430,537	0.5	0.6	32.8	35.5	Rupees
Indonesia	-	-	-	-	-	-	0.0	0.0	Rupiah*

WINE & ALCOHOLIC BEVERAGES WHOLESALES (NAICS 42482)

COUNTRY ESTIMATES

Country	Establishments 2018	Establishments 2019	Employment 2018	Employment 2019	Sales ($B) 2018	Sales ($B) 2019	Local Sales (B) 2018	Local Sales (B) 2019	Currency
Iran	-	-	-	-	-	-	0.0	0.0	Rial*
Iraq	-	-	-	-	-	-	0.0	0.0	Dinar*
Ireland	40	41	1,944	2,152	0.1	0.1	0.1	0.1	Euro
Israel	57	57	2,754	3,053	0.1	0.1	0.3	0.3	Shekel
Italy	402	400	19,516	21,242	0.4	0.4	0.3	0.4	Euro
Japan	846	837	41,074	44,458	1.0	1.0	111.7	115.1	Yen*
Kazakhstan	138	138	6,692	7,353	0.0	0.1	16.2	17.0	Tenge
Kuwait	-	-	-	-	-	-	0.0	0.0	Dinar
Malaysia	-	-	-	-	-	-	0.0	0.0	Ringgit
Mexico	859	869	41,712	46,143	0.3	0.3	5.2	5.4	New pesos
Netherlands	107	107	5,218	5,673	0.2	0.2	0.1	0.1	Euro
New Zealand	29	29	1,403	1,544	0.0	0.0	0.1	0.1	Dollar
Nigeria	1,482	1,506	71,949	79,999	0.1	0.1	49,001.9	51,321.3	Naira
Norway	40	40	1,928	2,115	0.1	0.1	0.8	0.9	Krone
Pakistan	-	-	-	-	-	-	0.0	0.0	Rupees
Peru	235	235	11,413	12,495	0.0	0.1	0.2	0.2	Nuevo Sol
Phillipines	640	651	31,076	34,574	0.1	0.1	3.7	4.0	Pesos
Poland	219	217	10,646	11,514	0.1	0.1	0.4	0.4	Zloty
Portugal	69	69	3,366	3,651	0.0	0.0	0.0	0.0	Euro
Puerto Rico	30	30	1,456	1,567	0.0	0.0	0.0	0.0	Dollar
Qatar	-	-	-	-	-	-	0.0	0.0	Riyal
Romania	158	155	7,662	8,247	0.0	0.1	0.2	0.2	New Leu
Russia	980	969	47,595	51,446	0.3	0.3	16.2	16.4	Rubles
Saudi Arabia	-	-	-	-	-	-	0.0	0.0	Rials*
Singapore	44	45	2,131	2,386	0.1	0.1	99.8	104.8	Dollar
South Africa	271	274	13,163	14,575	0.1	0.1	844.9	876.6	Rand
South Korea	383	382	18,605	20,265	0.4	0.4	397.7	418.8	Won*
Spain	318	320	15,444	16,985	0.3	0.3	238.3	244.6	Euro
Sweden	65	65	3,165	3,456	0.1	0.1	1,003.8	1,062.2	Krona
Switzerland	60	60	2,895	3,174	0.2	0.2	163.5	170.2	Swiss franc
Taiwan	239	247	11,595	13,100	0.1	0.1	3,757.3	3,923.5	Dollar
Thailand	577	580	28,027	30,801	0.1	0.1	3,458.2	3,602.7	Baht
Turkey	-	-	-	-	-	-	0.0	0.0	Euro
Ukraine	319	314	15,492	16,687	0.0	0.0	447.5	411.7	Hryvna
UAE	-	-	-	-	-	-	0.0	0.0	Dirham
United Kingdom	416	414	20,186	22,012	0.7	0.7	488.6	512.8	Pounds
United States	2,018	2,019	98,000	107,223	4.0	4.2	4,020.7	4,216.5	Dollars
Venezuela	206	209	9,997	11,098	0.1	0.1	1,094.2	1,091.7	Bolivar
Vietnam	724	725	35,172	38,484	0.1	0.1	1,305.9	1,418.4	Dong*

Note: Due to rounding, establishments will vary by + or - one establishment. Therefore, zero establishments may also be one establishment.

* Local Sales are in trillions

Book/Periodical/Newspaper Wholesales (NAICS 42492)

NAICS 42492: Book & Periodical & Newspaper Wholesales. Establishments primarily engaged in the wholesale distribution of books, periodicals, and newspapers.

COUNTRY ESTIMATES

Country	Establishments 2018	Establishments 2019	Employment 2018	Employment 2019	Sales ($B) 2018	Sales ($B) 2019	Local Sales (B) 2018	Local Sales (B) 2019	Currency
Algeria	371	373	3,382	3,508	0.1	0.1	9.8	9.6	Dinar
Argentina	257	258	2,345	2,419	0.2	0.2	3.8	3.7	Pesos
Australia	160	162	1,459	1,518	0.5	0.5	0.6	0.6	Dollars
Austria	57	57	522	536	0.1	0.1	0.1	0.1	Euro
Bangladesh	1,129	1,130	10,283	10,616	0.1	0.1	6.8	7.0	Taka
Belgium	72	72	654	675	0.2	0.2	0.1	0.1	Euro
Brazil	1,375	1,387	12,523	13,023	0.6	0.6	1,983.3	1,890.4	Real
Canada	241	242	2,195	2,269	0.6	0.6	0.7	0.7	Dollars
Chile	133	134	1,214	1,261	0.1	0.1	60.7	60.0	Pesos*
China	9,511	9,479	86,615	89,024	5.1	5.2	33.3	33.9	RMB
Colombia	286	286	2,604	2,686	0.1	0.1	0.3	0.3	Pesos*
Czech Republic	69	68	624	640	0.1	0.1	1.6	1.6	Koruna
Denmark	36	36	328	337	0.1	0.1	0.7	0.7	Kroner
Egypt	608	623	5,541	5,852	0.1	0.1	2.2	2.2	Pounds
Finland	36	36	325	334	0.1	0.1	0.1	0.1	Euro
France	399	398	3,633	3,739	0.8	0.8	0.7	0.7	Euro
Germany	508	501	4,625	4,709	1.3	1.3	1.1	1.0	Euro
Greece	67	66	609	623	0.1	0.1	0.1	0.1	Euro
Hong Kong	41	41	373	383	0.1	0.1	737.6	732.7	Dollar
Hungary	60	59	549	559	0.0	0.0	11.7	11.7	Forint*
India	7,986	8,107	72,735	76,139	0.8	0.8	52.1	53.4	Rupees
Indonesia	1,986	2,011	18,087	18,891	0.4	0.4	5.5	5.6	Rupiah*

Book/Periodical/Newspaper Wholesales (NAICS 42492)

Country Estimates

Country	Establishments 2018	Establishments 2019	Employment 2018	Employment 2019	Sales ($B) 2018	Sales ($B) 2019	Local Sales (B) 2018	Local Sales (B) 2019	Currency
Iran	544	550	4,954	5,169	0.1	0.1	5.3	5.1	Rial*
Iraq	285	290	2,598	2,720	0.1	0.1	0.1	0.1	Dinar*
Ireland	40	41	365	381	0.2	0.2	0.2	0.2	Euro
Israel	57	57	517	540	0.1	0.1	0.4	0.4	Shekel
Italy	402	400	3,660	3,757	0.7	0.6	0.6	0.5	Euro
Japan	846	837	7,703	7,862	1.6	1.5	177.5	173.2	Yen*
Kazakhstan	138	138	1,255	1,300	0.1	0.1	25.7	25.6	Tenge
Kuwait	32	34	293	316	0.0	0.0	0.0	0.0	Dinar
Malaysia	264	268	2,401	2,518	0.1	0.1	0.6	0.6	Ringgit
Mexico	859	869	7,822	8,160	0.4	0.4	8.2	8.1	New pesos
Netherlands	107	107	979	1,003	0.3	0.3	0.2	0.2	Euro
New Zealand	29	29	263	273	0.1	0.1	0.1	0.1	Dollar
Nigeria	1,482	1,506	13,493	14,147	0.2	0.2	77,827.9	77,237.8	Naira
Norway	40	40	361	374	0.2	0.2	1.3	1.3	Krone
Pakistan	1,187	1,212	10,812	11,382	0.1	0.1	10.6	10.8	Rupees
Peru	235	235	2,140	2,210	0.1	0.1	0.2	0.2	Nuevo Sol
Phillipines	640	651	5,828	6,114	0.1	0.1	5.8	6.0	Pesos
Poland	219	217	1,996	2,036	0.2	0.2	0.7	0.7	Zloty
Portugal	69	69	631	646	0.1	0.1	0.1	0.1	Euro
Puerto Rico	30	30	273	277	0.0	0.0	0.0	0.0	Dollar
Qatar	30	34	275	323	0.1	0.1	0.3	0.3	Riyal
Romania	158	155	1,437	1,458	0.1	0.1	0.3	0.3	New Leu
Russia	980	969	8,926	9,098	0.5	0.5	25.8	24.7	Rubles
Saudi Arabia	275	284	2,504	2,664	0.3	0.3	0.0	0.0	Rials*
Singapore	44	45	400	422	0.1	0.1	158.5	157.7	Dollar
South Africa	271	274	2,468	2,577	0.1	0.1	1,342.0	1,319.2	Rand
South Korea	383	382	3,489	3,584	0.6	0.6	631.6	630.3	Won*
Spain	318	320	2,896	3,004	0.5	0.4	378.5	368.1	Euro
Sweden	65	65	594	611	0.2	0.2	1,594.2	1,598.6	Krona
Switzerland	60	60	543	561	0.3	0.3	259.7	256.2	Swiss franc
Taiwan	239	247	2,174	2,317	0.2	0.2	5,967.5	5,904.9	Dollar
Thailand	577	580	5,256	5,447	0.2	0.2	5,492.6	5,422.0	Baht
Turkey	437	435	3,983	4,088	0.3	0.3	1,219.7	1,223.8	Euro
Ukraine	319	314	2,905	2,951	0.0	0.0	710.7	619.5	Hryvna
UAE	149	166	1,354	1,563	0.2	0.2	648.4	637.7	Dirham
United Kingdom	416	414	3,786	3,893	1.1	1.0	776.1	771.8	Pounds
United States	2,018	2,019	18,379	18,962	6.4	6.3	6,385.9	6,345.7	Dollars
Venezuela	206	209	1,875	1,963	0.2	0.2	1,737.9	1,643.0	Bolivar
Vietnam	724	725	6,596	6,806	0.1	0.1	2,074.1	2,134.6	Dong*

Note: Due to rounding, establishments will vary by + or - one establishment. Therefore, zero establishments may also be one establishment.

* Local Sales are in trillions

New Car Dealers Industry (NAICS 44111)

NAICS 44111: New Car Dealers. Establishments primarily engaged in the retail sale of new automobiles or new and used automobiles. These establishments frequently maintain repair departments and carry stocks of replacement parts, tires, batteries, and automotive accessories. These establishments also frequently sell pickups and vans at retail.

COUNTRY ESTIMATES

Country	Establishments 2018	Establishments 2019	Employment 2018	Employment 2019	Sales ($B) 2018	Sales ($B) 2019	Local Sales (B) 2018	Local Sales (B) 2019	Currency
Algeria	186	187	70,595	74,023	0.2	0.2	26.3	26.0	Dinar
Argentina	129	129	48,942	51,053	0.5	0.5	10.3	10.1	Pesos
Australia	80	81	30,455	32,031	1.3	1.3	1.7	1.7	Dollars
Austria	29	29	10,896	11,306	0.4	0.4	0.3	0.3	Euro
Bangladesh	565	565	214,640	224,042	0.2	0.2	18.4	19.0	Taka
Belgium	36	36	13,658	14,243	0.4	0.4	0.4	0.4	Euro
Brazil	688	693	261,392	274,836	1.7	1.6	5,338.1	5,115.1	Real
Canada	120	121	45,811	47,892	1.6	1.6	1.9	1.9	Dollars
Chile	67	67	25,344	26,617	0.3	0.3	163.3	162.3	Pesos*
China	4,755	4,739	1,807,910	1,878,766	13.8	14.1	89.6	91.7	RMB
Colombia	143	143	54,361	56,690	0.3	0.3	0.9	0.9	Pesos*
Czech Republic	34	34	13,030	13,510	0.2	0.2	4.3	4.3	Koruna
Denmark	18	18	6,855	7,109	0.3	0.3	1.8	1.8	Kroner
Egypt	304	312	115,650	123,494	0.3	0.3	6.0	5.9	Pounds
Finland	18	18	6,790	7,046	0.2	0.2	0.2	0.2	Euro
France	199	199	75,838	78,916	2.2	2.2	1.9	1.8	Euro
Germany	254	251	96,542	99,377	3.4	3.4	2.9	2.8	Euro
Greece	33	33	12,702	13,147	0.2	0.2	0.1	0.1	Euro
Hong Kong	20	20	7,790	8,086	0.3	0.3	1,985.2	1,982.5	Dollar
Hungary	30	30	11,456	11,793	0.1	0.1	31.4	31.7	Forint*
India	3,993	4,053	1,518,196	1,606,835	2.2	2.3	140.3	144.4	Rupees
Indonesia	993	1,006	377,523	398,680	1.1	1.1	14.7	15.0	Rupiah*

NEW CAR DEALERS INDUSTRY
(NAICS 44111)

COUNTRY ESTIMATES

Country	Establishments 2018	Establishments 2019	Employment 2018	Employment 2019	Sales ($B) 2018	Sales ($B) 2019	Local Sales (B) 2018	Local Sales (B) 2019	Currency
Iran	272	275	103,396	109,086	0.4	0.4	14.2	13.8	Rial*
Iraq	143	145	54,225	57,403	0.2	0.2	0.2	0.2	Dinar*
Ireland	20	20	7,608	8,033	0.5	0.6	0.4	0.5	Euro
Israel	28	29	10,781	11,396	0.3	0.3	1.1	1.1	Shekel
Italy	201	200	76,396	79,281	1.8	1.7	1.5	1.5	Euro
Japan	423	419	160,783	165,923	4.2	4.2	477.6	468.7	Yen*
Kazakhstan	69	69	26,196	27,442	0.2	0.2	69.2	69.2	Tenge
Kuwait	16	17	6,122	6,659	0.1	0.1	0.0	0.0	Dinar
Malaysia	132	134	50,119	53,139	0.4	0.4	1.6	1.6	Ringgit
Mexico	429	434	163,278	172,214	1.1	1.1	22.0	22.0	New pesos
Netherlands	54	53	20,424	21,173	0.7	0.7	0.6	0.6	Euro
New Zealand	14	15	5,492	5,761	0.2	0.2	0.2	0.2	Dollar
Nigeria	741	753	281,639	298,568	0.6	0.6	209,471.2	208,992.1	Naira
Norway	20	20	7,545	7,892	0.4	0.4	3.5	3.5	Krone
Pakistan	594	606	225,683	240,201	0.3	0.3	28.6	29.1	Rupees
Peru	118	118	44,674	46,635	0.2	0.2	0.7	0.7	Nuevo Sol
Phillipines	320	326	121,645	129,035	0.3	0.3	15.7	16.2	Pesos
Poland	110	108	41,671	42,973	0.5	0.5	1.8	1.8	Zloty
Portugal	35	34	13,175	13,627	0.2	0.2	0.2	0.2	Euro
Puerto Rico	15	15	5,700	5,850	0.1	0.1	0.1	0.1	Dollar
Qatar	15	17	5,739	6,816	0.2	0.2	0.7	0.7	Riyal
Romania	79	78	29,994	30,778	0.2	0.2	0.8	0.8	New Leu
Russia	490	484	186,307	192,005	1.4	1.3	69.3	66.8	Rubles
Saudi Arabia	137	142	52,266	56,229	0.8	0.8	0.0	0.0	Rials*
Singapore	22	22	8,343	8,906	0.3	0.3	426.7	426.8	Dollar
South Africa	136	137	51,525	54,396	0.3	0.3	3,611.9	3,569.6	Rand
South Korea	192	191	72,827	75,631	1.6	1.6	1,700.0	1,705.6	Won*
Spain	159	160	60,453	63,389	1.2	1.2	1,018.7	996.1	Euro
Sweden	33	33	12,389	12,898	0.5	0.5	4,290.8	4,325.6	Krona
Switzerland	30	30	11,334	11,847	0.7	0.7	699.0	693.1	Swiss franc
Taiwan	119	123	45,387	48,892	0.5	0.5	16,061.5	15,977.5	Dollar
Thailand	289	290	109,710	114,955	0.5	0.5	14,783.2	14,670.9	Baht
Turkey	219	218	83,133	86,271	0.9	0.9	3,282.8	3,311.4	Euro
Ukraine	160	157	60,644	62,277	0.1	0.1	1,912.8	1,676.4	Hryvna
UAE	74	83	28,263	32,995	0.5	0.5	1,745.0	1,725.6	Dirham
United Kingdom	208	207	79,017	82,152	2.8	2.8	2,088.8	2,088.4	Pounds
United States	2,018	2,019	767,228	800,349	34.4	34.3	34,375.0	34,340.9	Dollars
Venezuela	103	104	39,131	41,421	0.5	0.4	4,677.4	4,445.5	Bolivar
Vietnam	362	362	137,680	143,629	0.2	0.3	5,582.4	5,775.9	Dong*

Note: Due to rounding, establishments will vary by + or - one establishment. Therefore, zero establishments may also be one establishment.

* Local Sales are in trillions

NAICS 44211: Furniture Stores. Establishments primarily engaged in the retail sale of household furniture. These stores may also sell homefurnishings, major appliances, and floor coverings.

COUNTRY ESTIMATES

Country	Establishments		Employment		Sales ($B)		Local Sales (B)		Currency
	2018	2019	2018	2019	2018	2019	2018	2019	
Algeria	371	373	8,438	8,678	0.3	0.3	39.6	38.9	Dinar
Argentina	257	258	5,850	5,985	0.8	0.8	15.6	15.1	Pesos
Australia	160	162	3,640	3,755	2.0	2.0	2.6	2.6	Dollars
Austria	57	57	1,302	1,325	0.6	0.6	0.5	0.5	Euro
Bangladesh	1,129	1,130	25,654	26,265	0.3	0.3	27.7	28.4	Taka
Belgium	72	72	1,632	1,670	0.7	0.6	0.5	0.5	Euro
Brazil	1,375	1,387	31,242	32,219	2.5	2.4	8,038.5	7,653.2	Real
Canada	241	242	5,475	5,614	2.4	2.3	2.9	2.9	Dollars
Chile	133	134	3,029	3,120	0.4	0.4	245.9	242.8	Pesos*
China	9,511	9,479	216,082	220,250	20.8	21.1	135.0	137.2	RMB
Colombia	286	286	6,497	6,646	0.4	0.4	1.3	1.3	Pesos*
Czech Republic	69	68	1,557	1,584	0.3	0.3	6.4	6.5	Koruna
Denmark	36	36	819	833	0.4	0.4	2.7	2.7	Kroner
Egypt	608	623	13,822	14,477	0.5	0.5	9.0	8.8	Pounds
Finland	36	36	811	826	0.3	0.3	0.3	0.3	Euro
France	399	398	9,064	9,251	3.3	3.3	2.8	2.7	Euro
Germany	508	501	11,539	11,650	5.1	5.1	4.3	4.2	Euro
Greece	67	66	1,518	1,541	0.3	0.2	0.2	0.2	Euro
Hong Kong	41	41	931	948	0.4	0.4	2,989.6	2,966.3	Dollar
Hungary	60	59	1,369	1,382	0.2	0.2	47.2	47.4	Forint*
India	7,986	8,107	181,455	188,371	3.3	3.4	211.2	216.0	Rupees
Indonesia	1,986	2,011	45,122	46,738	1.6	1.7	22.2	22.5	Rupiah*

FURNITURE STORES INDUSTRY
(NAICS 44211)

COUNTRY ESTIMATES

Country	Establishments 2018	2019	Employment 2018	2019	Sales ($B) 2018	2019	Local Sales (B) 2018	2019	Currency
Iran	544	550	12,358	12,788	0.6	0.6	21.4	20.7	Rial*
Iraq	285	290	6,481	6,729	0.3	0.3	0.4	0.4	Dinar*
Ireland	40	41	909	942	0.8	0.8	0.6	0.7	Euro
Israel	57	57	1,289	1,336	0.5	0.5	1.7	1.7	Shekel
Italy	402	400	9,131	9,294	2.7	2.6	2.2	2.2	Euro
Japan	846	837	19,217	19,451	6.4	6.2	719.2	701.3	Yen*
Kazakhstan	138	138	3,131	3,217	0.3	0.3	104.2	103.5	Tenge
Kuwait	32	34	732	781	0.2	0.2	0.1	0.1	Dinar
Malaysia	264	268	5,990	6,230	0.6	0.6	2.4	2.4	Ringgit
Mexico	859	869	19,515	20,189	1.7	1.7	33.2	32.9	New pesos
Netherlands	107	107	2,441	2,482	1.1	1.1	0.9	0.9	Euro
New Zealand	29	29	656	675	0.2	0.2	0.3	0.3	Dollar
Nigeria	1,482	1,506	33,662	35,002	0.9	0.9	315,441.3	312,693.2	Naira
Norway	40	40	902	925	0.7	0.6	5.3	5.2	Krone
Pakistan	1,187	1,212	26,974	28,159	0.4	0.4	43.0	43.6	Rupees
Peru	235	235	5,339	5,467	0.3	0.3	1.0	1.0	Nuevo Sol
Phillipines	640	651	14,539	15,127	0.5	0.5	23.7	24.3	Pesos
Poland	219	217	4,981	5,038	0.8	0.8	2.7	2.7	Zloty
Portugal	69	69	1,575	1,598	0.3	0.3	0.2	0.2	Euro
Puerto Rico	30	30	681	686	0.2	0.2	0.2	0.2	Dollar
Qatar	30	34	686	799	0.3	0.3	1.1	1.1	Riyal
Romania	158	155	3,585	3,608	0.3	0.3	1.2	1.2	New Leu
Russia	980	969	22,267	22,509	2.0	2.0	104.4	100.0	Rubles
Saudi Arabia	275	284	6,247	6,592	1.3	1.2	0.0	0.0	Rials*
Singapore	44	45	997	1,044	0.5	0.5	642.6	638.6	Dollar
South Africa	271	274	6,158	6,377	0.4	0.4	5,439.1	5,340.8	Rand
South Korea	383	382	8,704	8,866	2.4	2.4	2,560.0	2,551.9	Won*
Spain	318	320	7,225	7,431	1.8	1.8	1,534.1	1,490.4	Euro
Sweden	65	65	1,481	1,512	0.8	0.8	6,461.5	6,471.9	Krona
Switzerland	60	60	1,355	1,389	1.1	1.1	1,052.7	1,037.0	Swiss franc
Taiwan	239	247	5,425	5,732	0.8	0.8	24,186.8	23,905.5	Dollar
Thailand	577	580	13,113	13,476	0.7	0.7	22,261.9	21,950.5	Baht
Turkey	437	435	9,936	10,114	1.3	1.3	4,943.6	4,954.5	Euro
Ukraine	319	314	7,248	7,301	0.1	0.1	2,880.5	2,508.2	Hryvna
UAE	149	166	3,378	3,868	0.7	0.7	2,627.8	2,581.8	Dirham
United Kingdom	416	414	9,444	9,631	4.3	4.2	3,145.5	3,124.7	Pounds
United States	2,018	2,019	45,850	46,913	25.9	25.7	25,882.6	25,690.3	Dollars
Venezuela	206	209	4,677	4,856	0.7	0.7	7,043.7	6,651.4	Bolivar
Vietnam	724	725	16,456	16,838	0.4	0.4	8,406.5	8,641.8	Dong*

Note: Due to rounding, establishments will vary by + or - one establishment. Therefore, zero establishments may also be one establishment.

* Local Sales are in trillions

HOME CENTERS INDUSTRY
(NAICS 44411)

NAICS 44411: Home Centers. This industry comprises establishments known as home centers primarily engaged in retailing a general line of new home repair and improvement materials and supplies, such as lumber, plumbing goods, electrical goods, tools, housewares, hardware, and lawn and garden supplies, with no one merchandise line predominating. The merchandise lines are normally arranged in separate departments.

COUNTRY ESTIMATES

Country	Establishments 2018	2019	Employment 2018	2019	Sales ($B) 2018	2019	Local Sales (B) 2018	2019	Currency
Algeria	186	187	15,598	16,403	0.1	0.1	5.8	5.8	Dinar
Argentina	129	129	10,814	11,313	0.1	0.1	2.3	2.2	Pesos
Australia	80	81	6,729	7,098	0.3	0.3	0.4	0.4	Dollars
Austria	29	29	2,408	2,505	0.1	0.1	0.1	0.1	Euro
Bangladesh	565	565	47,426	49,646	0.0	0.1	4.0	4.2	Taka
Belgium	36	36	3,018	3,156	0.1	0.1	0.1	0.1	Euro
Brazil	688	693	57,756	60,901	0.4	0.4	1,175.4	1,140.7	Real
Canada	120	121	10,122	10,613	0.3	0.3	0.4	0.4	Dollars
Chile	67	67	5,600	5,898	0.1	0.1	36.0	36.2	Pesos*
China	4,755	4,739	399,465	416,319	3.0	3.2	19.7	20.4	RMB
Colombia	143	143	12,011	12,562	0.1	0.1	0.2	0.2	Pesos*
Czech Republic	34	34	2,879	2,994	0.0	0.0	0.9	1.0	Koruna
Denmark	18	18	1,515	1,575	0.1	0.1	0.4	0.4	Kroner
Egypt	304	312	25,553	27,365	0.1	0.1	1.3	1.3	Pounds
Finland	18	18	1,500	1,561	0.0	0.0	0.0	0.0	Euro
France	199	199	16,757	17,487	0.5	0.5	0.4	0.4	Euro
Germany	254	251	21,331	22,021	0.8	0.8	0.6	0.6	Euro
Greece	33	33	2,806	2,913	0.0	0.0	0.0	0.0	Euro
Hong Kong	20	20	1,721	1,792	0.1	0.1	437.2	442.1	Dollar
Hungary	30	30	2,531	2,613	0.0	0.0	6.9	7.1	Forint*
India	3,993	4,053	335,452	356,062	0.5	0.5	30.9	32.2	Rupees
Indonesia	993	1,006	83,415	88,344	0.2	0.2	3.2	3.4	Rupiah*

HOME CENTERS INDUSTRY
(NAICS 44411)

COUNTRY ESTIMATES

Country	Establishments 2018	Establishments 2019	Employment 2018	Employment 2019	Sales ($B) 2018	Sales ($B) 2019	Local Sales (B) 2018	Local Sales (B) 2019	Currency
Iran	272	275	22,846	24,173	0.1	0.1	3.1	3.1	Rial*
Iraq	143	145	11,981	12,720	0.0	0.0	0.1	0.1	Dinar*
Ireland	20	20	1,681	1,780	0.1	0.1	0.1	0.1	Euro
Israel	28	29	2,382	2,525	0.1	0.1	0.2	0.2	Shekel
Italy	201	200	16,880	17,568	0.4	0.4	0.3	0.3	Euro
Japan	423	419	35,526	36,767	0.9	0.9	105.2	104.5	Yen*
Kazakhstan	69	69	5,788	6,081	0.0	0.0	15.2	15.4	Tenge
Kuwait	16	17	1,353	1,476	0.0	0.0	0.0	0.0	Dinar
Malaysia	132	134	11,074	11,775	0.1	0.1	0.3	0.4	Ringgit
Mexico	429	434	36,077	38,161	0.3	0.3	4.9	4.9	New pesos
Netherlands	54	53	4,513	4,692	0.2	0.2	0.1	0.1	Euro
New Zealand	14	15	1,214	1,277	0.0	0.0	0.1	0.1	Dollar
Nigeria	741	753	62,229	66,160	0.1	0.1	46,125.9	46,607.7	Naira
Norway	20	20	1,667	1,749	0.1	0.1	0.8	0.8	Krone
Pakistan	594	606	49,866	53,227	0.1	0.1	6.3	6.5	Rupees
Peru	118	118	9,871	10,334	0.0	0.0	0.1	0.1	Nuevo Sol
Phillipines	320	326	26,878	28,593	0.1	0.1	3.5	3.6	Pesos
Poland	110	108	9,207	9,522	0.1	0.1	0.4	0.4	Zloty
Portugal	35	34	2,911	3,020	0.0	0.0	0.0	0.0	Euro
Puerto Rico	15	15	1,259	1,296	0.0	0.0	0.0	0.0	Dollar
Qatar	15	17	1,268	1,510	0.0	0.0	0.2	0.2	Riyal
Romania	79	78	6,627	6,820	0.0	0.0	0.2	0.2	New Leu
Russia	490	484	41,165	42,547	0.3	0.3	15.3	14.9	Rubles
Saudi Arabia	137	142	11,548	12,460	0.2	0.2	0.0	0.0	Rials*
Singapore	22	22	1,843	1,974	0.1	0.1	94.0	95.2	Dollar
South Africa	136	137	11,385	12,054	0.1	0.1	795.3	796.1	Rand
South Korea	192	191	16,091	16,759	0.4	0.4	374.3	380.4	Won*
Spain	159	160	13,357	14,047	0.3	0.3	224.3	222.1	Euro
Sweden	33	33	2,737	2,858	0.1	0.1	944.8	964.7	Krona
Switzerland	30	30	2,504	2,625	0.2	0.2	153.9	154.6	Swiss franc
Taiwan	119	123	10,028	10,834	0.1	0.1	3,536.8	3,563.2	Dollar
Thailand	289	290	24,241	25,473	0.1	0.1	3,255.3	3,271.8	Baht
Turkey	219	218	18,369	19,117	0.2	0.2	722.9	738.5	Euro
Ukraine	160	157	13,400	13,800	0.0	0.0	421.2	373.9	Hryvna
UAE	74	83	6,245	7,311	0.1	0.1	384.3	384.8	Dirham
United Kingdom	208	207	17,459	18,204	0.6	0.6	460.0	465.7	Pounds
United States	2,018	2,019	169,522	177,351	7.6	7.7	7,569.4	7,658.4	Dollars
Venezuela	103	104	8,646	9,179	0.1	0.1	1,030.0	991.4	Bolivar
Vietnam	362	362	30,421	31,827	0.1	0.1	1,229.3	1,288.1	Dong*

Note: Due to rounding, establishments will vary by + or - one establishment. Therefore, zero establishments may also be one establishment.

* Local Sales are in trillions

HARDWARE STORES INDUSTRY (NAICS 44413)

NAICS 44413: Hardware Stores. Establishments primarily engaged in the retail sale of a number of basic hardware lines, such as tools, builders' hardware, paint and glass, housewares and household appliances, and cutlery.

COUNTRY ESTIMATES

Country	Establishments 2018	Establishments 2019	Employment 2018	Employment 2019	Sales ($B) 2018	Sales ($B) 2019	Local Sales (B) 2018	Local Sales (B) 2019	Currency
Algeria	371	373	4,404	4,647	0.2	0.2	27.1	27.6	Dinar
Argentina	257	258	3,053	3,205	0.6	0.6	10.7	10.7	Pesos
Australia	160	162	1,900	2,011	1.4	1.4	1.8	1.8	Dollars
Austria	57	57	680	710	0.4	0.4	0.3	0.3	Euro
Bangladesh	1,129	1,130	13,391	14,064	0.2	0.2	19.0	20.2	Taka
Belgium	72	72	852	894	0.4	0.5	0.4	0.4	Euro
Brazil	1,375	1,387	16,308	17,253	1.7	1.7	5,505.3	5,424.3	Real
Canada	241	242	2,858	3,006	1.6	1.6	2.0	2.0	Dollars
Chile	133	134	1,581	1,671	0.3	0.3	168.4	172.1	Pesos*
China	9,511	9,479	112,793	117,941	14.2	15.0	92.4	97.2	RMB
Colombia	286	286	3,391	3,559	0.3	0.3	0.9	0.9	Pesos*
Czech Republic	69	68	813	848	0.2	0.2	4.4	4.6	Koruna
Denmark	36	36	428	446	0.3	0.3	1.9	1.9	Kroner
Egypt	608	623	7,215	7,752	0.3	0.4	6.2	6.3	Pounds
Finland	36	36	424	442	0.2	0.2	0.2	0.2	Euro
France	399	398	4,731	4,954	2.3	2.3	1.9	1.9	Euro
Germany	508	501	6,023	6,238	3.5	3.6	2.9	3.0	Euro
Greece	67	66	792	825	0.2	0.2	0.1	0.1	Euro
Hong Kong	41	41	486	508	0.3	0.3	2,047.4	2,102.4	Dollar
Hungary	60	59	715	740	0.1	0.1	32.3	33.6	Forint*
India	7,986	8,107	94,718	100,870	2.3	2.4	144.7	153.1	Rupees
Indonesia	1,986	2,011	23,553	25,027	1.1	1.2	15.2	15.9	Rupiah*

COUNTRY ESTIMATES

Country	Establishments 2018	Establishments 2019	Employment 2018	Employment 2019	Sales ($B) 2018	Sales ($B) 2019	Local Sales (B) 2018	Local Sales (B) 2019	Currency
Iran	544	550	6,451	6,848	0.4	0.4	14.7	14.7	Rial*
Iraq	285	290	3,383	3,604	0.2	0.2	0.3	0.3	Dinar*
Ireland	40	41	475	504	0.5	0.6	0.4	0.5	Euro
Israel	57	57	673	715	0.3	0.3	1.1	1.2	Shekel
Italy	402	400	4,766	4,977	1.8	1.8	1.5	1.5	Euro
Japan	846	837	10,031	10,416	4.4	4.4	492.6	497.0	Yen*
Kazakhstan	138	138	1,634	1,723	0.2	0.2	71.4	73.4	Tenge
Kuwait	32	34	382	418	0.1	0.1	0.0	0.0	Dinar
Malaysia	264	268	3,127	3,336	0.4	0.4	1.6	1.7	Ringgit
Mexico	859	869	10,187	10,811	1.2	1.2	22.7	23.3	New pesos
Netherlands	107	107	1,274	1,329	0.8	0.8	0.6	0.6	Euro
New Zealand	29	29	343	362	0.2	0.2	0.2	0.2	Dollar
Nigeria	1,482	1,506	17,571	18,743	0.6	0.6	216,032.4	221,621.9	Naira
Norway	40	40	471	495	0.4	0.5	3.6	3.7	Krone
Pakistan	1,187	1,212	14,080	15,079	0.3	0.3	29.5	30.9	Rupees
Peru	235	235	2,787	2,928	0.2	0.2	0.7	0.7	Nuevo Sol
Phillipines	640	651	7,589	8,100	0.3	0.3	16.2	17.2	Pesos
Poland	219	217	2,600	2,698	0.5	0.6	1.8	1.9	Zloty
Portugal	69	69	822	855	0.2	0.2	0.2	0.2	Euro
Puerto Rico	30	30	356	367	0.1	0.1	0.1	0.1	Dollar
Qatar	30	34	358	428	0.2	0.2	0.7	0.7	Riyal
Romania	158	155	1,871	1,932	0.2	0.2	0.8	0.9	New Leu
Russia	980	969	11,623	12,053	1.4	1.4	71.5	70.9	Rubles
Saudi Arabia	275	284	3,261	3,530	0.9	0.9	0.0	0.0	Rials*
Singapore	44	45	520	559	0.3	0.3	440.1	452.6	Dollar
South Africa	271	274	3,215	3,415	0.3	0.3	3,725.0	3,785.3	Rand
South Korea	383	382	4,544	4,748	1.6	1.7	1,753.2	1,808.7	Won*
Spain	318	320	3,772	3,979	1.3	1.3	1,050.6	1,056.3	Euro
Sweden	65	65	773	810	0.5	0.6	4,425.2	4,587.0	Krona
Switzerland	60	60	707	744	0.7	0.8	720.9	735.0	Swiss franc
Taiwan	239	247	2,832	3,069	0.6	0.6	16,564.5	16,943.1	Dollar
Thailand	577	580	6,845	7,216	0.5	0.5	15,246.2	15,557.4	Baht
Turkey	437	435	5,187	5,416	0.9	0.9	3,385.7	3,511.5	Euro
Ukraine	319	314	3,783	3,910	0.1	0.1	1,972.7	1,777.7	Hryvna
UAE	149	166	1,763	2,071	0.5	0.5	1,799.7	1,829.8	Dirham
United Kingdom	416	414	4,930	5,157	2.9	3.0	2,154.2	2,214.6	Pounds
United States	2,018	2,019	23,933	25,121	17.7	18.2	17,725.9	18,208.1	Dollars
Venezuela	206	209	2,441	2,600	0.5	0.5	4,823.9	4,714.2	Bolivar
Vietnam	724	725	8,590	9,016	0.3	0.3	5,757.3	6,124.9	Dong*

Note: Due to rounding, establishments will vary by + or - one establishment. Therefore, zero establishments may also be one establishment.

* Local Sales are in trillions

GROCERY STORES INDUSTRY
(NAICS 44511)

NAICS 44511: Grocery Stores Industry. This industry comprises establishments generally known as supermarkets and grocery stores primarily engaged in retailing a general line of food, such as canned and frozen foods; fresh fruits and vegetables; and fresh and prepared meats, fish, and poultry. Included in this industry are delicatessen-type establishments primarily engaged in retailing a general line of food.

COUNTRY ESTIMATES

Country	Establishments 2018	2019	Employment 2018	2019	Sales ($B) 2018	2019	Local Sales (B) 2018	2019	Currency
Algeria	371	373	112,904	116,995	1.1	1.1	122.2	124.2	Dinar
Argentina	257	258	78,274	80,690	2.5	2.5	48.1	48.1	Pesos
Australia	160	162	48,707	50,626	6.3	6.4	8.0	8.1	Dollars
Austria	57	57	17,426	17,869	1.8	1.8	1.5	1.5	Euro
Bangladesh	1,129	1,130	343,278	354,101	1.0	1.1	85.5	90.7	Taka
Belgium	72	72	21,844	22,511	2.0	2.0	1.7	1.7	Euro
Brazil	1,375	1,387	418,050	434,380	7.7	7.6	24,843.1	24,402.9	Real
Canada	241	242	73,267	75,694	7.3	7.4	9.0	9.2	Dollars
Chile	133	134	40,533	42,068	1.3	1.3	759.9	774.2	Pesos*
China	9,511	9,479	2,891,433	2,969,405	64.3	67.4	417.1	437.4	RMB
Colombia	286	286	86,940	89,598	1.4	1.4	4.0	4.1	Pesos*
Czech Republic	69	68	20,839	21,353	0.9	1.0	19.9	20.7	Koruna
Denmark	36	36	10,963	11,236	1.3	1.4	8.4	8.5	Kroner
Egypt	608	623	184,962	195,183	1.6	1.6	27.8	28.2	Pounds
Finland	36	36	10,859	11,137	1.0	1.0	0.9	0.9	Euro
France	399	398	121,289	124,728	10.4	10.4	8.6	8.7	Euro
Germany	508	501	154,401	157,066	15.9	16.2	13.3	13.5	Euro
Greece	67	66	20,314	20,779	0.8	0.8	0.7	0.7	Euro
Hong Kong	41	41	12,459	12,780	1.2	1.2	9,239.2	9,458.2	Dollar
Hungary	60	59	18,322	18,638	0.6	0.6	146.0	151.2	Forint*
India	7,986	8,107	2,428,086	2,539,616	10.3	10.8	652.8	688.7	Rupees
Indonesia	1,986	2,011	603,781	630,117	5.1	5.3	68.5	71.7	Rupiah*

Grocery Stores Industry
(NAICS 44511)

Country Estimates

Country	Establishments 2018	2019	Employment 2018	2019	Sales ($B) 2018	2019	Local Sales (B) 2018	2019	Currency
Iran	544	550	165,364	172,411	1.8	1.8	66.3	65.9	Rial*
Iraq	285	290	86,723	90,726	1.0	1.0	1.1	1.2	Dinar*
Ireland	40	41	12,168	12,696	2.4	2.7	2.0	2.3	Euro
Israel	57	57	17,242	18,012	1.5	1.5	5.1	5.3	Shekel
Italy	402	400	122,181	125,304	8.3	8.3	6.9	6.9	Euro
Japan	846	837	257,144	262,242	19.7	19.8	2,222.8	2,236.1	Yen*
Kazakhstan	138	138	41,895	43,372	1.0	1.0	322.0	330.0	Tenge
Kuwait	32	34	9,792	10,525	0.6	0.6	0.2	0.2	Dinar
Malaysia	264	268	80,156	83,987	1.8	1.9	7.3	7.6	Ringgit
Mexico	859	869	261,134	272,185	5.3	5.5	102.6	104.9	New pesos
Netherlands	107	107	32,665	33,465	3.4	3.5	2.8	2.9	Euro
New Zealand	29	29	8,784	9,105	0.8	0.8	1.1	1.1	Dollar
Nigeria	1,482	1,506	450,432	471,890	2.7	2.8	974,871.9	997,042.9	Naira
Norway	40	40	12,067	12,473	2.0	2.1	16.4	16.7	Krone
Pakistan	1,187	1,212	360,940	379,640	1.2	1.3	133.0	138.9	Rupees
Peru	235	235	71,448	73,707	1.0	1.0	3.1	3.2	Nuevo Sol
Phillipines	640	651	194,549	203,941	1.5	1.5	73.1	77.4	Pesos
Poland	219	217	66,646	67,919	2.4	2.5	8.3	8.6	Zloty
Portugal	69	69	21,071	21,538	0.9	0.9	0.8	0.7	Euro
Puerto Rico	30	30	9,116	9,245	0.5	0.5	0.5	0.5	Dollar
Qatar	30	34	9,179	10,772	0.9	0.9	3.3	3.4	Riyal
Romania	158	155	47,971	48,645	1.0	1.0	3.7	3.9	New Leu
Russia	980	969	297,965	303,466	6.3	6.2	322.6	318.7	Rubles
Saudi Arabia	275	284	83,591	88,870	3.9	3.9	0.0	0.0	Rials*
Singapore	44	45	13,343	14,077	1.5	1.5	1,985.9	2,036.3	Dollar
South Africa	271	274	82,404	85,973	1.4	1.4	16,809.5	17,029.4	Rand
South Korea	383	382	116,474	119,536	7.4	7.6	7,911.6	8,137.0	Won*
Spain	318	320	96,684	100,187	5.7	5.7	4,741.1	4,752.1	Euro
Sweden	65	65	19,814	20,385	2.4	2.5	19,969.3	20,636.0	Krona
Switzerland	60	60	18,126	18,724	3.3	3.4	3,253.3	3,306.7	Swiss franc
Taiwan	239	247	72,589	77,274	2.5	2.6	74,749.5	76,224.3	Dollar
Thailand	577	580	175,462	181,688	2.1	2.2	68,800.3	69,990.6	Baht
Turkey	437	435	132,956	136,352	4.1	4.2	15,278.2	15,797.7	Euro
Ukraine	319	314	96,989	98,430	0.3	0.3	8,902.3	7,997.6	Hryvna
UAE	149	166	45,202	52,149	2.2	2.2	8,121.3	8,232.2	Dirham
United Kingdom	416	414	126,373	129,842	13.2	13.5	9,721.2	9,963.3	Pounds
United States	2,018	2,019	613,523	632,479	80.0	81.9	79,990.1	81,915.3	Dollars
Venezuela	206	209	62,583	65,467	2.2	2.1	21,768.6	21,208.4	Bolivar
Vietnam	724	725	220,195	227,007	1.1	1.2	25,980.3	27,555.1	Dong*

Note: Due to rounding, establishments will vary by + or - one establishment. Therefore, zero establishments may also be one establishment.

* Local Sales are in trillions

Beer & Wine & Liquor Stores Industry (NAICS 44531)

NAICS 44531: Beer & Wine & Liquor Stores. Establishments primarily engaged in the retail sale of packaged alcoholic beverages, such as ale, beer, wine, and liquor, for consumption off the premises. Stores selling prepared drinks for consumption on the premises are classified in SIC 5813.

COUNTRY ESTIMATES

Country	Establishments 2018	2019	Employment 2018	2019	Sales ($B) 2018	2019	Local Sales (B) 2018	2019	Currency
Algeria	-	-	-	-	-	-	0.0	0.0	Dinar
Argentina	129	129	3,066	3,273	0.6	0.6	11.6	11.7	Pesos
Australia	80	81	1,908	2,054	1.5	1.6	1.9	2.0	Dollars
Austria	29	29	683	725	0.4	0.4	0.4	0.4	Euro
Bangladesh	565	565	13,447	14,365	0.2	0.3	20.7	22.1	Taka
Belgium	36	36	856	913	0.5	0.5	0.4	0.4	Euro
Brazil	688	693	16,376	17,622	1.9	1.8	6,011.7	5,958.3	Real
Canada	120	121	2,870	3,071	1.8	1.8	2.2	2.2	Dollars
Chile	67	67	1,588	1,707	0.3	0.3	183.9	189.0	Pesos*
China	4,755	4,739	113,268	120,462	15.6	16.5	100.9	106.8	RMB
Colombia	143	143	3,406	3,635	0.3	0.3	1.0	1.0	Pesos*
Czech Republic	34	34	816	866	0.2	0.2	4.8	5.0	Koruna
Denmark	18	18	429	456	0.3	0.3	2.0	2.1	Kroner
Egypt	-	-	-	-	-	-	0.0	0.0	Pounds
Finland	18	18	425	452	0.2	0.2	0.2	0.2	Euro
France	199	199	4,751	5,060	2.5	2.5	2.1	2.1	Euro
Germany	254	251	6,048	6,372	3.8	3.9	3.2	3.3	Euro
Greece	33	33	796	843	0.2	0.2	0.2	0.2	Euro
Hong Kong	20	20	488	518	0.3	0.3	2,235.8	2,309.4	Dollar
Hungary	30	30	718	756	0.1	0.1	35.3	36.9	Forint*
India	3,993	4,053	95,117	103,027	2.5	2.6	158.0	168.2	Rupees
Indonesia	-	-	-	-	-	-	0.0	0.0	Rupiah*

Beer & Wine & Liquor Stores Industry (NAICS 44531)

Country Estimates

Country	Establishments 2018	2019	Employment 2018	2019	Sales ($B) 2018	2019	Local Sales (B) 2018	2019	Currency
Iran	-	-	-	-	-	-	0.0	0.0	Rial*
Iraq	-	-	-	-	-	-	0.0	0.0	Dinar*
Ireland	20	20	477	515	0.6	0.7	0.5	0.6	Euro
Israel	28	29	675	731	0.4	0.4	1.2	1.3	Shekel
Italy	201	200	4,786	5,083	2.0	2.0	1.7	1.7	Euro
Japan	423	419	10,073	10,639	4.8	4.8	537.9	546.0	Yen*
Kazakhstan	69	69	1,641	1,760	0.2	0.2	77.9	80.6	Tenge
Kuwait	-	-	-	-	-	-	0.0	0.0	Dinar
Malaysia	-	-	-	-	-	-	0.0	0.0	Ringgit
Mexico	429	434	10,230	11,042	1.3	1.3	24.8	25.6	New pesos
Netherlands	54	53	1,280	1,358	0.8	0.8	0.7	0.7	Euro
New Zealand	14	15	344	369	0.2	0.2	0.3	0.3	Dollar
Nigeria	741	753	17,645	19,144	0.7	0.7	235,905.2	243,443.2	Naira
Norway	20	20	473	506	0.5	0.5	4.0	4.1	Krone
Pakistan	-	-	-	-	-	-	0.0	0.0	Rupees
Peru	118	118	2,799	2,990	0.2	0.2	0.8	0.8	Nuevo Sol
Phillipines	320	326	7,621	8,273	0.4	0.4	17.7	18.9	Pesos
Poland	110	108	2,611	2,755	0.6	0.6	2.0	2.1	Zloty
Portugal	35	34	825	874	0.2	0.2	0.2	0.2	Euro
Puerto Rico	15	15	357	375	0.1	0.1	0.1	0.1	Dollar
Qatar	-	-	-	-	-	-	0.0	0.0	Riyal
Romania	79	78	1,879	1,973	0.2	0.2	0.9	0.9	New Leu
Russia	490	484	11,672	12,311	1.5	1.5	78.1	77.8	Rubles
Saudi Arabia	-	-	-	-	-	-	0.0	0.0	Rials*
Singapore	22	22	523	571	0.4	0.4	480.6	497.2	Dollar
South Africa	136	137	3,228	3,488	0.3	0.3	4,067.7	4,158.0	Rand
South Korea	192	191	4,563	4,849	1.8	1.9	1,914.5	1,986.8	Won*
Spain	159	160	3,787	4,064	1.4	1.4	1,147.3	1,160.3	Euro
Sweden	33	33	776	827	0.6	0.6	4,832.3	5,038.6	Krona
Switzerland	30	30	710	760	0.8	0.8	787.2	807.4	Swiss franc
Taiwan	119	123	2,844	3,135	0.6	0.6	18,088.3	18,611.3	Dollar
Thailand	289	290	6,873	7,371	0.5	0.5	16,648.7	17,089.3	Baht
Turkey	-	-	-	-	-	-	0.0	0.0	Euro
Ukraine	160	157	3,799	3,993	0.1	0.1	2,154.2	1,952.7	Hryvna
UAE	-	-	-	-	-	-	0.0	0.0	Dirham
United Kingdom	208	207	4,950	5,267	3.2	3.3	2,352.4	2,432.7	Pounds
United States	2,018	2,019	48,068	51,317	38.7	40.0	38,712.9	40,001.7	Dollars
Venezuela	103	104	2,452	2,656	0.5	0.5	5,267.7	5,178.4	Bolivar
Vietnam	362	362	8,626	9,209	0.3	0.3	6,286.9	6,728.0	Dong*

Note: Due to rounding, establishments will vary by + or - one establishment. Therefore, zero establishments may also be one establishment.

* Local Sales are in trillions

PHARMACIES & DRUG STORES INDUSTRY (NAICS 44611)

NAICS 44611 Pharmacies and Drug Stores – This industry comprises establishments known as pharmacies and drug stores engaged in retailing prescription or nonprescription drugs and medicines.

COUNTRY ESTIMATES

Country	Establishments 2018	2019	Employment 2018	2019	Sales ($B) 2018	2019	Local Sales (B) 2018	2019	Currency
Algeria	371	373	43,643	46,846	0.7	0.7	75.4	76.8	Dinar
Argentina	257	258	30,257	32,309	1.6	1.6	29.7	29.7	Pesos
Australia	160	162	18,828	20,271	3.9	4.0	4.9	5.0	Dollars
Austria	29	29	3,368	3,577	0.5	0.5	0.5	0.5	Euro
Bangladesh	565	565	66,348	70,893	0.3	0.3	26.4	28.1	Taka
Belgium	36	36	4,222	4,507	0.6	0.6	0.5	0.5	Euro
Brazil	1,375	1,387	161,598	173,930	4.7	4.7	15,330.6	15,099.2	Real
Canada	120	121	14,161	15,154	2.2	2.3	2.8	2.8	Dollars
Chile	133	134	15,668	16,844	0.8	0.8	468.9	479.0	Pesos*
China	9,511	9,479	1,117,692	1,188,980	39.7	41.7	257.4	270.6	RMB
Colombia	286	286	33,607	35,876	0.9	0.9	2.5	2.6	Pesos*
Czech Republic	69	68	8,055	8,550	0.6	0.6	12.3	12.8	Koruna
Denmark	18	18	2,119	2,250	0.4	0.4	2.6	2.6	Kroner
Egypt	608	623	71,497	78,153	1.0	1.0	17.1	17.4	Pounds
Finland	18	18	2,099	2,230	0.3	0.3	0.3	0.3	Euro
France	199	199	23,442	24,971	3.2	3.2	2.7	2.7	Euro
Germany	254	251	29,842	31,445	4.9	5.0	4.1	4.2	Euro
Greece	33	33	3,926	4,160	0.2	0.2	0.2	0.2	Euro
Hong Kong	41	41	4,816	5,117	0.7	0.7	5,701.5	5,852.2	Dollar
Hungary	60	59	7,082	7,463	0.3	0.4	90.1	93.5	Forint*
India	7,986	8,107	938,583	1,016,888	6.3	6.7	402.9	426.1	Rupees
Indonesia	1,986	2,011	233,393	252,305	3.1	3.3	42.2	44.3	Rupiah*

Pharmacies & Drug Stores Industry (NAICS 44611)

Country Estimates

Country	Establishments 2018	2019	Employment 2018	2019	Sales ($B) 2018	2019	Local Sales (B) 2018	2019	Currency
Iran	544	550	63,922	69,035	1.1	1.1	40.9	40.8	Rial*
Iraq	143	145	16,762	18,164	0.3	0.3	0.4	0.4	Dinar*
Ireland	20	20	2,352	2,542	0.7	0.8	0.6	0.7	Euro
Israel	57	57	6,665	7,212	0.9	1.0	3.2	3.3	Shekel
Italy	201	200	23,615	25,086	2.6	2.6	2.1	2.1	Euro
Japan	846	837	99,400	105,005	12.1	12.3	1,371.7	1,383.6	Yen*
Kazakhstan	138	138	16,195	17,367	0.6	0.6	198.7	204.2	Tenge
Kuwait	32	34	3,785	4,214	0.4	0.4	0.1	0.1	Dinar
Malaysia	264	268	30,985	33,629	1.1	1.2	4.5	4.7	Ringgit
Mexico	859	869	100,942	108,986	3.3	3.4	63.3	64.9	New pesos
Netherlands	54	53	6,313	6,700	1.0	1.1	0.9	0.9	Euro
New Zealand	29	29	3,395	3,646	0.5	0.5	0.7	0.7	Dollar
Nigeria	741	753	87,058	94,475	0.8	0.9	300,794.7	308,457.5	Naira
Norway	20	20	2,332	2,497	0.6	0.6	5.1	5.2	Krone
Pakistan	1,187	1,212	139,522	152,012	0.7	0.8	82.0	85.9	Rupees
Peru	235	235	27,618	29,513	0.6	0.6	1.9	2.0	Nuevo Sol
Phillipines	640	651	75,204	81,660	0.9	1.0	45.1	47.9	Pesos
Poland	219	217	25,762	27,196	1.5	1.5	5.1	5.3	Zloty
Portugal	35	34	4,073	4,312	0.3	0.3	0.2	0.2	Euro
Puerto Rico	30	30	3,524	3,702	0.3	0.3	0.3	0.3	Dollar
Qatar	30	34	3,548	4,313	0.6	0.6	2.0	2.1	Riyal
Romania	158	155	18,543	19,478	0.6	0.6	2.3	2.4	New Leu
Russia	980	969	115,179	121,511	3.9	3.9	199.1	197.2	Rubles
Saudi Arabia	275	284	32,312	35,584	2.4	2.4	0.0	0.0	Rials*
Singapore	44	45	5,158	5,636	0.9	0.9	1,225.5	1,260.0	Dollar
South Africa	271	274	31,854	34,424	0.8	0.8	10,373.1	10,536.9	Rand
South Korea	383	382	45,023	47,863	4.6	4.7	4,882.2	5,034.7	Won*
Spain	159	160	18,687	20,058	1.8	1.8	1,462.9	1,470.2	Euro
Sweden	33	33	3,829	4,081	0.8	0.8	6,161.5	6,384.2	Krona
Switzerland	30	30	3,503	3,749	1.0	1.0	1,003.8	1,023.0	Swiss franc
Taiwan	239	247	28,059	30,941	1.6	1.6	46,127.6	47,163.4	Dollar
Thailand	577	580	67,825	72,750	1.3	1.3	42,456.4	43,306.3	Baht
Turkey	437	435	51,395	54,597	2.5	2.6	9,428.1	9,774.8	Euro
Ukraine	160	157	18,746	19,706	0.1	0.1	2,746.8	2,474.2	Hryvna
UAE	74	83	8,736	10,440	0.7	0.7	2,505.8	2,546.8	Dirham
United Kingdom	208	207	24,425	25,995	4.1	4.2	2,999.5	3,082.4	Pounds
United States	2,018	2,019	237,159	253,251	49.4	50.7	49,361.5	50,684.7	Dollars
Venezuela	206	209	24,192	26,214	1.3	1.3	13,433.3	13,122.6	Bolivar
Vietnam	724	725	85,117	90,896	0.7	0.8	16,032.3	17,049.6	Dong*

Note: Due to rounding, establishments will vary by + or - one establishment. Therefore, zero establishments may also be one establishment.

* Local Sales are in trillions

NAICS 44711: Gas Stations with Convenience Stores. This industry comprises establishments primarily engaged in selling gasoline and lubricating oils. These establishments frequently sell other merchandise, such as tires, batteries, and other automobile parts, or perform minor repair work. Gasoline stations combined with other activities, such as grocery stores, convenience stores, or carwashes, are classified according to the primary activity.

COUNTRY ESTIMATES

Country	Establishments 2018	2019	Employment 2018	2019	Sales ($B) 2018	2019	Local Sales (B) 2018	2019	Currency
Algeria	186	187	43,716	47,174	0.7	0.7	77.9	79.2	Dinar
Argentina	129	129	30,307	32,536	1.6	1.6	30.7	30.7	Pesos
Australia	80	81	18,859	20,413	4.0	4.1	5.1	5.2	Dollars
Austria	29	29	6,747	7,205	1.1	1.1	0.9	0.9	Euro
Bangladesh	565	565	132,915	142,780	0.7	0.7	54.5	57.8	Taka
Belgium	36	36	8,458	9,077	1.3	1.3	1.1	1.1	Euro
Brazil	688	693	161,866	175,150	4.9	4.8	15,837.9	15,560.6	Real
Canada	120	121	28,368	30,521	4.6	4.7	5.8	5.9	Dollars
Chile	67	67	15,694	16,963	0.8	0.8	484.5	493.7	Pesos*
China	4,755	4,739	1,119,540	1,197,317	41.0	43.0	265.9	278.9	RMB
Colombia	143	143	33,663	36,128	0.9	0.9	2.6	2.6	Pesos*
Czech Republic	34	34	8,069	8,610	0.6	0.6	12.7	13.2	Koruna
Denmark	18	18	4,245	4,531	0.9	0.9	5.3	5.4	Kroner
Egypt	304	312	71,616	78,701	1.0	1.0	17.7	18.0	Pounds
Finland	18	18	4,204	4,490	0.7	0.7	0.5	0.5	Euro
France	199	199	46,962	50,292	6.6	6.7	5.5	5.6	Euro
Germany	254	251	59,783	63,332	10.1	10.3	8.5	8.6	Euro
Greece	33	33	7,865	8,378	0.5	0.5	0.4	0.4	Euro
Hong Kong	20	20	4,824	5,153	0.8	0.8	5,890.1	6,031.1	Dollar
Hungary	30	30	7,094	7,515	0.4	0.4	93.1	96.4	Forint*
India	3,993	4,053	940,135	1,024,019	6.6	6.9	416.2	439.2	Rupees
Indonesia	993	1,006	233,779	254,074	3.2	3.4	43.6	45.7	Rupiah*

Gas Stations with Convenience Stores (NAICS 44711)

Country Estimates

Country	Establishments 2018	Establishments 2019	Employment 2018	Employment 2019	Sales ($B) 2018	Sales ($B) 2019	Local Sales (B) 2018	Local Sales (B) 2019	Currency
Iran	272	275	64,028	69,519	1.2	1.2	42.2	42.0	Rial*
Iraq	143	145	33,579	36,582	0.6	0.6	0.7	0.7	Dinar*
Ireland	20	20	4,711	5,119	1.5	1.7	1.3	1.4	Euro
Israel	28	29	6,676	7,263	1.0	1.0	3.3	3.4	Shekel
Italy	201	200	47,308	50,525	5.3	5.3	4.4	4.4	Euro
Japan	423	419	99,564	105,741	12.6	12.6	1,417.1	1,425.9	Yen*
Kazakhstan	69	69	16,222	17,489	0.6	0.6	205.3	210.5	Tenge
Kuwait	16	17	3,791	4,244	0.4	0.4	0.1	0.1	Dinar
Malaysia	132	134	31,036	33,865	1.2	1.2	4.6	4.9	Ringgit
Mexico	429	434	101,109	109,750	3.4	3.5	65.4	66.9	New pesos
Netherlands	54	53	12,648	13,494	2.2	2.2	1.8	1.8	Euro
New Zealand	14	15	3,401	3,671	0.5	0.5	0.7	0.7	Dollar
Nigeria	741	753	174,404	190,274	1.7	1.8	621,496.0	635,770.4	Naira
Norway	20	20	4,672	5,029	1.3	1.3	10.4	10.6	Krone
Pakistan	594	606	139,753	153,078	0.8	0.8	84.8	88.6	Rupees
Peru	118	118	27,664	29,720	0.6	0.6	2.0	2.0	Nuevo Sol
Phillipines	320	326	75,328	82,233	0.9	1.0	46.6	49.3	Pesos
Poland	110	108	25,805	27,386	1.5	1.6	5.3	5.5	Zloty
Portugal	35	34	8,159	8,685	0.6	0.6	0.5	0.5	Euro
Puerto Rico	15	15	3,530	3,728	0.3	0.3	0.3	0.3	Dollar
Qatar	15	17	3,554	4,343	0.6	0.6	2.1	2.1	Riyal
Romania	79	78	18,574	19,615	0.6	0.6	2.4	2.5	New Leu
Russia	490	484	115,370	122,363	4.0	4.0	205.7	203.3	Rubles
Saudi Arabia	137	142	32,366	35,834	2.5	2.5	0.0	0.0	Rials*
Singapore	22	22	5,166	5,676	1.0	1.0	1,266.0	1,298.5	Dollar
South Africa	136	137	31,906	34,666	0.9	0.9	10,716.3	10,858.9	Rand
South Korea	192	191	45,098	48,199	4.7	4.9	5,043.8	5,188.6	Won*
Spain	159	160	37,435	40,397	3.6	3.6	3,022.5	3,030.2	Euro
Sweden	33	33	7,672	8,219	1.6	1.6	12,730.8	13,158.7	Krona
Switzerland	30	30	7,018	7,550	2.1	2.2	2,074.0	2,108.5	Swiss franc
Taiwan	119	123	28,106	31,158	1.6	1.6	47,653.9	48,604.9	Dollar
Thailand	289	290	67,937	73,260	1.4	1.4	43,861.3	44,629.9	Baht
Turkey	219	218	51,480	54,979	2.6	2.7	9,740.1	10,073.5	Euro
Ukraine	160	157	37,554	39,689	0.2	0.2	5,675.3	5,099.7	Hryvna
UAE	74	83	17,502	21,027	1.4	1.4	5,177.5	5,249.3	Dirham
United Kingdom	208	207	48,931	52,354	8.4	8.6	6,197.4	6,353.1	Pounds
United States	2,018	2,019	475,102	510,054	102.0	104.5	101,989.8	104,467.6	Dollars
Venezuela	103	104	24,232	26,397	1.4	1.4	13,877.8	13,523.7	Bolivar
Vietnam	362	362	85,258	91,533	0.7	0.8	16,562.9	17,570.7	Dong*

Note: Due to rounding, establishments will vary by + or - one establishment. Therefore, zero establishments may also be one establishment.

* Local Sales are in trillions

MEN'S CLOTHING STORES INDUSTRY
(NAICS 44811)

NAICS 44811: Men's Clothing Stores. This industry comprises establishments primarily engaged in retailing a general line of new men's and boys' clothing. These establishments may provide basic alterations, such as hemming, taking in or letting out seams, or lengthening or shortening sleeves.

COUNTRY ESTIMATES

Country	Establishments 2018	2019	Employment 2018	2019	Sales ($B) 2018	2019	Local Sales (B) 2018	2019	Currency
Algeria	371	373	1,452	1,517	0.1	0.1	12.3	12.1	Dinar
Argentina	257	258	1,007	1,046	0.3	0.2	4.8	4.7	Pesos
Australia	160	162	626	656	0.6	0.6	0.8	0.8	Dollars
Austria	57	57	224	232	0.2	0.2	0.1	0.1	Euro
Bangladesh	1,129	1,130	4,415	4,592	0.1	0.1	8.6	8.9	Taka
Belgium	72	72	281	292	0.2	0.2	0.2	0.2	Euro
Brazil	1,375	1,387	5,377	5,633	0.8	0.7	2,500.7	2,387.0	Real
Canada	241	242	942	982	0.7	0.7	0.9	0.9	Dollars
Chile	133	134	521	546	0.1	0.1	76.5	75.7	Pesos*
China	9,511	9,479	37,189	38,505	6.5	6.6	42.0	42.8	RMB
Colombia	286	286	1,118	1,162	0.1	0.1	0.4	0.4	Pesos*
Czech Republic	69	68	268	277	0.1	0.1	2.0	2.0	Koruna
Denmark	36	36	141	146	0.1	0.1	0.8	0.8	Kroner
Egypt	608	623	2,379	2,531	0.2	0.2	2.8	2.8	Pounds
Finland	36	36	140	144	0.1	0.1	0.1	0.1	Euro
France	399	398	1,560	1,617	1.0	1.0	0.9	0.9	Euro
Germany	508	501	1,986	2,037	1.6	1.6	1.3	1.3	Euro
Greece	67	66	261	269	0.1	0.1	0.1	0.1	Euro
Hong Kong	41	41	160	166	0.1	0.1	930.0	925.2	Dollar
Hungary	60	59	236	242	0.1	0.1	14.7	14.8	Forint*
India	7,986	8,107	31,230	32,932	1.0	1.1	65.7	67.4	Rupees
Indonesia	1,986	2,011	7,766	8,171	0.5	0.5	6.9	7.0	Rupiah*

MEN'S CLOTHING STORES INDUSTRY
(NAICS 44811)

COUNTRY ESTIMATES

Country	Establishments 2018	Establishments 2019	Employment 2018	Employment 2019	Sales ($B) 2018	Sales ($B) 2019	Local Sales (B) 2018	Local Sales (B) 2019	Currency
Iran	544	550	2,127	2,236	0.2	0.2	6.7	6.4	Rial*
Iraq	285	290	1,115	1,176	0.1	0.1	0.1	0.1	Dinar*
Ireland	40	41	157	165	0.2	0.3	0.2	0.2	Euro
Israel	57	57	222	234	0.2	0.2	0.5	0.5	Shekel
Italy	402	400	1,571	1,625	0.8	0.8	0.7	0.7	Euro
Japan	846	837	3,307	3,401	2.0	1.9	223.7	218.7	Yen*
Kazakhstan	138	138	539	562	0.1	0.1	32.4	32.3	Tenge
Kuwait	32	34	126	136	0.1	0.1	0.0	0.0	Dinar
Malaysia	264	268	1,031	1,089	0.2	0.2	0.7	0.7	Ringgit
Mexico	859	869	3,359	3,530	0.5	0.5	10.3	10.3	New pesos
Netherlands	107	107	420	434	0.3	0.3	0.3	0.3	Euro
New Zealand	29	29	113	118	0.1	0.1	0.1	0.1	Dollar
Nigeria	1,482	1,506	5,793	6,119	0.3	0.3	98,129.8	97,528.6	Naira
Norway	40	40	155	162	0.2	0.2	1.6	1.6	Krone
Pakistan	1,187	1,212	4,642	4,923	0.1	0.1	13.4	13.6	Rupees
Peru	235	235	919	956	0.1	0.1	0.3	0.3	Nuevo Sol
Phillipines	640	651	2,502	2,645	0.1	0.2	7.4	7.6	Pesos
Poland	219	217	857	881	0.2	0.2	0.8	0.8	Zloty
Portugal	69	69	271	279	0.1	0.1	0.1	0.1	Euro
Puerto Rico	30	30	117	120	0.1	0.1	0.1	0.1	Dollar
Qatar	30	34	118	140	0.1	0.1	0.3	0.3	Riyal
Romania	158	155	617	631	0.1	0.1	0.4	0.4	New Leu
Russia	980	969	3,832	3,935	0.6	0.6	32.5	31.2	Rubles
Saudi Arabia	275	284	1,075	1,152	0.4	0.4	0.0	0.0	Rials*
Singapore	44	45	172	183	0.2	0.1	199.9	199.2	Dollar
South Africa	271	274	1,060	1,115	0.1	0.1	1,692.0	1,665.8	Rand
South Korea	383	382	1,498	1,550	0.7	0.7	796.4	795.9	Won*
Spain	318	320	1,244	1,299	0.6	0.6	477.2	464.8	Euro
Sweden	65	65	255	264	0.2	0.2	2,010.1	2,018.6	Krona
Switzerland	60	60	233	243	0.3	0.3	327.5	323.4	Swiss franc
Taiwan	239	247	934	1,002	0.3	0.3	7,524.2	7,456.1	Dollar
Thailand	577	580	2,257	2,356	0.2	0.2	6,925.4	6,846.3	Baht
Turkey	437	435	1,710	1,768	0.4	0.4	1,537.9	1,545.3	Euro
Ukraine	319	314	1,247	1,276	0.0	0.0	896.1	782.3	Hryvna
UAE	149	166	581	676	0.2	0.2	817.5	805.3	Dirham
United Kingdom	416	414	1,625	1,684	1.3	1.3	978.5	974.6	Pounds
United States	2,018	2,019	7,891	8,202	8.1	8.0	8,051.7	8,012.8	Dollars
Venezuela	206	209	805	849	0.2	0.2	2,191.2	2,074.6	Bolivar
Vietnam	724	725	2,832	2,944	0.1	0.1	2,615.2	2,695.4	Dong*

Note: Due to rounding, establishments will vary by + or - one establishment. Therefore, zero establishments may also be one establishment.

* Local Sales are in trillions

WOMEN'S CLOTHING STORES INDUSTRY (NAICS 44812)

NAICS 44812: Women's Clothing Stores . This industry comprises establishments primarily engaged in retailing a general line of new women's, misses' and juniors' clothing, including maternity wear. These establishments may provide basic alterations, such as hemming, taking in or letting out seams, or lengthening or shortening sleeves.

COUNTRY ESTIMATES

Country	Establishments 2018	Establishments 2019	Employment 2018	Employment 2019	Sales ($B) 2018	Sales ($B) 2019	Local Sales (B) 2018	Local Sales (B) 2019	Currency
Algeria	371	373	9,173	9,807	0.6	0.6	70.7	71.9	Dinar
Argentina	257	258	6,359	6,764	1.5	1.5	27.8	27.8	Pesos
Australia	160	162	3,957	4,244	3.6	3.7	4.6	4.7	Dollars
Austria	57	57	1,416	1,498	1.0	1.0	0.8	0.9	Euro
Bangladesh	1,129	1,130	27,889	29,682	0.6	0.6	49.5	52.5	Taka
Belgium	72	72	1,775	1,887	1.2	1.2	1.0	1.0	Euro
Brazil	1,375	1,387	33,964	36,411	4.4	4.4	14,372.5	14,122.1	Real
Canada	241	242	5,953	6,345	4.2	4.3	5.2	5.3	Dollars
Chile	133	134	3,293	3,526	0.7	0.7	439.6	448.0	Pesos*
China	9,511	9,479	234,913	248,904	37.2	39.0	241.3	253.1	RMB
Colombia	286	286	7,063	7,510	0.8	0.8	2.3	2.4	Pesos*
Czech Republic	69	68	1,693	1,790	0.5	0.6	11.5	12.0	Koruna
Denmark	36	36	891	942	0.8	0.8	4.8	4.9	Kroner
Egypt	608	623	15,027	16,361	0.9	0.9	16.1	16.3	Pounds
Finland	36	36	882	933	0.6	0.6	0.5	0.5	Euro
France	399	398	9,854	10,455	6.0	6.0	5.0	5.0	Euro
Germany	508	501	12,544	13,166	9.2	9.4	7.7	7.8	Euro
Greece	67	66	1,650	1,742	0.5	0.5	0.4	0.4	Euro
Hong Kong	41	41	1,012	1,071	0.7	0.7	5,345.2	5,473.5	Dollar
Hungary	60	59	1,489	1,562	0.3	0.3	84.4	87.5	Forint*
India	7,986	8,107	197,269	212,877	5.9	6.3	377.7	398.6	Rupees
Indonesia	1,986	2,011	49,054	52,818	2.9	3.1	39.6	41.5	Rupiah*

WOMEN'S CLOTHING STORES INDUSTRY
(NAICS 44812)

COUNTRY ESTIMATES

Country	Establishments 2018	2019	Employment 2018	2019	Sales ($B) 2018	2019	Local Sales (B) 2018	2019	Currency
Iran	544	550	13,435	14,452	1.1	1.1	38.3	38.1	Rial*
Iraq	285	290	7,046	7,605	0.6	0.6	0.7	0.7	Dinar*
Ireland	40	41	989	1,064	1.4	1.6	1.1	1.3	Euro
Israel	57	57	1,401	1,510	0.9	0.9	3.0	3.1	Shekel
Italy	402	400	9,927	10,503	4.8	4.8	4.0	4.0	Euro
Japan	846	837	20,891	21,982	11.4	11.5	1,285.9	1,294.0	Yen*
Kazakhstan	138	138	3,404	3,636	0.6	0.6	186.3	191.0	Tenge
Kuwait	32	34	796	882	0.3	0.3	0.1	0.1	Dinar
Malaysia	264	268	6,512	7,040	1.0	1.1	4.2	4.4	Ringgit
Mexico	859	869	21,216	22,815	3.1	3.2	59.3	60.7	New pesos
Netherlands	107	107	2,654	2,805	2.0	2.0	1.6	1.7	Euro
New Zealand	29	29	714	763	0.4	0.5	0.6	0.6	Dollar
Nigeria	1,482	1,506	36,595	39,555	1.6	1.6	563,991.6	576,994.0	Naira
Norway	40	40	980	1,046	1.2	1.2	9.5	9.7	Krone
Pakistan	1,187	1,212	29,324	31,822	0.7	0.7	76.9	80.4	Rupees
Peru	235	235	5,805	6,178	0.6	0.6	1.8	1.9	Nuevo Sol
Phillipines	640	651	15,806	17,095	0.8	0.9	42.3	44.8	Pesos
Poland	219	217	5,415	5,693	1.4	1.4	4.8	5.0	Zloty
Portugal	69	69	1,712	1,805	0.5	0.5	0.4	0.4	Euro
Puerto Rico	30	30	741	775	0.3	0.3	0.3	0.3	Dollar
Qatar	30	34	746	903	0.5	0.5	1.9	1.9	Riyal
Romania	158	155	3,897	4,078	0.6	0.6	2.2	2.2	New Leu
Russia	980	969	24,208	25,437	3.7	3.6	186.6	184.5	Rubles
Saudi Arabia	275	284	6,791	7,449	2.2	2.3	0.0	0.0	Rials*
Singapore	44	45	1,084	1,180	0.9	0.9	1,148.9	1,178.4	Dollar
South Africa	271	274	6,695	7,206	0.8	0.8	9,724.8	9,855.0	Rand
South Korea	383	382	9,463	10,020	4.3	4.4	4,577.1	4,708.9	Won*
Spain	318	320	7,855	8,398	3.3	3.3	2,742.9	2,750.1	Euro
Sweden	65	65	1,610	1,709	1.4	1.5	11,552.8	11,942.2	Krona
Switzerland	60	60	1,473	1,570	1.9	2.0	1,882.1	1,913.6	Swiss franc
Taiwan	239	247	5,897	6,477	1.5	1.5	43,244.7	44,111.4	Dollar
Thailand	577	580	14,255	15,230	1.2	1.3	39,803.0	40,503.9	Baht
Turkey	437	435	10,802	11,429	2.4	2.4	8,838.9	9,142.2	Euro
Ukraine	319	314	7,880	8,251	0.2	0.2	5,150.2	4,628.2	Hryvna
UAE	149	166	3,672	4,371	1.3	1.3	4,698.4	4,764.0	Dirham
United Kingdom	416	414	10,267	10,884	7.6	7.8	5,624.0	5,765.8	Pounds
United States	2,018	2,019	49,845	53,016	46.3	47.4	46,276.6	47,404.8	Dollars
Venezuela	206	209	5,085	5,488	1.3	1.2	12,593.8	12,273.4	Bolivar
Vietnam	724	725	17,890	19,028	0.7	0.7	15,030.4	15,946.3	Dong*

Note: Due to rounding, establishments will vary by + or - one establishment. Therefore, zero establishments may also be one establishment.

* Local Sales are in trillions

FAMILY CLOTHING STORES INDUSTRY (NAICS 44814)

NAICS 44814: Family Clothing Stores . This industry comprises establishments primarily engaged in retailing a general line of new clothing for men, women, and children, without specializing in sales for an individual gender or age group. These establishments may provide basic alterations, such as hemming, taking in or letting out seams, or lengthening or shortening sleeves.

COUNTRY ESTIMATES

Country	Establishments		Employment		Sales ($B)		Local Sales (B)		
	2018	2019	2018	2019	2018	2019	2018	2019	Currency
Algeria	371	373	20,788	22,208	0.5	0.5	53.6	54.6	Dinar
Argentina	257	258	14,412	15,316	1.1	1.1	21.1	21.1	Pesos
Australia	160	162	8,968	9,610	2.7	2.8	3.5	3.6	Dollars
Austria	57	57	3,209	3,392	0.8	0.8	0.6	0.6	Euro
Bangladesh	1,129	1,130	63,204	67,215	0.5	0.5	37.5	39.8	Taka
Belgium	72	72	4,022	4,273	0.9	0.9	0.7	0.7	Euro
Brazil	1,375	1,387	76,971	82,453	3.4	3.3	10,896.5	10,720.9	Real
Canada	241	242	13,490	14,368	3.2	3.3	4.0	4.0	Dollars
Chile	133	134	7,463	7,985	0.5	0.6	333.3	340.1	Pesos*
China	9,511	9,479	532,367	563,647	28.2	29.6	183.0	192.1	RMB
Colombia	286	286	16,007	17,007	0.6	0.6	1.8	1.8	Pesos*
Czech Republic	69	68	3,837	4,053	0.4	0.4	8.7	9.1	Koruna
Denmark	36	36	2,018	2,133	0.6	0.6	3.7	3.7	Kroner
Egypt	608	623	34,055	37,049	0.7	0.7	12.2	12.4	Pounds
Finland	36	36	1,999	2,114	0.5	0.4	0.4	0.4	Euro
France	399	398	22,332	23,676	4.5	4.6	3.8	3.8	Euro
Germany	508	501	28,428	29,814	7.0	7.1	5.8	5.9	Euro
Greece	67	66	3,740	3,944	0.4	0.3	0.3	0.3	Euro
Hong Kong	41	41	2,294	2,426	0.5	0.5	4,052.4	4,155.3	Dollar
Hungary	60	59	3,373	3,538	0.2	0.3	64.0	66.4	Forint*
India	7,986	8,107	447,056	482,065	4.5	4.8	286.3	302.6	Rupees
Indonesia	1,986	2,011	111,167	119,608	2.2	2.3	30.0	31.5	Rupiah*

FAMILY CLOTHING STORES INDUSTRY
(NAICS 44814)

COUNTRY ESTIMATES

Country	Establishments 2018	2019	Employment 2018	2019	Sales ($B) 2018	2019	Local Sales (B) 2018	2019	Currency
Iran	544	550	30,447	32,727	0.8	0.8	29.1	29.0	Rial*
Iraq	285	290	15,967	17,221	0.4	0.4	0.5	0.5	Dinar*
Ireland	40	41	2,240	2,410	1.0	1.2	0.9	1.0	Euro
Israel	57	57	3,175	3,419	0.7	0.7	2.3	2.3	Shekel
Italy	402	400	22,496	23,785	3.6	3.6	3.0	3.0	Euro
Japan	846	837	47,345	49,778	8.6	8.7	974.9	982.4	Yen*
Kazakhstan	138	138	7,714	8,233	0.4	0.4	141.2	145.0	Tenge
Kuwait	32	34	1,803	1,998	0.3	0.2	0.1	0.1	Dinar
Malaysia	264	268	14,758	15,942	0.8	0.8	3.2	3.4	Ringgit
Mexico	859	869	48,080	51,666	2.3	2.4	45.0	46.1	New pesos
Netherlands	107	107	6,014	6,352	1.5	1.5	1.2	1.3	Euro
New Zealand	29	29	1,617	1,728	0.3	0.3	0.5	0.5	Dollar
Nigeria	1,482	1,506	82,933	89,573	1.2	1.2	427,589.3	438,031.0	Naira
Norway	40	40	2,222	2,368	0.9	0.9	7.2	7.3	Krone
Pakistan	1,187	1,212	66,456	72,063	0.5	0.6	58.3	61.0	Rupees
Peru	235	235	13,155	13,991	0.4	0.4	1.4	1.4	Nuevo Sol
Phillipines	640	651	35,820	38,712	0.6	0.7	32.1	34.0	Pesos
Poland	219	217	12,271	12,892	1.1	1.1	3.7	3.8	Zloty
Portugal	69	69	3,880	4,088	0.4	0.4	0.3	0.3	Euro
Puerto Rico	30	30	1,678	1,755	0.2	0.2	0.2	0.2	Dollar
Qatar	30	34	1,690	2,045	0.4	0.4	1.4	1.5	Riyal
Romania	158	155	8,832	9,234	0.4	0.4	1.6	1.7	New Leu
Russia	980	969	54,861	57,603	2.8	2.7	141.5	140.0	Rubles
Saudi Arabia	275	284	15,391	16,869	1.7	1.7	0.0	0.0	Rials*
Singapore	44	45	2,457	2,672	0.7	0.7	871.0	894.6	Dollar
South Africa	271	274	15,172	16,319	0.6	0.6	7,372.8	7,481.5	Rand
South Korea	383	382	21,445	22,690	3.3	3.4	3,470.1	3,574.8	Won*
Spain	318	320	17,801	19,017	2.5	2.5	2,079.5	2,087.8	Euro
Sweden	65	65	3,648	3,869	1.1	1.1	8,758.8	9,066.0	Krona
Switzerland	60	60	3,337	3,554	1.5	1.5	1,426.9	1,452.7	Swiss franc
Taiwan	239	247	13,365	14,668	1.1	1.1	32,785.9	33,487.6	Dollar
Thailand	577	580	32,306	34,488	0.9	1.0	30,176.6	30,749.0	Baht
Turkey	437	435	24,480	25,882	1.8	1.9	6,701.2	6,940.4	Euro
Ukraine	319	314	17,858	18,684	0.1	0.1	3,904.6	3,513.6	Hryvna
UAE	149	166	8,323	9,899	1.0	1.0	3,562.1	3,616.7	Dirham
United Kingdom	416	414	23,268	24,646	5.8	5.9	4,263.8	4,377.2	Pounds
United States	2,018	2,019	112,961	120,056	35.1	36.0	35,084.5	35,987.9	Dollars
Venezuela	206	209	11,523	12,427	1.0	0.9	9,547.9	9,317.5	Bolivar
Vietnam	724	725	40,542	43,090	0.5	0.5	11,395.2	12,105.8	Dong*

Note: Due to rounding, establishments will vary by + or - one establishment. Therefore, zero establishments may also be one establishment.

* Local Sales are in trillions

BOOK STORES RETAILING INDUSTRY
(NAICS 451211)

NAICS 451211: Book Stores. This industry comprises establishments primarily engaged in the retail sale of new books and magazines. Establishments primarily engaged in the retail sale of used books are classified in 5932.

COUNTRY ESTIMATES

Country	Establishments 2018	2019	Employment 2018	2019	Sales ($B) 2018	2019	Local Sales (B) 2018	2019	Currency
Algeria	371	373	2,217	2,330	0.1	0.1	15.1	14.9	Dinar
Argentina	257	258	1,537	1,607	0.3	0.3	5.9	5.8	Pesos
Australia	160	162	956	1,008	0.8	0.8	1.0	1.0	Dollars
Austria	57	57	342	356	0.2	0.2	0.2	0.2	Euro
Bangladesh	1,129	1,130	6,740	7,052	0.1	0.1	10.6	10.9	Taka
Belgium	72	72	429	448	0.2	0.2	0.2	0.2	Euro
Brazil	1,375	1,387	8,208	8,651	1.0	0.9	3,069.1	2,929.4	Real
Canada	241	242	1,438	1,508	0.9	0.9	1.1	1.1	Dollars
Chile	133	134	796	838	0.2	0.2	93.9	92.9	Pesos*
China	9,511	9,479	56,769	59,140	7.9	8.1	51.5	52.5	RMB
Colombia	286	286	1,707	1,784	0.2	0.2	0.5	0.5	Pesos*
Czech Republic	69	68	409	425	0.1	0.1	2.5	2.5	Koruna
Denmark	36	36	215	224	0.2	0.2	1.0	1.0	Kroner
Egypt	608	623	3,631	3,887	0.2	0.2	3.4	3.4	Pounds
Finland	36	36	213	222	0.1	0.1	0.1	0.1	Euro
France	399	398	2,381	2,484	1.3	1.3	1.1	1.0	Euro
Germany	508	501	3,031	3,128	2.0	1.9	1.6	1.6	Euro
Greece	67	66	399	414	0.1	0.1	0.1	0.1	Euro
Hong Kong	41	41	245	255	0.1	0.1	1,141.4	1,135.4	Dollar
Hungary	60	59	360	371	0.1	0.1	18.0	18.1	Forint*
India	7,986	8,107	47,672	50,580	1.3	1.3	80.6	82.7	Rupees
Indonesia	1,986	2,011	11,854	12,550	0.6	0.6	8.5	8.6	Rupiah*

BOOK STORES RETAILING INDUSTRY
(NAICS 451211)

COUNTRY ESTIMATES

Country	Establishments 2018	Establishments 2019	Employment 2018	Employment 2019	Sales ($B) 2018	Sales ($B) 2019	Local Sales (B) 2018	Local Sales (B) 2019	Currency
Iran	544	550	3,247	3,434	0.2	0.2	8.2	7.9	Rial*
Iraq	285	290	1,703	1,807	0.1	0.1	0.1	0.1	Dinar*
Ireland	40	41	239	253	0.3	0.3	0.2	0.3	Euro
Israel	57	57	339	359	0.2	0.2	0.6	0.6	Shekel
Italy	402	400	2,399	2,496	1.0	1.0	0.9	0.8	Euro
Japan	846	837	5,049	5,223	2.4	2.4	274.6	268.4	Yen*
Kazakhstan	138	138	823	864	0.1	0.1	39.8	39.6	Tenge
Kuwait	32	34	192	210	0.1	0.1	0.0	0.0	Dinar
Malaysia	264	268	1,574	1,673	0.2	0.2	0.9	0.9	Ringgit
Mexico	859	869	5,127	5,421	0.7	0.7	12.7	12.6	New pesos
Netherlands	107	107	641	666	0.4	0.4	0.4	0.3	Euro
New Zealand	29	29	172	181	0.1	0.1	0.1	0.1	Dollar
Nigeria	1,482	1,506	8,844	9,398	0.3	0.3	120,433.0	119,686.3	Naira
Norway	40	40	237	248	0.3	0.2	2.0	2.0	Krone
Pakistan	1,187	1,212	7,087	7,561	0.1	0.2	16.4	16.7	Rupees
Peru	235	235	1,403	1,468	0.1	0.1	0.4	0.4	Nuevo Sol
Phillipines	640	651	3,820	4,062	0.2	0.2	9.0	9.3	Pesos
Poland	219	217	1,308	1,353	0.3	0.3	1.0	1.0	Zloty
Portugal	69	69	414	429	0.1	0.1	0.1	0.1	Euro
Puerto Rico	30	30	179	184	0.1	0.1	0.1	0.1	Dollar
Qatar	30	34	180	215	0.1	0.1	0.4	0.4	Riyal
Romania	158	155	942	969	0.1	0.1	0.5	0.5	New Leu
Russia	980	969	5,850	6,044	0.8	0.7	39.9	38.3	Rubles
Saudi Arabia	275	284	1,641	1,770	0.5	0.5	0.0	0.0	Rials*
Singapore	44	45	262	280	0.2	0.2	245.3	244.4	Dollar
South Africa	271	274	1,618	1,712	0.2	0.2	2,076.6	2,044.2	Rand
South Korea	383	382	2,287	2,381	0.9	0.9	977.4	976.8	Won*
Spain	318	320	1,898	1,995	0.7	0.7	585.7	570.5	Euro
Sweden	65	65	389	406	0.3	0.3	2,467.0	2,477.2	Krona
Switzerland	60	60	356	373	0.4	0.4	401.9	396.9	Swiss franc
Taiwan	239	247	1,425	1,539	0.3	0.3	9,234.3	9,150.1	Dollar
Thailand	577	580	3,445	3,619	0.3	0.3	8,499.4	8,401.8	Baht
Turkey	437	435	2,610	2,716	0.5	0.5	1,887.4	1,896.4	Euro
Ukraine	319	314	1,904	1,960	0.0	0.0	1,099.8	960.0	Hryvna
UAE	149	166	887	1,039	0.3	0.3	1,003.3	988.2	Dirham
United Kingdom	416	414	2,481	2,586	1.6	1.6	1,200.9	1,196.0	Pounds
United States	2,018	2,019	12,046	12,597	9.9	9.8	9,881.8	9,833.2	Dollars
Venezuela	206	209	1,229	1,304	0.3	0.3	2,689.2	2,545.9	Bolivar
Vietnam	724	725	4,323	4,521	0.1	0.1	3,209.5	3,307.7	Dong*

Note: Due to rounding, establishments will vary by + or - one establishment. Therefore, zero establishments may also be one establishment.

* Local Sales are in trillions

Department Stores Industry (NAICS 45211)

NAICS 45211: Department Stores Industry . This industry comprises establishments known as department stores primarily engaged in retailing a wide range of the following new products with no one merchandise line predominating: apparel, furniture, appliances and home furnishings; and selected additional items, such as paint, hardware, toiletries, cosmetics, photographic equipment, jewelry, toys, and sporting goods. Merchandise lines are normally arranged in separate departments.

Country Estimates

Country	Establishments 2018	2019	Employment 2018	2019	Sales ($B) 2018	2019	Local Sales (B) 2018	2019	Currency
Algeria	371	373	23,218	23,571	0.1	0.1	14.2	14.0	Dinar
Argentina	257	258	16,097	16,256	0.3	0.3	5.6	5.4	Pesos
Australia	160	162	10,016	10,199	0.7	0.7	0.9	0.9	Dollars
Austria	57	57	3,584	3,600	0.2	0.2	0.2	0.2	Euro
Bangladesh	1,129	1,130	70,594	71,340	0.1	0.1	9.9	10.2	Taka
Belgium	72	72	4,492	4,535	0.2	0.2	0.2	0.2	Euro
Brazil	1,375	1,387	85,970	87,514	0.9	0.9	2,883.8	2,748.2	Real
Canada	241	242	15,067	15,250	0.8	0.8	1.0	1.0	Dollars
Chile	133	134	8,336	8,475	0.1	0.1	88.2	87.2	Pesos*
China	9,511	9,479	594,613	598,239	7.5	7.6	48.4	49.3	RMB
Colombia	286	286	17,879	18,051	0.2	0.2	0.5	0.5	Pesos*
Czech Republic	69	68	4,285	4,302	0.1	0.1	2.3	2.3	Koruna
Denmark	36	36	2,254	2,264	0.2	0.2	1.0	1.0	Kroner
Egypt	608	623	38,037	39,323	0.2	0.2	3.2	3.2	Pounds
Finland	36	36	2,233	2,244	0.1	0.1	0.1	0.1	Euro
France	399	398	24,943	25,129	1.2	1.2	1.0	1.0	Euro
Germany	508	501	31,752	31,644	1.8	1.8	1.5	1.5	Euro
Greece	67	66	4,177	4,186	0.1	0.1	0.1	0.1	Euro
Hong Kong	41	41	2,562	2,575	0.1	0.1	1,072.5	1,065.2	Dollar
Hungary	60	59	3,768	3,755	0.1	0.1	16.9	17.0	Forint*
India	7,986	8,107	499,327	511,650	1.2	1.2	75.8	77.6	Rupees
Indonesia	1,986	2,011	124,165	126,948	0.6	0.6	7.9	8.1	Rupiah*

Department Stores Industry
(NAICS 45211)

Country Estimates

Country	Establishments 2018	Establishments 2019	Employment 2018	Employment 2019	Sales ($B) 2018	Sales ($B) 2019	Local Sales (B) 2018	Local Sales (B) 2019	Currency
Iran	544	550	34,006	34,735	0.2	0.2	7.7	7.4	Rial*
Iraq	285	290	17,834	18,278	0.1	0.1	0.1	0.1	Dinar*
Ireland	40	41	2,502	2,558	0.3	0.3	0.2	0.3	Euro
Israel	57	57	3,546	3,629	0.2	0.2	0.6	0.6	Shekel
Italy	402	400	25,126	25,245	1.0	0.9	0.8	0.8	Euro
Japan	846	837	52,881	52,833	2.3	2.2	258.0	251.8	Yen*
Kazakhstan	138	138	8,616	8,738	0.1	0.1	37.4	37.2	Tenge
Kuwait	32	34	2,014	2,120	0.1	0.1	0.0	0.0	Dinar
Malaysia	264	268	16,484	16,921	0.2	0.2	0.8	0.9	Ringgit
Mexico	859	869	53,701	54,836	0.6	0.6	11.9	11.8	New pesos
Netherlands	107	107	6,717	6,742	0.4	0.4	0.3	0.3	Euro
New Zealand	29	29	1,806	1,834	0.1	0.1	0.1	0.1	Dollar
Nigeria	1,482	1,506	92,630	95,070	0.3	0.3	113,162.1	112,285.3	Naira
Norway	40	40	2,482	2,513	0.2	0.2	1.9	1.9	Krone
Pakistan	1,187	1,212	74,226	76,485	0.1	0.1	15.4	15.6	Rupees
Peru	235	235	14,693	14,850	0.1	0.1	0.4	0.4	Nuevo Sol
Phillipines	640	651	40,008	41,088	0.2	0.2	8.5	8.7	Pesos
Poland	219	217	13,705	13,684	0.3	0.3	1.0	1.0	Zloty
Portugal	69	69	4,333	4,339	0.1	0.1	0.1	0.1	Euro
Puerto Rico	30	30	1,875	1,863	0.1	0.1	0.1	0.1	Dollar
Qatar	30	34	1,888	2,170	0.1	0.1	0.4	0.4	Riyal
Romania	158	155	9,865	9,800	0.1	0.1	0.4	0.4	New Leu
Russia	980	969	61,276	61,138	0.7	0.7	37.4	35.9	Rubles
Saudi Arabia	275	284	17,190	17,904	0.4	0.4	0.0	0.0	Rials*
Singapore	44	45	2,744	2,836	0.2	0.2	230.5	229.3	Dollar
South Africa	271	274	16,946	17,321	0.2	0.2	1,951.2	1,917.8	Rand
South Korea	383	382	23,953	24,083	0.9	0.9	918.4	916.4	Won*
Spain	318	320	19,883	20,185	0.7	0.6	550.3	535.2	Euro
Sweden	65	65	4,075	4,107	0.3	0.3	2,318.0	2,324.0	Krona
Switzerland	60	60	3,728	3,772	0.4	0.4	377.6	372.4	Swiss franc
Taiwan	239	247	14,928	15,568	0.3	0.3	8,676.8	8,584.3	Dollar
Thailand	577	580	36,083	36,604	0.2	0.2	7,986.3	7,882.2	Baht
Turkey	437	435	27,342	27,470	0.5	0.5	1,773.5	1,779.1	Euro
Ukraine	319	314	19,946	19,830	0.0	0.0	1,033.4	900.7	Hryvna
UAE	149	166	9,296	10,506	0.3	0.3	942.7	927.1	Dirham
United Kingdom	416	414	25,988	26,159	1.5	1.5	1,128.4	1,122.0	Pounds
United States	2,018	2,019	126,169	127,424	9.3	9.2	9,285.2	9,225.2	Dollars
Venezuela	206	209	12,870	13,189	0.3	0.2	2,526.9	2,388.5	Bolivar
Vietnam	724	725	45,282	45,734	0.1	0.1	3,015.8	3,103.2	Dong*

Note: Due to rounding, establishments will vary by + or - one establishment. Therefore, zero establishments may also be one establishment.

* Local Sales are in trillions

Warehouse Clubs & Superstores Industry (NAICS 45291)

NAICS 45291: Warehouse Clubs and Superstores This industry comprises establishments known as warehouse clubs, superstores or supercenters primarily engaged in retailing a general line of groceries in combination with general lines of new merchandise, such as apparel, furniture, and appliances.

COUNTRY ESTIMATES

Country	Establishments 2018	Establishments 2019	Employment 2018	Employment 2019	Sales ($B) 2018	Sales ($B) 2019	Local Sales (B) 2018	Local Sales (B) 2019	Currency
Algeria	186	187	51,100	54,407	0.1	0.1	6.3	6.4	Dinar
Argentina	129	129	35,427	37,524	0.1	0.1	2.5	2.5	Pesos
Australia	80	81	22,045	23,543	0.3	0.3	0.4	0.4	Dollars
Austria	29	29	7,887	8,310	0.1	0.1	0.1	0.1	Euro
Bangladesh	565	565	155,366	164,670	0.1	0.1	4.4	4.6	Taka
Belgium	36	36	9,886	10,469	0.1	0.1	0.1	0.1	Euro
Brazil	688	693	189,207	202,003	0.4	0.4	1,275.7	1,249.9	Real
Canada	120	121	33,160	35,201	0.4	0.4	0.5	0.5	Dollars
Chile	67	67	18,345	19,563	0.1	0.1	39.0	39.7	Pesos*
China	4,755	4,739	1,308,647	1,380,884	3.3	3.5	21.4	22.4	RMB
Colombia	143	143	39,349	41,667	0.1	0.1	0.2	0.2	Pesos*
Czech Republic	34	34	9,431	9,930	0.0	0.0	1.0	1.1	Koruna
Denmark	18	18	4,962	5,225	0.1	0.1	0.4	0.4	Kroner
Egypt	304	312	83,713	90,767	0.1	0.1	1.4	1.4	Pounds
Finland	18	18	4,915	5,179	0.1	0.1	0.0	0.0	Euro
France	199	199	54,895	58,003	0.5	0.5	0.4	0.4	Euro
Germany	254	251	69,881	73,042	0.8	0.8	0.7	0.7	Euro
Greece	33	33	9,194	9,663	0.0	0.0	0.0	0.0	Euro
Hong Kong	20	20	5,639	5,943	0.1	0.1	474.4	484.4	Dollar
Hungary	30	30	8,292	8,667	0.0	0.0	7.5	7.7	Forint*
India	3,993	4,053	1,098,939	1,181,016	0.5	0.6	33.5	35.3	Rupees
Indonesia	993	1,006	273,268	293,028	0.3	0.3	3.5	3.7	Rupiah*

WAREHOUSE CLUBS & SUPERSTORES INDUSTRY
(NAICS 45291)

COUNTRY ESTIMATES

Country	Establishments 2018	2019	Employment 2018	2019	Sales ($B) 2018	2019	Local Sales (B) 2018	2019	Currency
Iran	272	275	74,843	80,178	0.1	0.1	3.4	3.4	Rial*
Iraq	143	145	39,251	42,191	0.0	0.0	0.1	0.1	Dinar*
Ireland	20	20	5,507	5,904	0.1	0.1	0.1	0.1	Euro
Israel	28	29	7,804	8,376	0.1	0.1	0.3	0.3	Shekel
Italy	201	200	55,299	58,271	0.4	0.4	0.4	0.4	Euro
Japan	423	419	116,382	121,953	1.0	1.0	114.1	114.5	Yen*
Kazakhstan	69	69	18,962	20,170	0.1	0.1	16.5	16.9	Tenge
Kuwait	16	17	4,432	4,894	0.0	0.0	0.0	0.0	Dinar
Malaysia	132	134	36,278	39,057	0.1	0.1	0.4	0.4	Ringgit
Mexico	429	434	118,188	126,576	0.3	0.3	5.3	5.4	New pesos
Netherlands	54	53	14,784	15,562	0.2	0.2	0.1	0.1	Euro
New Zealand	14	15	3,976	4,234	0.0	0.0	0.1	0.1	Dollar
Nigeria	741	753	203,863	219,446	0.1	0.1	50,059.1	51,068.8	Naira
Norway	20	20	5,461	5,800	0.1	0.1	0.8	0.9	Krone
Pakistan	594	606	163,359	176,547	0.1	0.1	6.8	7.1	Rupees
Peru	118	118	32,337	34,277	0.0	0.1	0.2	0.2	Nuevo Sol
Phillipines	320	326	88,052	94,840	0.1	0.1	3.8	4.0	Pesos
Poland	110	108	30,164	31,585	0.1	0.1	0.4	0.4	Zloty
Portugal	35	34	9,537	10,016	0.0	0.0	0.0	0.0	Euro
Puerto Rico	15	15	4,126	4,299	0.0	0.0	0.0	0.0	Dollar
Qatar	15	17	4,154	5,009	0.0	0.0	0.2	0.2	Riyal
Romania	79	78	21,711	22,622	0.0	0.1	0.2	0.2	New Leu
Russia	490	484	134,858	141,123	0.3	0.3	16.6	16.3	Rubles
Saudi Arabia	137	142	37,833	41,328	0.2	0.2	0.0	0.0	Rials*
Singapore	22	22	6,039	6,546	0.1	0.1	102.0	104.3	Dollar
South Africa	136	137	37,296	39,980	0.1	0.1	863.2	872.3	Rand
South Korea	192	191	52,716	55,589	0.4	0.4	406.3	416.8	Won*
Spain	159	160	43,758	46,591	0.3	0.3	243.5	243.4	Euro
Sweden	33	33	8,968	9,480	0.1	0.1	1,025.4	1,057.0	Krona
Switzerland	30	30	8,204	8,708	0.2	0.2	167.1	169.4	Swiss franc
Taiwan	119	123	32,853	35,935	0.1	0.1	3,838.3	3,904.2	Dollar
Thailand	289	290	79,413	84,492	0.1	0.1	3,532.9	3,584.9	Baht
Turkey	219	218	60,175	63,409	0.2	0.2	784.5	809.2	Euro
Ukraine	160	157	43,897	45,774	0.0	0.0	457.1	409.6	Hryvna
UAE	74	83	20,458	24,251	0.1	0.1	417.0	421.7	Dirham
United Kingdom	208	207	57,196	60,381	0.7	0.7	499.2	510.3	Pounds
United States	2,018	2,019	555,354	588,253	8.2	8.4	8,214.9	8,391.4	Dollars
Venezuela	103	104	28,325	30,444	0.1	0.1	1,117.8	1,086.3	Bolivar
Vietnam	362	362	99,659	105,567	0.1	0.1	1,334.1	1,411.4	Dong*

Note: Due to rounding, establishments will vary by + or - one establishment. Therefore, zero establishments may also be one establishment.

* Local Sales are in trillions

© Barnes Reports: 2018 World Industry & Market Outlook

Office Supplies & Stationery Stores Industry (NAICS 45321)

NAICS 45321: Office Supplies and Stationery Stores . This industry comprises establishments primarily engaged in one or more of the following: (1) retailing new stationery, school supplies, and office supplies; (2) selling a combination of new office equipment, furniture, and supplies; and (3) selling new office equipment, furniture, and supplies in combination with selling new computers.

Country Estimates

Country	Establishments 2018	Establishments 2019	Employment 2018	Employment 2019	Sales ($B) 2018	Sales ($B) 2019	Local Sales (B) 2018	Local Sales (B) 2019	Currency
Algeria	371	373	2,436	2,393	0.1	0.1	11.3	10.9	Dinar
Argentina	257	258	1,689	1,651	0.2	0.2	4.5	4.2	Pesos
Australia	160	162	1,051	1,036	0.6	0.6	0.7	0.7	Dollars
Austria	57	57	376	366	0.2	0.2	0.1	0.1	Euro
Bangladesh	1,129	1,130	7,407	7,244	0.1	0.1	7.9	8.0	Taka
Belgium	72	72	471	461	0.2	0.2	0.2	0.2	Euro
Brazil	1,375	1,387	9,020	8,886	0.7	0.7	2,302.9	2,148.6	Real
Canada	241	242	1,581	1,548	0.7	0.7	0.8	0.8	Dollars
Chile	133	134	875	861	0.1	0.1	70.4	68.2	Pesos*
China	9,511	9,479	62,390	60,745	6.0	5.9	38.7	38.5	RMB
Colombia	286	286	1,876	1,833	0.1	0.1	0.4	0.4	Pesos*
Czech Republic	69	68	450	437	0.1	0.1	1.8	1.8	Koruna
Denmark	36	36	237	230	0.1	0.1	0.8	0.7	Kroner
Egypt	608	623	3,991	3,993	0.1	0.1	2.6	2.5	Pounds
Finland	36	36	234	228	0.1	0.1	0.1	0.1	Euro
France	399	398	2,617	2,552	1.0	0.9	0.8	0.8	Euro
Germany	508	501	3,332	3,213	1.5	1.4	1.2	1.2	Euro
Greece	67	66	438	425	0.1	0.1	0.1	0.1	Euro
Hong Kong	41	41	269	261	0.1	0.1	856.4	832.8	Dollar
Hungary	60	59	395	381	0.1	0.1	13.5	13.3	Forint*
India	7,986	8,107	52,392	51,953	1.0	1.0	60.5	60.6	Rupees
Indonesia	1,986	2,011	13,028	12,890	0.5	0.5	6.3	6.3	Rupiah*

OFFICE SUPPLIES & STATIONERY STORES INDUSTRY
(NAICS 45321)

COUNTRY ESTIMATES

Country	Establishments 2018	Establishments 2019	Employment 2018	Employment 2019	Sales ($B) 2018	Sales ($B) 2019	Local Sales (B) 2018	Local Sales (B) 2019	Currency
Iran	544	550	3,568	3,527	0.2	0.2	6.1	5.8	Rial*
Iraq	285	290	1,871	1,856	0.1	0.1	0.1	0.1	Dinar*
Ireland	40	41	263	260	0.2	0.2	0.2	0.2	Euro
Israel	57	57	372	368	0.1	0.1	0.5	0.5	Shekel
Italy	402	400	2,636	2,563	0.8	0.7	0.6	0.6	Euro
Japan	846	837	5,549	5,365	1.8	1.7	206.0	196.9	Yen*
Kazakhstan	138	138	904	887	0.1	0.1	29.9	29.1	Tenge
Kuwait	32	34	211	215	0.1	0.0	0.0	0.0	Dinar
Malaysia	264	268	1,730	1,718	0.2	0.2	0.7	0.7	Ringgit
Mexico	859	869	5,635	5,568	0.5	0.5	9.5	9.2	New pesos
Netherlands	107	107	705	685	0.3	0.3	0.3	0.3	Euro
New Zealand	29	29	190	186	0.1	0.1	0.1	0.1	Dollar
Nigeria	1,482	1,506	9,719	9,653	0.3	0.2	90,367.6	87,788.2	Naira
Norway	40	40	260	255	0.2	0.2	1.5	1.5	Krone
Pakistan	1,187	1,212	7,788	7,766	0.1	0.1	12.3	12.2	Rupees
Peru	235	235	1,542	1,508	0.1	0.1	0.3	0.3	Nuevo Sol
Phillipines	640	651	4,198	4,172	0.1	0.1	6.8	6.8	Pesos
Poland	219	217	1,438	1,389	0.2	0.2	0.8	0.8	Zloty
Portugal	69	69	455	441	0.1	0.1	0.1	0.1	Euro
Puerto Rico	30	30	197	189	0.1	0.0	0.1	0.0	Dollar
Qatar	30	34	198	220	0.1	0.1	0.3	0.3	Riyal
Romania	158	155	1,035	995	0.1	0.1	0.3	0.3	New Leu
Russia	980	969	6,429	6,208	0.6	0.5	29.9	28.1	Rubles
Saudi Arabia	275	284	1,804	1,818	0.4	0.3	0.0	0.0	Rials*
Singapore	44	45	288	288	0.1	0.1	184.1	179.3	Dollar
South Africa	271	274	1,778	1,759	0.1	0.1	1,558.2	1,499.4	Rand
South Korea	383	382	2,513	2,445	0.7	0.7	733.4	716.5	Won*
Spain	318	320	2,086	2,050	0.5	0.5	439.5	418.4	Euro
Sweden	65	65	428	417	0.2	0.2	1,851.1	1,817.0	Krona
Switzerland	60	60	391	383	0.3	0.3	301.6	291.1	Swiss franc
Taiwan	239	247	1,566	1,581	0.2	0.2	6,929.0	6,711.4	Dollar
Thailand	577	580	3,786	3,717	0.2	0.2	6,377.6	6,162.6	Baht
Turkey	437	435	2,869	2,789	0.4	0.4	1,416.2	1,391.0	Euro
Ukraine	319	314	2,093	2,014	0.0	0.0	825.2	704.2	Hryvna
UAE	149	166	975	1,067	0.2	0.2	752.8	724.8	Dirham
United Kingdom	416	414	2,727	2,656	1.2	1.2	901.1	877.3	Pounds
United States	2,018	2,019	13,238	12,939	7.4	7.2	7,414.8	7,212.5	Dollars
Venezuela	206	209	1,350	1,339	0.2	0.2	2,017.9	1,867.4	Bolivar
Vietnam	724	725	4,751	4,644	0.1	0.1	2,408.3	2,426.2	Dong*

Note: Due to rounding, establishments will vary by + or - one establishment. Therefore, zero establishments may also be one establishment.

* Local Sales are in trillions

Electronic Shopping & Mail Order Houses (NAICS 45411)

NAICS 45411: Electronic Shopping and Mail-Order Houses This industry comprises establishments primarily engaged in retailing all types of merchandise by means of mail or by electronic media, such as interactive television or computer. Included in this industry are establishments primarily engaged in retailing from catalogue showrooms of mail-order houses.

COUNTRY ESTIMATES

Country	Establishments 2018	2019	Employment 2018	2019	Sales ($B) 2018	2019	Local Sales (B) 2018	2019	Currency
Algeria	371	373	94,853	105,569	1.3	1.4	153.1	159.4	Dinar
Argentina	257	258	65,760	72,810	3.2	3.2	60.3	61.7	Pesos
Australia	160	162	40,920	45,682	7.8	8.2	10.0	10.5	Dollars
Austria	57	57	14,640	16,124	2.2	2.3	1.8	1.9	Euro
Bangladesh	1,129	1,130	288,394	319,519	1.3	1.4	107.2	116.4	Taka
Belgium	72	72	18,352	20,313	2.5	2.6	2.1	2.2	Euro
Brazil	1,375	1,387	351,211	391,959	9.6	9.7	31,125.8	31,328.9	Real
Canada	241	242	61,553	68,302	9.1	9.5	11.3	11.8	Dollars
Chile	133	134	34,053	37,960	1.6	1.6	952.1	994.0	Pesos*
China	9,511	9,479	2,429,146	2,679,416	80.5	86.5	522.6	561.5	RMB
Colombia	286	286	73,040	80,848	1.7	1.8	5.0	5.3	Pesos*
Czech Republic	69	68	17,507	19,267	1.2	1.2	25.0	26.5	Koruna
Denmark	36	36	9,210	10,139	1.7	1.8	10.5	10.9	Kroner
Egypt	608	623	155,390	176,122	2.0	2.1	34.8	36.2	Pounds
Finland	36	36	9,123	10,049	1.3	1.3	1.1	1.1	Euro
France	399	398	101,897	112,547	13.0	13.4	10.8	11.2	Euro
Germany	508	501	129,715	141,727	19.9	20.8	16.6	17.3	Euro
Greece	67	66	17,066	18,750	1.0	1.0	0.8	0.8	Euro
Hong Kong	41	41	10,467	11,532	1.5	1.6	11,575.8	12,142.6	Dollar
Hungary	60	59	15,393	16,818	0.7	0.8	182.9	194.1	Forint*
India	7,986	8,107	2,039,879	2,291,600	12.9	13.9	817.9	884.2	Rupees
Indonesia	1,986	2,011	507,247	568,580	6.4	6.9	85.8	92.0	Rupiah*

ELECTRONIC SHOPPING & MAIL ORDER HOUSES (NAICS 45411)

COUNTRY ESTIMATES

Country	Establishments 2018	Establishments 2019	Employment 2018	Employment 2019	Sales ($B) 2018	Sales ($B) 2019	Local Sales (B) 2018	Local Sales (B) 2019	Currency
Iran	544	550	138,925	155,574	2.3	2.3	83.0	84.6	Rial*
Iraq	285	290	72,858	81,866	1.2	1.2	1.4	1.5	Dinar*
Ireland	40	41	10,223	11,456	3.0	3.5	2.5	2.9	Euro
Israel	57	57	14,486	16,253	1.9	2.0	6.4	6.8	Shekel
Italy	402	400	102,647	113,067	10.4	10.7	8.7	8.9	Euro
Japan	846	837	216,031	236,632	24.7	25.4	2,784.9	2,870.7	Yen*
Kazakhstan	138	138	35,197	39,137	1.2	1.3	403.5	423.7	Tenge
Kuwait	32	34	8,226	9,497	0.7	0.7	0.2	0.2	Dinar
Malaysia	264	268	67,341	75,785	2.3	2.5	9.1	9.8	Ringgit
Mexico	859	869	219,384	245,604	6.7	7.0	128.5	134.6	New pesos
Netherlands	107	107	27,443	30,197	4.3	4.4	3.6	3.7	Euro
New Zealand	29	29	7,379	8,216	1.0	1.0	1.3	1.4	Dollar
Nigeria	1,482	1,506	378,416	425,805	3.4	3.6	1,221,411.9	1,280,024.1	Naira
Norway	40	40	10,138	11,255	2.5	2.7	20.5	21.4	Krone
Pakistan	1,187	1,212	303,232	342,565	1.5	1.6	166.6	178.3	Rupees
Peru	235	235	60,024	66,509	1.2	1.3	3.9	4.1	Nuevo Sol
Phillipines	640	651	163,445	184,025	1.8	2.0	91.6	99.4	Pesos
Poland	219	217	55,990	61,286	3.0	3.2	10.5	11.1	Zloty
Portugal	69	69	17,702	19,435	1.1	1.1	0.9	1.0	Euro
Puerto Rico	30	30	7,659	8,342	0.7	0.7	0.7	0.7	Dollar
Qatar	30	34	7,711	9,720	1.1	1.2	4.1	4.3	Riyal
Romania	158	155	40,301	43,895	1.2	1.3	4.7	4.9	New Leu
Russia	980	969	250,326	273,829	7.9	8.0	404.2	409.2	Rubles
Saudi Arabia	275	284	70,226	80,191	4.8	5.1	0.0	0.0	Rials*
Singapore	44	45	11,209	12,702	1.9	2.0	2,488.1	2,614.3	Dollar
South Africa	271	274	69,230	77,577	1.7	1.8	21,060.5	21,862.7	Rand
South Korea	383	382	97,852	107,862	9.3	9.8	9,912.4	10,446.5	Won*
Spain	318	320	81,226	90,403	7.1	7.3	5,940.1	6,100.9	Euro
Sweden	65	65	16,646	18,394	3.1	3.2	25,019.5	26,492.9	Krona
Switzerland	60	60	15,228	16,896	4.2	4.3	4,076.0	4,245.1	Swiss franc
Taiwan	239	247	60,983	69,727	3.2	3.3	93,653.2	97,858.3	Dollar
Thailand	577	580	147,409	163,944	2.7	2.8	86,199.5	89,855.3	Baht
Turkey	437	435	111,699	123,036	5.1	5.4	19,142.0	20,281.4	Euro
Ukraine	319	314	81,483	88,817	0.4	0.4	11,153.6	10,267.5	Hryvna
UAE	149	166	37,975	47,056	2.8	2.9	10,175.2	10,568.7	Dirham
United Kingdom	416	414	106,168	117,161	16.5	17.4	12,179.7	12,791.0	Pounds
United States	2,018	2,019	515,432	570,711	100.2	105.2	100,219.1	105,164.6	Dollars
Venezuela	206	209	52,577	59,073	2.7	2.7	27,273.8	27,227.8	Bolivar
Vietnam	724	725	184,990	204,837	1.4	1.6	32,550.6	35,375.8	Dong*

Note: Due to rounding, establishments will vary by + or - one establishment. Therefore, zero establishments may also be one establishment.

* Local Sales are in trillions

NAICS 48111: Scheduled Air Transportation Industry. This industry comprises establishments primarily engaged in providing air transportation of passengers and/or cargo over regular routes and on regular schedules. Establishments in this industry operate flights even if partially loaded. Establishments primarily engaged in providing scheduled air transportation of mail on a contract basis are included in this industry.

COUNTRY ESTIMATES

Country	Establishments 2018	2019	Employment 2018	2019	Sales ($B) 2018	2019	Local Sales (B) 2018	2019	Currency
Algeria	186	187	15,068	16,116	0.0	0.0	4.3	4.1	Dinar
Argentina	129	129	10,446	11,115	0.1	0.1	1.7	1.6	Pesos
Australia	80	81	6,500	6,974	0.2	0.2	0.3	0.3	Dollars
Austria	29	29	2,326	2,461	0.1	0.1	0.1	0.0	Euro
Bangladesh	565	565	45,813	48,778	0.0	0.0	3.0	3.0	Taka
Belgium	36	36	2,915	3,101	0.1	0.1	0.1	0.1	Euro
Brazil	688	693	55,791	59,837	0.3	0.3	868.3	815.0	Real
Canada	120	121	9,778	10,427	0.3	0.2	0.3	0.3	Dollars
Chile	67	67	5,409	5,795	0.0	0.0	26.6	25.9	Pesos*
China	4,755	4,739	385,880	409,044	2.2	2.3	14.6	14.6	RMB
Colombia	143	143	11,603	12,342	0.0	0.0	0.1	0.1	Pesos*
Czech Republic	34	34	2,781	2,941	0.0	0.0	0.7	0.7	Koruna
Denmark	18	18	1,463	1,548	0.0	0.0	0.3	0.3	Kroner
Egypt	304	312	24,684	26,887	0.1	0.1	1.0	0.9	Pounds
Finland	18	18	1,449	1,534	0.0	0.0	0.0	0.0	Euro
France	199	199	16,187	17,182	0.4	0.3	0.3	0.3	Euro
Germany	254	251	20,606	21,636	0.6	0.5	0.5	0.5	Euro
Greece	33	33	2,711	2,862	0.0	0.0	0.0	0.0	Euro
Hong Kong	20	20	1,663	1,760	0.0	0.0	322.9	315.9	Dollar
Hungary	30	30	2,445	2,567	0.0	0.0	5.1	5.0	Forint*
India	3,993	4,053	324,043	349,840	0.4	0.4	22.8	23.0	Rupees
Indonesia	993	1,006	80,578	86,800	0.2	0.2	2.4	2.4	Rupiah*

Scheduled Air Transportation Industry
(NAICS 48111)

Country Estimates

Country	Establishments 2018	2019	Employment 2018	2019	Sales ($B) 2018	2019	Local Sales (B) 2018	2019	Currency
Iran	272	275	22,069	23,750	0.1	0.1	2.3	2.2	Rial*
Iraq	143	145	11,574	12,498	0.0	0.0	0.0	0.0	Dinar*
Ireland	20	20	1,624	1,749	0.1	0.1	0.1	0.1	Euro
Israel	28	29	2,301	2,481	0.1	0.1	0.2	0.2	Shekel
Italy	201	200	16,306	17,261	0.3	0.3	0.2	0.2	Euro
Japan	423	419	34,317	36,125	0.7	0.7	77.7	74.7	Yen*
Kazakhstan	69	69	5,591	5,975	0.0	0.0	11.3	11.0	Tenge
Kuwait	16	17	1,307	1,450	0.0	0.0	0.0	0.0	Dinar
Malaysia	132	134	10,697	11,569	0.1	0.1	0.3	0.3	Ringgit
Mexico	429	434	34,850	37,494	0.2	0.2	3.6	3.5	New pesos
Netherlands	54	53	4,359	4,610	0.1	0.1	0.1	0.1	Euro
New Zealand	14	15	1,172	1,254	0.0	0.0	0.0	0.0	Dollar
Nigeria	741	753	60,113	65,004	0.1	0.1	34,074.5	33,298.8	Naira
Norway	20	20	1,610	1,718	0.1	0.1	0.6	0.6	Krone
Pakistan	594	606	48,170	52,297	0.0	0.0	4.6	4.6	Rupees
Peru	118	118	9,535	10,153	0.0	0.0	0.1	0.1	Nuevo Sol
Phillipines	320	326	25,964	28,094	0.1	0.1	2.6	2.6	Pesos
Poland	110	108	8,894	9,356	0.1	0.1	0.3	0.3	Zloty
Portugal	35	34	2,812	2,967	0.0	0.0	0.0	0.0	Euro
Puerto Rico	15	15	1,217	1,274	0.0	0.0	0.0	0.0	Dollar
Qatar	15	17	1,225	1,484	0.0	0.0	0.1	0.1	Riyal
Romania	79	78	6,402	6,701	0.0	0.0	0.1	0.1	New Leu
Russia	490	484	39,765	41,803	0.2	0.2	11.3	10.6	Rubles
Saudi Arabia	137	142	11,156	12,242	0.1	0.1	0.0	0.0	Rials*
Singapore	22	22	1,781	1,939	0.1	0.1	69.4	68.0	Dollar
South Africa	136	137	10,997	11,843	0.0	0.0	587.5	568.7	Rand
South Korea	192	191	15,544	16,466	0.3	0.3	276.5	271.8	Won*
Spain	159	160	12,903	13,801	0.2	0.2	165.7	158.7	Euro
Sweden	33	33	2,644	2,808	0.1	0.1	698.0	689.2	Krona
Switzerland	30	30	2,419	2,579	0.1	0.1	113.7	110.4	Swiss franc
Taiwan	119	123	9,687	10,645	0.1	0.1	2,612.7	2,545.7	Dollar
Thailand	289	290	23,416	25,028	0.1	0.1	2,404.8	2,337.5	Baht
Turkey	219	218	17,744	18,783	0.1	0.1	534.0	527.6	Euro
Ukraine	160	157	12,944	13,559	0.0	0.0	311.2	267.1	Hryvna
UAE	74	83	6,032	7,184	0.1	0.1	283.9	274.9	Dirham
United Kingdom	208	207	16,865	17,886	0.5	0.5	339.8	332.7	Pounds
United States	2,018	2,019	163,757	174,252	5.6	5.5	5,591.8	5,471.5	Dollars
Venezuela	103	104	8,352	9,018	0.1	0.1	760.9	708.3	Bolivar
Vietnam	362	362	29,386	31,271	0.0	0.0	908.1	920.3	Dong*

Note: Due to rounding, establishments will vary by + or - one establishment. Therefore, zero establishments may also be one establishment.

* Local Sales are in trillions

Local Freight Trucking Industry (NAICS 48411)

NAICS 48411: Freight Trucking, Local. This industry comprises establishments primarily engaged in providing local general freight trucking. General freight establishments handle a wide variety of commodities, generally palletized and transported in a container or van trailer. Local general freight trucking establishments usually provide trucking within a metropolitan area which may cross state lines. Generally the trips are same-day return.

Country Estimates

Country	Establishments 2018	Establishments 2019	Employment 2018	Employment 2019	Sales ($B) 2018	Sales ($B) 2019	Local Sales (B) 2018	Local Sales (B) 2019	Currency
Algeria	371	373	4,303	4,408	0.8	0.8	94.9	96.0	Dinar
Argentina	257	258	2,984	3,040	2.0	1.9	37.4	37.2	Pesos
Australia	160	162	1,857	1,907	4.9	5.0	6.2	6.3	Dollars
Austria	57	57	664	673	1.4	1.4	1.1	1.1	Euro
Bangladesh	1,129	1,130	13,085	13,341	0.8	0.8	66.4	70.1	Taka
Belgium	72	72	833	848	1.6	1.6	1.3	1.3	Euro
Brazil	1,375	1,387	15,935	16,365	6.0	5.8	19,286.2	18,865.6	Real
Canada	241	242	2,793	2,852	5.7	5.7	7.0	7.1	Dollars
Chile	133	134	1,545	1,585	1.0	1.0	589.9	598.5	Pesos*
China	9,511	9,479	110,211	111,871	49.9	52.1	323.8	338.1	RMB
Colombia	286	286	3,314	3,376	1.1	1.1	3.1	3.2	Pesos*
Czech Republic	69	68	794	804	0.7	0.8	15.5	16.0	Koruna
Denmark	36	36	418	423	1.0	1.1	6.5	6.6	Kroner
Egypt	608	623	7,050	7,353	1.2	1.2	21.6	21.8	Pounds
Finland	36	36	414	420	0.8	0.8	0.7	0.7	Euro
France	399	398	4,623	4,699	8.0	8.1	6.7	6.7	Euro
Germany	508	501	5,885	5,917	12.3	12.5	10.3	10.4	Euro
Greece	67	66	774	783	0.6	0.6	0.5	0.5	Euro
Hong Kong	41	41	475	481	0.9	0.9	7,172.6	7,312.0	Dollar
Hungary	60	59	698	702	0.4	0.5	113.3	116.9	Forint*
India	7,986	8,107	92,550	95,679	8.0	8.4	506.8	532.4	Rupees
Indonesia	1,986	2,011	23,014	23,739	4.0	4.1	53.1	55.4	Rupiah*

LOCAL FREIGHT TRUCKING INDUSTRY
(NAICS 48411)

COUNTRY ESTIMATES

Country	Establishments 2018	2019	Employment 2018	2019	Sales ($B) 2018	2019	Local Sales (B) 2018	2019	Currency
Iran	544	550	6,303	6,496	1.4	1.4	51.4	51.0	Rial*
Iraq	285	290	3,306	3,418	0.7	0.7	0.9	0.9	Dinar*
Ireland	40	41	464	478	1.8	2.1	1.5	1.7	Euro
Israel	57	57	657	679	1.2	1.2	4.0	4.1	Shekel
Italy	402	400	4,657	4,721	6.4	6.4	5.4	5.4	Euro
Japan	846	837	9,801	9,880	15.3	15.3	1,725.6	1,728.7	Yen*
Kazakhstan	138	138	1,597	1,634	0.8	0.8	250.0	255.2	Tenge
Kuwait	32	34	373	397	0.4	0.4	0.1	0.1	Dinar
Malaysia	264	268	3,055	3,164	1.4	1.5	5.6	5.9	Ringgit
Mexico	859	869	9,953	10,254	4.1	4.2	79.6	81.1	New pesos
Netherlands	107	107	1,245	1,261	2.6	2.7	2.2	2.2	Euro
New Zealand	29	29	335	343	0.6	0.6	0.8	0.9	Dollar
Nigeria	1,482	1,506	17,169	17,778	2.1	2.1	756,810.9	770,801.1	Naira
Norway	40	40	460	470	1.6	1.6	12.7	12.9	Krone
Pakistan	1,187	1,212	13,758	14,303	0.9	1.0	103.2	107.4	Rupees
Peru	235	235	2,723	2,777	0.8	0.8	2.4	2.5	Nuevo Sol
Phillipines	640	651	7,416	7,683	1.1	1.2	56.8	59.8	Pesos
Poland	219	217	2,540	2,559	1.9	1.9	6.5	6.7	Zloty
Portugal	69	69	803	811	0.7	0.7	0.6	0.6	Euro
Puerto Rico	30	30	347	348	0.4	0.4	0.4	0.4	Dollar
Qatar	30	34	350	406	0.7	0.7	2.6	2.6	Riyal
Romania	158	155	1,828	1,833	0.7	0.8	2.9	3.0	New Leu
Russia	980	969	11,357	11,433	4.9	4.8	250.4	246.4	Rubles
Saudi Arabia	275	284	3,186	3,348	3.0	3.0	0.0	0.0	Rials*
Singapore	44	45	509	530	1.2	1.2	1,541.7	1,574.3	Dollar
South Africa	271	274	3,141	3,239	1.1	1.1	13,049.5	13,165.2	Rand
South Korea	383	382	4,440	4,503	5.8	5.9	6,141.9	6,290.6	Won*
Spain	318	320	3,685	3,775	4.4	4.4	3,680.6	3,673.8	Euro
Sweden	65	65	755	768	1.9	1.9	15,502.6	15,953.4	Krona
Switzerland	60	60	691	705	2.6	2.6	2,525.6	2,556.3	Swiss franc
Taiwan	239	247	2,767	2,911	2.0	2.0	58,029.4	58,928.0	Dollar
Thailand	577	580	6,688	6,845	1.7	1.7	53,410.9	54,108.8	Baht
Turkey	437	435	5,068	5,137	3.2	3.3	11,860.7	12,213.0	Euro
Ukraine	319	314	3,697	3,708	0.2	0.2	6,911.0	6,182.8	Hryvna
UAE	149	166	1,723	1,965	1.7	1.7	6,304.7	6,364.2	Dirham
United Kingdom	416	414	4,817	4,892	10.2	10.5	7,546.8	7,702.5	Pounds
United States	2,018	2,019	23,385	23,828	62.1	63.3	62,097.8	63,327.7	Dollars
Venezuela	206	209	2,385	2,466	1.7	1.6	16,899.4	16,396.0	Bolivar
Vietnam	724	725	8,393	8,552	0.9	0.9	20,169.0	21,302.5	Dong*

Note: Due to rounding, establishments will vary by + or - one establishment. Therefore, zero establishments may also be one establishment.

* Local Sales are in trillions

© Barnes Reports: 2018 World Industry & Market Outlook

FREIGHT TRUCKING LONG DISTANCE INDUSTRY (NAICS 48412)

NAICS 48412: Freight Trucking, Long-Distance. This industry comprises establishments primarily engaged in providing long-distance general freight trucking. General freight establishments handle a wide variety of commodities, generally palletized and transported in a container or van trailer. Long-distance general freight trucking establishments usually provide trucking between metropolitan areas which may cross North American country borders. Included in this industry are establishments operating as truckload (TL) or less than truckload (LTL) carriers.

COUNTRY ESTIMATES

Country	Establishments		Employment		Sales ($B)		Local Sales (B)		Currency
	2018	2019	2018	2019	2018	2019	2018	2019	
Algeria	371	373	30,022	33,430	1.1	1.1	121.7	127.9	Dinar
Argentina	257	258	20,814	23,056	2.5	2.6	47.9	49.5	Pesos
Australia	160	162	12,952	14,466	6.2	6.6	7.9	8.4	Dollars
Austria	57	57	4,634	5,106	1.8	1.8	1.5	1.5	Euro
Bangladesh	1,129	1,130	91,280	101,181	1.0	1.1	85.1	93.4	Taka
Belgium	72	72	5,808	6,432	2.0	2.1	1.7	1.8	Euro
Brazil	1,375	1,387	111,163	124,120	7.7	7.8	24,730.0	25,136.5	Real
Canada	241	242	19,482	21,629	7.3	7.6	9.0	9.5	Dollars
Chile	133	134	10,778	12,021	1.2	1.3	756.5	797.5	Pesos*
China	9,511	9,479	768,855	848,478	64.0	69.4	415.2	450.5	RMB
Colombia	286	286	23,118	25,602	1.4	1.5	4.0	4.3	Pesos*
Czech Republic	69	68	5,541	6,101	0.9	1.0	19.8	21.3	Koruna
Denmark	36	36	2,915	3,211	1.3	1.4	8.3	8.7	Kroner
Egypt	608	623	49,183	55,772	1.6	1.6	27.6	29.0	Pounds
Finland	36	36	2,887	3,182	1.0	1.1	0.9	0.9	Euro
France	399	398	32,252	35,640	10.3	10.7	8.6	9.0	Euro
Germany	508	501	41,056	44,880	15.8	16.7	13.2	13.9	Euro
Greece	67	66	5,402	5,937	0.8	0.8	0.7	0.7	Euro
Hong Kong	41	41	3,313	3,652	1.2	1.2	9,197.2	9,742.5	Dollar
Hungary	60	59	4,872	5,326	0.6	0.6	145.3	155.7	Forint*
India	7,986	8,107	645,647	725,670	10.2	11.2	649.9	709.4	Rupees
Indonesia	1,986	2,011	160,550	180,050	5.1	5.5	68.1	73.8	Rupiah*

FREIGHT TRUCKING LONG DISTANCE INDUSTRY (NAICS 48412)

COUNTRY ESTIMATES

Country	Establishments		Employment		Sales ($B)		Local Sales (B)		Currency
	2018	2019	2018	2019	2018	2019	2018	2019	
Iran	544	550	43,972	49,265	1.8	1.9	66.0	67.9	Rial*
Iraq	285	290	23,060	25,924	1.0	1.0	1.1	1.2	Dinar*
Ireland	40	41	3,236	3,628	2.3	2.8	2.0	2.3	Euro
Israel	57	57	4,585	5,147	1.5	1.6	5.1	5.5	Shekel
Italy	402	400	32,489	35,804	8.2	8.6	6.9	7.1	Euro
Japan	846	837	68,377	74,933	19.6	20.4	2,212.7	2,303.3	Yen*
Kazakhstan	138	138	11,140	12,393	1.0	1.0	320.6	340.0	Tenge
Kuwait	32	34	2,604	3,007	0.6	0.6	0.2	0.2	Dinar
Malaysia	264	268	21,314	23,999	1.8	2.0	7.2	7.9	Ringgit
Mexico	859	869	69,438	77,774	5.3	5.6	102.1	108.0	New pesos
Netherlands	107	107	8,686	9,562	3.4	3.6	2.8	3.0	Euro
New Zealand	29	29	2,336	2,602	0.8	0.8	1.1	1.1	Dollar
Nigeria	1,482	1,506	119,773	134,838	2.7	2.9	970,434.9	1,027,017.1	Naira
Norway	40	40	3,209	3,564	2.0	2.1	16.3	17.2	Krone
Pakistan	1,187	1,212	95,977	108,478	1.2	1.3	132.4	143.1	Rupees
Peru	235	235	18,998	21,061	1.0	1.0	3.1	3.3	Nuevo Sol
Phillipines	640	651	51,732	58,274	1.5	1.6	72.8	79.7	Pesos
Poland	219	217	17,722	19,407	2.4	2.6	8.3	8.9	Zloty
Portugal	69	69	5,603	6,154	0.9	0.9	0.7	0.8	Euro
Puerto Rico	30	30	2,424	2,642	0.5	0.5	0.5	0.5	Dollar
Qatar	30	34	2,441	3,078	0.9	0.9	3.3	3.5	Riyal
Romania	158	155	12,756	13,900	1.0	1.0	3.7	4.0	New Leu
Russia	980	969	79,231	86,712	6.3	6.4	321.1	328.3	Rubles
Saudi Arabia	275	284	22,228	25,394	3.9	4.1	0.0	0.0	Rials*
Singapore	44	45	3,548	4,022	1.5	1.6	1,976.8	2,097.6	Dollar
South Africa	271	274	21,912	24,566	1.3	1.4	16,733.0	17,541.4	Rand
South Korea	383	382	30,971	34,156	7.4	7.9	7,875.6	8,381.6	Won*
Spain	318	320	25,709	28,628	5.7	5.9	4,719.5	4,895.0	Euro
Sweden	65	65	5,269	5,825	2.4	2.6	19,878.5	21,256.4	Krona
Switzerland	60	60	4,820	5,350	3.3	3.5	3,238.4	3,406.1	Swiss franc
Taiwan	239	247	19,302	22,080	2.5	2.7	74,409.2	78,515.9	Dollar
Thailand	577	580	46,657	51,916	2.1	2.2	68,487.2	72,094.7	Baht
Turkey	437	435	35,354	38,961	4.1	4.3	15,208.6	16,272.6	Euro
Ukraine	319	314	25,790	28,125	0.3	0.3	8,861.7	8,238.0	Hryvna
UAE	149	166	12,020	14,901	2.2	2.3	8,084.4	8,479.7	Dirham
United Kingdom	416	414	33,604	37,101	13.1	13.9	9,677.0	10,262.8	Pounds
United States	2,018	2,019	163,141	180,725	79.6	84.4	79,626.0	84,377.9	Dollars
Venezuela	206	209	16,641	18,706	2.2	2.2	21,669.5	21,846.0	Bolivar
Vietnam	724	725	58,552	64,865	1.1	1.2	25,862.1	28,383.5	Dong*

Note: Due to rounding, establishments will vary by + or - one establishment. Therefore, zero establishments may also be one establishment.

* Local Sales are in trillions

GENERAL WAREHOUSING & STORAGE INDUSTRY (NAICS 49311)

NAICS 49311: General Warehousing and Storage . This industry comprises establishments primarily engaged in operating merchandise warehousing and storage facilities. These establishments generally handle goods in containers, such as boxes, barrels, and/or drums, using equipment, such as forklifts, pallets, and racks. They are not specialized in handling bulk products of any particular type, size, or quantity of goods or products.

COUNTRY ESTIMATES

Country	Establishments		Employment		Sales ($B)		Local Sales (B)		
	2018	2019	2018	2019	2018	2019	2018	2019	Currency
Algeria	371	373	9,881	10,614	0.2	0.2	20.7	21.0	Dinar
Argentina	257	258	6,851	7,320	0.4	0.4	8.2	8.1	Pesos
Australia	160	162	4,263	4,593	1.1	1.1	1.3	1.4	Dollars
Austria	57	57	1,525	1,621	0.3	0.3	0.2	0.3	Euro
Bangladesh	1,129	1,130	30,044	32,124	0.2	0.2	14.5	15.4	Taka
Belgium	72	72	1,912	2,042	0.3	0.3	0.3	0.3	Euro
Brazil	1,375	1,387	36,588	39,407	1.3	1.3	4,215.1	4,131.2	Real
Canada	241	242	6,412	6,867	1.2	1.3	1.5	1.6	Dollars
Chile	133	134	3,547	3,816	0.2	0.2	128.9	131.1	Pesos*
China	9,511	9,479	253,059	269,386	10.9	11.4	70.8	74.0	RMB
Colombia	286	286	7,609	8,128	0.2	0.2	0.7	0.7	Pesos*
Czech Republic	69	68	1,824	1,937	0.2	0.2	3.4	3.5	Koruna
Denmark	36	36	959	1,019	0.2	0.2	1.4	1.4	Kroner
Egypt	608	623	16,188	17,707	0.3	0.3	4.7	4.8	Pounds
Finland	36	36	950	1,010	0.2	0.2	0.1	0.1	Euro
France	399	398	10,615	11,315	1.8	1.8	1.5	1.5	Euro
Germany	508	501	13,513	14,249	2.7	2.7	2.3	2.3	Euro
Greece	67	66	1,778	1,885	0.1	0.1	0.1	0.1	Euro
Hong Kong	41	41	1,090	1,159	0.2	0.2	1,567.6	1,601.2	Dollar
Hungary	60	59	1,604	1,691	0.1	0.1	24.8	25.6	Forint*
India	7,986	8,107	212,507	230,395	1.7	1.8	110.8	116.6	Rupees
Indonesia	1,986	2,011	52,843	57,165	0.9	0.9	11.6	12.1	Rupiah*

GENERAL WAREHOUSING & STORAGE INDUSTRY
(NAICS 49311)

COUNTRY ESTIMATES

Country	Establishments 2018	Establishments 2019	Employment 2018	Employment 2019	Sales ($B) 2018	Sales ($B) 2019	Local Sales (B) 2018	Local Sales (B) 2019	Currency
Iran	544	550	14,473	15,641	0.3	0.3	11.2	11.2	Rial*
Iraq	285	290	7,590	8,231	0.2	0.2	0.2	0.2	Dinar*
Ireland	40	41	1,065	1,152	0.4	0.5	0.3	0.4	Euro
Israel	57	57	1,509	1,634	0.3	0.3	0.9	0.9	Shekel
Italy	402	400	10,693	11,368	1.4	1.4	1.2	1.2	Euro
Japan	846	837	22,505	23,791	3.3	3.4	377.1	378.5	Yen*
Kazakhstan	138	138	3,667	3,935	0.2	0.2	54.6	55.9	Tenge
Kuwait	32	34	857	955	0.1	0.1	0.0	0.0	Dinar
Malaysia	264	268	7,015	7,619	0.3	0.3	1.2	1.3	Ringgit
Mexico	859	869	22,855	24,693	0.9	0.9	17.4	17.8	New pesos
Netherlands	107	107	2,859	3,036	0.6	0.6	0.5	0.5	Euro
New Zealand	29	29	769	826	0.1	0.1	0.2	0.2	Dollar
Nigeria	1,482	1,506	39,422	42,810	0.5	0.5	165,403.6	168,789.7	Naira
Norway	40	40	1,056	1,132	0.3	0.3	2.8	2.8	Krone
Pakistan	1,187	1,212	31,590	34,441	0.2	0.2	22.6	23.5	Rupees
Peru	235	235	6,253	6,687	0.2	0.2	0.5	0.5	Nuevo Sol
Phillipines	640	651	17,027	18,502	0.2	0.3	12.4	13.1	Pesos
Poland	219	217	5,833	6,162	0.4	0.4	1.4	1.5	Zloty
Portugal	69	69	1,844	1,954	0.2	0.2	0.1	0.1	Euro
Puerto Rico	30	30	798	839	0.1	0.1	0.1	0.1	Dollar
Qatar	30	34	803	977	0.2	0.2	0.6	0.6	Riyal
Romania	158	155	4,198	4,413	0.2	0.2	0.6	0.7	New Leu
Russia	980	969	26,078	27,531	1.1	1.1	54.7	54.0	Rubles
Saudi Arabia	275	284	7,316	8,062	0.7	0.7	0.0	0.0	Rials*
Singapore	44	45	1,168	1,277	0.3	0.3	336.9	344.7	Dollar
South Africa	271	274	7,212	7,799	0.2	0.2	2,852.0	2,882.9	Rand
South Korea	383	382	10,194	10,844	1.3	1.3	1,342.3	1,377.5	Won*
Spain	318	320	8,462	9,089	1.0	1.0	804.4	804.5	Euro
Sweden	65	65	1,734	1,849	0.4	0.4	3,388.1	3,493.5	Krona
Switzerland	60	60	1,586	1,699	0.6	0.6	552.0	559.8	Swiss franc
Taiwan	239	247	6,353	7,010	0.4	0.4	12,682.5	12,904.0	Dollar
Thailand	577	580	15,356	16,483	0.4	0.4	11,673.1	11,848.7	Baht
Turkey	437	435	11,636	12,370	0.7	0.7	2,592.2	2,674.4	Euro
Ukraine	319	314	8,489	8,930	0.1	0.0	1,510.4	1,353.9	Hryvna
UAE	149	166	3,956	4,731	0.4	0.4	1,377.9	1,393.6	Dirham
United Kingdom	416	414	11,060	11,779	2.2	2.3	1,649.4	1,686.7	Pounds
United States	2,018	2,019	53,696	57,379	13.6	13.9	13,571.7	13,867.5	Dollars
Venezuela	206	209	5,477	5,939	0.4	0.4	3,693.4	3,590.4	Bolivar
Vietnam	724	725	19,272	20,594	0.2	0.2	4,408.0	4,664.8	Dong*

Note: Due to rounding, establishments will vary by + or - one establishment. Therefore, zero establishments may also be one establishment.

* Local Sales are in trillions

NEWSPAPER PUBLISHING INDUSTRY (NAICS 51111)

NAICS 51111: Newspaper Publishers . Establishments primarily engaged in publishing newspapers, or in publishing and printing newspapers.
These establishments carry on the various operations necessary for issuing newspapers, including the gathering of news and the preparation of editorials and advertisements, but may or may not perform their own printing.

COUNTRY ESTIMATES

Country	Establishments 2018	Establishments 2019	Employment 2018	Employment 2019	Sales ($B) 2018	Sales ($B) 2019	Local Sales (B) 2018	Local Sales (B) 2019	Currency
Algeria	371	373	5,695	5,830	0.2	0.2	26.1	25.9	Dinar
Argentina	257	258	3,948	4,021	0.5	0.5	10.3	10.0	Pesos
Australia	160	162	2,457	2,523	1.3	1.3	1.7	1.7	Dollars
Austria	57	57	879	890	0.4	0.4	0.3	0.3	Euro
Bangladesh	1,129	1,130	17,315	17,646	0.2	0.2	18.3	19.0	Taka
Belgium	72	72	1,102	1,122	0.4	0.4	0.4	0.4	Euro
Brazil	1,375	1,387	21,086	21,647	1.6	1.6	5,306.3	5,099.7	Real
Canada	241	242	3,696	3,772	1.6	1.5	1.9	1.9	Dollars
Chile	133	134	2,044	2,096	0.3	0.3	162.3	161.8	Pesos*
China	9,511	9,479	145,843	147,976	13.7	14.1	89.1	91.4	RMB
Colombia	286	286	4,385	4,465	0.3	0.3	0.9	0.9	Pesos*
Czech Republic	69	68	1,051	1,064	0.2	0.2	4.3	4.3	Koruna
Denmark	36	36	553	560	0.3	0.3	1.8	1.8	Kroner
Egypt	608	623	9,329	9,727	0.3	0.3	5.9	5.9	Pounds
Finland	36	36	548	555	0.2	0.2	0.2	0.2	Euro
France	399	398	6,118	6,216	2.2	2.2	1.8	1.8	Euro
Germany	508	501	7,788	7,827	3.4	3.4	2.8	2.8	Euro
Greece	67	66	1,025	1,035	0.2	0.2	0.1	0.1	Euro
Hong Kong	41	41	628	637	0.3	0.3	1,973.4	1,976.5	Dollar
Hungary	60	59	924	929	0.1	0.1	31.2	31.6	Forint*
India	7,986	8,107	122,472	126,558	2.2	2.3	139.4	143.9	Rupees
Indonesia	1,986	2,011	30,455	31,401	1.1	1.1	14.6	15.0	Rupiah*

NEWSPAPER PUBLISHING INDUSTRY
(NAICS 51111)

COUNTRY ESTIMATES

Country	Establishments 2018	2019	Employment 2018	2019	Sales ($B) 2018	2019	Local Sales (B) 2018	2019	Currency
Iran	544	550	8,341	8,592	0.4	0.4	14.2	13.8	Rial*
Iraq	285	290	4,374	4,521	0.2	0.2	0.2	0.2	Dinar*
Ireland	40	41	614	633	0.5	0.6	0.4	0.5	Euro
Israel	57	57	870	898	0.3	0.3	1.1	1.1	Shekel
Italy	402	400	6,163	6,244	1.8	1.7	1.5	1.4	Euro
Japan	846	837	12,970	13,068	4.2	4.1	474.8	467.3	Yen*
Kazakhstan	138	138	2,113	2,161	0.2	0.2	68.8	69.0	Tenge
Kuwait	32	34	494	524	0.1	0.1	0.0	0.0	Dinar
Malaysia	264	268	4,043	4,185	0.4	0.4	1.6	1.6	Ringgit
Mexico	859	869	13,172	13,564	1.1	1.1	21.9	21.9	New pesos
Netherlands	107	107	1,648	1,668	0.7	0.7	0.6	0.6	Euro
New Zealand	29	29	443	454	0.2	0.2	0.2	0.2	Dollar
Nigeria	1,482	1,506	22,720	23,516	0.6	0.6	208,223.2	208,360.1	Naira
Norway	40	40	609	622	0.4	0.4	3.5	3.5	Krone
Pakistan	1,187	1,212	18,206	18,919	0.3	0.3	28.4	29.0	Rupees
Peru	235	235	3,604	3,673	0.2	0.2	0.7	0.7	Nuevo Sol
Phillipines	640	651	9,813	10,163	0.3	0.3	15.6	16.2	Pesos
Poland	219	217	3,362	3,385	0.5	0.5	1.8	1.8	Zloty
Portugal	69	69	1,063	1,073	0.2	0.2	0.2	0.2	Euro
Puerto Rico	30	30	460	461	0.1	0.1	0.1	0.1	Dollar
Qatar	30	34	463	537	0.2	0.2	0.7	0.7	Riyal
Romania	158	155	2,420	2,424	0.2	0.2	0.8	0.8	New Leu
Russia	980	969	15,029	15,123	1.3	1.3	68.9	66.6	Rubles
Saudi Arabia	275	284	4,216	4,429	0.8	0.8	0.0	0.0	Rials*
Singapore	44	45	673	701	0.3	0.3	424.2	425.6	Dollar
South Africa	271	274	4,156	4,284	0.3	0.3	3,590.3	3,558.8	Rand
South Korea	383	382	5,875	5,957	1.6	1.6	1,689.8	1,700.5	Won*
Spain	318	320	4,877	4,993	1.2	1.2	1,012.6	993.1	Euro
Sweden	65	65	999	1,016	0.5	0.5	4,265.3	4,312.5	Krona
Switzerland	60	60	914	933	0.7	0.7	694.9	691.0	Swiss franc
Taiwan	239	247	3,661	3,851	0.5	0.5	15,965.8	15,929.2	Dollar
Thailand	577	580	8,850	9,054	0.5	0.5	14,695.1	14,626.5	Baht
Turkey	437	435	6,706	6,795	0.9	0.9	3,263.3	3,301.4	Euro
Ukraine	319	314	4,892	4,905	0.1	0.1	1,901.4	1,671.3	Hryvna
UAE	149	166	2,280	2,599	0.5	0.5	1,734.6	1,720.3	Dirham
United Kingdom	416	414	6,374	6,470	2.8	2.8	2,076.4	2,082.1	Pounds
United States	2,018	2,019	30,946	31,519	17.1	17.1	17,085.1	17,118.5	Dollars
Venezuela	206	209	3,157	3,262	0.5	0.4	4,649.6	4,432.1	Bolivar
Vietnam	724	725	11,107	11,313	0.2	0.3	5,549.1	5,758.4	Dong*

Note: Due to rounding, establishments will vary by + or - one establishment. Therefore, zero establishments may also be one establishment.

* Local Sales are in trillions

PERIODICAL PUBLISHING INDUSTRY (NAICS 51112)

NAICS 51112: Periodical Publishing . Establishments primarily engaged in publishing periodicals, or in publishing and printing periodicals. These establishments carry on the various operations necessary for issuing periodicals, but may or may not perform their own printing. Establishments not engaged in publishing periodicals, but which print periodicals for publishers, are classified in SIC 2752-2759.

COUNTRY ESTIMATES

Country	Establishments		Employment		Sales ($B)		Local Sales (B)		Currency
	2018	2019	2018	2019	2018	2019	2018	2019	
Algeria	371	373	4,525	4,551	0.2	0.2	20.2	19.7	Dinar
Argentina	257	258	3,137	3,139	0.4	0.4	7.9	7.6	Pesos
Australia	160	162	1,952	1,969	1.0	1.0	1.3	1.3	Dollars
Austria	57	57	698	695	0.3	0.3	0.2	0.2	Euro
Bangladesh	1,129	1,130	13,759	13,776	0.2	0.2	14.1	14.4	Taka
Belgium	72	72	876	876	0.3	0.3	0.3	0.3	Euro
Brazil	1,375	1,387	16,756	16,899	1.3	1.2	4,100.8	3,870.8	Real
Canada	241	242	2,937	2,945	1.2	1.2	1.5	1.5	Dollars
Chile	133	134	1,625	1,637	0.2	0.2	125.4	122.8	Pesos*
China	9,511	9,479	115,895	115,519	10.6	10.7	68.9	69.4	RMB
Colombia	286	286	3,485	3,486	0.2	0.2	0.7	0.7	Pesos*
Czech Republic	69	68	835	831	0.2	0.2	3.3	3.3	Koruna
Denmark	36	36	439	437	0.2	0.2	1.4	1.3	Kroner
Egypt	608	623	7,414	7,593	0.3	0.3	4.6	4.5	Pounds
Finland	36	36	435	433	0.2	0.2	0.1	0.1	Euro
France	399	398	4,862	4,852	1.7	1.7	1.4	1.4	Euro
Germany	508	501	6,189	6,110	2.6	2.6	2.2	2.1	Euro
Greece	67	66	814	808	0.1	0.1	0.1	0.1	Euro
Hong Kong	41	41	499	497	0.2	0.2	1,525.1	1,500.2	Dollar
Hungary	60	59	734	725	0.1	0.1	24.1	24.0	Forint*
India	7,986	8,107	97,323	98,799	1.7	1.7	107.8	109.2	Rupees
Indonesia	1,986	2,011	24,201	24,513	0.8	0.8	11.3	11.4	Rupiah*

PERIODICAL PUBLISHING INDUSTRY
(NAICS 51112)

COUNTRY ESTIMATES

Country	Establishments 2018	Establishments 2019	Employment 2018	Employment 2019	Sales ($B) 2018	Sales ($B) 2019	Local Sales (B) 2018	Local Sales (B) 2019	Currency
Iran	544	550	6,628	6,707	0.3	0.3	10.9	10.5	Rial*
Iraq	285	290	3,476	3,530	0.2	0.2	0.2	0.2	Dinar*
Ireland	40	41	488	494	0.4	0.4	0.3	0.4	Euro
Israel	57	57	691	701	0.2	0.2	0.8	0.8	Shekel
Italy	402	400	4,897	4,875	1.4	1.3	1.1	1.1	Euro
Japan	846	837	10,307	10,202	3.2	3.1	366.9	354.7	Yen*
Kazakhstan	138	138	1,679	1,687	0.2	0.2	53.2	52.4	Tenge
Kuwait	32	34	392	409	0.1	0.1	0.0	0.0	Dinar
Malaysia	264	268	3,213	3,267	0.3	0.3	1.2	1.2	Ringgit
Mexico	859	869	10,467	10,589	0.9	0.9	16.9	16.6	New pesos
Netherlands	107	107	1,309	1,302	0.6	0.5	0.5	0.5	Euro
New Zealand	29	29	352	354	0.1	0.1	0.2	0.2	Dollar
Nigeria	1,482	1,506	18,054	18,358	0.4	0.4	160,920.6	158,149.9	Naira
Norway	40	40	484	485	0.3	0.3	2.7	2.6	Krone
Pakistan	1,187	1,212	14,467	14,769	0.2	0.2	21.9	22.0	Rupees
Peru	235	235	2,864	2,867	0.2	0.2	0.5	0.5	Nuevo Sol
Phillipines	640	651	7,798	7,934	0.2	0.2	12.1	12.3	Pesos
Poland	219	217	2,671	2,642	0.4	0.4	1.4	1.4	Zloty
Portugal	69	69	845	838	0.1	0.1	0.1	0.1	Euro
Puerto Rico	30	30	365	360	0.1	0.1	0.1	0.1	Dollar
Qatar	30	34	368	419	0.1	0.1	0.5	0.5	Riyal
Romania	158	155	1,923	1,892	0.2	0.2	0.6	0.6	New Leu
Russia	980	969	11,943	11,806	1.0	1.0	53.3	50.6	Rubles
Saudi Arabia	275	284	3,351	3,457	0.6	0.6	0.0	0.0	Rials*
Singapore	44	45	535	548	0.2	0.2	327.8	323.0	Dollar
South Africa	271	274	3,303	3,345	0.2	0.2	2,774.7	2,701.2	Rand
South Korea	383	382	4,669	4,650	1.2	1.2	1,306.0	1,290.7	Won*
Spain	318	320	3,875	3,898	0.9	0.9	782.6	753.8	Euro
Sweden	65	65	794	793	0.4	0.4	3,296.3	3,273.3	Krona
Switzerland	60	60	727	728	0.5	0.5	537.0	524.5	Swiss franc
Taiwan	239	247	2,910	3,006	0.4	0.4	12,338.8	12,090.6	Dollar
Thailand	577	580	7,033	7,068	0.4	0.3	11,356.8	11,101.8	Baht
Turkey	437	435	5,329	5,305	0.7	0.7	2,521.9	2,505.8	Euro
Ukraine	319	314	3,888	3,829	0.1	0.0	1,469.5	1,268.6	Hryvna
UAE	149	166	1,812	2,029	0.4	0.4	1,340.6	1,305.8	Dirham
United Kingdom	416	414	5,065	5,051	2.2	2.1	1,604.7	1,580.4	Pounds
United States	2,018	2,019	24,591	24,605	13.2	13.0	13,203.8	12,993.3	Dollars
Venezuela	206	209	2,508	2,547	0.4	0.3	3,593.3	3,364.1	Bolivar
Vietnam	724	725	8,826	8,831	0.2	0.2	4,288.5	4,370.8	Dong*

Note: Due to rounding, establishments will vary by + or - one establishment. Therefore, zero establishments may also be one establishment.

* Local Sales are in trillions

NAICS 51113: Book Publishers . This U.S. industry comprises establishments known as book publishers. Establishments in this industry carry out design, editing, and marketing activities necessary for producing and distributing books. These establishments may publish books in print, electronic, or audio form.

COUNTRY ESTIMATES

Country	Establishments 2018	2019	Employment 2018	2019	Sales ($B) 2018	2019	Local Sales (B) 2018	2019	Currency
Algeria	371	373	3,736	3,856	0.1	0.1	8.8	8.7	Dinar
Argentina	257	258	2,590	2,659	0.2	0.2	3.5	3.4	Pesos
Australia	160	162	1,612	1,668	0.5	0.4	0.6	0.6	Dollars
Austria	57	57	577	589	0.1	0.1	0.1	0.1	Euro
Bangladesh	1,129	1,130	11,360	11,669	0.1	0.1	6.2	6.3	Taka
Belgium	72	72	723	742	0.1	0.1	0.1	0.1	Euro
Brazil	1,375	1,387	13,835	14,315	0.6	0.5	1,792.5	1,703.0	Real
Canada	241	242	2,425	2,495	0.5	0.5	0.7	0.6	Dollars
Chile	133	134	1,341	1,386	0.1	0.1	54.8	54.0	Pesos*
China	9,511	9,479	95,689	97,857	4.6	4.7	30.1	30.5	RMB
Colombia	286	286	2,877	2,953	0.1	0.1	0.3	0.3	Pesos*
Czech Republic	69	68	690	704	0.1	0.1	1.4	1.4	Koruna
Denmark	36	36	363	370	0.1	0.1	0.6	0.6	Kroner
Egypt	608	623	6,121	6,432	0.1	0.1	2.0	2.0	Pounds
Finland	36	36	359	367	0.1	0.1	0.1	0.1	Euro
France	399	398	4,014	4,110	0.7	0.7	0.6	0.6	Euro
Germany	508	501	5,110	5,176	1.1	1.1	1.0	0.9	Euro
Greece	67	66	672	685	0.1	0.1	0.0	0.0	Euro
Hong Kong	41	41	412	421	0.1	0.1	666.6	660.1	Dollar
Hungary	60	59	606	614	0.0	0.0	10.5	10.6	Forint*
India	7,986	8,107	80,355	83,694	0.7	0.8	47.1	48.1	Rupees
Indonesia	1,986	2,011	19,982	20,766	0.4	0.4	4.9	5.0	Rupiah*

COUNTRY ESTIMATES

Country	Establishments 2018	2019	Employment 2018	2019	Sales ($B) 2018	2019	Local Sales (B) 2018	2019	Currency
Iran	544	550	5,473	5,682	0.1	0.1	4.8	4.6	Rial*
Iraq	285	290	2,870	2,990	0.1	0.1	0.1	0.1	Dinar*
Ireland	40	41	403	418	0.2	0.2	0.1	0.2	Euro
Israel	57	57	571	594	0.1	0.1	0.4	0.4	Shekel
Italy	402	400	4,043	4,129	0.6	0.6	0.5	0.5	Euro
Japan	846	837	8,510	8,642	1.4	1.4	160.4	156.1	Yen*
Kazakhstan	138	138	1,386	1,429	0.1	0.1	23.2	23.0	Tenge
Kuwait	32	34	324	347	0.0	0.0	0.0	0.0	Dinar
Malaysia	264	268	2,653	2,768	0.1	0.1	0.5	0.5	Ringgit
Mexico	859	869	8,642	8,970	0.4	0.4	7.4	7.3	New pesos
Netherlands	107	107	1,081	1,103	0.2	0.2	0.2	0.2	Euro
New Zealand	29	29	291	300	0.1	0.1	0.1	0.1	Dollar
Nigeria	1,482	1,506	14,907	15,551	0.2	0.2	70,339.5	69,580.5	Naira
Norway	40	40	399	411	0.1	0.1	1.2	1.2	Krone
Pakistan	1,187	1,212	11,945	12,511	0.1	0.1	9.6	9.7	Rupees
Peru	235	235	2,364	2,429	0.1	0.1	0.2	0.2	Nuevo Sol
Phillipines	640	651	6,438	6,721	0.1	0.1	5.3	5.4	Pesos
Poland	219	217	2,206	2,238	0.2	0.2	0.6	0.6	Zloty
Portugal	69	69	697	710	0.1	0.1	0.1	0.1	Euro
Puerto Rico	30	30	302	305	0.0	0.0	0.0	0.0	Dollar
Qatar	30	34	304	355	0.1	0.1	0.2	0.2	Riyal
Romania	158	155	1,588	1,603	0.1	0.1	0.3	0.3	New Leu
Russia	980	969	9,861	10,001	0.5	0.4	23.3	22.2	Rubles
Saudi Arabia	275	284	2,766	2,929	0.3	0.3	0.0	0.0	Rials*
Singapore	44	45	442	464	0.1	0.1	143.3	142.1	Dollar
South Africa	271	274	2,727	2,833	0.1	0.1	1,212.8	1,188.4	Rand
South Korea	383	382	3,855	3,939	0.5	0.5	570.8	567.9	Won*
Spain	318	320	3,200	3,302	0.4	0.4	342.1	331.6	Euro
Sweden	65	65	656	672	0.2	0.2	1,440.8	1,440.1	Krona
Switzerland	60	60	600	617	0.2	0.2	234.7	230.8	Swiss franc
Taiwan	239	247	2,402	2,547	0.2	0.2	5,393.4	5,319.5	Dollar
Thailand	577	580	5,807	5,988	0.2	0.2	4,964.1	4,884.4	Baht
Turkey	437	435	4,400	4,494	0.3	0.3	1,102.4	1,102.5	Euro
Ukraine	319	314	3,210	3,244	0.0	0.0	642.3	558.1	Hryvna
UAE	149	166	1,496	1,719	0.2	0.2	586.0	574.5	Dirham
United Kingdom	416	414	4,182	4,279	1.0	0.9	701.4	695.3	Pounds
United States	2,018	2,019	20,304	20,843	5.8	5.7	5,771.5	5,716.6	Dollars
Venezuela	206	209	2,071	2,157	0.2	0.1	1,570.7	1,480.1	Bolivar
Vietnam	724	725	7,287	7,481	0.1	0.1	1,874.5	1,923.0	Dong*

Note: Due to rounding, establishments will vary by + or - one establishment. Therefore, zero establishments may also be one establishment.

* Local Sales are in trillions

DATABASE & DIRECTORY PUBLISHING INDUSTRY (NAICS 51114)

NAICS 51114: Database and Directory Publishers . This U.S. industry comprises establishments primarily engaged in publishing compilations and collections of information or facts that are logically organized to facilitate their use. These collections may be published in print or electronic form. Electronic versions may be provided directly to customers by the establishment or offered through on-line services or third-party vendors.

COUNTRY ESTIMATES

Country	Establishments 2018	Establishments 2019	Employment 2018	Employment 2019	Sales ($B) 2018	Sales ($B) 2019	Local Sales (B) 2018	Local Sales (B) 2019	Currency
Algeria	371	373	953	925	0.0	0.0	2.8	2.6	Dinar
Argentina	257	258	661	638	0.1	0.1	1.1	1.0	Pesos
Australia	160	162	411	400	0.1	0.1	0.2	0.2	Dollars
Austria	57	57	147	141	0.0	0.0	0.0	0.0	Euro
Bangladesh	1,129	1,130	2,898	2,801	0.0	0.0	2.0	1.9	Taka
Belgium	72	72	184	178	0.0	0.0	0.0	0.0	Euro
Brazil	1,375	1,387	3,530	3,436	0.2	0.2	570.9	513.3	Real
Canada	241	242	619	599	0.2	0.2	0.2	0.2	Dollars
Chile	133	134	342	333	0.0	0.0	17.5	16.3	Pesos*
China	9,511	9,479	24,413	23,490	1.5	1.4	9.6	9.2	RMB
Colombia	286	286	734	709	0.0	0.0	0.1	0.1	Pesos*
Czech Republic	69	68	176	169	0.0	0.0	0.5	0.4	Koruna
Denmark	36	36	93	89	0.0	0.0	0.2	0.2	Kroner
Egypt	608	623	1,562	1,544	0.0	0.0	0.6	0.6	Pounds
Finland	36	36	92	88	0.0	0.0	0.0	0.0	Euro
France	399	398	1,024	987	0.2	0.2	0.2	0.2	Euro
Germany	508	501	1,304	1,242	0.4	0.3	0.3	0.3	Euro
Greece	67	66	172	164	0.0	0.0	0.0	0.0	Euro
Hong Kong	41	41	105	101	0.0	0.0	212.3	198.9	Dollar
Hungary	60	59	155	147	0.0	0.0	3.4	3.2	Forint*
India	7,986	8,107	20,501	20,090	0.2	0.2	15.0	14.5	Rupees
Indonesia	1,986	2,011	5,098	4,985	0.1	0.1	1.6	1.5	Rupiah*

DATABASE & DIRECTORY PUBLISHING INDUSTRY
(NAICS 51114)

COUNTRY ESTIMATES

Country	Establishments 2018	Establishments 2019	Employment 2018	Employment 2019	Sales ($B) 2018	Sales ($B) 2019	Local Sales (B) 2018	Local Sales (B) 2019	Currency
Iran	544	550	1,396	1,364	0.0	0.0	1.5	1.4	Rial*
Iraq	285	290	732	718	0.0	0.0	0.0	0.0	Dinar*
Ireland	40	41	103	100	0.1	0.1	0.0	0.0	Euro
Israel	57	57	146	142	0.0	0.0	0.1	0.1	Shekel
Italy	402	400	1,032	991	0.2	0.2	0.2	0.1	Euro
Japan	846	837	2,171	2,074	0.5	0.4	51.1	47.0	Yen*
Kazakhstan	138	138	354	343	0.0	0.0	7.4	6.9	Tenge
Kuwait	32	34	83	83	0.0	0.0	0.0	0.0	Dinar
Malaysia	264	268	677	664	0.0	0.0	0.2	0.2	Ringgit
Mexico	859	869	2,205	2,153	0.1	0.1	2.4	2.2	New pesos
Netherlands	107	107	276	265	0.1	0.1	0.1	0.1	Euro
New Zealand	29	29	74	72	0.0	0.0	0.0	0.0	Dollar
Nigeria	1,482	1,506	3,803	3,733	0.1	0.1	22,403.4	20,970.2	Naira
Norway	40	40	102	99	0.0	0.0	0.4	0.4	Krone
Pakistan	1,187	1,212	3,047	3,003	0.0	0.0	3.1	2.9	Rupees
Peru	235	235	603	583	0.0	0.0	0.1	0.1	Nuevo Sol
Phillipines	640	651	1,643	1,613	0.0	0.0	1.7	1.6	Pesos
Poland	219	217	563	537	0.1	0.1	0.2	0.2	Zloty
Portugal	69	69	178	170	0.0	0.0	0.0	0.0	Euro
Puerto Rico	30	30	77	73	0.0	0.0	0.0	0.0	Dollar
Qatar	30	34	77	85	0.0	0.0	0.1	0.1	Riyal
Romania	158	155	405	385	0.0	0.0	0.1	0.1	New Leu
Russia	980	969	2,516	2,401	0.1	0.1	7.4	6.7	Rubles
Saudi Arabia	275	284	706	703	0.1	0.1	0.0	0.0	Rials*
Singapore	44	45	113	111	0.0	0.0	45.6	42.8	Dollar
South Africa	271	274	696	680	0.0	0.0	386.3	358.2	Rand
South Korea	383	382	983	946	0.2	0.2	181.8	171.1	Won*
Spain	318	320	816	793	0.1	0.1	109.0	99.9	Euro
Sweden	65	65	167	161	0.1	0.1	458.9	434.0	Krona
Switzerland	60	60	153	148	0.1	0.1	74.8	69.5	Swiss franc
Taiwan	239	247	613	611	0.1	0.1	1,717.8	1,603.2	Dollar
Thailand	577	580	1,481	1,437	0.0	0.0	1,581.1	1,472.1	Baht
Turkey	437	435	1,123	1,079	0.1	0.1	351.1	332.3	Euro
Ukraine	319	314	819	779	0.0	0.0	204.6	168.2	Hryvna
UAE	149	166	382	413	0.1	0.0	186.6	173.1	Dirham
United Kingdom	416	414	1,067	1,027	0.3	0.3	223.4	209.6	Pounds
United States	2,018	2,019	5,180	5,003	1.8	1.7	1,838.2	1,722.9	Dollars
Venezuela	206	209	528	518	0.1	0.0	500.3	446.1	Bolivar
Vietnam	724	725	1,859	1,796	0.0	0.0	597.1	579.6	Dong*

Note: Due to rounding, establishments will vary by + or - one establishment. Therefore, zero establishments may also be one establishment.

* Local Sales are in trillions

SOFTWARE PUBLISHING INDUSTRY
(NAICS 51121)

NAICS 51121: Software Publishers . This industry comprises establishments primarily engaged in computer software publishing or publishing and reproduction. Establishments in this industry carry out operations necessary for producing and distributing computer software, such as designing, providing documentation, assisting in installation, and providing support services to software purchasers. These establishments may design, develop, and publish, or publish only.

COUNTRY ESTIMATES

Country	Establishments 2018	2019	Employment 2018	2019	Sales ($B) 2018	2019	Local Sales (B) 2018	2019	Currency
Algeria	371	373	45,551	51,255	0.3	0.3	35.8	36.8	Dinar
Argentina	257	258	31,579	35,350	0.7	0.7	14.1	14.3	Pesos
Australia	160	162	19,651	22,179	1.8	1.9	2.3	2.4	Dollars
Austria	57	57	7,031	7,828	0.5	0.5	0.4	0.4	Euro
Bangladesh	1,129	1,130	138,494	155,131	0.3	0.3	25.1	26.9	Taka
Belgium	72	72	8,813	9,862	0.6	0.6	0.5	0.5	Euro
Brazil	1,375	1,387	168,660	190,301	2.3	2.2	7,278.0	7,236.7	Real
Canada	241	242	29,559	33,162	2.1	2.2	2.6	2.7	Dollars
Chile	133	134	16,353	18,430	0.4	0.4	222.6	229.6	Pesos*
China	9,511	9,479	1,166,536	1,300,889	18.8	20.0	122.2	129.7	RMB
Colombia	286	286	35,076	39,253	0.4	0.4	1.2	1.2	Pesos*
Czech Republic	69	68	8,407	9,355	0.3	0.3	5.8	6.1	Koruna
Denmark	36	36	4,423	4,923	0.4	0.4	2.5	2.5	Kroner
Egypt	608	623	74,622	85,509	0.5	0.5	8.1	8.4	Pounds
Finland	36	36	4,381	4,879	0.3	0.3	0.3	0.3	Euro
France	399	398	48,933	54,643	3.0	3.1	2.5	2.6	Euro
Germany	508	501	62,292	68,810	4.7	4.8	3.9	4.0	Euro
Greece	67	66	8,196	9,103	0.2	0.2	0.2	0.2	Euro
Hong Kong	41	41	5,026	5,599	0.3	0.4	2,706.7	2,804.8	Dollar
Hungary	60	59	7,392	8,165	0.2	0.2	42.8	44.8	Forint*
India	7,986	8,107	979,600	1,112,599	3.0	3.2	191.3	204.2	Rupees
Indonesia	1,986	2,011	243,593	276,052	1.5	1.6	20.1	21.3	Rupiah*

Software Publishing Industry
(NAICS 51121)

Country Estimates

Country	Establishments 2018	Establishments 2019	Employment 2018	Employment 2019	Sales ($B) 2018	Sales ($B) 2019	Local Sales (B) 2018	Local Sales (B) 2019	Currency
Iran	544	550	66,715	75,533	0.5	0.5	19.4	19.5	Rial*
Iraq	285	290	34,988	39,747	0.3	0.3	0.3	0.3	Dinar*
Ireland	40	41	4,909	5,562	0.7	0.8	0.6	0.7	Euro
Israel	57	57	6,956	7,891	0.4	0.5	1.5	1.6	Shekel
Italy	402	400	49,293	54,895	2.4	2.5	2.0	2.1	Euro
Japan	846	837	103,743	114,888	5.8	5.9	651.2	663.1	Yen*
Kazakhstan	138	138	16,903	19,001	0.3	0.3	94.3	97.9	Tenge
Kuwait	32	34	3,950	4,611	0.2	0.2	0.1	0.1	Dinar
Malaysia	264	268	32,339	36,795	0.5	0.6	2.1	2.3	Ringgit
Mexico	859	869	105,353	119,244	1.6	1.6	30.0	31.1	New pesos
Netherlands	107	107	13,179	14,661	1.0	1.0	0.8	0.9	Euro
New Zealand	29	29	3,544	3,989	0.2	0.2	0.3	0.3	Dollar
Nigeria	1,482	1,506	181,725	206,734	0.8	0.8	285,598.3	295,674.1	Naira
Norway	40	40	4,868	5,464	0.6	0.6	4.8	4.9	Krone
Pakistan	1,187	1,212	145,619	166,319	0.4	0.4	39.0	41.2	Rupees
Peru	235	235	28,825	32,291	0.3	0.3	0.9	0.9	Nuevo Sol
Phillipines	640	651	78,490	89,346	0.4	0.5	21.4	23.0	Pesos
Poland	219	217	26,888	29,755	0.7	0.7	2.4	2.6	Zloty
Portugal	69	69	8,501	9,436	0.3	0.3	0.2	0.2	Euro
Puerto Rico	30	30	3,678	4,050	0.2	0.2	0.2	0.2	Dollar
Qatar	30	34	3,703	4,719	0.3	0.3	1.0	1.0	Riyal
Romania	158	155	19,354	21,311	0.3	0.3	1.1	1.1	New Leu
Russia	980	969	120,213	132,947	1.8	1.8	94.5	94.5	Rubles
Saudi Arabia	275	284	33,724	38,934	1.1	1.2	0.0	0.0	Rials*
Singapore	44	45	5,383	6,167	0.4	0.5	581.8	603.9	Dollar
South Africa	271	274	33,246	37,664	0.4	0.4	4,924.5	5,050.1	Rand
South Korea	383	382	46,991	52,368	2.2	2.3	2,317.8	2,413.0	Won*
Spain	318	320	39,007	43,892	1.7	1.7	1,388.9	1,409.3	Euro
Sweden	65	65	7,994	8,930	0.7	0.7	5,850.2	6,119.6	Krona
Switzerland	60	60	7,313	8,203	1.0	1.0	953.1	980.6	Swiss franc
Taiwan	239	247	29,286	33,853	0.7	0.8	21,898.6	22,604.4	Dollar
Thailand	577	580	70,789	79,597	0.6	0.6	20,155.7	20,755.8	Baht
Turkey	437	435	53,641	59,735	1.2	1.2	4,475.9	4,684.8	Euro
Ukraine	319	314	39,130	43,122	0.1	0.1	2,608.0	2,371.7	Hryvna
UAE	149	166	18,237	22,846	0.6	0.7	2,379.2	2,441.3	Dirham
United Kingdom	416	414	50,985	56,883	3.9	4.0	2,847.9	2,954.6	Pounds
United States	2,018	2,019	247,523	277,087	23.4	24.3	23,433.9	24,292.1	Dollars
Venezuela	206	209	25,249	28,681	0.6	0.6	6,377.3	6,289.4	Bolivar
Vietnam	724	725	88,837	99,451	0.3	0.4	7,611.2	8,171.5	Dong*

Note: Due to rounding, establishments will vary by + or - one establishment. Therefore, zero establishments may also be one establishment.

* Local Sales are in trillions

NAICS 51211: Motion Picture and Video Production Industry . This industry comprises establishments primarily engaged in producing, or producing and distributing motion pictures, videos, television programs, or television and video commercials.

COUNTRY ESTIMATES

Country	Establishments 2018	2019	Employment 2018	2019	Sales ($B) 2018	2019	Local Sales (B) 2018	2019	Currency
Algeria	186	187	6,425	7,020	0.2	0.3	28.3	29.1	Dinar
Argentina	129	129	4,454	4,842	0.6	0.6	11.1	11.3	Pesos
Australia	80	81	2,772	3,038	1.4	1.5	1.8	1.9	Dollars
Austria	29	29	992	1,072	0.4	0.4	0.3	0.3	Euro
Bangladesh	565	565	19,535	21,248	0.2	0.3	19.8	21.3	Taka
Belgium	36	36	1,243	1,351	0.5	0.5	0.4	0.4	Euro
Brazil	688	693	23,790	26,065	1.8	1.8	5,747.6	5,724.6	Real
Canada	120	121	4,169	4,542	1.7	1.7	2.1	2.2	Dollars
Chile	67	67	2,307	2,524	0.3	0.3	175.8	181.6	Pesos*
China	4,755	4,739	164,541	178,182	14.9	15.8	96.5	102.6	RMB
Colombia	143	143	4,947	5,376	0.3	0.3	0.9	1.0	Pesos*
Czech Republic	34	34	1,186	1,281	0.2	0.2	4.6	4.9	Koruna
Denmark	18	18	624	674	0.3	0.3	1.9	2.0	Kroner
Egypt	304	312	10,526	11,712	0.4	0.4	6.4	6.6	Pounds
Finland	18	18	618	668	0.2	0.2	0.2	0.2	Euro
France	199	199	6,902	7,484	2.4	2.4	2.0	2.0	Euro
Germany	254	251	8,786	9,425	3.7	3.8	3.1	3.2	Euro
Greece	33	33	1,156	1,247	0.2	0.2	0.2	0.2	Euro
Hong Kong	20	20	709	767	0.3	0.3	2,137.5	2,218.8	Dollar
Hungary	30	30	1,043	1,118	0.1	0.1	33.8	35.5	Forint*
India	7,986	8,107	276,348	304,784	4.8	5.1	302.1	323.1	Rupees
Indonesia	993	1,006	34,359	37,811	1.2	1.3	15.8	16.8	Rupiah*

Motion Pictures & Video Production Industry
(NAICS 51211)

Country Estimates

Country	Establishments 2018	2019	Employment 2018	2019	Sales ($B) 2018	2019	Local Sales (B) 2018	2019	Currency
Iran	272	275	9,410	10,346	0.4	0.4	15.3	15.5	Rial*
Iraq	143	145	4,935	5,444	0.2	0.2	0.3	0.3	Dinar*
Ireland	20	20	692	762	0.5	0.6	0.5	0.5	Euro
Israel	28	29	981	1,081	0.3	0.4	1.2	1.2	Shekel
Italy	201	200	6,953	7,519	1.9	1.9	1.6	1.6	Euro
Japan	423	419	14,633	15,736	4.6	4.6	514.3	524.6	Yen*
Kazakhstan	69	69	2,384	2,603	0.2	0.2	74.5	77.4	Tenge
Kuwait	16	17	557	632	0.1	0.1	0.0	0.0	Dinar
Malaysia	132	134	4,561	5,040	0.4	0.4	1.7	1.8	Ringgit
Mexico	429	434	14,860	16,333	1.2	1.3	23.7	24.6	New pesos
Netherlands	54	53	1,859	2,008	0.8	0.8	0.7	0.7	Euro
New Zealand	14	15	500	546	0.2	0.2	0.2	0.3	Dollar
Nigeria	741	753	25,633	28,316	0.6	0.6	225,540.7	233,894.5	Naira
Norway	20	20	687	748	0.5	0.5	3.8	3.9	Krone
Pakistan	594	606	20,540	22,781	0.3	0.3	30.8	32.6	Rupees
Peru	118	118	4,066	4,423	0.2	0.2	0.7	0.7	Nuevo Sol
Phillipines	320	326	11,071	12,238	0.3	0.4	16.9	18.2	Pesos
Poland	110	108	3,793	4,076	0.6	0.6	1.9	2.0	Zloty
Portugal	35	34	1,199	1,292	0.2	0.2	0.2	0.2	Euro
Puerto Rico	15	15	519	555	0.1	0.1	0.1	0.1	Dollar
Qatar	15	17	522	646	0.2	0.2	0.8	0.8	Riyal
Romania	79	78	2,730	2,919	0.2	0.2	0.9	0.9	New Leu
Russia	490	484	16,956	18,210	1.5	1.5	74.6	74.8	Rubles
Saudi Arabia	137	142	4,757	5,333	0.9	0.9	0.0	0.0	Rials*
Singapore	22	22	759	845	0.3	0.4	459.4	477.7	Dollar
South Africa	136	137	4,689	5,159	0.3	0.3	3,889.0	3,994.9	Rand
South Korea	192	191	6,628	7,173	1.7	1.8	1,830.4	1,908.8	Won*
Spain	159	160	5,502	6,012	1.3	1.3	1,096.9	1,114.8	Euro
Sweden	33	33	1,128	1,223	0.6	0.6	4,620.0	4,841.0	Krona
Switzerland	30	30	1,032	1,124	0.8	0.8	752.7	775.7	Swiss franc
Taiwan	119	123	4,131	4,637	0.6	0.6	17,293.6	17,881.3	Dollar
Thailand	289	290	9,985	10,902	0.5	0.5	15,917.2	16,419.0	Baht
Turkey	219	218	7,566	8,182	0.9	1.0	3,534.7	3,706.0	Euro
Ukraine	160	157	5,519	5,906	0.1	0.1	2,059.6	1,876.1	Hryvna
UAE	74	83	2,572	3,129	0.5	0.5	1,878.9	1,931.2	Dirham
United Kingdom	208	207	7,191	7,791	3.1	3.2	2,249.1	2,337.3	Pounds
United States	2,018	2,019	69,827	75,905	37.0	38.4	37,012.1	38,432.7	Dollars
Venezuela	103	104	3,561	3,928	0.5	0.5	5,036.3	4,975.2	Bolivar
Vietnam	362	362	12,531	13,622	0.3	0.3	6,010.7	6,464.1	Dong*

Note: Due to rounding, establishments will vary by + or - one establishment. Therefore, zero establishments may also be one establishment.

* Local Sales are in trillions

NAICS 51223: Music Publishers . This U.S. industry comprises establishments known as music publishers. Establishments in this industry carry out design, editing, and marketing activities necessary for producing and distributing music books. These establishments may publish books in print, electronic, or audio form.

COUNTRY ESTIMATES

Country	Establishments 2018	2019	Employment 2018	2019	Sales ($B) 2018	2019	Local Sales (B) 2018	2019	Currency
Algeria	371	373	656	699	0.0	0.0	5.2	5.3	Dinar
Argentina	257	258	455	482	0.1	0.1	2.0	2.1	Pesos
Australia	160	162	283	302	0.3	0.3	0.3	0.3	Dollars
Austria	57	57	101	107	0.1	0.1	0.1	0.1	Euro
Bangladesh	1,129	1,130	1,994	2,116	0.0	0.0	3.6	3.9	Taka
Belgium	72	72	127	135	0.1	0.1	0.1	0.1	Euro
Brazil	1,375	1,387	2,428	2,595	0.3	0.3	1,056.8	1,044.0	Real
Canada	241	242	426	452	0.3	0.3	0.4	0.4	Dollars
Chile	133	134	235	251	0.1	0.1	32.3	33.1	Pesos*
China	9,511	9,479	16,794	17,742	2.7	2.9	17.7	18.7	RMB
Colombia	286	286	505	535	0.1	0.1	0.2	0.2	Pesos*
Czech Republic	69	68	121	128	0.0	0.0	0.8	0.9	Koruna
Denmark	36	36	64	67	0.1	0.1	0.4	0.4	Kroner
Egypt	608	623	1,074	1,166	0.1	0.1	1.2	1.2	Pounds
Finland	36	36	63	67	0.0	0.0	0.0	0.0	Euro
France	399	398	704	745	0.4	0.4	0.4	0.4	Euro
Germany	508	501	897	938	0.7	0.7	0.6	0.6	Euro
Greece	67	66	118	124	0.0	0.0	0.0	0.0	Euro
Hong Kong	41	41	72	76	0.1	0.1	393.0	404.6	Dollar
Hungary	60	59	106	111	0.0	0.0	6.2	6.5	Forint*
India	7,986	8,107	14,103	15,174	0.4	0.5	27.8	29.5	Rupees
Indonesia	1,986	2,011	3,507	3,765	0.2	0.2	2.9	3.1	Rupiah*

MUSIC PUBLISHING INDUSTRY
(NAICS 51223)

COUNTRY ESTIMATES

Country	Establishments		Employment		Sales ($B)		Local Sales (B)		
	2018	2019	2018	2019	2018	2019	2018	2019	Currency
Iran	544	550	960	1,030	0.1	0.1	2.8	2.8	Rial*
Iraq	285	290	504	542	0.0	0.0	0.0	0.0	Dinar*
Ireland	40	41	71	76	0.1	0.1	0.1	0.1	Euro
Israel	57	57	100	108	0.1	0.1	0.2	0.2	Shekel
Italy	402	400	710	749	0.4	0.4	0.3	0.3	Euro
Japan	846	837	1,494	1,567	0.8	0.8	94.6	95.7	Yen*
Kazakhstan	138	138	243	259	0.0	0.0	13.7	14.1	Tenge
Kuwait	32	34	57	63	0.0	0.0	0.0	0.0	Dinar
Malaysia	264	268	466	502	0.1	0.1	0.3	0.3	Ringgit
Mexico	859	869	1,517	1,626	0.2	0.2	4.4	4.5	New pesos
Netherlands	107	107	190	200	0.1	0.1	0.1	0.1	Euro
New Zealand	29	29	51	54	0.0	0.0	0.0	0.0	Dollar
Nigeria	1,482	1,506	2,616	2,820	0.1	0.1	41,469.6	42,656.2	Naira
Norway	40	40	70	75	0.1	0.1	0.7	0.7	Krone
Pakistan	1,187	1,212	2,096	2,268	0.1	0.1	5.7	5.9	Rupees
Peru	235	235	415	440	0.0	0.0	0.1	0.1	Nuevo Sol
Phillipines	640	651	1,130	1,219	0.1	0.1	3.1	3.3	Pesos
Poland	219	217	387	406	0.1	0.1	0.4	0.4	Zloty
Portugal	69	69	122	129	0.0	0.0	0.0	0.0	Euro
Puerto Rico	30	30	53	55	0.0	0.0	0.0	0.0	Dollar
Qatar	30	34	53	64	0.0	0.0	0.1	0.1	Riyal
Romania	158	155	279	291	0.0	0.0	0.2	0.2	New Leu
Russia	980	969	1,731	1,813	0.3	0.3	13.7	13.6	Rubles
Saudi Arabia	275	284	486	531	0.2	0.2	0.0	0.0	Rials*
Singapore	44	45	77	84	0.1	0.1	84.5	87.1	Dollar
South Africa	271	274	479	514	0.1	0.1	715.1	728.6	Rand
South Korea	383	382	676	714	0.3	0.3	336.5	348.1	Won*
Spain	318	320	562	599	0.2	0.2	201.7	203.3	Euro
Sweden	65	65	115	122	0.1	0.1	849.5	882.9	Krona
Switzerland	60	60	105	112	0.1	0.1	138.4	141.5	Swiss franc
Taiwan	239	247	422	462	0.1	0.1	3,179.7	3,261.1	Dollar
Thailand	577	580	1,019	1,086	0.1	0.1	2,926.7	2,994.4	Baht
Turkey	437	435	772	815	0.2	0.2	649.9	675.9	Euro
Ukraine	319	314	563	588	0.0	0.0	378.7	342.2	Hryvna
UAE	149	166	263	312	0.1	0.1	345.5	352.2	Dirham
United Kingdom	416	414	734	776	0.6	0.6	413.5	426.3	Pounds
United States	2,018	2,019	3,563	3,779	3.4	3.5	3,402.7	3,504.6	Dollars
Venezuela	206	209	363	391	0.1	0.1	926.0	907.4	Bolivar
Vietnam	724	725	1,279	1,356	0.0	0.1	1,105.2	1,178.9	Dong*

Note: Due to rounding, establishments will vary by + or - one establishment. Therefore, zero establishments may also be one establishment.

* Local Sales are in trillions

Radio Broadcasting Industry (NAICS 51511)

NAICS 51511: Radio Broadcasting . This industry comprises establishments primarily engaged in broadcasting audio signals. These establishments operate radio broadcasting studios and facilities for the transmission of aural programming by radio to the public, to affiliates, or to subscribers. The radio programs may include entertainment, news, talk shows, business data, or religious services.

COUNTRY ESTIMATES

Country	Establishments 2018	2019	Employment 2018	2019	Sales ($B) 2018	2019	Local Sales (B) 2018	2019	Currency
Algeria	371	373	2,821	2,922	0.2	0.2	17.8	17.7	Dinar
Argentina	257	258	1,955	2,015	0.4	0.4	7.0	6.8	Pesos
Australia	160	162	1,217	1,264	0.9	0.9	1.2	1.2	Dollars
Austria	57	57	435	446	0.3	0.3	0.2	0.2	Euro
Bangladesh	1,129	1,130	8,576	8,843	0.2	0.2	12.5	12.9	Taka
Belgium	72	72	546	562	0.3	0.3	0.2	0.2	Euro
Brazil	1,375	1,387	10,444	10,847	1.1	1.1	3,624.3	3,471.5	Real
Canada	241	242	1,830	1,890	1.1	1.1	1.3	1.3	Dollars
Chile	133	134	1,013	1,051	0.2	0.2	110.9	110.1	Pesos*
China	9,511	9,479	72,234	74,152	9.4	9.6	60.9	62.2	RMB
Colombia	286	286	2,172	2,237	0.2	0.2	0.6	0.6	Pesos*
Czech Republic	69	68	521	533	0.1	0.1	2.9	2.9	Koruna
Denmark	36	36	274	281	0.2	0.2	1.2	1.2	Kroner
Egypt	608	623	4,621	4,874	0.2	0.2	4.1	4.0	Pounds
Finland	36	36	271	278	0.1	0.1	0.1	0.1	Euro
France	399	398	3,030	3,115	1.5	1.5	1.3	1.2	Euro
Germany	508	501	3,857	3,922	2.3	2.3	1.9	1.9	Euro
Greece	67	66	507	519	0.1	0.1	0.1	0.1	Euro
Hong Kong	41	41	311	319	0.2	0.2	1,347.9	1,345.5	Dollar
Hungary	60	59	458	465	0.1	0.1	21.3	21.5	Forint*
India	7,986	8,107	60,659	63,419	1.5	1.5	95.2	98.0	Rupees
Indonesia	1,986	2,011	15,084	15,735	0.7	0.8	10.0	10.2	Rupiah*

RADIO BROADCASTING INDUSTRY
(NAICS 51511)

COUNTRY ESTIMATES

Country	Establishments 2018	Establishments 2019	Employment 2018	Employment 2019	Sales ($B) 2018	Sales ($B) 2019	Local Sales (B) 2018	Local Sales (B) 2019	Currency
Iran	544	550	4,131	4,305	0.3	0.3	9.7	9.4	Rial*
Iraq	285	290	2,167	2,266	0.1	0.1	0.2	0.2	Dinar*
Ireland	40	41	304	317	0.3	0.4	0.3	0.3	Euro
Israel	57	57	431	450	0.2	0.2	0.8	0.8	Shekel
Italy	402	400	3,052	3,129	1.2	1.2	1.0	1.0	Euro
Japan	846	837	6,424	6,549	2.9	2.8	324.3	318.1	Yen*
Kazakhstan	138	138	1,047	1,083	0.1	0.1	47.0	47.0	Tenge
Kuwait	32	34	245	263	0.1	0.1	0.0	0.0	Dinar
Malaysia	264	268	2,002	2,097	0.3	0.3	1.1	1.1	Ringgit
Mexico	859	869	6,524	6,797	0.8	0.8	15.0	14.9	New pesos
Netherlands	107	107	816	836	0.5	0.5	0.4	0.4	Euro
New Zealand	29	29	219	227	0.1	0.1	0.2	0.2	Dollar
Nigeria	1,482	1,506	11,253	11,784	0.4	0.4	142,222.1	141,837.8	Naira
Norway	40	40	301	311	0.3	0.3	2.4	2.4	Krone
Pakistan	1,187	1,212	9,017	9,480	0.2	0.2	19.4	19.8	Rupees
Peru	235	235	1,785	1,841	0.1	0.1	0.5	0.5	Nuevo Sol
Phillipines	640	651	4,860	5,093	0.2	0.2	10.7	11.0	Pesos
Poland	219	217	1,665	1,696	0.3	0.4	1.2	1.2	Zloty
Portugal	69	69	526	538	0.1	0.1	0.1	0.1	Euro
Puerto Rico	30	30	228	231	0.1	0.1	0.1	0.1	Dollar
Qatar	30	34	229	269	0.1	0.1	0.5	0.5	Riyal
Romania	158	155	1,198	1,215	0.1	0.1	0.5	0.5	New Leu
Russia	980	969	7,444	7,578	0.9	0.9	47.1	45.3	Rubles
Saudi Arabia	275	284	2,088	2,219	0.6	0.6	0.0	0.0	Rials*
Singapore	44	45	333	352	0.2	0.2	289.7	289.7	Dollar
South Africa	271	274	2,059	2,147	0.2	0.2	2,452.3	2,422.6	Rand
South Korea	383	382	2,910	2,985	1.1	1.1	1,154.2	1,157.6	Won*
Spain	318	320	2,415	2,502	0.8	0.8	691.7	676.0	Euro
Sweden	65	65	495	509	0.4	0.4	2,913.3	2,935.6	Krona
Switzerland	60	60	453	468	0.5	0.5	474.6	470.4	Swiss franc
Taiwan	239	247	1,813	1,930	0.4	0.4	10,905.1	10,843.6	Dollar
Thailand	577	580	4,383	4,537	0.3	0.3	10,037.1	9,956.8	Baht
Turkey	437	435	3,322	3,405	0.6	0.6	2,228.9	2,247.4	Euro
Ukraine	319	314	2,423	2,458	0.0	0.0	1,298.7	1,137.7	Hryvna
UAE	149	166	1,129	1,302	0.3	0.3	1,184.8	1,171.1	Dirham
United Kingdom	416	414	3,157	3,242	1.9	1.9	1,418.2	1,417.4	Pounds
United States	2,018	2,019	15,327	15,794	11.7	11.7	11,669.6	11,653.1	Dollars
Venezuela	206	209	1,563	1,635	0.3	0.3	3,175.8	3,017.1	Bolivar
Vietnam	724	725	5,501	5,669	0.2	0.2	3,790.2	3,919.9	Dong*

Note: Due to rounding, establishments will vary by + or - one establishment. Therefore, zero establishments may also be one establishment.

* Local Sales are in trillions

TELEVISION BROADCASTING SERVICES INDUSTRY (NAICS 51512)

NAICS 51512: Television Broadcasting . This industry comprises establishments primarily engaged in broadcasting images together with sound. These establishments operate television broadcasting studios and facilities for the programming and transmission of programs to the public. These establishments also produce or transmit visual programming to affiliated broadcast television stations, which in turn broadcast the programs to the public on a predetermined schedule. Programming may originate in their own studios, from an affiliated network, or from external sources.

COUNTRY ESTIMATES

Country	Establishments		Employment		Sales ($B)		Local Sales (B)		Currency
	2018	2019	2018	2019	2018	2019	2018	2019	
Algeria	371	373	6,623	6,724	0.1	0.1	6.5	6.5	Dinar
Argentina	257	258	4,592	4,637	0.1	0.1	2.5	2.5	Pesos
Australia	160	162	2,857	2,910	0.3	0.3	0.4	0.4	Dollars
Austria	57	57	1,022	1,027	0.1	0.1	0.1	0.1	Euro
Bangladesh	1,129	1,130	20,137	20,351	0.1	0.1	4.5	4.8	Taka
Belgium	72	72	1,281	1,294	0.1	0.1	0.1	0.1	Euro
Brazil	1,375	1,387	24,523	24,965	0.4	0.4	1,313.1	1,278.2	Real
Canada	241	242	4,298	4,350	0.4	0.4	0.5	0.5	Dollars
Chile	133	134	2,378	2,418	0.1	0.1	40.2	40.6	Pesos*
China	9,511	9,479	169,613	170,660	3.4	3.5	22.0	22.9	RMB
Colombia	286	286	5,100	5,149	0.1	0.1	0.2	0.2	Pesos*
Czech Republic	69	68	1,222	1,227	0.0	0.1	1.1	1.1	Koruna
Denmark	36	36	643	646	0.1	0.1	0.4	0.4	Kroner
Egypt	608	623	10,850	11,218	0.1	0.1	1.5	1.5	Pounds
Finland	36	36	637	640	0.1	0.1	0.0	0.0	Euro
France	399	398	7,115	7,168	0.5	0.5	0.5	0.5	Euro
Germany	508	501	9,057	9,027	0.8	0.8	0.7	0.7	Euro
Greece	67	66	1,192	1,194	0.0	0.0	0.0	0.0	Euro
Hong Kong	41	41	731	734	0.1	0.1	488.3	495.4	Dollar
Hungary	60	59	1,075	1,071	0.0	0.0	7.7	7.9	Forint*
India	7,986	8,107	142,433	145,959	0.5	0.6	34.5	36.1	Rupees
Indonesia	1,986	2,011	35,418	36,215	0.3	0.3	3.6	3.8	Rupiah*

TELEVISION BROADCASTING SERVICES INDUSTRY (NAICS 51512)

COUNTRY ESTIMATES

Country	Establishments 2018	2019	Employment 2018	2019	Sales ($B) 2018	2019	Local Sales (B) 2018	2019	Currency
Iran	544	550	9,700	9,909	0.1	0.1	3.5	3.5	Rial*
Iraq	285	290	5,087	5,214	0.1	0.1	0.1	0.1	Dinar*
Ireland	40	41	714	730	0.1	0.1	0.1	0.1	Euro
Israel	57	57	1,011	1,035	0.1	0.1	0.3	0.3	Shekel
Italy	402	400	7,167	7,202	0.4	0.4	0.4	0.4	Euro
Japan	846	837	15,084	15,072	1.0	1.0	117.5	117.1	Yen*
Kazakhstan	138	138	2,458	2,493	0.1	0.1	17.0	17.3	Tenge
Kuwait	32	34	574	605	0.0	0.0	0.0	0.0	Dinar
Malaysia	264	268	4,702	4,827	0.1	0.1	0.4	0.4	Ringgit
Mexico	859	869	15,318	15,643	0.3	0.3	5.4	5.5	New pesos
Netherlands	107	107	1,916	1,923	0.2	0.2	0.2	0.2	Euro
New Zealand	29	29	515	523	0.0	0.0	0.1	0.1	Dollar
Nigeria	1,482	1,506	26,423	27,121	0.1	0.1	51,527.0	52,224.1	Naira
Norway	40	40	708	717	0.1	0.1	0.9	0.9	Krone
Pakistan	1,187	1,212	21,173	21,819	0.1	0.1	7.0	7.3	Rupees
Peru	235	235	4,191	4,236	0.1	0.1	0.2	0.2	Nuevo Sol
Phillipines	640	651	11,412	11,721	0.1	0.1	3.9	4.1	Pesos
Poland	219	217	3,909	3,904	0.1	0.1	0.4	0.5	Zloty
Portugal	69	69	1,236	1,238	0.0	0.0	0.0	0.0	Euro
Puerto Rico	30	30	535	531	0.0	0.0	0.0	0.0	Dollar
Qatar	30	34	538	619	0.0	0.0	0.2	0.2	Riyal
Romania	158	155	2,814	2,796	0.1	0.1	0.2	0.2	New Leu
Russia	980	969	17,479	17,441	0.3	0.3	17.1	16.7	Rubles
Saudi Arabia	275	284	4,903	5,108	0.2	0.2	0.0	0.0	Rials*
Singapore	44	45	783	809	0.1	0.1	105.0	106.7	Dollar
South Africa	271	274	4,834	4,941	0.1	0.1	888.5	892.0	Rand
South Korea	383	382	6,832	6,870	0.4	0.4	418.2	426.2	Won*
Spain	318	320	5,672	5,758	0.3	0.3	250.6	248.9	Euro
Sweden	65	65	1,162	1,172	0.1	0.1	1,055.5	1,080.9	Krona
Switzerland	60	60	1,063	1,076	0.2	0.2	172.0	173.2	Swiss franc
Taiwan	239	247	4,258	4,441	0.1	0.1	3,950.9	3,992.6	Dollar
Thailand	577	580	10,293	10,442	0.1	0.1	3,636.5	3,666.0	Baht
Turkey	437	435	7,799	7,837	0.2	0.2	807.5	827.5	Euro
Ukraine	319	314	5,689	5,657	0.0	0.0	470.5	418.9	Hryvna
UAE	149	166	2,652	2,997	0.1	0.1	429.3	431.2	Dirham
United Kingdom	416	414	7,413	7,462	0.7	0.7	513.8	521.9	Pounds
United States	2,018	2,019	35,990	36,350	4.2	4.3	4,227.9	4,290.6	Dollars
Venezuela	206	209	3,671	3,763	0.1	0.1	1,150.6	1,110.9	Bolivar
Vietnam	724	725	12,917	13,047	0.1	0.1	1,373.2	1,443.3	Dong*

Note: Due to rounding, establishments will vary by + or - one establishment. Therefore, zero establishments may also be one establishment.

* Local Sales are in trillions

Cable Television Networks Industry (NAICS 51521)

NAICS 51521: Cable Networks . This industry comprises establishments primarily engaged in operating studios and facilities for the broadcasting of programs on a subscription or fee basis. The broadcast programming is typically narrowcast in nature (e.g., limited format, such as news, sports, education, or youth-oriented). These establishments produce programming in their own facilities or acquire programming from external sources. The programming material is usually delivered to a third party, such as cable systems or direct-to-home satellite systems, for transmission to viewers.

COUNTRY ESTIMATES

Country	Establishments 2018	Establishments 2019	Employment 2018	Employment 2019	Sales ($B) 2018	Sales ($B) 2019	Local Sales (B) 2018	Local Sales (B) 2019	Currency
Algeria	371	373	14,770	16,208	0.0	0.0	2.5	2.6	Dinar
Argentina	257	258	10,239	11,178	0.1	0.1	1.0	1.0	Pesos
Australia	160	162	6,372	7,013	0.1	0.1	0.2	0.2	Dollars
Austria	57	57	2,280	2,475	0.0	0.0	0.0	0.0	Euro
Bangladesh	1,129	1,130	44,906	49,055	0.0	0.0	1.7	1.9	Taka
Belgium	72	72	2,858	3,119	0.0	0.0	0.0	0.0	Euro
Brazil	1,375	1,387	54,687	60,177	0.2	0.2	506.3	504.9	Real
Canada	241	242	9,584	10,486	0.1	0.2	0.2	0.2	Dollars
Chile	133	134	5,302	5,828	0.0	0.0	15.5	16.0	Pesos*
China	9,511	9,479	378,242	411,368	1.3	1.4	8.5	9.0	RMB
Colombia	286	286	11,373	12,413	0.0	0.0	0.1	0.1	Pesos*
Czech Republic	69	68	2,726	2,958	0.0	0.0	0.4	0.4	Koruna
Denmark	36	36	1,434	1,557	0.0	0.0	0.2	0.2	Kroner
Egypt	608	623	24,196	27,040	0.0	0.0	0.6	0.6	Pounds
Finland	36	36	1,420	1,543	0.0	0.0	0.0	0.0	Euro
France	399	398	15,866	17,279	0.2	0.2	0.2	0.2	Euro
Germany	508	501	20,198	21,759	0.3	0.3	0.3	0.3	Euro
Greece	67	66	2,657	2,879	0.0	0.0	0.0	0.0	Euro
Hong Kong	41	41	1,630	1,770	0.0	0.0	188.3	195.7	Dollar
Hungary	60	59	2,397	2,582	0.0	0.0	3.0	3.1	Forint*
India	7,986	8,107	317,629	351,827	0.2	0.2	13.3	14.2	Rupees
Indonesia	1,986	2,011	78,983	87,293	0.1	0.1	1.4	1.5	Rupiah*

Cable Television Networks Industry (NAICS 51521)

Country Estimates

Country	Establishments 2018	Establishments 2019	Employment 2018	Employment 2019	Sales ($B) 2018	Sales ($B) 2019	Local Sales (B) 2018	Local Sales (B) 2019	Currency
Iran	544	550	21,632	23,885	0.0	0.0	1.4	1.4	Rial*
Iraq	285	290	11,345	12,569	0.0	0.0	0.0	0.0	Dinar*
Ireland	40	41	1,592	1,759	0.0	0.1	0.0	0.0	Euro
Israel	57	57	2,256	2,495	0.0	0.0	0.1	0.1	Shekel
Italy	402	400	15,983	17,359	0.2	0.2	0.1	0.1	Euro
Japan	846	837	33,638	36,330	0.4	0.4	45.3	46.3	Yen*
Kazakhstan	138	138	5,481	6,009	0.0	0.0	6.6	6.8	Tenge
Kuwait	32	34	1,281	1,458	0.0	0.0	0.0	0.0	Dinar
Malaysia	264	268	10,486	11,635	0.0	0.0	0.1	0.2	Ringgit
Mexico	859	869	34,160	37,707	0.1	0.1	2.1	2.2	New pesos
Netherlands	107	107	4,273	4,636	0.1	0.1	0.1	0.1	Euro
New Zealand	29	29	1,149	1,261	0.0	0.0	0.0	0.0	Dollar
Nigeria	1,482	1,506	58,923	65,373	0.1	0.1	19,868.1	20,628.5	Naira
Norway	40	40	1,579	1,728	0.0	0.0	0.3	0.3	Krone
Pakistan	1,187	1,212	47,216	52,594	0.0	0.0	2.7	2.9	Rupees
Peru	235	235	9,346	10,211	0.0	0.0	0.1	0.1	Nuevo Sol
Phillipines	640	651	25,450	28,253	0.0	0.0	1.5	1.6	Pesos
Poland	219	217	8,718	9,409	0.0	0.1	0.2	0.2	Zloty
Portugal	69	69	2,756	2,984	0.0	0.0	0.0	0.0	Euro
Puerto Rico	30	30	1,193	1,281	0.0	0.0	0.0	0.0	Dollar
Qatar	30	34	1,201	1,492	0.0	0.0	0.1	0.1	Riyal
Romania	158	155	6,275	6,739	0.0	0.0	0.1	0.1	New Leu
Russia	980	969	38,978	42,041	0.1	0.1	6.6	6.6	Rubles
Saudi Arabia	275	284	10,935	12,312	0.1	0.1	0.0	0.0	Rials*
Singapore	44	45	1,745	1,950	0.0	0.0	40.5	42.1	Dollar
South Africa	271	274	10,780	11,910	0.0	0.0	342.6	352.3	Rand
South Korea	383	382	15,237	16,560	0.2	0.2	161.2	168.4	Won*
Spain	318	320	12,648	13,880	0.1	0.1	96.6	98.3	Euro
Sweden	65	65	2,592	2,824	0.0	0.1	407.0	427.0	Krona
Switzerland	60	60	2,371	2,594	0.1	0.1	66.3	68.4	Swiss franc
Taiwan	239	247	9,496	10,705	0.1	0.1	1,523.4	1,577.1	Dollar
Thailand	577	580	22,953	25,170	0.0	0.0	1,402.2	1,448.1	Baht
Turkey	437	435	17,393	18,890	0.1	0.1	311.4	326.9	Euro
Ukraine	319	314	12,688	13,636	0.0	0.0	181.4	165.5	Hryvna
UAE	149	166	5,913	7,224	0.0	0.0	165.5	170.3	Dirham
United Kingdom	416	414	16,531	17,988	0.3	0.3	198.1	206.1	Pounds
United States	2,018	2,019	80,258	87,621	1.6	1.7	1,630.2	1,694.8	Dollars
Venezuela	206	209	8,187	9,069	0.0	0.0	443.6	438.8	Bolivar
Vietnam	724	725	28,805	31,448	0.0	0.0	529.5	570.1	Dong*

Note: Due to rounding, establishments will vary by + or - one establishment. Therefore, zero establishments may also be one establishment.

* Local Sales are in trillions

WIRED TELECOMMUNICATIONS CARRIERS INDUSTRY (NAICS 51711)

NAICS 51711: Wired Telecommunications Carriers . This industry comprises establishments engaged in (1) operating and maintaining switching and transmission facilities to provide direct communications via landlines, microwave, or a combination of landlines and satellite linkups or (2) furnishing telegraph and other nonvocal communications using their own facilities.

COUNTRY ESTIMATES

Country	Establishments 2018	2019	Employment 2018	2019	Sales ($B) 2018	2019	Local Sales (B) 2018	2019	Currency
Algeria	371	373	68,143	70,746	0.6	0.6	65.5	66.6	Dinar
Argentina	257	258	47,242	48,793	1.4	1.4	25.8	25.8	Pesos
Australia	160	162	29,397	30,613	3.4	3.4	4.3	4.4	Dollars
Austria	57	57	10,518	10,805	0.9	0.9	0.8	0.8	Euro
Bangladesh	1,129	1,130	207,185	214,124	0.6	0.6	45.8	48.7	Taka
Belgium	72	72	13,184	13,613	1.1	1.1	0.9	0.9	Euro
Brazil	1,375	1,387	252,313	262,669	4.1	4.1	13,304.3	13,090.6	Real
Canada	241	242	44,220	45,772	3.9	4.0	4.8	4.9	Dollars
Chile	133	134	24,464	25,439	0.7	0.7	407.0	415.3	Pesos*
China	9,511	9,479	1,745,119	1,795,597	34.4	36.1	223.4	234.6	RMB
Colombia	286	286	52,473	54,180	0.7	0.8	2.1	2.2	Pesos*
Czech Republic	69	68	12,577	12,912	0.5	0.5	10.7	11.1	Koruna
Denmark	36	36	6,617	6,795	0.7	0.7	4.5	4.6	Kroner
Egypt	608	623	111,633	118,027	0.8	0.9	14.9	15.1	Pounds
Finland	36	36	6,554	6,734	0.5	0.5	0.5	0.5	Euro
France	399	398	73,204	75,423	5.5	5.6	4.6	4.7	Euro
Germany	508	501	93,188	94,978	8.5	8.7	7.1	7.2	Euro
Greece	67	66	12,260	12,565	0.4	0.4	0.4	0.4	Euro
Hong Kong	41	41	7,519	7,728	0.6	0.6	4,947.9	5,073.7	Dollar
Hungary	60	59	11,058	11,271	0.3	0.3	78.2	81.1	Forint*
India	7,986	8,107	1,465,466	1,535,704	5.5	5.8	349.6	369.5	Rupees
Indonesia	1,986	2,011	364,411	381,031	2.7	2.9	36.7	38.4	Rupiah*

WIRED TELECOMMUNICATIONS CARRIERS INDUSTRY (NAICS 51711)

COUNTRY ESTIMATES

Country	Establishments 2018	2019	Employment 2018	2019	Sales ($B) 2018	2019	Local Sales (B) 2018	2019	Currency
Iran	544	550	99,805	104,257	1.0	1.0	35.5	35.4	Rial*
Iraq	285	290	52,342	54,862	0.5	0.5	0.6	0.6	Dinar*
Ireland	40	41	7,344	7,677	1.3	1.5	1.1	1.2	Euro
Israel	57	57	10,407	10,892	0.8	0.8	2.8	2.8	Shekel
Italy	402	400	73,742	75,771	4.4	4.5	3.7	3.7	Euro
Japan	846	837	155,199	158,578	10.5	10.6	1,190.4	1,199.5	Yen*
Kazakhstan	138	138	25,286	26,227	0.5	0.5	172.5	177.1	Tenge
Kuwait	32	34	5,910	6,364	0.3	0.3	0.1	0.1	Dinar
Malaysia	264	268	48,378	50,787	1.0	1.0	3.9	4.1	Ringgit
Mexico	859	869	157,607	164,590	2.9	2.9	54.9	56.3	New pesos
Netherlands	107	107	19,715	20,236	1.8	1.9	1.5	1.5	Euro
New Zealand	29	29	5,301	5,506	0.4	0.4	0.6	0.6	Dollar
Nigeria	1,482	1,506	271,857	285,351	1.5	1.5	522,077.1	534,851.2	Naira
Norway	40	40	7,283	7,542	1.1	1.1	8.8	8.9	Krone
Pakistan	1,187	1,212	217,844	229,568	0.6	0.7	71.2	74.5	Rupees
Peru	235	235	43,122	44,571	0.5	0.5	1.7	1.7	Nuevo Sol
Phillipines	640	651	117,420	123,323	0.8	0.8	39.2	41.5	Pesos
Poland	219	217	40,224	41,071	1.3	1.3	4.5	4.6	Zloty
Portugal	69	69	12,718	13,024	0.5	0.5	0.4	0.4	Euro
Puerto Rico	30	30	5,502	5,591	0.3	0.3	0.3	0.3	Dollar
Qatar	30	34	5,540	6,514	0.5	0.5	1.8	1.8	Riyal
Romania	158	155	28,953	29,416	0.5	0.5	2.0	2.1	New Leu
Russia	980	969	179,836	183,505	3.4	3.3	172.8	171.0	Rubles
Saudi Arabia	275	284	50,451	53,740	2.1	2.1	0.0	0.0	Rials*
Singapore	44	45	8,053	8,512	0.8	0.8	1,063.5	1,092.4	Dollar
South Africa	271	274	49,735	51,988	0.7	0.7	9,002.1	9,135.2	Rand
South Korea	383	382	70,298	72,283	4.0	4.1	4,236.9	4,365.0	Won*
Spain	318	320	58,353	60,583	3.0	3.1	2,539.0	2,549.2	Euro
Sweden	65	65	11,958	12,327	1.3	1.3	10,694.3	11,069.9	Krona
Switzerland	60	60	10,940	11,323	1.8	1.8	1,742.2	1,773.8	Swiss franc
Taiwan	239	247	43,811	46,727	1.4	1.4	40,030.9	40,889.6	Dollar
Thailand	577	580	105,900	109,866	1.1	1.2	36,844.9	37,545.6	Baht
Turkey	437	435	80,245	82,452	2.2	2.3	8,182.0	8,474.5	Euro
Ukraine	319	314	58,538	59,520	0.2	0.2	4,767.5	4,290.2	Hryvna
UAE	149	166	27,282	31,534	1.2	1.2	4,349.3	4,416.1	Dirham
United Kingdom	416	414	76,272	78,515	7.1	7.3	5,206.1	5,344.7	Pounds
United States	2,018	2,019	370,291	382,459	42.8	43.9	42,837.4	43,942.4	Dollars
Venezuela	206	209	37,772	39,588	1.2	1.1	11,657.8	11,377.0	Bolivar
Vietnam	724	725	132,898	137,271	0.6	0.7	13,913.3	14,781.6	Dong*

Note: Due to rounding, establishments will vary by + or - one establishment. Therefore, zero establishments may also be one establishment.

* Local Sales are in trillions

Wireless Telecommunications Carriers (NAICS 51721)

NAICS 51721: Wireless Telecommunications Carriers. This industry comprises establishments primarily engaged in providing two-way radiotelephone communications services, such as cellular telephone services. This business also includes establishments primarily engaged in providing telephone paging and beeper services and those engaged in leasing telephone lines or other methods of telephone transmission, such as optical fiber lines and microwave or satellite facilities, and reselling the use of such methods to others.

COUNTRY ESTIMATES

Country	Establishments		Employment		Sales ($B)		Local Sales (B)		Currency
	2018	2019	2018	2019	2018	2019	2018	2019	
Algeria	371	373	31,140	34,796	0.2	0.2	23.9	24.8	Dinar
Argentina	257	258	21,589	23,999	0.5	0.5	9.4	9.6	Pesos
Australia	160	162	13,434	15,057	1.2	1.3	1.6	1.6	Dollars
Austria	57	57	4,806	5,314	0.3	0.4	0.3	0.3	Euro
Bangladesh	1,129	1,130	94,679	105,316	0.2	0.2	16.7	18.1	Taka
Belgium	72	72	6,025	6,695	0.4	0.4	0.3	0.3	Euro
Brazil	1,375	1,387	115,302	129,193	1.5	1.5	4,853.1	4,882.2	Real
Canada	241	242	20,208	22,513	1.4	1.5	1.8	1.8	Dollars
Chile	133	134	11,179	12,512	0.2	0.3	148.5	154.9	Pesos*
China	9,511	9,479	797,484	883,155	12.6	13.5	81.5	87.5	RMB
Colombia	286	286	23,979	26,648	0.3	0.3	0.8	0.8	Pesos*
Czech Republic	69	68	5,748	6,351	0.2	0.2	3.9	4.1	Koruna
Denmark	36	36	3,024	3,342	0.3	0.3	1.6	1.7	Kroner
Egypt	608	623	51,014	58,051	0.3	0.3	5.4	5.6	Pounds
Finland	36	36	2,995	3,312	0.2	0.2	0.2	0.2	Euro
France	399	398	33,453	37,096	2.0	2.1	1.7	1.7	Euro
Germany	508	501	42,585	46,714	3.1	3.2	2.6	2.7	Euro
Greece	67	66	5,603	6,180	0.2	0.2	0.1	0.1	Euro
Hong Kong	41	41	3,436	3,801	0.2	0.2	1,804.9	1,892.3	Dollar
Hungary	60	59	5,053	5,543	0.1	0.1	28.5	30.2	Forint*
India	7,986	8,107	669,689	755,328	2.0	2.2	127.5	137.8	Rupees
Indonesia	1,986	2,011	166,528	187,408	1.0	1.1	13.4	14.3	Rupiah*

Wireless Telecommunications Carriers (NAICS 51721)

Country Estimates

Country	Establishments 2018	Establishments 2019	Employment 2018	Employment 2019	Sales ($B) 2018	Sales ($B) 2019	Local Sales (B) 2018	Local Sales (B) 2019	Currency
Iran	544	550	45,609	51,278	0.4	0.4	12.9	13.2	Rial*
Iraq	285	290	23,919	26,984	0.2	0.2	0.2	0.2	Dinar*
Ireland	40	41	3,356	3,776	0.5	0.5	0.4	0.5	Euro
Israel	57	57	4,756	5,357	0.3	0.3	1.0	1.1	Shekel
Italy	402	400	33,699	37,268	1.6	1.7	1.3	1.4	Euro
Japan	846	837	70,923	77,996	3.8	4.0	434.2	447.4	Yen*
Kazakhstan	138	138	11,555	12,900	0.2	0.2	62.9	66.0	Tenge
Kuwait	32	34	2,701	3,130	0.1	0.1	0.0	0.0	Dinar
Malaysia	264	268	22,108	24,979	0.4	0.4	1.4	1.5	Ringgit
Mexico	859	869	72,023	80,953	1.0	1.1	20.0	21.0	New pesos
Netherlands	107	107	9,009	9,953	0.7	0.7	0.6	0.6	Euro
New Zealand	29	29	2,423	2,708	0.1	0.2	0.2	0.2	Dollar
Nigeria	1,482	1,506	124,233	140,348	0.5	0.6	190,442.9	199,475.8	Naira
Norway	40	40	3,328	3,710	0.4	0.4	3.2	3.3	Krone
Pakistan	1,187	1,212	99,551	112,912	0.2	0.3	26.0	27.8	Rupees
Peru	235	235	19,706	21,922	0.2	0.2	0.6	0.6	Nuevo Sol
Phillipines	640	651	53,659	60,656	0.3	0.3	14.3	15.5	Pesos
Poland	219	217	18,382	20,200	0.5	0.5	1.6	1.7	Zloty
Portugal	69	69	5,812	6,406	0.2	0.2	0.1	0.1	Euro
Puerto Rico	30	30	2,514	2,750	0.1	0.1	0.1	0.1	Dollar
Qatar	30	34	2,532	3,204	0.2	0.2	0.6	0.7	Riyal
Romania	158	155	13,231	14,468	0.2	0.2	0.7	0.8	New Leu
Russia	980	969	82,182	90,256	1.2	1.2	63.0	63.8	Rubles
Saudi Arabia	275	284	23,055	26,432	0.8	0.8	0.0	0.0	Rials*
Singapore	44	45	3,680	4,187	0.3	0.3	387.9	407.4	Dollar
South Africa	271	274	22,728	25,570	0.3	0.3	3,283.8	3,407.0	Rand
South Korea	383	382	32,125	35,552	1.4	1.5	1,545.5	1,628.0	Won*
Spain	318	320	26,666	29,798	1.1	1.1	926.2	950.7	Euro
Sweden	65	65	5,465	6,063	0.5	0.5	3,901.0	4,128.6	Krona
Switzerland	60	60	4,999	5,569	0.7	0.7	635.5	661.6	Swiss franc
Taiwan	239	247	20,021	22,983	0.5	0.5	14,602.4	15,250.0	Dollar
Thailand	577	580	48,394	54,037	0.4	0.4	13,440.3	14,002.8	Baht
Turkey	437	435	36,671	40,553	0.8	0.8	2,984.6	3,160.6	Euro
Ukraine	319	314	26,751	29,275	0.1	0.1	1,739.1	1,600.1	Hryvna
UAE	149	166	12,467	15,510	0.4	0.4	1,586.5	1,647.0	Dirham
United Kingdom	416	414	34,855	38,617	2.6	2.7	1,899.1	1,993.3	Pounds
United States	2,018	2,019	169,215	188,111	15.6	16.4	15,626.2	16,388.6	Dollars
Venezuela	206	209	17,261	19,471	0.4	0.4	4,252.5	4,243.1	Bolivar
Vietnam	724	725	60,732	67,516	0.2	0.2	5,075.3	5,512.9	Dong*

Note: Due to rounding, establishments will vary by + or - one establishment. Therefore, zero establishments may also be one establishment.

* Local Sales are in trillions

Data Processing Services Industry (NAICS 51821)

NAICS 51821: Data Processing Services. This industry comprises establishments primarily engaged in providing computer processing and data preparation services. The service may consist of complete processing and preparation of reports from data supplied by the customer or a specialized service, such as data entry or making data processing equipment available on an hourly or time-sharing basis.

COUNTRY ESTIMATES

Country	Establishments 2018	Establishments 2019	Employment 2018	Employment 2019	Sales ($B) 2018	Sales ($B) 2019	Local Sales (B) 2018	Local Sales (B) 2019	Currency
Algeria	371	373	18,876	19,631	0.6	0.6	63.6	65.8	Dinar
Argentina	257	258	13,087	13,539	1.3	1.3	25.0	25.5	Pesos
Australia	160	162	8,143	8,494	3.3	3.4	4.1	4.3	Dollars
Austria	57	57	2,913	2,998	0.9	0.9	0.8	0.8	Euro
Bangladesh	1,129	1,130	57,392	59,415	0.5	0.6	44.5	48.1	Taka
Belgium	72	72	3,652	3,777	1.0	1.1	0.9	0.9	Euro
Brazil	1,375	1,387	69,893	72,885	4.0	4.0	12,919.8	12,932.6	Real
Canada	241	242	12,249	12,701	3.8	3.9	4.7	4.9	Dollars
Chile	133	134	6,777	7,059	0.7	0.7	395.2	410.3	Pesos*
China	9,511	9,479	483,414	498,236	33.4	35.7	216.9	231.8	RMB
Colombia	286	286	14,535	15,034	0.7	0.8	2.1	2.2	Pesos*
Czech Republic	69	68	3,484	3,583	0.5	0.5	10.4	11.0	Koruna
Denmark	36	36	1,833	1,885	0.7	0.7	4.4	4.5	Kroner
Egypt	608	623	30,923	32,750	0.8	0.8	14.4	14.9	Pounds
Finland	36	36	1,815	1,869	0.5	0.5	0.4	0.5	Euro
France	399	398	20,278	20,928	5.4	5.5	4.5	4.6	Euro
Germany	508	501	25,814	26,354	8.3	8.6	6.9	7.2	Euro
Greece	67	66	3,396	3,486	0.4	0.4	0.3	0.3	Euro
Hong Kong	41	41	2,083	2,144	0.6	0.6	4,804.9	5,012.5	Dollar
Hungary	60	59	3,063	3,127	0.3	0.3	75.9	80.1	Forint*
India	7,986	8,107	405,947	426,122	5.3	5.7	339.5	365.0	Rupees
Indonesia	1,986	2,011	100,945	105,727	2.7	2.8	35.6	38.0	Rupiah*

DATA PROCESSING SERVICES INDUSTRY
(NAICS 51821)

COUNTRY ESTIMATES

Country	Establishments 2018	2019	Employment 2018	2019	Sales ($B) 2018	2019	Local Sales (B) 2018	2019	Currency
Iran	544	550	27,647	28,929	1.0	1.0	34.5	34.9	Rial*
Iraq	285	290	14,499	15,223	0.5	0.5	0.6	0.6	Dinar*
Ireland	40	41	2,034	2,130	1.2	1.4	1.0	1.2	Euro
Israel	57	57	2,883	3,022	0.8	0.8	2.7	2.8	Shekel
Italy	402	400	20,427	21,025	4.3	4.4	3.6	3.7	Euro
Japan	846	837	42,991	44,002	10.2	10.5	1,156.0	1,185.1	Yen*
Kazakhstan	138	138	7,004	7,277	0.5	0.5	167.5	174.9	Tenge
Kuwait	32	34	1,637	1,766	0.3	0.3	0.1	0.1	Dinar
Malaysia	264	268	13,401	14,092	0.9	1.0	3.8	4.1	Ringgit
Mexico	859	869	43,659	45,670	2.8	2.9	53.3	55.6	New pesos
Netherlands	107	107	5,461	5,615	1.8	1.8	1.5	1.5	Euro
New Zealand	29	29	1,469	1,528	0.4	0.4	0.6	0.6	Dollar
Nigeria	1,482	1,506	75,307	79,178	1.4	1.5	506,989.1	528,396.8	Naira
Norway	40	40	2,017	2,093	1.1	1.1	8.5	8.8	Krone
Pakistan	1,187	1,212	60,345	63,700	0.6	0.7	69.1	73.6	Rupees
Peru	235	235	11,945	12,367	0.5	0.5	1.6	1.7	Nuevo Sol
Phillipines	640	651	32,526	34,219	0.8	0.8	38.0	41.0	Pesos
Poland	219	217	11,142	11,396	1.2	1.3	4.3	4.6	Zloty
Portugal	69	69	3,523	3,614	0.5	0.5	0.4	0.4	Euro
Puerto Rico	30	30	1,524	1,551	0.3	0.3	0.3	0.3	Dollar
Qatar	30	34	1,535	1,807	0.5	0.5	1.7	1.8	Riyal
Romania	158	155	8,020	8,162	0.5	0.5	1.9	2.0	New Leu
Russia	980	969	49,816	50,918	3.3	3.3	167.8	168.9	Rubles
Saudi Arabia	275	284	13,975	14,912	2.0	2.1	0.0	0.0	Rials*
Singapore	44	45	2,231	2,362	0.8	0.8	1,032.8	1,079.2	Dollar
South Africa	271	274	13,777	14,425	0.7	0.7	8,741.9	9,025.0	Rand
South Korea	383	382	19,473	20,057	3.9	4.0	4,114.5	4,312.3	Won*
Spain	318	320	16,164	16,810	3.0	3.0	2,465.6	2,518.5	Euro
Sweden	65	65	3,313	3,420	1.3	1.3	10,385.2	10,936.3	Krona
Switzerland	60	60	3,031	3,142	1.7	1.8	1,691.9	1,752.4	Swiss franc
Taiwan	239	247	12,136	12,966	1.3	1.4	38,874.0	40,396.1	Dollar
Thailand	577	580	29,335	30,485	1.1	1.2	35,780.1	37,092.5	Baht
Turkey	437	435	22,229	22,878	2.1	2.2	7,945.5	8,372.2	Euro
Ukraine	319	314	16,215	16,516	0.2	0.2	4,629.7	4,238.4	Hryvna
UAE	149	166	7,557	8,750	1.2	1.2	4,223.6	4,362.8	Dirham
United Kingdom	416	414	21,128	21,786	6.9	7.2	5,055.6	5,280.2	Pounds
United States	2,018	2,019	102,574	106,124	41.6	43.4	41,599.4	43,412.2	Dollars
Venezuela	206	209	10,463	10,985	1.1	1.1	11,320.9	11,239.7	Bolivar
Vietnam	724	725	36,814	38,089	0.6	0.6	13,511.3	14,603.2	Dong*

Note: Due to rounding, establishments will vary by + or - one establishment. Therefore, zero establishments may also be one establishment.

* Local Sales are in trillions

NAICS 52211: Commercial Banking. This industry comprises commercial banks and trust companies (accepting deposits) chartered under the National Bank Act. Trust companies engaged in fiduciary business, but not regularly engaged in deposit banking, are classified in 6091.

COUNTRY ESTIMATES

Country	Establishments 2018	2019	Employment 2018	2019	Sales ($B) 2018	2019	Local Sales (B) 2018	2019	Currency
Algeria	371	373	93,989	98,620	1.3	1.3	147.6	149.2	Dinar
Argentina	257	258	65,161	68,017	3.0	3.0	58.1	57.8	Pesos
Australia	160	162	40,547	42,675	7.6	7.7	9.6	9.8	Dollars
Austria	57	57	14,507	15,062	2.1	2.1	1.8	1.8	Euro
Bangladesh	1,129	1,130	285,768	298,486	1.2	1.3	103.3	109.0	Taka
Belgium	72	72	18,184	18,976	2.4	2.5	2.0	2.0	Euro
Brazil	1,375	1,387	348,013	366,157	9.3	9.1	29,990.3	29,316.2	Real
Canada	120	121	30,496	31,903	4.4	4.4	5.5	5.5	Dollars
Chile	133	134	33,743	35,461	1.5	1.5	917.4	930.1	Pesos*
China	9,511	9,479	2,407,023	2,503,035	77.6	81.0	503.5	525.4	RMB
Colombia	286	286	72,375	75,526	1.7	1.7	4.8	5.0	Pesos*
Czech Republic	69	68	17,348	17,999	1.1	1.2	24.1	24.8	Koruna
Denmark	36	36	9,126	9,471	1.6	1.6	10.1	10.2	Kroner
Egypt	608	623	153,974	164,528	1.9	1.9	33.5	33.8	Pounds
Finland	36	36	9,039	9,387	1.2	1.2	1.0	1.0	Euro
France	399	398	100,969	105,138	12.5	12.5	10.4	10.5	Euro
Germany	508	501	128,534	132,398	19.2	19.4	16.0	16.2	Euro
Greece	67	66	16,911	17,515	1.0	0.9	0.8	0.8	Euro
Hong Kong	41	41	10,372	10,773	1.4	1.5	11,153.4	11,362.5	Dollar
Hungary	60	59	15,252	15,711	0.7	0.7	176.2	181.6	Forint*
India	7,986	8,107	2,021,301	2,140,748	12.4	13.0	788.1	827.4	Rupees
Indonesia	1,986	2,011	502,628	531,151	6.2	6.4	82.6	86.1	Rupiah*

COMMERCIAL BANKING INDUSTRY
(NAICS 52211)

COUNTRY ESTIMATES

Country	Establishments 2018	Establishments 2019	Employment 2018	Employment 2019	Sales ($B) 2018	Sales ($B) 2019	Local Sales (B) 2018	Local Sales (B) 2019	Currency
Iran	544	550	137,660	145,333	2.2	2.2	80.0	79.2	Rial*
Iraq	285	290	72,194	76,477	1.2	1.2	1.4	1.4	Dinar*
Ireland	40	41	10,129	10,702	2.8	3.2	2.4	2.7	Euro
Israel	57	57	14,354	15,183	1.8	1.9	6.2	6.4	Shekel
Italy	402	400	101,712	105,624	10.0	10.0	8.3	8.3	Euro
Japan	846	837	214,064	221,055	23.8	23.8	2,683.3	2,686.3	Yen*
Kazakhstan	138	138	34,877	36,560	1.2	1.2	388.8	396.5	Tenge
Kuwait	32	34	8,151	8,872	0.7	0.7	0.2	0.2	Dinar
Malaysia	264	268	66,727	70,796	2.2	2.3	8.8	9.2	Ringgit
Mexico	859	869	217,386	229,436	6.4	6.6	123.8	126.0	New pesos
Netherlands	107	107	27,193	28,209	4.1	4.2	3.4	3.5	Euro
New Zealand	29	29	7,312	7,675	0.9	1.0	1.3	1.3	Dollar
Nigeria	1,482	1,506	374,970	397,775	3.3	3.3	1,176,851.2	1,197,789.7	Naira
Norway	40	40	10,045	10,514	2.4	2.5	19.8	20.0	Krone
Pakistan	1,187	1,212	300,470	320,014	1.4	1.5	160.5	166.9	Rupees
Peru	235	235	59,478	62,131	1.2	1.2	3.8	3.8	Nuevo Sol
Phillipines	640	651	161,956	171,911	1.8	1.9	88.3	93.0	Pesos
Poland	219	217	55,480	57,252	2.9	3.0	10.1	10.4	Zloty
Portugal	69	69	17,541	18,155	1.1	1.1	0.9	0.9	Euro
Puerto Rico	30	30	7,589	7,793	0.7	0.6	0.7	0.6	Dollar
Qatar	30	34	7,641	9,080	1.1	1.1	4.0	4.0	Riyal
Romania	158	155	39,934	41,005	1.2	1.2	4.5	4.6	New Leu
Russia	980	969	248,046	255,804	7.6	7.5	389.4	382.9	Rubles
Saudi Arabia	275	284	69,587	74,912	4.7	4.7	0.0	0.0	Rials*
Singapore	44	45	11,107	11,866	1.8	1.8	2,397.3	2,446.4	Dollar
South Africa	271	274	68,599	72,470	1.6	1.6	20,292.2	20,458.2	Rand
South Korea	383	382	96,961	100,762	9.0	9.2	9,550.8	9,775.3	Won*
Spain	318	320	80,486	84,452	6.9	6.8	5,723.4	5,708.9	Euro
Sweden	65	65	16,494	17,183	2.9	3.0	24,106.7	24,790.9	Krona
Switzerland	60	60	15,090	15,784	4.0	4.1	3,927.3	3,972.4	Swiss franc
Taiwan	239	247	60,428	65,137	3.1	3.1	90,236.5	91,571.5	Dollar
Thailand	577	580	146,066	153,152	2.6	2.6	83,054.7	84,082.6	Baht
Turkey	437	435	110,682	114,937	4.9	5.1	18,443.6	18,978.5	Euro
Ukraine	319	314	80,740	82,971	0.4	0.3	10,746.7	9,607.8	Hryvna
UAE	149	166	37,629	43,958	2.7	2.7	9,804.0	9,889.7	Dirham
United Kingdom	416	414	105,201	109,449	15.9	16.2	11,735.4	11,969.3	Pounds
United States	2,018	2,019	510,738	533,143	96.6	98.4	96,562.8	98,408.3	Dollars
Venezuela	206	209	52,099	55,185	2.6	2.6	26,278.7	25,478.6	Bolivar
Vietnam	724	725	183,305	191,353	1.4	1.5	31,363.1	33,103.1	Dong*

Note: Due to rounding, establishments will vary by + or - one establishment. Therefore, zero establishments may also be one establishment.

* Local Sales are in trillions

Mortgage & Non-Mortgage Loan Brokers (NAICS 52231)

NAICS 52231: Mortgage & Non-Mortgage Loan Brokers. This industry comprises establishments primarily engaged in arranging loans for others. These establishments operate mostly on a commission or fee basis and do not ordinarily have any continuing relationship with either borrower or lender.

Country Estimates

Country	Establishments 2018	2019	Employment 2018	2019	Sales ($B) 2018	2019	Local Sales (B) 2018	2019	Currency
Algeria	371	373	1,436	1,418	0.1	0.1	11.4	11.2	Dinar
Argentina	257	258	996	978	0.2	0.2	4.5	4.3	Pesos
Australia	160	162	620	614	0.6	0.6	0.7	0.7	Dollars
Austria	57	57	222	217	0.2	0.2	0.1	0.1	Euro
Bangladesh	1,129	1,130	4,366	4,291	0.1	0.1	7.9	8.2	Taka
Belgium	72	72	278	273	0.2	0.2	0.2	0.2	Euro
Brazil	1,375	1,387	5,317	5,264	0.7	0.7	2,307.7	2,194.7	Real
Canada	241	242	932	917	0.7	0.7	0.8	0.8	Dollars
Chile	133	134	516	510	0.1	0.1	70.6	69.6	Pesos*
China	9,511	9,479	36,778	35,987	6.0	6.1	38.7	39.3	RMB
Colombia	286	286	1,106	1,086	0.1	0.1	0.4	0.4	Pesos*
Czech Republic	69	68	265	259	0.1	0.1	1.9	1.9	Koruna
Denmark	36	36	139	136	0.1	0.1	0.8	0.8	Kroner
Egypt	608	623	2,353	2,365	0.1	0.1	2.6	2.5	Pounds
Finland	36	36	138	135	0.1	0.1	0.1	0.1	Euro
France	399	398	1,543	1,512	1.0	0.9	0.8	0.8	Euro
Germany	508	501	1,964	1,904	1.5	1.5	1.2	1.2	Euro
Greece	67	66	258	252	0.1	0.1	0.1	0.1	Euro
Hong Kong	41	41	158	155	0.1	0.1	858.3	850.6	Dollar
Hungary	60	59	233	226	0.1	0.1	13.6	13.6	Forint*
India	7,986	8,107	30,884	30,778	1.0	1.0	60.6	61.9	Rupees
Indonesia	1,986	2,011	7,680	7,637	0.5	0.5	6.4	6.4	Rupiah*

Mortgage & Non-Mortgage Loan Brokers (NAICS 52231)

Country Estimates

Country	Establishments 2018	2019	Employment 2018	2019	Sales ($B) 2018	2019	Local Sales (B) 2018	2019	Currency
Iran	544	550	2,103	2,090	0.2	0.2	6.2	5.9	Rial*
Iraq	285	290	1,103	1,100	0.1	0.1	0.1	0.1	Dinar*
Ireland	40	41	155	154	0.2	0.2	0.2	0.2	Euro
Israel	57	57	219	218	0.1	0.1	0.5	0.5	Shekel
Italy	402	400	1,554	1,519	0.8	0.7	0.6	0.6	Euro
Japan	846	837	3,271	3,178	1.8	1.8	206.5	201.1	Yen*
Kazakhstan	138	138	533	526	0.1	0.1	29.9	29.7	Tenge
Kuwait	32	34	125	128	0.1	0.1	0.0	0.0	Dinar
Malaysia	264	268	1,020	1,018	0.2	0.2	0.7	0.7	Ringgit
Mexico	859	869	3,322	3,299	0.5	0.5	9.5	9.4	New pesos
Netherlands	107	107	415	406	0.3	0.3	0.3	0.3	Euro
New Zealand	29	29	112	110	0.1	0.1	0.1	0.1	Dollar
Nigeria	1,482	1,506	5,729	5,719	0.3	0.2	90,558.2	89,671.9	Naira
Norway	40	40	153	151	0.2	0.2	1.5	1.5	Krone
Pakistan	1,187	1,212	4,591	4,601	0.1	0.1	12.4	12.5	Rupees
Peru	235	235	909	893	0.1	0.1	0.3	0.3	Nuevo Sol
Phillipines	640	651	2,475	2,472	0.1	0.1	6.8	7.0	Pesos
Poland	219	217	848	823	0.2	0.2	0.8	0.8	Zloty
Portugal	69	69	268	261	0.1	0.1	0.1	0.1	Euro
Puerto Rico	30	30	116	112	0.1	0.0	0.1	0.0	Dollar
Qatar	30	34	117	131	0.1	0.1	0.3	0.3	Riyal
Romania	158	155	610	590	0.1	0.1	0.3	0.3	New Leu
Russia	980	969	3,790	3,678	0.6	0.6	30.0	28.7	Rubles
Saudi Arabia	275	284	1,063	1,077	0.4	0.4	0.0	0.0	Rials*
Singapore	44	45	170	171	0.1	0.1	184.5	183.1	Dollar
South Africa	271	274	1,048	1,042	0.1	0.1	1,561.5	1,531.6	Rand
South Korea	383	382	1,482	1,449	0.7	0.7	734.9	731.8	Won*
Spain	318	320	1,230	1,214	0.5	0.5	440.4	427.4	Euro
Sweden	65	65	252	247	0.2	0.2	1,855.0	1,856.0	Krona
Switzerland	60	60	231	227	0.3	0.3	302.2	297.4	Swiss franc
Taiwan	239	247	923	937	0.2	0.2	6,943.7	6,855.5	Dollar
Thailand	577	580	2,232	2,202	0.2	0.2	6,391.0	6,294.8	Baht
Turkey	437	435	1,691	1,652	0.4	0.4	1,419.2	1,420.8	Euro
Ukraine	319	314	1,234	1,193	0.0	0.0	827.0	719.3	Hryvna
UAE	149	166	575	632	0.2	0.2	754.4	740.4	Dirham
United Kingdom	416	414	1,607	1,574	1.2	1.2	903.0	896.1	Pounds
United States	2,018	2,019	7,804	7,665	7.4	7.4	7,430.5	7,367.3	Dollars
Venezuela	206	209	796	793	0.2	0.2	2,022.1	1,907.4	Bolivar
Vietnam	724	725	2,801	2,751	0.1	0.1	2,413.4	2,478.2	Dong*

Note: Due to rounding, establishments will vary by + or - one establishment. Therefore, zero establishments may also be one establishment.

* Local Sales are in trillions

NAICS 52311: Investment Banking & Securities Dealing. This industry compromises establishments primarily engaged in the purchase, sale, and brokerage of securities; and those, generally known as investment bankers, primarily engaged in originating, underwriting, and distributing issues of securities. Establishments primarily engaged in issuing shares of mutual and money market funds, unit investment trusts, and face amount certificates are classified in 6722 or 6726.

COUNTRY ESTIMATES

Country	Establishments 2018	Establishments 2019	Employment 2018	Employment 2019	Sales ($B) 2018	Sales ($B) 2019	Local Sales (B) 2018	Local Sales (B) 2019	Currency
Algeria	186	187	11,711	12,822	0.0	0.0	3.8	3.7	Dinar
Argentina	129	129	8,119	8,843	0.1	0.1	1.5	1.4	Pesos
Australia	80	81	5,052	5,548	0.2	0.2	0.2	0.2	Dollars
Austria	29	29	1,807	1,958	0.1	0.1	0.0	0.0	Euro
Bangladesh	565	565	35,606	38,807	0.0	0.0	2.7	2.7	Taka
Belgium	36	36	2,266	2,467	0.1	0.1	0.1	0.1	Euro
Brazil	688	693	43,361	47,606	0.2	0.2	776.1	733.1	Real
Canada	120	121	7,599	8,296	0.2	0.2	0.3	0.3	Dollars
Chile	67	67	4,204	4,610	0.0	0.0	23.7	23.3	Pesos*
China	4,755	4,739	299,905	325,430	2.0	2.0	13.0	13.1	RMB
Colombia	143	143	9,018	9,819	0.0	0.0	0.1	0.1	Pesos*
Czech Republic	34	34	2,161	2,340	0.0	0.0	0.6	0.6	Koruna
Denmark	18	18	1,137	1,231	0.0	0.0	0.3	0.3	Kroner
Egypt	304	312	19,185	21,391	0.0	0.0	0.9	0.8	Pounds
Finland	18	18	1,126	1,221	0.0	0.0	0.0	0.0	Euro
France	199	199	12,580	13,669	0.3	0.3	0.3	0.3	Euro
Germany	254	251	16,015	17,214	0.5	0.5	0.4	0.4	Euro
Greece	33	33	2,107	2,277	0.0	0.0	0.0	0.0	Euro
Hong Kong	20	20	1,292	1,401	0.0	0.0	288.6	284.1	Dollar
Hungary	30	30	1,900	2,043	0.0	0.0	4.6	4.5	Forint*
India	3,993	4,053	251,846	278,327	0.3	0.3	20.4	20.7	Rupees
Indonesia	993	1,006	62,625	69,057	0.2	0.2	2.1	2.2	Rupiah*

Investment Banking & Securities Dealing (NAICS 52311)

Country Estimates

Country	Establishments 2018	2019	Employment 2018	2019	Sales ($B) 2018	2019	Local Sales (B) 2018	2019	Currency
Iran	272	275	17,152	18,895	0.1	0.1	2.1	2.0	Rial*
Iraq	143	145	8,995	9,943	0.0	0.0	0.0	0.0	Dinar*
Ireland	20	20	1,262	1,391	0.1	0.1	0.1	0.1	Euro
Israel	28	29	1,788	1,974	0.0	0.0	0.2	0.2	Shekel
Italy	201	200	12,673	13,733	0.3	0.2	0.2	0.2	Euro
Japan	423	419	26,671	28,740	0.6	0.6	69.4	67.2	Yen*
Kazakhstan	69	69	4,345	4,753	0.0	0.0	10.1	9.9	Tenge
Kuwait	16	17	1,016	1,153	0.0	0.0	0.0	0.0	Dinar
Malaysia	132	134	8,314	9,205	0.1	0.1	0.2	0.2	Ringgit
Mexico	429	434	27,085	29,830	0.2	0.2	3.2	3.2	New pesos
Netherlands	54	53	3,388	3,668	0.1	0.1	0.1	0.1	Euro
New Zealand	14	15	911	998	0.0	0.0	0.0	0.0	Dollar
Nigeria	741	753	46,720	51,716	0.1	0.1	30,453.2	29,950.8	Naira
Norway	20	20	1,252	1,367	0.1	0.1	0.5	0.5	Krone
Pakistan	594	606	37,437	41,606	0.0	0.0	4.2	4.2	Rupees
Peru	118	118	7,411	8,078	0.0	0.0	0.1	0.1	Nuevo Sol
Phillipines	320	326	20,179	22,351	0.0	0.0	2.3	2.3	Pesos
Poland	110	108	6,913	7,444	0.1	0.1	0.3	0.3	Zloty
Portugal	35	34	2,186	2,360	0.0	0.0	0.0	0.0	Euro
Puerto Rico	15	15	946	1,013	0.0	0.0	0.0	0.0	Dollar
Qatar	15	17	952	1,181	0.0	0.0	0.1	0.1	Riyal
Romania	79	78	4,976	5,331	0.0	0.0	0.1	0.1	New Leu
Russia	490	484	30,906	33,258	0.2	0.2	10.1	9.6	Rubles
Saudi Arabia	137	142	8,670	9,740	0.1	0.1	0.0	0.0	Rials*
Singapore	22	22	1,384	1,543	0.0	0.0	62.0	61.2	Dollar
South Africa	136	137	8,547	9,422	0.0	0.0	525.1	511.6	Rand
South Korea	192	191	12,081	13,100	0.2	0.2	247.1	244.4	Won*
Spain	159	160	10,028	10,980	0.2	0.2	148.1	142.8	Euro
Sweden	33	33	2,055	2,234	0.1	0.1	623.8	619.9	Krona
Switzerland	30	30	1,880	2,052	0.1	0.1	101.6	99.3	Swiss franc
Taiwan	119	123	7,529	8,469	0.1	0.1	2,335.0	2,289.7	Dollar
Thailand	289	290	18,199	19,912	0.1	0.1	2,149.2	2,102.5	Baht
Turkey	219	218	13,790	14,943	0.1	0.1	477.3	474.6	Euro
Ukraine	160	157	10,060	10,787	0.0	0.0	278.1	240.2	Hryvna
UAE	74	83	4,688	5,715	0.1	0.1	253.7	247.3	Dirham
United Kingdom	208	207	13,108	14,230	0.4	0.4	303.7	299.3	Pounds
United States	2,018	2,019	127,272	138,632	5.0	4.9	4,997.5	4,921.4	Dollars
Venezuela	103	104	6,491	7,175	0.1	0.1	680.0	637.1	Bolivar
Vietnam	362	362	22,839	24,879	0.0	0.0	811.6	827.7	Dong*

Note: Due to rounding, establishments will vary by + or - one establishment. Therefore, zero establishments may also be one establishment.

* Local Sales are in trillions

Securities Brokerage Industry (NAICS 52312)

NAICS 52312: Securities Brokerage Industry. This industry comprises establishments primarily engaged in the purchase, sale, and brokerage of securities; and those, generally known as investment bankers, primarily engaged in originating, underwriting, and distributing issues of securities. Establishments primarily engaged in issuing shares of mutual and money market funds, unit investment trusts, and face amount certificates are classified in 6722 or 6726.

COUNTRY ESTIMATES

Country	Establishments 2018	Establishments 2019	Employment 2018	Employment 2019	Sales ($B) 2018	Sales ($B) 2019	Local Sales (B) 2018	Local Sales (B) 2019	Currency
Algeria	186	187	16,943	18,586	0.3	0.3	35.2	36.2	Dinar
Argentina	129	129	11,746	12,819	0.7	0.7	13.8	14.0	Pesos
Australia	80	81	7,309	8,043	1.8	1.9	2.3	2.4	Dollars
Austria	29	29	2,615	2,839	0.5	0.5	0.4	0.4	Euro
Bangladesh	565	565	51,515	56,254	0.3	0.3	24.6	26.5	Taka
Belgium	36	36	3,278	3,576	0.6	0.6	0.5	0.5	Euro
Brazil	688	693	62,736	69,008	2.2	2.2	7,149.3	7,124.2	Real
Canada	120	121	10,995	12,025	2.1	2.2	2.6	2.7	Dollars
Chile	67	67	6,083	6,683	0.4	0.4	218.7	226.0	Pesos*
China	4,755	4,739	433,909	471,734	18.5	19.7	120.0	127.7	RMB
Colombia	143	143	13,047	14,234	0.4	0.4	1.2	1.2	Pesos*
Czech Republic	34	34	3,127	3,392	0.3	0.3	5.7	6.0	Koruna
Denmark	18	18	1,645	1,785	0.4	0.4	2.4	2.5	Kroner
Egypt	304	312	27,757	31,008	0.5	0.5	8.0	8.2	Pounds
Finland	18	18	1,630	1,769	0.3	0.3	0.2	0.2	Euro
France	199	199	18,201	19,815	3.0	3.0	2.5	2.5	Euro
Germany	254	251	23,171	24,952	4.6	4.7	3.8	3.9	Euro
Greece	33	33	3,048	3,301	0.2	0.2	0.2	0.2	Euro
Hong Kong	20	20	1,870	2,030	0.3	0.4	2,658.9	2,761.2	Dollar
Hungary	30	30	2,750	2,961	0.2	0.2	42.0	44.1	Forint*
India	3,993	4,053	364,376	403,456	3.0	3.2	187.9	201.1	Rupees
Indonesia	993	1,006	90,608	100,103	1.5	1.6	19.7	20.9	Rupiah*

SECURITIES BROKERAGE INDUSTRY
(NAICS 52312)

COUNTRY ESTIMATES

Country	Establishments 2018	2019	Employment 2018	2019	Sales ($B) 2018	2019	Local Sales (B) 2018	2019	Currency
Iran	272	275	24,816	27,390	0.5	0.5	19.1	19.2	Rial*
Iraq	143	145	13,014	14,413	0.3	0.3	0.3	0.3	Dinar*
Ireland	20	20	1,826	2,017	0.7	0.8	0.6	0.7	Euro
Israel	28	29	2,588	2,861	0.4	0.4	1.5	1.5	Shekel
Italy	201	200	18,335	19,906	2.4	2.4	2.0	2.0	Euro
Japan	423	419	38,589	41,661	5.7	5.8	639.7	652.8	Yen*
Kazakhstan	69	69	6,287	6,890	0.3	0.3	92.7	96.4	Tenge
Kuwait	16	17	1,469	1,672	0.2	0.2	0.0	0.0	Dinar
Malaysia	132	134	12,029	13,343	0.5	0.6	2.1	2.2	Ringgit
Mexico	429	434	39,188	43,241	1.5	1.6	29.5	30.6	New pesos
Netherlands	54	53	4,902	5,316	1.0	1.0	0.8	0.8	Euro
New Zealand	14	15	1,318	1,446	0.2	0.2	0.3	0.3	Dollar
Nigeria	741	753	67,595	74,967	0.8	0.8	280,548.0	291,078.0	Naira
Norway	20	20	1,811	1,982	0.6	0.6	4.7	4.9	Krone
Pakistan	594	606	54,165	60,311	0.3	0.4	38.3	40.5	Rupees
Peru	118	118	10,722	11,709	0.3	0.3	0.9	0.9	Nuevo Sol
Phillipines	320	326	29,195	32,399	0.4	0.5	21.0	22.6	Pesos
Poland	110	108	10,001	10,790	0.7	0.7	2.4	2.5	Zloty
Portugal	35	34	3,162	3,422	0.3	0.3	0.2	0.2	Euro
Puerto Rico	15	15	1,368	1,469	0.2	0.2	0.2	0.2	Dollar
Qatar	15	17	1,377	1,711	0.3	0.3	1.0	1.0	Riyal
Romania	79	78	7,199	7,728	0.3	0.3	1.1	1.1	New Leu
Russia	490	484	44,715	48,210	1.8	1.8	92.8	93.1	Rubles
Saudi Arabia	137	142	12,544	14,118	1.1	1.1	0.0	0.0	Rials*
Singapore	22	22	2,002	2,236	0.4	0.4	571.5	594.5	Dollar
South Africa	136	137	12,366	13,658	0.4	0.4	4,837.4	4,971.6	Rand
South Korea	192	191	17,479	18,990	2.1	2.2	2,276.8	2,375.5	Won*
Spain	159	160	14,509	15,916	1.6	1.7	1,364.4	1,387.3	Euro
Sweden	33	33	2,973	3,238	0.7	0.7	5,746.8	6,024.5	Krona
Switzerland	30	30	2,720	2,975	1.0	1.0	936.2	965.3	Swiss franc
Taiwan	119	123	10,893	12,276	0.7	0.8	21,511.3	22,253.0	Dollar
Thailand	289	290	26,331	28,864	0.6	0.6	19,799.3	20,433.1	Baht
Turkey	219	218	19,952	21,662	1.2	1.2	4,396.7	4,612.0	Euro
Ukraine	160	157	14,555	15,637	0.1	0.1	2,561.9	2,334.8	Hryvna
UAE	74	83	6,783	8,285	0.6	0.7	2,337.2	2,403.3	Dirham
United Kingdom	208	207	18,964	20,627	3.8	3.9	2,797.6	2,908.7	Pounds
United States	2,018	2,019	184,139	200,957	46.0	47.8	46,039.0	47,828.9	Dollars
Venezuela	103	104	9,392	10,400	0.6	0.6	6,264.5	6,191.6	Bolivar
Vietnam	362	362	33,044	36,063	0.3	0.4	7,476.6	8,044.5	Dong*

Note: Due to rounding, establishments will vary by + or - one establishment. Therefore, zero establishments may also be one establishment.

* Local Sales are in trillions

LIFE INSURANCE CARRIERS INDUSTRY
(NAICS 524113)

NAICS 524113: Life Insurance Carriers. This industry comprises establishments primarily engaged in underwriting life insurance. These establishments are operated by enterprises that may be owned by stockholders, policyholders, or other carriers.

COUNTRY ESTIMATES

Country	Establishments 2018	2019	Employment 2018	2019	Sales ($B) 2018	2019	Local Sales (B) 2018	2019	Currency
Algeria	371	373	117,939	124,344	0.1	0.1	15.0	15.3	Dinar
Argentina	257	258	81,765	85,758	0.3	0.3	5.9	5.9	Pesos
Australia	160	162	50,879	53,806	0.8	0.8	1.0	1.0	Dollars
Austria	57	57	18,203	18,991	0.2	0.2	0.2	0.2	Euro
Bangladesh	1,129	1,130	358,587	376,345	0.1	0.1	10.5	11.2	Taka
Belgium	72	72	22,818	23,925	0.2	0.3	0.2	0.2	Euro
Brazil	1,375	1,387	436,693	461,668	0.9	0.9	3,051.2	3,006.4	Real
Canada	241	242	76,535	80,449	0.9	0.9	1.1	1.1	Dollars
Chile	133	134	42,341	44,711	0.2	0.2	93.3	95.4	Pesos*
China	9,511	9,479	3,020,379	3,155,939	7.9	8.3	51.2	53.9	RMB
Colombia	286	286	90,818	95,227	0.2	0.2	0.5	0.5	Pesos*
Czech Republic	69	68	21,768	22,694	0.1	0.1	2.4	2.5	Koruna
Denmark	36	36	11,452	11,942	0.2	0.2	1.0	1.0	Kroner
Egypt	608	623	193,210	207,444	0.2	0.2	3.4	3.5	Pounds
Finland	36	36	11,343	11,836	0.1	0.1	0.1	0.1	Euro
France	399	398	126,698	132,563	1.3	1.3	1.1	1.1	Euro
Germany	508	501	161,287	166,933	2.0	2.0	1.6	1.7	Euro
Greece	67	66	21,220	22,084	0.1	0.1	0.1	0.1	Euro
Hong Kong	41	41	13,014	13,583	0.1	0.1	1,134.7	1,165.2	Dollar
Hungary	60	59	19,139	19,809	0.1	0.1	17.9	18.6	Forint*
India	7,986	8,107	2,536,368	2,699,151	1.3	1.3	80.2	84.8	Rupees
Indonesia	1,986	2,011	630,707	669,700	0.6	0.7	8.4	8.8	Rupiah*

LIFE INSURANCE CARRIERS INDUSTRY
(NAICS 524113)

COUNTRY ESTIMATES

Country	Establishments 2018	2019	Employment 2018	2019	Sales ($B) 2018	2019	Local Sales (B) 2018	2019	Currency
Iran	544	550	172,738	183,242	0.2	0.2	8.1	8.1	Rial*
Iraq	285	290	90,591	96,425	0.1	0.1	0.1	0.1	Dinar*
Ireland	40	41	12,711	13,493	0.3	0.3	0.2	0.3	Euro
Israel	57	57	18,011	19,143	0.2	0.2	0.6	0.7	Shekel
Italy	402	400	127,630	133,175	1.0	1.0	0.8	0.9	Euro
Japan	846	837	268,611	278,716	2.4	2.4	273.0	275.5	Yen*
Kazakhstan	138	138	43,764	46,097	0.1	0.1	39.6	40.7	Tenge
Kuwait	32	34	10,228	11,186	0.1	0.1	0.0	0.0	Dinar
Malaysia	264	268	83,731	89,263	0.2	0.2	0.9	0.9	Ringgit
Mexico	859	869	272,780	289,284	0.7	0.7	12.6	12.9	New pesos
Netherlands	107	107	34,122	35,567	0.4	0.4	0.3	0.4	Euro
New Zealand	29	29	9,176	9,677	0.1	0.1	0.1	0.1	Dollar
Nigeria	1,482	1,506	470,519	501,533	0.3	0.3	119,731.1	122,832.6	Naira
Norway	40	40	12,605	13,256	0.2	0.3	2.0	2.1	Krone
Pakistan	1,187	1,212	377,036	403,488	0.1	0.2	16.3	17.1	Rupees
Peru	235	235	74,634	78,337	0.1	0.1	0.4	0.4	Nuevo Sol
Phillipines	640	651	203,226	216,753	0.2	0.2	9.0	9.5	Pesos
Poland	219	217	69,618	72,186	0.3	0.3	1.0	1.1	Zloty
Portugal	69	69	22,011	22,891	0.1	0.1	0.1	0.1	Euro
Puerto Rico	30	30	9,523	9,826	0.1	0.1	0.1	0.1	Dollar
Qatar	30	34	9,588	11,449	0.1	0.1	0.4	0.4	Riyal
Romania	158	155	50,110	51,701	0.1	0.1	0.5	0.5	New Leu
Russia	980	969	311,253	322,529	0.8	0.8	39.6	39.3	Rubles
Saudi Arabia	275	284	87,319	94,453	0.5	0.5	0.0	0.0	Rials*
Singapore	44	45	13,938	14,961	0.2	0.2	243.9	250.9	Dollar
South Africa	271	274	86,079	91,373	0.2	0.2	2,064.5	2,098.0	Rand
South Korea	383	382	121,669	127,045	0.9	0.9	971.7	1,002.5	Won*
Spain	318	320	100,995	106,481	0.7	0.7	582.3	585.4	Euro
Sweden	65	65	20,697	21,665	0.3	0.3	2,452.6	2,542.3	Krona
Switzerland	60	60	18,935	19,901	0.4	0.4	399.6	407.4	Swiss franc
Taiwan	239	247	75,826	82,128	0.3	0.3	9,180.5	9,390.6	Dollar
Thailand	577	580	183,287	193,101	0.3	0.3	8,449.9	8,622.6	Baht
Turkey	437	435	138,886	144,917	0.5	0.5	1,876.4	1,946.2	Euro
Ukraine	319	314	101,315	104,613	0.0	0.0	1,093.4	985.3	Hryvna
UAE	149	166	47,218	55,425	0.3	0.3	997.4	1,014.2	Dirham
United Kingdom	416	414	132,009	137,998	1.6	1.7	1,193.9	1,227.4	Pounds
United States	2,018	2,019	640,883	672,210	9.8	10.1	9,824.2	10,091.7	Dollars
Venezuela	206	209	65,374	69,579	0.3	0.3	2,673.6	2,612.8	Bolivar
Vietnam	724	725	230,014	241,267	0.1	0.1	3,190.8	3,394.7	Dong*

Note: Due to rounding, establishments will vary by + or - one establishment. Therefore, zero establishments may also be one establishment.

* Local Sales are in trillions

© Barnes Reports: 2018 World Industry & Market Outlook

Health & Medical Insurance Carriers (NAICS 524114)

NAICS 524114: Health & Medical Insurance Carrier. This industry comprises establishments primarily engaged in providing hospital, medical, and other health services to subscribers or members in accordance with prearranged agreements or service plans, generally in return for specified subscription charges. The plans may be through a contract with a participating hospital or physician. Other plans provide for partial indemnity and service benefits. Includes separate establishments of HMOs which provide insurance.

COUNTRY ESTIMATES

Country	Establishments 2018	Establishments 2019	Employment 2018	Employment 2019	Sales ($B) 2018	Sales ($B) 2019	Local Sales (B) 2018	Local Sales (B) 2019	Currency
Algeria	371	373	126,873	139,500	0.1	0.1	8.6	8.8	Dinar
Argentina	257	258	87,959	96,212	0.2	0.2	3.4	3.4	Pesos
Australia	160	162	54,733	60,364	0.4	0.5	0.6	0.6	Dollars
Austria	29	29	9,791	10,653	0.1	0.1	0.1	0.1	Euro
Bangladesh	565	565	192,875	211,109	0.0	0.0	3.0	3.2	Taka
Belgium	36	36	12,273	13,421	0.1	0.1	0.1	0.1	Euro
Brazil	1,375	1,387	469,773	517,941	0.5	0.5	1,740.9	1,735.5	Real
Canada	120	121	41,166	45,128	0.3	0.3	0.3	0.3	Dollars
Chile	133	134	45,548	50,161	0.1	0.1	53.3	55.1	Pesos*
China	9,511	9,479	3,249,177	3,540,622	4.5	4.8	29.2	31.1	RMB
Colombia	286	286	97,697	106,834	0.1	0.1	0.3	0.3	Pesos*
Czech Republic	69	68	23,417	25,460	0.1	0.1	1.4	1.5	Koruna
Denmark	18	18	6,160	6,699	0.0	0.0	0.3	0.3	Kroner
Egypt	608	623	207,846	232,730	0.1	0.1	1.9	2.0	Pounds
Finland	18	18	6,101	6,639	0.0	0.0	0.0	0.0	Euro
France	199	199	68,148	74,361	0.4	0.4	0.3	0.3	Euro
Germany	254	251	86,752	93,640	0.6	0.6	0.5	0.5	Euro
Greece	33	33	11,414	12,388	0.0	0.0	0.0	0.0	Euro
Hong Kong	41	41	14,000	15,238	0.1	0.1	647.5	672.6	Dollar
Hungary	60	59	20,589	22,224	0.0	0.0	10.2	10.8	Forint*
India	7,986	8,107	2,728,502	3,028,156	0.7	0.8	45.7	49.0	Rupees
Indonesia	1,986	2,011	678,484	751,331	0.4	0.4	4.8	5.1	Rupiah*

HEALTH & MEDICAL INSURANCE CARRIERS (NAICS 524114)

COUNTRY ESTIMATES

Country	Establishments 2018	2019	Employment 2018	2019	Sales ($B) 2018	2019	Local Sales (B) 2018	2019	Currency
Iran	544	550	185,823	205,578	0.1	0.1	4.6	4.7	Rial*
Iraq	143	145	48,727	54,089	0.0	0.0	0.0	0.0	Dinar*
Ireland	20	20	6,837	7,569	0.1	0.1	0.1	0.1	Euro
Israel	57	57	19,376	21,476	0.1	0.1	0.4	0.4	Shekel
Italy	201	200	68,649	74,704	0.3	0.3	0.2	0.2	Euro
Japan	846	837	288,959	312,689	1.4	1.4	155.8	159.0	Yen*
Kazakhstan	138	138	47,079	51,716	0.1	0.1	22.6	23.5	Tenge
Kuwait	32	34	11,003	12,550	0.0	0.0	0.0	0.0	Dinar
Malaysia	264	268	90,073	100,144	0.1	0.1	0.5	0.5	Ringgit
Mexico	859	869	293,443	324,545	0.4	0.4	7.2	7.5	New pesos
Netherlands	54	53	18,353	19,951	0.1	0.1	0.1	0.1	Euro
New Zealand	29	29	9,871	10,857	0.1	0.1	0.1	0.1	Dollar
Nigeria	741	753	253,081	281,333	0.1	0.1	34,158.2	35,453.4	Naira
Norway	20	20	6,780	7,436	0.1	0.1	0.6	0.6	Krone
Pakistan	1,187	1,212	405,597	452,670	0.1	0.1	9.3	9.9	Rupees
Peru	235	235	80,288	87,886	0.1	0.1	0.2	0.2	Nuevo Sol
Phillipines	640	651	218,620	243,173	0.1	0.1	5.1	5.5	Pesos
Poland	219	217	74,892	80,985	0.2	0.2	0.6	0.6	Zloty
Portugal	35	34	11,839	12,841	0.0	0.0	0.0	0.0	Euro
Puerto Rico	30	30	10,244	11,024	0.0	0.0	0.0	0.0	Dollar
Qatar	30	34	10,314	12,844	0.1	0.1	0.2	0.2	Riyal
Romania	158	155	53,906	58,003	0.1	0.1	0.3	0.3	New Leu
Russia	980	969	334,831	361,843	0.4	0.4	22.6	22.7	Rubles
Saudi Arabia	275	284	93,933	105,966	0.3	0.3	0.0	0.0	Rials*
Singapore	44	45	14,993	16,784	0.1	0.1	139.2	144.8	Dollar
South Africa	271	274	92,600	102,511	0.1	0.1	1,178.0	1,211.1	Rand
South Korea	383	382	130,885	142,531	0.5	0.5	554.4	578.7	Won*
Spain	159	160	54,323	59,730	0.2	0.2	166.1	169.0	Euro
Sweden	33	33	11,132	12,153	0.1	0.1	699.7	733.8	Krona
Switzerland	30	30	10,185	11,163	0.1	0.1	114.0	117.6	Swiss franc
Taiwan	239	247	81,570	92,139	0.2	0.2	5,238.2	5,420.9	Dollar
Thailand	577	580	197,171	216,639	0.1	0.2	4,821.3	4,977.5	Baht
Turkey	437	435	149,406	162,581	0.3	0.3	1,070.7	1,123.5	Euro
Ukraine	160	157	54,495	58,682	0.0	0.0	311.9	284.4	Hryvna
UAE	74	83	25,397	31,090	0.1	0.1	284.6	292.7	Dirham
United Kingdom	208	207	71,004	77,409	0.5	0.5	340.6	354.3	Pounds
United States	2,018	2,019	689,431	754,147	5.6	5.8	5,605.5	5,825.6	Dollars
Venezuela	206	209	70,326	78,060	0.2	0.2	1,525.5	1,508.3	Bolivar
Vietnam	724	725	247,438	270,675	0.1	0.1	1,820.6	1,959.6	Dong*

Note: Due to rounding, establishments will vary by + or - one establishment. Therefore, zero establishments may also be one establishment.

* Local Sales are in trillions

PROPERTY & CASUALTY INSURANCE CARRIERS (NAICS 524126)

NAICS 524126: Property & Casualty Insurance Carriers. This industry comprises establishments primarily engaged in underwriting fire, marine, and casualty insurance. These establishments are operated by enterprises that may be owned by stockholders, policyholders, or other carriers.

COUNTRY ESTIMATES

Country	Establishments 2018	2019	Employment 2018	2019	Sales ($B) 2018	2019	Local Sales (B) 2018	2019	Currency
Algeria	371	373	90,558	95,651	0.2	0.2	18.6	18.2	Dinar
Argentina	257	258	62,782	65,969	0.4	0.4	7.3	7.0	Pesos
Australia	160	162	39,067	41,390	1.0	0.9	1.2	1.2	Dollars
Austria	57	57	13,977	14,609	0.3	0.3	0.2	0.2	Euro
Bangladesh	1,129	1,130	275,336	289,502	0.2	0.2	13.0	13.3	Taka
Belgium	72	72	17,521	18,405	0.3	0.3	0.3	0.2	Euro
Brazil	1,375	1,387	335,309	355,136	1.2	1.1	3,780.0	3,577.3	Real
Canada	241	242	58,766	61,885	1.1	1.1	1.4	1.3	Dollars
Chile	133	134	32,511	34,394	0.2	0.2	115.6	113.5	Pesos*
China	9,511	9,479	2,319,156	2,427,695	9.8	9.9	63.5	64.1	RMB
Colombia	286	286	69,733	73,253	0.2	0.2	0.6	0.6	Pesos*
Czech Republic	69	68	16,714	17,457	0.1	0.1	3.0	3.0	Koruna
Denmark	36	36	8,793	9,186	0.2	0.2	1.3	1.2	Kroner
Egypt	608	623	148,354	159,576	0.2	0.2	4.2	4.1	Pounds
Finland	36	36	8,709	9,105	0.2	0.1	0.1	0.1	Euro
France	399	398	97,283	101,974	1.6	1.5	1.3	1.3	Euro
Germany	508	501	123,842	128,413	2.4	2.4	2.0	2.0	Euro
Greece	67	66	16,293	16,988	0.1	0.1	0.1	0.1	Euro
Hong Kong	41	41	9,993	10,448	0.2	0.2	1,405.8	1,386.5	Dollar
Hungary	60	59	14,696	15,238	0.1	0.1	22.2	22.2	Forint*
India	7,986	8,107	1,947,515	2,076,313	1.6	1.6	99.3	101.0	Rupees
Indonesia	1,986	2,011	484,279	515,164	0.8	0.8	10.4	10.5	Rupiah*

Property & Casualty Insurance Carriers (NAICS 524126)

Country Estimates

Country	Establishments 2018	2019	Employment 2018	2019	Sales ($B) 2018	2019	Local Sales (B) 2018	2019	Currency
Iran	544	550	132,635	140,958	0.3	0.3	10.1	9.7	Rial*
Iraq	285	290	69,559	74,175	0.1	0.1	0.2	0.2	Dinar*
Ireland	40	41	9,760	10,380	0.4	0.4	0.3	0.3	Euro
Israel	57	57	13,830	14,726	0.2	0.2	0.8	0.8	Shekel
Italy	402	400	97,999	102,444	1.3	1.2	1.1	1.0	Euro
Japan	846	837	206,249	214,401	3.0	2.9	338.2	327.8	Yen*
Kazakhstan	138	138	33,603	35,460	0.1	0.1	49.0	48.4	Tenge
Kuwait	32	34	7,854	8,605	0.1	0.1	0.0	0.0	Dinar
Malaysia	264	268	64,291	68,665	0.3	0.3	1.1	1.1	Ringgit
Mexico	859	869	209,450	222,530	0.8	0.8	15.6	15.4	New pesos
Netherlands	107	107	26,200	27,360	0.5	0.5	0.4	0.4	Euro
New Zealand	29	29	7,045	7,444	0.1	0.1	0.2	0.2	Dollar
Nigeria	1,482	1,506	361,282	385,803	0.4	0.4	148,329.5	146,158.0	Naira
Norway	40	40	9,679	10,197	0.3	0.3	2.5	2.4	Krone
Pakistan	1,187	1,212	289,502	310,382	0.2	0.2	20.2	20.4	Rupees
Peru	235	235	57,307	60,261	0.1	0.1	0.5	0.5	Nuevo Sol
Phillipines	640	651	156,044	166,736	0.2	0.2	11.1	11.3	Pesos
Poland	219	217	53,455	55,529	0.4	0.4	1.3	1.3	Zloty
Portugal	69	69	16,901	17,609	0.1	0.1	0.1	0.1	Euro
Puerto Rico	30	30	7,312	7,559	0.1	0.1	0.1	0.1	Dollar
Qatar	30	34	7,362	8,807	0.1	0.1	0.5	0.5	Riyal
Romania	158	155	38,476	39,771	0.1	0.1	0.6	0.6	New Leu
Russia	980	969	238,992	248,104	1.0	0.9	49.1	46.7	Rubles
Saudi Arabia	275	284	67,047	72,657	0.6	0.6	0.0	0.0	Rials*
Singapore	44	45	10,702	11,509	0.2	0.2	302.2	298.5	Dollar
South Africa	271	274	66,095	70,289	0.2	0.2	2,557.6	2,496.4	Rand
South Korea	383	382	93,421	97,729	1.1	1.1	1,203.8	1,192.8	Won*
Spain	318	320	77,548	81,910	0.9	0.8	721.4	696.6	Euro
Sweden	65	65	15,892	16,666	0.4	0.4	3,038.4	3,025.1	Krona
Switzerland	60	60	14,539	15,309	0.5	0.5	495.0	484.7	Swiss franc
Taiwan	239	247	58,222	63,177	0.4	0.4	11,373.3	11,173.8	Dollar
Thailand	577	580	140,734	148,542	0.3	0.3	10,468.2	10,260.0	Baht
Turkey	437	435	106,641	111,477	0.6	0.6	2,324.6	2,315.8	Euro
Ukraine	319	314	77,793	80,473	0.0	0.0	1,354.5	1,172.4	Hryvna
UAE	149	166	36,256	42,635	0.3	0.3	1,235.7	1,206.8	Dirham
United Kingdom	416	414	101,361	106,154	2.0	2.0	1,479.1	1,460.5	Pounds
United States	2,018	2,019	492,093	517,095	12.2	12.0	12,170.7	12,008.1	Dollars
Venezuela	206	209	50,197	53,524	0.3	0.3	3,312.2	3,109.0	Bolivar
Vietnam	724	725	176,613	185,594	0.2	0.2	3,953.0	4,039.3	Dong*

Note: Due to rounding, establishments will vary by + or - one establishment. Therefore, zero establishments may also be one establishment.

* Local Sales are in trillions

Insurance Agencies & Brokerages Industry (NAICS 52421)

NAICS 52421: Insurance Agencies & Brokerages. This industry comprises establishments primarily representing one or more insurance carriers, or brokers not representing any particular carriers primarily engaged as independent contractors in the sale or placement of insurance contracts with carriers, but not employees of the insurance carriers they represent. This business also includes independent organizations concerned with insurance services.

Country Estimates

Country	Establishments 2018	Establishments 2019	Employment 2018	Employment 2019	Sales ($B) 2018	Sales ($B) 2019	Local Sales (B) 2018	Local Sales (B) 2019	Currency
Algeria	371	373	25,733	27,287	3.1	3.1	353.0	355.8	Dinar
Argentina	257	258	17,840	18,820	7.3	7.2	139.0	137.8	Pesos
Australia	160	162	11,101	11,808	18.1	18.4	23.0	23.3	Dollars
Austria	57	57	3,972	4,168	5.1	5.1	4.2	4.2	Euro
Bangladesh	1,129	1,130	78,239	82,589	3.0	3.1	247.0	259.9	Taka
Belgium	72	72	4,979	5,250	5.8	5.8	4.9	4.9	Euro
Brazil	1,375	1,387	95,281	101,314	22.2	21.7	71,745.5	69,930.2	Real
Canada	241	242	16,699	17,655	21.0	21.2	26.1	26.3	Dollars
Chile	133	134	9,238	9,812	3.6	3.7	2,194.6	2,218.6	Pesos*
China	9,511	9,479	659,008	692,576	185.6	193.1	1,204.6	1,253.3	RMB
Colombia	286	286	19,815	20,898	4.0	4.1	11.6	11.9	Pesos*
Czech Republic	69	68	4,749	4,980	2.7	2.8	57.5	59.3	Koruna
Denmark	36	36	2,499	2,621	3.9	3.9	24.2	24.3	Kroner
Egypt	608	623	42,156	45,524	4.6	4.6	80.2	80.7	Pounds
Finland	36	36	2,475	2,597	3.0	2.9	2.5	2.4	Euro
France	399	398	27,644	29,091	29.9	29.9	25.0	25.0	Euro
Germany	508	501	35,191	36,634	45.9	46.3	38.4	38.7	Euro
Greece	67	66	4,630	4,846	2.3	2.3	1.9	1.9	Euro
Hong Kong	41	41	2,840	2,981	3.4	3.5	26,682.3	27,103.8	Dollar
Hungary	60	59	4,176	4,347	1.6	1.7	421.6	433.2	Forint*
India	7,986	8,107	553,403	592,333	29.7	31.1	1,885.4	1,973.6	Rupees
Indonesia	1,986	2,011	137,612	146,967	14.7	15.3	197.7	205.4	Rupiah*

Insurance Agencies & Brokerages Industry (NAICS 52421)

Country Estimates

Country	Establishments 2018	2019	Employment 2018	2019	Sales ($B) 2018	2019	Local Sales (B) 2018	2019	Currency
Iran	544	550	37,689	40,213	5.3	5.2	191.4	188.9	Rial*
Iraq	285	290	19,766	21,161	2.8	2.8	3.3	3.3	Dinar*
Ireland	40	41	2,773	2,961	6.8	7.7	5.7	6.5	Euro
Israel	57	57	3,930	4,201	4.3	4.4	14.9	15.2	Shekel
Italy	402	400	27,847	29,225	23.9	23.8	20.0	19.9	Euro
Japan	846	837	58,607	61,165	56.9	56.8	6,419.3	6,407.9	Yen*
Kazakhstan	138	138	9,549	10,116	2.8	2.9	930.0	945.8	Tenge
Kuwait	32	34	2,232	2,455	1.7	1.6	0.5	0.5	Dinar
Malaysia	264	268	18,269	19,589	5.2	5.5	21.0	21.9	Ringgit
Mexico	859	869	59,517	63,484	15.4	15.7	296.2	300.5	New pesos
Netherlands	107	107	7,445	7,805	9.8	9.9	8.2	8.3	Euro
New Zealand	29	29	2,002	2,124	2.2	2.3	3.1	3.2	Dollar
Nigeria	1,482	1,506	102,661	110,062	7.8	7.9	2,815,375.4	2,857,177.7	Naira
Norway	40	40	2,750	2,909	5.9	5.9	47.3	47.8	Krone
Pakistan	1,187	1,212	82,264	88,546	3.5	3.6	384.0	398.0	Rupees
Peru	235	235	16,284	17,191	2.8	2.9	9.0	9.2	Nuevo Sol
Phillipines	640	651	44,341	47,567	4.2	4.4	211.2	221.8	Pesos
Poland	219	217	15,190	15,841	6.9	7.1	24.1	24.7	Zloty
Portugal	69	69	4,803	5,023	2.6	2.6	2.2	2.1	Euro
Puerto Rico	30	30	2,078	2,156	1.6	1.5	1.6	1.5	Dollar
Qatar	30	34	2,092	2,512	2.6	2.6	9.5	9.6	Riyal
Romania	158	155	10,933	11,346	2.8	2.9	10.8	11.0	New Leu
Russia	980	969	67,911	70,780	18.2	17.9	931.6	913.4	Rubles
Saudi Arabia	275	284	19,052	20,728	11.2	11.3	0.0	0.0	Rials*
Singapore	44	45	3,041	3,283	4.3	4.4	5,735.1	5,835.5	Dollar
South Africa	271	274	18,781	20,052	3.9	3.9	48,544.9	48,800.4	Rand
South Korea	383	382	26,546	27,880	21.4	21.9	22,848.2	23,317.8	Won*
Spain	318	320	22,036	23,367	16.4	16.3	13,692.0	13,618.0	Euro
Sweden	65	65	4,516	4,754	7.0	7.2	57,670.4	59,135.6	Krona
Switzerland	60	60	4,131	4,367	9.6	9.7	9,395.2	9,475.7	Swiss franc
Taiwan	239	247	16,544	18,023	7.3	7.4	215,872.3	218,432.4	Dollar
Thailand	577	580	39,991	42,376	6.2	6.2	198,691.4	200,568.5	Baht
Turkey	437	435	30,303	31,802	11.8	12.1	44,122.5	45,270.8	Euro
Ukraine	319	314	22,106	22,958	0.9	0.8	25,709.2	22,918.3	Hryvna
UAE	149	166	10,302	12,163	6.4	6.4	23,454.0	23,590.6	Dirham
United Kingdom	416	414	28,803	30,284	38.1	38.7	28,074.4	28,551.2	Pounds
United States	2,018	2,019	139,832	147,518	231.0	234.7	231,006.8	234,740.7	Dollars
Venezuela	206	209	14,264	15,269	6.3	6.1	62,866.5	60,776.0	Bolivar
Vietnam	724	725	50,186	52,946	3.3	3.5	75,029.7	78,963.2	Dong*

Note: Due to rounding, establishments will vary by + or - one establishment. Therefore, zero establishments may also be one establishment.

* Local Sales are in trillions

OFFICES OF REAL ESTATE AGENTS & BROKERS (NAICS 53121)

NAICS 53121: Real Estate Agents & Brokers. This industry comprises establishments primarily engaged in renting, buying, selling, managing, and appraising real estate for others.

COUNTRY ESTIMATES

Country	Establishments 2018	Establishments 2019	Employment 2018	Employment 2019	Sales ($B) 2018	Sales ($B) 2019	Local Sales (B) 2018	Local Sales (B) 2019	Currency
Algeria	371	373	16,927	17,868	3.9	4.1	454.2	472.1	Dinar
Argentina	257	258	11,735	12,323	9.4	9.6	178.8	182.8	Pesos
Australia	160	162	7,302	7,732	23.3	24.4	29.6	30.9	Dollars
Austria	57	57	2,613	2,729	6.5	6.7	5.5	5.6	Euro
Bangladesh	1,129	1,130	51,466	54,080	3.8	4.2	317.8	344.8	Taka
Belgium	72	72	3,275	3,438	7.5	7.8	6.3	6.5	Euro
Brazil	1,375	1,387	62,677	66,341	28.6	28.7	92,311.4	92,779.8	Real
Canada	241	242	10,985	11,560	27.1	28.1	33.6	34.9	Dollars
Chile	133	134	6,077	6,425	4.7	4.9	2,823.7	2,943.6	Pesos*
China	9,511	9,479	433,501	453,503	238.8	256.2	1,549.9	1,662.8	RMB
Colombia	286	286	13,035	13,684	5.1	5.4	14.9	15.8	Pesos*
Czech Republic	69	68	3,124	3,261	3.5	3.7	74.0	78.6	Koruna
Denmark	36	36	1,644	1,716	5.0	5.2	31.1	32.3	Kroner
Egypt	608	623	27,731	29,809	5.9	6.1	103.2	107.1	Pounds
Finland	36	36	1,628	1,701	3.8	3.9	3.2	3.2	Euro
France	399	398	18,184	19,049	38.5	39.7	32.1	33.1	Euro
Germany	508	501	23,149	23,988	59.1	61.5	49.3	51.3	Euro
Greece	67	66	3,046	3,173	3.0	3.0	2.5	2.5	Euro
Hong Kong	41	41	1,868	1,952	4.4	4.6	34,330.8	35,960.0	Dollar
Hungary	60	59	2,747	2,847	2.1	2.2	542.4	574.8	Forint*
India	7,986	8,107	364,033	387,863	38.2	41.2	2,425.8	2,618.5	Rupees
Indonesia	1,986	2,011	90,522	96,235	18.9	20.3	254.4	272.5	Rupiah*

Offices of Real Estate Agents & Brokers (NAICS 53121)

Country Estimates

Country	Establishments 2018	Establishments 2019	Employment 2018	Employment 2019	Sales ($B) 2018	Sales ($B) 2019	Local Sales (B) 2018	Local Sales (B) 2019	Currency
Iran	544	550	24,792	26,332	6.8	6.9	246.2	250.6	Rial*
Iraq	285	290	13,002	13,856	3.6	3.7	4.3	4.4	Dinar*
Ireland	40	41	1,824	1,939	8.8	10.3	7.3	8.6	Euro
Israel	57	57	2,585	2,751	5.6	5.9	19.1	20.1	Shekel
Italy	402	400	18,318	19,137	30.8	31.6	25.7	26.4	Euro
Japan	846	837	38,553	40,051	73.2	75.3	8,259.4	8,501.6	Yen*
Kazakhstan	138	138	6,281	6,624	3.6	3.8	1,196.6	1,254.8	Tenge
Kuwait	32	34	1,468	1,607	2.1	2.2	0.6	0.6	Dinar
Malaysia	264	268	12,017	12,827	6.7	7.3	27.0	29.1	Ringgit
Mexico	859	869	39,151	41,570	19.8	20.8	381.1	398.7	New pesos
Netherlands	107	107	4,897	5,111	12.6	13.1	10.6	11.0	Euro
New Zealand	29	29	1,317	1,391	2.9	3.0	4.0	4.2	Dollar
Nigeria	1,482	1,506	67,531	72,069	10.1	10.5	3,622,403.1	3,790,757.9	Naira
Norway	40	40	1,809	1,905	7.5	7.8	60.9	63.4	Krone
Pakistan	1,187	1,212	54,114	57,981	4.5	4.8	494.0	528.1	Rupees
Peru	235	235	10,712	11,257	3.6	3.8	11.6	12.2	Nuevo Sol
Phillipines	640	651	29,168	31,147	5.4	5.9	271.7	294.2	Pesos
Poland	219	217	9,992	10,373	8.9	9.4	31.0	32.8	Zloty
Portugal	69	69	3,159	3,289	3.3	3.4	2.8	2.8	Euro
Puerto Rico	30	30	1,367	1,412	2.0	2.0	2.0	2.0	Dollar
Qatar	30	34	1,376	1,645	3.4	3.5	12.3	12.8	Riyal
Romania	158	155	7,192	7,429	3.6	3.8	13.9	14.7	New Leu
Russia	980	969	44,673	46,347	23.5	23.7	1,198.7	1,211.9	Rubles
Saudi Arabia	275	284	12,532	13,573	14.4	15.0	0.1	0.1	Rials*
Singapore	44	45	2,000	2,150	5.5	5.8	7,379.1	7,742.2	Dollar
South Africa	271	274	12,355	13,130	5.0	5.2	62,460.3	64,746.0	Rand
South Korea	383	382	17,463	18,256	27.6	29.0	29,397.7	30,936.9	Won*
Spain	318	320	14,495	15,301	21.1	21.6	17,616.8	18,067.6	Euro
Sweden	65	65	2,971	3,113	9.0	9.6	74,201.6	78,458.1	Krona
Switzerland	60	60	2,718	2,860	12.4	12.9	12,088.4	12,571.9	Swiss franc
Taiwan	239	247	10,883	11,802	9.4	9.8	277,752.1	289,804.9	Dollar
Thailand	577	580	26,306	27,748	7.9	8.3	255,646.3	266,104.1	Baht
Turkey	437	435	19,934	20,824	15.1	16.0	56,770.3	60,063.0	Euro
Ukraine	319	314	14,541	15,033	1.2	1.1	33,078.8	30,406.8	Hryvna
UAE	149	166	6,777	7,964	8.2	8.5	30,177.0	31,298.8	Dirham
United Kingdom	416	414	18,947	19,830	49.0	51.4	36,122.0	37,880.3	Pounds
United States	2,018	2,019	91,983	96,595	297.2	311.4	297,225.0	311,442.1	Dollars
Venezuela	206	209	9,383	9,998	8.1	8.1	80,887.1	80,634.5	Bolivar
Vietnam	724	725	33,013	34,670	4.3	4.6	96,537.0	104,764.4	Dong*

Note: Due to rounding, establishments will vary by + or - one establishment. Therefore, zero establishments may also be one establishment.

* Local Sales are in trillions

REAL ESTATE PROPERTY MANAGERS INDUSTRY (NAICS 53131)

NAICS 53131: Real Estate Property Managers. This industry comprises establishments primarily engaged in renting, buying, selling, managing, and appraising real estate for others.

COUNTRY ESTIMATES

Country	Establishments 2018	Establishments 2019	Employment 2018	Employment 2019	Sales ($B) 2018	Sales ($B) 2019	Local Sales (B) 2018	Local Sales (B) 2019	Currency
Algeria	371	373	9,358	9,747	1.7	1.8	194.9	201.6	Dinar
Argentina	257	258	6,487	6,722	4.0	4.1	76.7	78.1	Pesos
Australia	160	162	4,037	4,218	10.0	10.4	12.7	13.2	Dollars
Austria	57	57	1,444	1,489	2.8	2.9	2.3	2.4	Euro
Bangladesh	1,129	1,130	28,451	29,500	1.6	1.8	136.4	147.3	Taka
Belgium	72	72	1,810	1,875	3.2	3.3	2.7	2.8	Euro
Brazil	1,375	1,387	34,648	36,188	12.3	12.3	39,607.3	39,629.0	Real
Canada	241	242	6,072	6,306	11.6	12.0	14.4	14.9	Dollars
Chile	133	134	3,359	3,505	2.0	2.1	1,211.5	1,257.3	Pesos*
China	9,511	9,479	239,642	247,382	102.5	109.4	665.0	710.2	RMB
Colombia	286	286	7,206	7,464	2.2	2.3	6.4	6.7	Pesos*
Czech Republic	69	68	1,727	1,779	1.5	1.6	31.8	33.6	Koruna
Denmark	36	36	909	936	2.1	2.2	13.3	13.8	Kroner
Egypt	608	623	15,330	16,261	2.5	2.6	44.3	45.8	Pounds
Finland	36	36	900	928	1.6	1.7	1.4	1.4	Euro
France	399	398	10,052	10,391	16.5	16.9	13.8	14.2	Euro
Germany	508	501	12,797	13,085	25.4	26.3	21.2	21.9	Euro
Greece	67	66	1,684	1,731	1.3	1.3	1.1	1.1	Euro
Hong Kong	41	41	1,033	1,065	1.9	2.0	14,730.1	15,359.6	Dollar
Hungary	60	59	1,519	1,553	0.9	1.0	232.7	245.5	Forint*
India	7,986	8,107	201,240	211,576	16.4	17.6	1,040.8	1,118.5	Rupees
Indonesia	1,986	2,011	50,041	52,495	8.1	8.7	109.1	116.4	Rupiah*

REAL ESTATE PROPERTY MANAGERS INDUSTRY
(NAICS 53131)

COUNTRY ESTIMATES

Country	Establishments 2018	Establishments 2019	Employment 2018	Employment 2019	Sales ($B) 2018	Sales ($B) 2019	Local Sales (B) 2018	Local Sales (B) 2019	Currency
Iran	544	550	13,705	14,364	2.9	3.0	105.6	107.0	Rial*
Iraq	285	290	7,188	7,558	1.5	1.6	1.8	1.9	Dinar*
Ireland	40	41	1,008	1,058	3.8	4.4	3.1	3.7	Euro
Israel	57	57	1,429	1,501	2.4	2.5	8.2	8.6	Shekel
Italy	402	400	10,126	10,439	13.2	13.5	11.0	11.3	Euro
Japan	846	837	21,312	21,847	31.4	32.2	3,543.8	3,631.3	Yen*
Kazakhstan	138	138	3,472	3,613	1.6	1.6	513.4	536.0	Tenge
Kuwait	32	34	812	877	0.9	0.9	0.3	0.3	Dinar
Malaysia	264	268	6,643	6,997	2.9	3.1	11.6	12.4	Ringgit
Mexico	859	869	21,643	22,676	8.5	8.9	163.5	170.3	New pesos
Netherlands	107	107	2,707	2,788	5.4	5.6	4.5	4.7	Euro
New Zealand	29	29	728	759	1.2	1.3	1.7	1.8	Dollar
Nigeria	1,482	1,506	37,332	39,313	4.3	4.5	1,554,235.8	1,619,144.9	Naira
Norway	40	40	1,000	1,039	3.2	3.4	26.1	27.1	Krone
Pakistan	1,187	1,212	29,915	31,628	1.9	2.0	212.0	225.5	Rupees
Peru	235	235	5,922	6,141	1.5	1.6	5.0	5.2	Nuevo Sol
Phillipines	640	651	16,124	16,990	2.3	2.5	116.6	125.7	Pesos
Poland	219	217	5,524	5,658	3.8	4.0	13.3	14.0	Zloty
Portugal	69	69	1,746	1,794	1.4	1.4	1.2	1.2	Euro
Puerto Rico	30	30	756	770	0.9	0.9	0.9	0.9	Dollar
Qatar	30	34	761	897	1.4	1.5	5.3	5.5	Riyal
Romania	158	155	3,976	4,053	1.5	1.6	5.9	6.3	New Leu
Russia	980	969	24,695	25,282	10.1	10.1	514.3	517.6	Rubles
Saudi Arabia	275	284	6,928	7,404	6.2	6.4	0.0	0.0	Rials*
Singapore	44	45	1,106	1,173	2.4	2.5	3,166.1	3,306.9	Dollar
South Africa	271	274	6,830	7,162	2.2	2.2	26,799.4	27,654.9	Rand
South Korea	383	382	9,653	9,959	11.8	12.4	12,613.4	13,214.1	Won*
Spain	318	320	8,013	8,347	9.1	9.2	7,558.7	7,717.2	Euro
Sweden	65	65	1,642	1,698	3.9	4.1	31,837.1	33,511.8	Krona
Switzerland	60	60	1,502	1,560	5.3	5.5	5,186.7	5,369.8	Swiss franc
Taiwan	239	247	6,016	6,438	4.0	4.2	119,172.9	123,784.3	Dollar
Thailand	577	580	14,542	15,136	3.4	3.5	109,688.2	113,661.0	Baht
Turkey	437	435	11,019	11,359	6.5	6.8	24,358.0	25,654.7	Euro
Ukraine	319	314	8,038	8,200	0.5	0.5	14,192.8	12,987.7	Hryvna
UAE	149	166	3,746	4,345	3.5	3.6	12,947.8	13,368.7	Dirham
United Kingdom	416	414	10,474	10,817	21.0	22.0	15,498.6	16,179.8	Pounds
United States	2,018	2,019	50,849	52,692	127.5	133.0	127,528.0	133,026.1	Dollars
Venezuela	206	209	5,187	5,454	3.5	3.5	34,705.6	34,441.4	Bolivar
Vietnam	724	725	18,250	18,912	1.8	2.0	41,420.4	44,748.0	Dong*

Note: Due to rounding, establishments will vary by + or - one establishment. Therefore, zero establishments may also be one establishment.

* Local Sales are in trillions

OFFICES OF LAWYERS INDUSTRY (NAICS 54111)

NAICS 54111: Offices of Lawyers. This industry comprises offices of legal practitioners known as lawyers or attorneys (i.e., counselors-at-law) primarily engaged in the practice of law. Establishments in this industry may provide expertise in a range or in specific areas of law, such as criminal law, corporate law, family and estate law, patent law, real estate law, or tax law.

COUNTRY ESTIMATES

Country	Establishments 2018	Establishments 2019	Employment 2018	Employment 2019	Sales ($B) 2018	Sales ($B) 2019	Local Sales (B) 2018	Local Sales (B) 2019	Currency
Algeria	186	187	21,336	22,916	1.7	1.7	197.6	199.0	Dinar
Argentina	129	129	14,792	15,805	4.1	4.0	77.8	77.1	Pesos
Australia	80	81	9,204	9,916	10.1	10.3	12.9	13.0	Dollars
Austria	29	29	3,293	3,500	2.8	2.8	2.4	2.4	Euro
Bangladesh	565	565	64,871	69,358	1.7	1.8	138.3	145.4	Taka
Belgium	36	36	4,128	4,409	3.3	3.3	2.7	2.7	Euro
Brazil	688	693	79,001	85,082	12.4	12.1	40,166.7	39,118.2	Real
Canada	120	121	13,846	14,826	11.8	11.9	14.6	14.7	Dollars
Chile	67	67	7,660	8,240	2.0	2.0	1,228.7	1,241.1	Pesos*
China	4,755	4,739	546,409	581,617	103.9	108.0	674.4	701.1	RMB
Colombia	143	143	16,430	17,550	2.2	2.3	6.5	6.6	Pesos*
Czech Republic	34	34	3,938	4,182	1.5	1.6	32.2	33.1	Koruna
Denmark	18	18	2,072	2,201	2.2	2.2	13.5	13.6	Kroner
Egypt	304	312	34,953	38,230	2.6	2.6	44.9	45.2	Pounds
Finland	18	18	2,052	2,181	1.7	1.6	1.4	1.4	Euro
France	199	199	22,921	24,430	16.7	16.7	14.0	14.0	Euro
Germany	254	251	29,178	30,765	25.7	25.9	21.5	21.6	Euro
Greece	33	33	3,839	4,070	1.3	1.3	1.1	1.1	Euro
Hong Kong	20	20	2,354	2,503	1.9	1.9	14,938.1	15,161.6	Dollar
Hungary	30	30	3,462	3,651	0.9	0.9	236.0	242.3	Forint*
India	3,993	4,053	458,848	497,434	16.6	17.4	1,055.5	1,104.0	Rupees
Indonesia	993	1,006	114,100	123,421	8.2	8.6	110.7	114.9	Rupiah*

OFFICES OF LAWYERS INDUSTRY
(NAICS 54111)

COUNTRY ESTIMATES

Country	Establishments 2018	Establishments 2019	Employment 2018	Employment 2019	Sales ($B) 2018	Sales ($B) 2019	Local Sales (B) 2018	Local Sales (B) 2019	Currency
Iran	272	275	31,250	33,770	3.0	2.9	107.1	105.7	Rial*
Iraq	143	145	16,389	17,771	1.6	1.6	1.9	1.8	Dinar*
Ireland	20	20	2,299	2,487	3.8	4.3	3.2	3.6	Euro
Israel	28	29	3,258	3,528	2.4	2.5	8.3	8.5	Shekel
Italy	201	200	23,089	24,543	13.4	13.3	11.2	11.1	Euro
Japan	423	419	48,594	51,365	31.8	31.7	3,593.8	3,584.5	Yen*
Kazakhstan	69	69	7,917	8,495	1.6	1.6	520.7	529.1	Tenge
Kuwait	16	17	1,850	2,062	0.9	0.9	0.3	0.3	Dinar
Malaysia	132	134	15,148	16,451	2.9	3.1	11.7	12.3	Ringgit
Mexico	429	434	49,348	53,313	8.6	8.8	165.8	168.1	New pesos
Netherlands	54	53	6,173	6,555	5.5	5.5	4.6	4.6	Euro
New Zealand	14	15	1,660	1,783	1.2	1.3	1.7	1.8	Dollar
Nigeria	741	753	85,120	92,429	4.4	4.4	1,576,186.4	1,598,274.0	Naira
Norway	20	20	2,280	2,443	3.3	3.3	26.5	26.7	Krone
Pakistan	594	606	68,209	74,360	1.9	2.0	215.0	222.6	Rupees
Peru	118	118	13,502	14,437	1.6	1.6	5.0	5.1	Nuevo Sol
Phillipines	320	326	36,765	39,946	2.4	2.5	118.2	124.1	Pesos
Poland	110	108	12,594	13,303	3.9	4.0	13.5	13.8	Zloty
Portugal	35	34	3,982	4,219	1.5	1.4	1.2	1.2	Euro
Puerto Rico	15	15	1,723	1,811	0.9	0.8	0.9	0.8	Dollar
Qatar	15	17	1,735	2,110	1.5	1.5	5.3	5.4	Riyal
Romania	79	78	9,065	9,528	1.6	1.6	6.0	6.2	New Leu
Russia	490	484	56,308	59,440	10.2	10.0	521.6	511.0	Rubles
Saudi Arabia	137	142	15,797	17,407	6.3	6.3	0.0	0.0	Rials*
Singapore	22	22	2,521	2,757	2.4	2.5	3,210.8	3,264.3	Dollar
South Africa	136	137	15,572	16,839	2.2	2.2	27,177.8	27,298.4	Rand
South Korea	192	191	22,011	23,413	12.0	12.2	12,791.6	13,043.7	Won*
Spain	159	160	18,271	19,624	9.2	9.1	7,665.4	7,617.7	Euro
Sweden	33	33	3,744	3,993	3.9	4.0	32,286.7	33,079.8	Krona
Switzerland	30	30	3,425	3,668	5.4	5.4	5,259.9	5,300.6	Swiss franc
Taiwan	119	123	13,717	15,136	4.1	4.1	120,856.0	122,188.7	Dollar
Thailand	289	290	33,158	35,587	3.5	3.5	111,237.3	112,195.9	Baht
Turkey	219	218	25,125	26,707	6.6	6.8	24,702.0	25,324.0	Euro
Ukraine	160	157	18,329	19,279	0.5	0.5	14,393.3	12,820.2	Hryvna
UAE	74	83	8,542	10,214	3.6	3.6	13,130.7	13,196.3	Dirham
United Kingdom	208	207	23,881	25,432	21.3	21.7	15,717.5	15,971.3	Pounds
United States	2,018	2,019	231,881	247,767	258.7	262.6	258,658.1	262,622.8	Dollars
Venezuela	103	104	11,827	12,823	3.5	3.4	35,195.8	33,997.4	Bolivar
Vietnam	362	362	41,611	44,464	1.8	1.9	42,005.3	44,171.2	Dong*

Note: Due to rounding, establishments will vary by + or - one establishment. Therefore, zero establishments may also be one establishment.

* Local Sales are in trillions

OFFICES OF CERTIFIED PUBLIC ACCOUNTANTS (NAICS 541211)

NAICS 541211: Offices of Certified Public Accountants This U.S. industry comprises establishments of accountants that are certified to audit the accounting records of public and private organizations and to attest to compliance with generally accepted accounting practices. Offices of certified public accountants (CPAs) may provide one or more of the following accounting services: (1) auditing financial statements; (2) designing accounting systems; (3) preparing financial statements; (4) developing budgets; and (5) providing advice on matters related to accounting.

COUNTRY ESTIMATES

Country	Establishments 2018	Establishments 2019	Employment 2018	Employment 2019	Sales ($B) 2018	Sales ($B) 2019	Local Sales (B) 2018	Local Sales (B) 2019	Currency
Algeria	371	373	14,868	16,078	0.9	0.9	108.1	108.8	Dinar
Argentina	257	258	10,308	11,089	2.2	2.2	42.6	42.1	Pesos
Australia	160	162	6,414	6,957	5.5	5.6	7.0	7.1	Dollars
Austria	57	57	2,295	2,456	1.6	1.6	1.3	1.3	Euro
Bangladesh	1,129	1,130	45,206	48,662	0.9	1.0	75.6	79.5	Taka
Belgium	72	72	2,877	3,094	1.8	1.8	1.5	1.5	Euro
Brazil	1,375	1,387	55,053	59,695	6.8	6.6	21,964.5	21,384.2	Real
Canada	241	242	9,648	10,402	6.4	6.5	8.0	8.0	Dollars
Chile	133	134	5,338	5,781	1.1	1.1	671.9	678.4	Pesos*
China	9,511	9,479	380,770	408,072	56.8	59.1	368.8	383.3	RMB
Colombia	286	286	11,449	12,313	1.2	1.3	3.5	3.6	Pesos*
Czech Republic	69	68	2,744	2,934	0.8	0.9	17.6	18.1	Koruna
Denmark	36	36	1,444	1,544	1.2	1.2	7.4	7.4	Kroner
Egypt	608	623	24,357	26,823	1.4	1.4	24.6	24.7	Pounds
Finland	36	36	1,430	1,530	0.9	0.9	0.8	0.7	Euro
France	399	398	15,972	17,141	9.2	9.1	7.6	7.6	Euro
Germany	508	501	20,333	21,585	14.1	14.2	11.7	11.8	Euro
Greece	67	66	2,675	2,856	0.7	0.7	0.6	0.6	Euro
Hong Kong	41	41	1,641	1,756	1.0	1.1	8,168.7	8,288.2	Dollar
Hungary	60	59	2,413	2,561	0.5	0.5	129.1	132.5	Forint*
India	7,986	8,107	319,752	349,008	9.1	9.5	577.2	603.5	Rupees
Indonesia	1,986	2,011	79,511	86,594	4.5	4.7	60.5	62.8	Rupiah*

Offices of Certified Public Accountants (NAICS 541211)

Country Estimates

Country	Establishments 2018	2019	Employment 2018	2019	Sales ($B) 2018	2019	Local Sales (B) 2018	2019	Currency
Iran	544	550	21,777	23,694	1.6	1.6	58.6	57.8	Rial*
Iraq	285	290	11,421	12,468	0.9	0.8	1.0	1.0	Dinar*
Ireland	40	41	1,602	1,745	2.1	2.4	1.7	2.0	Euro
Israel	57	57	2,271	2,475	1.3	1.4	4.5	4.6	Shekel
Italy	402	400	16,090	17,220	7.3	7.3	6.1	6.1	Euro
Japan	846	837	33,863	36,039	17.4	17.4	1,965.2	1,959.5	Yen*
Kazakhstan	138	138	5,517	5,960	0.9	0.9	284.7	289.2	Tenge
Kuwait	32	34	1,289	1,446	0.5	0.5	0.2	0.1	Dinar
Malaysia	264	268	10,556	11,542	1.6	1.7	6.4	6.7	Ringgit
Mexico	859	869	34,389	37,405	4.7	4.8	90.7	91.9	New pesos
Netherlands	107	107	4,302	4,599	3.0	3.0	2.5	2.5	Euro
New Zealand	29	29	1,157	1,251	0.7	0.7	0.9	1.0	Dollar
Nigeria	1,482	1,506	59,317	64,850	2.4	2.4	861,913.0	873,706.6	Naira
Norway	40	40	1,589	1,714	1.8	1.8	14.5	14.6	Krone
Pakistan	1,187	1,212	47,532	52,172	1.1	1.1	117.6	121.7	Rupees
Peru	235	235	9,409	10,129	0.9	0.9	2.8	2.8	Nuevo Sol
Phillipines	640	651	25,620	28,027	1.3	1.4	64.6	67.8	Pesos
Poland	219	217	8,777	9,334	2.1	2.2	7.4	7.6	Zloty
Portugal	69	69	2,775	2,960	0.8	0.8	0.7	0.7	Euro
Puerto Rico	30	30	1,201	1,271	0.5	0.5	0.5	0.5	Dollar
Qatar	30	34	1,209	1,480	0.8	0.8	2.9	2.9	Riyal
Romania	158	155	6,317	6,685	0.9	0.9	3.3	3.4	New Leu
Russia	980	969	39,239	41,704	5.6	5.5	285.2	279.3	Rubles
Saudi Arabia	275	284	11,008	12,213	3.4	3.4	0.0	0.0	Rials*
Singapore	44	45	1,757	1,934	1.3	1.3	1,755.8	1,784.4	Dollar
South Africa	271	274	10,852	11,815	1.2	1.2	14,861.8	14,922.9	Rand
South Korea	383	382	15,338	16,427	6.6	6.7	6,994.9	7,130.4	Won*
Spain	318	320	12,732	13,768	5.0	5.0	4,191.7	4,164.3	Euro
Sweden	65	65	2,609	2,801	2.2	2.2	17,655.5	18,083.3	Krona
Switzerland	60	60	2,387	2,573	2.9	3.0	2,876.3	2,897.6	Swiss franc
Taiwan	239	247	9,559	10,619	2.2	2.3	66,088.2	66,795.2	Dollar
Thailand	577	580	23,106	24,969	1.9	1.9	60,828.4	61,332.6	Baht
Turkey	437	435	17,509	18,738	3.6	3.7	13,507.9	13,843.5	Euro
Ukraine	319	314	12,772	13,527	0.3	0.2	7,870.7	7,008.3	Hryvna
UAE	149	166	5,953	7,167	2.0	2.0	7,180.3	7,213.9	Dirham
United Kingdom	416	414	16,642	17,844	11.7	11.8	8,594.8	8,730.8	Pounds
United States	2,018	2,019	80,794	86,919	70.7	71.8	70,721.6	71,782.2	Dollars
Venezuela	206	209	8,242	8,997	1.9	1.9	19,246.3	18,584.9	Bolivar
Vietnam	724	725	28,997	31,197	1.0	1.1	22,970.0	24,146.5	Dong*

Note: Due to rounding, establishments will vary by + or - one establishment. Therefore, zero establishments may also be one establishment.

* Local Sales are in trillions

NAICS 54131: Architectural Services. This industry comprises establishments primarily engaged in planning and designing residential, institutional, leisure, commercial, and industrial buildings and structures by applying knowledge of design, construction procedures, zoning regulations, building codes, and building materials.

COUNTRY ESTIMATES

Country	Establishments 2018	2019	Employment 2018	2019	Sales ($B) 2018	2019	Local Sales (B) 2018	2019	Currency
Algeria	371	373	5,379	5,695	0.4	0.4	50.9	50.1	Dinar
Argentina	257	258	3,729	3,928	1.1	1.0	20.1	19.4	Pesos
Australia	160	162	2,321	2,464	2.6	2.6	3.3	3.3	Dollars
Austria	57	57	830	870	0.7	0.7	0.6	0.6	Euro
Bangladesh	1,129	1,130	16,355	17,237	0.4	0.4	35.6	36.6	Taka
Belgium	72	72	1,041	1,096	0.8	0.8	0.7	0.7	Euro
Brazil	1,375	1,387	19,917	21,145	3.2	3.0	10,349.9	9,840.7	Real
Canada	241	242	3,491	3,685	3.0	3.0	3.8	3.7	Dollars
Chile	133	134	1,931	2,048	0.5	0.5	316.6	312.2	Pesos*
China	9,511	9,479	137,757	144,547	26.8	27.2	173.8	176.4	RMB
Colombia	286	286	4,142	4,362	0.6	0.6	1.7	1.7	Pesos*
Czech Republic	69	68	993	1,039	0.4	0.4	8.3	8.3	Koruna
Denmark	36	36	522	547	0.6	0.6	3.5	3.4	Kroner
Egypt	608	623	8,812	9,501	0.7	0.6	11.6	11.4	Pounds
Finland	36	36	517	542	0.4	0.4	0.4	0.3	Euro
France	399	398	5,779	6,072	4.3	4.2	3.6	3.5	Euro
Germany	508	501	7,356	7,646	6.6	6.5	5.5	5.4	Euro
Greece	67	66	968	1,011	0.3	0.3	0.3	0.3	Euro
Hong Kong	41	41	594	622	0.5	0.5	3,849.2	3,814.1	Dollar
Hungary	60	59	873	907	0.2	0.2	60.8	61.0	Forint*
India	7,986	8,107	115,682	123,625	4.3	4.4	272.0	277.7	Rupees
Indonesia	1,986	2,011	28,766	30,673	2.1	2.2	28.5	28.9	Rupiah*

Architectural Services Industry
(NAICS 54131)

Country Estimates

Country	Establishments 2018	2019	Employment 2018	2019	Sales ($B) 2018	2019	Local Sales (B) 2018	2019	Currency
Iran	544	550	7,878	8,393	0.8	0.7	27.6	26.6	Rial*
Iraq	285	290	4,132	4,416	0.4	0.4	0.5	0.5	Dinar*
Ireland	40	41	580	618	1.0	1.1	0.8	0.9	Euro
Israel	57	57	821	877	0.6	0.6	2.1	2.1	Shekel
Italy	402	400	5,821	6,100	3.4	3.3	2.9	2.8	Euro
Japan	846	837	12,251	12,766	8.2	8.0	926.0	901.7	Yen*
Kazakhstan	138	138	1,996	2,111	0.4	0.4	134.2	133.1	Tenge
Kuwait	32	34	467	512	0.2	0.2	0.1	0.1	Dinar
Malaysia	264	268	3,819	4,088	0.8	0.8	3.0	3.1	Ringgit
Mexico	859	869	12,441	13,250	2.2	2.2	42.7	42.3	New pesos
Netherlands	107	107	1,556	1,629	1.4	1.4	1.2	1.2	Euro
New Zealand	29	29	418	443	0.3	0.3	0.4	0.4	Dollar
Nigeria	1,482	1,506	21,460	22,971	1.1	1.1	406,143.6	402,067.1	Naira
Norway	40	40	575	607	0.8	0.8	6.8	6.7	Krone
Pakistan	1,187	1,212	17,196	18,480	0.5	0.5	55.4	56.0	Rupees
Peru	235	235	3,404	3,588	0.4	0.4	1.3	1.3	Nuevo Sol
Phillipines	640	651	9,269	9,928	0.6	0.6	30.5	31.2	Pesos
Poland	219	217	3,175	3,306	1.0	1.0	3.5	3.5	Zloty
Portugal	69	69	1,004	1,048	0.4	0.4	0.3	0.3	Euro
Puerto Rico	30	30	434	450	0.2	0.2	0.2	0.2	Dollar
Qatar	30	34	437	524	0.4	0.4	1.4	1.4	Riyal
Romania	158	155	2,285	2,368	0.4	0.4	1.6	1.6	New Leu
Russia	980	969	14,196	14,772	2.6	2.5	134.4	128.5	Rubles
Saudi Arabia	275	284	3,983	4,326	1.6	1.6	0.0	0.0	Rials*
Singapore	44	45	636	685	0.6	0.6	827.3	821.2	Dollar
South Africa	271	274	3,926	4,185	0.6	0.6	7,003.0	6,867.3	Rand
South Korea	383	382	5,549	5,819	3.1	3.1	3,296.1	3,281.3	Won*
Spain	318	320	4,606	4,877	2.4	2.3	1,975.2	1,916.3	Euro
Sweden	65	65	944	992	1.0	1.0	8,319.5	8,321.7	Krona
Switzerland	60	60	864	911	1.4	1.4	1,355.3	1,333.4	Swiss franc
Taiwan	239	247	3,458	3,762	1.1	1.0	31,141.5	30,738.2	Dollar
Thailand	577	580	8,360	8,844	0.9	0.9	28,663.1	28,224.4	Baht
Turkey	437	435	6,334	6,637	1.7	1.7	6,365.1	6,370.6	Euro
Ukraine	319	314	4,621	4,791	0.1	0.1	3,708.8	3,225.1	Hryvna
UAE	149	166	2,154	2,539	0.9	0.9	3,383.4	3,319.7	Dirham
United Kingdom	416	414	6,021	6,321	5.5	5.5	4,050.0	4,017.8	Pounds
United States	2,018	2,019	29,230	30,788	33.3	33.0	33,324.8	33,033.1	Dollars
Venezuela	206	209	2,982	3,187	0.9	0.9	9,069.1	8,552.5	Bolivar
Vietnam	724	725	10,491	11,050	0.5	0.5	10,823.7	11,111.8	Dong*

Note: Due to rounding, establishments will vary by + or - one establishment. Therefore, zero establishments may also be one establishment.

* Local Sales are in trillions

ENGINEERING SERVICES INDUSTRY
(NAICS 54133)

NAICS 54133: Engineering Services. This industry comprises establishments primarily engaged in applying physical laws and principles of engineering in the design, development, and utilization of machines, materials, instruments, structures, processes, and systems. The assignments undertaken by these establishments may involve any of the following activities: provision of advice, preparation of feasibility studies, preparation of preliminary and final plans and designs, provision of technical services during the construction or installation phase, inspection and evaluation of engineering projects, and related services.

COUNTRY ESTIMATES

Country	Establishments 2018	2019	Employment 2018	2019	Sales ($B) 2018	2019	Local Sales (B) 2018	2019	Currency
Algeria	371	373	42,998	46,396	1.2	1.2	137.4	138.3	Dinar
Argentina	257	258	29,809	31,999	2.8	2.8	54.1	53.6	Pesos
Australia	160	162	18,549	20,076	7.0	7.1	8.9	9.1	Dollars
Austria	57	57	6,637	7,086	2.0	2.0	1.7	1.6	Euro
Bangladesh	1,129	1,130	130,732	140,424	1.2	1.2	96.1	101.0	Taka
Belgium	72	72	8,319	8,927	2.3	2.3	1.9	1.9	Euro
Brazil	1,375	1,387	159,207	172,260	8.6	8.4	27,924.3	27,185.2	Real
Canada	241	242	27,903	30,018	8.2	8.2	10.2	10.2	Dollars
Chile	133	134	15,436	16,683	1.4	1.4	854.2	862.5	Pesos*
China	9,511	9,479	1,101,154	1,177,561	72.2	75.1	468.9	487.2	RMB
Colombia	286	286	33,110	35,532	1.6	1.6	4.5	4.6	Pesos*
Czech Republic	69	68	7,936	8,468	1.1	1.1	22.4	23.0	Koruna
Denmark	36	36	4,175	4,456	1.5	1.5	9.4	9.5	Kroner
Egypt	608	623	70,440	77,403	1.8	1.8	31.2	31.4	Pounds
Finland	36	36	4,135	4,416	1.2	1.1	1.0	1.0	Euro
France	399	398	46,191	49,463	11.6	11.6	9.7	9.7	Euro
Germany	508	501	58,801	62,287	17.9	18.0	14.9	15.0	Euro
Greece	67	66	7,736	8,240	0.9	0.9	0.8	0.7	Euro
Hong Kong	41	41	4,745	5,068	1.3	1.3	10,385.1	10,536.5	Dollar
Hungary	60	59	6,978	7,391	0.6	0.7	164.1	168.4	Forint*
India	7,986	8,107	924,696	1,007,122	11.6	12.1	733.8	767.2	Rupees
Indonesia	1,986	2,011	229,940	249,882	5.7	5.9	76.9	79.8	Rupiah*

ENGINEERING SERVICES INDUSTRY
(NAICS 54133)

COUNTRY ESTIMATES

Country	Establishments 2018	Establishments 2019	Employment 2018	Employment 2019	Sales ($B) 2018	Sales ($B) 2019	Local Sales (B) 2018	Local Sales (B) 2019	Currency
Iran	544	550	62,976	68,372	2.1	2.0	74.5	73.4	Rial*
Iraq	285	290	33,027	35,979	1.1	1.1	1.3	1.3	Dinar*
Ireland	40	41	4,634	5,035	2.7	3.0	2.2	2.5	Euro
Israel	57	57	6,566	7,143	1.7	1.7	5.8	5.9	Shekel
Italy	402	400	46,531	49,691	9.3	9.3	7.8	7.7	Euro
Japan	846	837	97,929	103,996	22.1	22.1	2,498.5	2,491.0	Yen*
Kazakhstan	138	138	15,955	17,200	1.1	1.1	362.0	367.7	Tenge
Kuwait	32	34	3,729	4,174	0.6	0.6	0.2	0.2	Dinar
Malaysia	264	268	30,526	33,306	2.0	2.1	8.2	8.5	Ringgit
Mexico	859	869	99,449	107,939	6.0	6.1	115.3	116.8	New pesos
Netherlands	107	107	12,440	13,271	3.8	3.9	3.2	3.2	Euro
New Zealand	29	29	3,345	3,611	0.9	0.9	1.2	1.2	Dollar
Nigeria	1,482	1,506	171,540	187,135	3.0	3.1	1,095,779.8	1,110,719.8	Naira
Norway	40	40	4,596	4,946	2.3	2.3	18.4	18.6	Krone
Pakistan	1,187	1,212	137,458	150,552	1.4	1.4	149.5	154.7	Rupees
Peru	235	235	27,210	29,230	1.1	1.1	3.5	3.6	Nuevo Sol
Phillipines	640	651	74,091	80,876	1.6	1.7	82.2	86.2	Pesos
Poland	219	217	25,381	26,934	2.7	2.8	9.4	9.6	Zloty
Portugal	69	69	8,025	8,541	1.0	1.0	0.8	0.8	Euro
Puerto Rico	30	30	3,472	3,666	0.6	0.6	0.6	0.6	Dollar
Qatar	30	34	3,496	4,272	1.0	1.0	3.7	3.7	Riyal
Romania	158	155	18,269	19,291	1.1	1.1	4.2	4.3	New Leu
Russia	980	969	113,475	120,344	7.1	6.9	362.6	355.1	Rubles
Saudi Arabia	275	284	31,834	35,243	4.3	4.4	0.0	0.0	Rials*
Singapore	44	45	5,081	5,582	1.7	1.7	2,232.2	2,268.5	Dollar
South Africa	271	274	31,382	34,094	1.5	1.5	18,894.3	18,971.0	Rand
South Korea	383	382	44,357	47,404	8.3	8.5	8,892.8	9,064.7	Won*
Spain	318	320	36,820	39,731	6.4	6.3	5,329.1	5,294.0	Euro
Sweden	65	65	7,546	8,084	2.7	2.8	22,446.0	22,988.8	Krona
Switzerland	60	60	6,903	7,425	3.7	3.8	3,656.7	3,683.7	Swiss franc
Taiwan	239	247	27,644	30,644	2.8	2.9	84,020.2	84,915.0	Dollar
Thailand	577	580	66,822	72,051	2.4	2.4	77,333.2	77,970.5	Baht
Turkey	437	435	50,634	54,072	4.6	4.7	17,173.0	17,598.9	Euro
Ukraine	319	314	36,937	39,034	0.4	0.3	10,006.3	8,909.4	Hryvna
UAE	149	166	17,214	20,680	2.5	2.5	9,128.6	9,170.8	Dirham
United Kingdom	416	414	48,127	51,491	14.8	15.1	10,926.9	11,099.2	Pounds
United States	2,018	2,019	233,650	250,819	89.9	91.3	89,910.8	91,254.8	Dollars
Venezuela	206	209	23,834	25,962	2.5	2.4	24,468.4	23,626.5	Bolivar
Vietnam	724	725	83,857	90,023	1.3	1.4	29,202.5	30,696.7	Dong*

Note: Due to rounding, establishments will vary by + or - one establishment. Therefore, zero establishments may also be one establishment.

* Local Sales are in trillions

INTERIOR DESIGN SERVICES INDUSTRY (NAICS 54141)

NAICS 54141: Interior Design Services . This industry comprises establishments primarily engaged in planning, designing, and administering projects in interior spaces to meet the physical and aesthetic needs of people using them, taking into consideration building codes, health and safety regulations, traffic patterns and floor planning, mechanical and electrical needs, and interior fittings and furniture. Interior designers and interior design consultants work in areas, such as hospitality design, health care design, institutional design, commercial and corporate design, and residential design.

COUNTRY ESTIMATES

Country	Establishments 2018	Establishments 2019	Employment 2018	Employment 2019	Sales ($B) 2018	Sales ($B) 2019	Local Sales (B) 2018	Local Sales (B) 2019	Currency
Algeria	371	373	1,817	1,877	0.6	0.6	73.5	72.4	Dinar
Argentina	257	258	1,259	1,295	1.5	1.5	29.0	28.0	Pesos
Australia	160	162	784	812	3.8	3.7	4.8	4.7	Dollars
Austria	57	57	280	287	1.1	1.0	0.9	0.9	Euro
Bangladesh	1,129	1,130	5,524	5,681	0.6	0.6	51.5	52.9	Taka
Belgium	72	72	351	361	1.2	1.2	1.0	1.0	Euro
Brazil	1,375	1,387	6,727	6,969	4.6	4.4	14,946.9	14,233.5	Real
Canada	241	242	1,179	1,214	4.4	4.3	5.4	5.4	Dollars
Chile	133	134	652	675	0.8	0.7	457.2	451.6	Pesos*
China	9,511	9,479	46,525	47,641	38.7	39.3	251.0	255.1	RMB
Colombia	286	286	1,399	1,437	0.8	0.8	2.4	2.4	Pesos*
Czech Republic	69	68	335	343	0.6	0.6	12.0	12.1	Koruna
Denmark	36	36	176	180	0.8	0.8	5.0	5.0	Kroner
Egypt	608	623	2,976	3,131	0.9	0.9	16.7	16.4	Pounds
Finland	36	36	175	179	0.6	0.6	0.5	0.5	Euro
France	399	398	1,952	2,001	6.2	6.1	5.2	5.1	Euro
Germany	508	501	2,484	2,520	9.6	9.4	8.0	7.9	Euro
Greece	67	66	327	333	0.5	0.5	0.4	0.4	Euro
Hong Kong	41	41	200	205	0.7	0.7	5,558.8	5,516.7	Dollar
Hungary	60	59	295	299	0.3	0.3	87.8	88.2	Forint*
India	7,986	8,107	39,069	40,745	6.2	6.3	392.8	401.7	Rupees
Indonesia	1,986	2,011	9,715	10,109	3.1	3.1	41.2	41.8	Rupiah*

INTERIOR DESIGN SERVICES INDUSTRY
(NAICS 54141)

COUNTRY ESTIMATES

Country	Establishments 2018	2019	Employment 2018	2019	Sales ($B) 2018	2019	Local Sales (B) 2018	2019	Currency
Iran	544	550	2,661	2,766	1.1	1.1	39.9	38.4	Rial*
Iraq	285	290	1,395	1,456	0.6	0.6	0.7	0.7	Dinar*
Ireland	40	41	196	204	1.4	1.6	1.2	1.3	Euro
Israel	57	57	277	289	0.9	0.9	3.1	3.1	Shekel
Italy	402	400	1,966	2,010	5.0	4.8	4.2	4.0	Euro
Japan	846	837	4,138	4,207	11.8	11.6	1,337.3	1,304.3	Yen*
Kazakhstan	138	138	674	696	0.6	0.6	193.8	192.5	Tenge
Kuwait	32	34	158	169	0.3	0.3	0.1	0.1	Dinar
Malaysia	264	268	1,290	1,347	1.1	1.1	4.4	4.5	Ringgit
Mexico	859	869	4,202	4,367	3.2	3.2	61.7	61.2	New pesos
Netherlands	107	107	526	537	2.0	2.0	1.7	1.7	Euro
New Zealand	29	29	141	146	0.5	0.5	0.6	0.6	Dollar
Nigeria	1,482	1,506	7,248	7,571	1.6	1.6	586,532.3	581,548.1	Naira
Norway	40	40	194	200	1.2	1.2	9.9	9.7	Krone
Pakistan	1,187	1,212	5,808	6,091	0.7	0.7	80.0	81.0	Rupees
Peru	235	235	1,150	1,183	0.6	0.6	1.9	1.9	Nuevo Sol
Phillipines	640	651	3,130	3,272	0.9	0.9	44.0	45.1	Pesos
Poland	219	217	1,072	1,090	1.4	1.4	5.0	5.0	Zloty
Portugal	69	69	339	346	0.5	0.5	0.5	0.4	Euro
Puerto Rico	30	30	147	148	0.3	0.3	0.3	0.3	Dollar
Qatar	30	34	148	173	0.5	0.5	2.0	2.0	Riyal
Romania	158	155	772	780	0.6	0.6	2.2	2.2	New Leu
Russia	980	969	4,794	4,869	3.8	3.6	194.1	185.9	Rubles
Saudi Arabia	275	284	1,345	1,426	2.3	2.3	0.0	0.0	Rials*
Singapore	44	45	215	226	0.9	0.9	1,194.8	1,187.7	Dollar
South Africa	271	274	1,326	1,379	0.8	0.8	10,113.5	9,932.8	Rand
South Korea	383	382	1,874	1,918	4.5	4.4	4,760.0	4,746.1	Won*
Spain	318	320	1,556	1,607	3.4	3.3	2,852.5	2,771.8	Euro
Sweden	65	65	319	327	1.5	1.5	12,014.6	12,036.4	Krona
Switzerland	60	60	292	300	2.0	2.0	1,957.3	1,928.7	Swiss franc
Taiwan	239	247	1,168	1,240	1.5	1.5	44,973.1	44,459.6	Dollar
Thailand	577	580	2,823	2,915	1.3	1.3	41,393.7	40,823.6	Baht
Turkey	437	435	2,139	2,188	2.5	2.5	9,192.1	9,214.4	Euro
Ukraine	319	314	1,561	1,579	0.2	0.2	5,356.0	4,664.8	Hryvna
UAE	149	166	727	837	1.3	1.3	4,886.2	4,801.6	Dirham
United Kingdom	416	414	2,033	2,083	7.9	7.9	5,848.8	5,811.3	Pounds
United States	2,018	2,019	9,872	10,147	48.1	47.8	48,126.1	47,779.0	Dollars
Venezuela	206	209	1,007	1,050	1.3	1.2	13,097.1	12,370.3	Bolivar
Vietnam	724	725	3,543	3,642	0.7	0.7	15,631.1	16,072.1	Dong*

Note: Due to rounding, establishments will vary by + or - one establishment. Therefore, zero establishments may also be one establishment.

* Local Sales are in trillions

GRAPHIC DESIGNS SERVICES INDUSTRY (NAICS 54143)

NAICS 54143: Graphic Design Services . This industry comprises establishments primarily engaged in planning, designing, and managing the production of visual communication in order to convey specific messages or concepts, clarify complex information, or project visual identities. These services can include the design of printed materials, packaging, advertising, signage systems, and corporate identification (logos). This industry also includes commercial artists engaged exclusively in generating drawings and illustrations requiring technical accuracy or interpretative skills.

COUNTRY ESTIMATES

Country	Establishments 2018	2019	Employment 2018	2019	Sales ($B) 2018	2019	Local Sales (B) 2018	2019	Currency
Algeria	371	373	1,858	1,882	0.8	0.8	96.0	95.6	Dinar
Argentina	257	258	1,288	1,298	2.0	1.9	37.8	37.0	Pesos
Australia	160	162	802	815	4.9	4.9	6.2	6.3	Dollars
Austria	57	57	287	287	1.4	1.4	1.2	1.1	Euro
Bangladesh	1,129	1,130	5,649	5,697	0.8	0.8	67.2	69.9	Taka
Belgium	72	72	359	362	1.6	1.6	1.3	1.3	Euro
Brazil	1,375	1,387	6,880	6,989	6.0	5.8	19,513.3	18,797.3	Real
Canada	241	242	1,206	1,218	5.7	5.7	7.1	7.1	Dollars
Chile	133	134	667	677	1.0	1.0	596.9	596.4	Pesos*
China	9,511	9,479	47,583	47,775	50.5	51.9	327.6	336.9	RMB
Colombia	286	286	1,431	1,442	1.1	1.1	3.1	3.2	Pesos*
Czech Republic	69	68	343	344	0.7	0.7	15.6	15.9	Koruna
Denmark	36	36	180	181	1.1	1.1	6.6	6.5	Kroner
Egypt	608	623	3,044	3,140	1.2	1.2	21.8	21.7	Pounds
Finland	36	36	179	179	0.8	0.8	0.7	0.7	Euro
France	399	398	1,996	2,007	8.1	8.0	6.8	6.7	Euro
Germany	508	501	2,541	2,527	12.5	12.5	10.4	10.4	Euro
Greece	67	66	334	334	0.6	0.6	0.5	0.5	Euro
Hong Kong	41	41	205	206	0.9	0.9	7,257.0	7,285.5	Dollar
Hungary	60	59	302	300	0.4	0.5	114.7	116.5	Forint*
India	7,986	8,107	39,958	40,860	8.1	8.4	512.8	530.5	Rupees
Indonesia	1,986	2,011	9,936	10,138	4.0	4.1	53.8	55.2	Rupiah*

GRAPHIC DESIGNS SERVICES INDUSTRY
(NAICS 54143)

COUNTRY ESTIMATES

Country	Establishments 2018	Establishments 2019	Employment 2018	Employment 2019	Sales ($B) 2018	Sales ($B) 2019	Local Sales (B) 2018	Local Sales (B) 2019	Currency
Iran	544	550	2,721	2,774	1.4	1.4	52.0	50.8	Rial*
Iraq	285	290	1,427	1,460	0.8	0.7	0.9	0.9	Dinar*
Ireland	40	41	200	204	1.9	2.1	1.5	1.7	Euro
Israel	57	57	284	290	1.2	1.2	4.0	4.1	Shekel
Italy	402	400	2,011	2,016	6.5	6.4	5.4	5.3	Euro
Japan	846	837	4,232	4,219	15.5	15.3	1,745.9	1,722.4	Yen*
Kazakhstan	138	138	689	698	0.8	0.8	252.9	254.2	Tenge
Kuwait	32	34	161	169	0.5	0.4	0.1	0.1	Dinar
Malaysia	264	268	1,319	1,351	1.4	1.5	5.7	5.9	Ringgit
Mexico	859	869	4,297	4,379	4.2	4.2	80.6	80.8	New pesos
Netherlands	107	107	538	538	2.7	2.7	2.2	2.2	Euro
New Zealand	29	29	145	146	0.6	0.6	0.8	0.8	Dollar
Nigeria	1,482	1,506	7,413	7,592	2.1	2.1	765,722.4	768,012.8	Naira
Norway	40	40	199	201	1.6	1.6	12.9	12.8	Krone
Pakistan	1,187	1,212	5,940	6,108	0.9	1.0	104.4	107.0	Rupees
Peru	235	235	1,176	1,186	0.8	0.8	2.4	2.5	Nuevo Sol
Phillipines	640	651	3,202	3,281	1.1	1.2	57.4	59.6	Pesos
Poland	219	217	1,097	1,093	1.9	1.9	6.6	6.6	Zloty
Portugal	69	69	347	347	0.7	0.7	0.6	0.6	Euro
Puerto Rico	30	30	150	149	0.4	0.4	0.4	0.4	Dollar
Qatar	30	34	151	173	0.7	0.7	2.6	2.6	Riyal
Romania	158	155	789	783	0.8	0.8	2.9	3.0	New Leu
Russia	980	969	4,904	4,882	5.0	4.8	253.4	245.5	Rubles
Saudi Arabia	275	284	1,376	1,430	3.0	3.0	0.0	0.0	Rials*
Singapore	44	45	220	226	1.2	1.2	1,559.8	1,568.6	Dollar
South Africa	271	274	1,356	1,383	1.1	1.1	13,203.2	13,117.6	Rand
South Korea	383	382	1,917	1,923	5.8	5.9	6,214.2	6,267.9	Won*
Spain	318	320	1,591	1,612	4.5	4.4	3,723.9	3,660.5	Euro
Sweden	65	65	326	328	1.9	1.9	15,685.1	15,895.7	Krona
Switzerland	60	60	298	301	2.6	2.6	2,555.3	2,547.1	Swiss franc
Taiwan	239	247	1,195	1,243	2.0	2.0	58,712.7	58,714.9	Dollar
Thailand	577	580	2,888	2,923	1.7	1.7	54,039.9	53,913.1	Baht
Turkey	437	435	2,188	2,194	3.2	3.2	12,000.4	12,168.8	Euro
Ukraine	319	314	1,596	1,584	0.2	0.2	6,992.4	6,160.5	Hryvna
UAE	149	166	744	839	1.7	1.7	6,379.0	6,341.2	Dirham
United Kingdom	416	414	2,080	2,089	10.4	10.4	7,635.6	7,674.6	Pounds
United States	2,018	2,019	10,097	10,176	62.8	63.1	62,829.0	63,098.6	Dollars
Venezuela	206	209	1,030	1,053	1.7	1.6	17,098.3	16,336.7	Bolivar
Vietnam	724	725	3,624	3,652	0.9	0.9	20,406.5	21,225.4	Dong*

Note: Due to rounding, establishments will vary by + or - one establishment. Therefore, zero establishments may also be one establishment.

* Local Sales are in trillions

COMPUTER SYSTEMS DESIGNS SERVICES INDUSTRY (NAICS 54151)

NAICS 54151: Computer Systems Design and Related Services .
This industry comprises establishments primarily engaged in providing expertise in the field of information technologies through one or more of the following activities: (1) writing, modifying, testing, and supporting software to meet the needs of a particular customer; (2) planning and designing computer systems that integrate computer hardware, software, and communication technologies; (3) on-site management and operation of clients' computer systems and/or data processing facilities; and (4) other professional and technical computer-related advice and services.

COUNTRY ESTIMATES

Country	Establishments 2018	2019	Employment 2018	2019	Sales ($B) 2018	2019	Local Sales (B) 2018	2019	Currency
Algeria	371	373	73,418	80,086	3.9	4.1	453.7	467.4	Dinar
Argentina	257	258	50,899	55,234	9.4	9.5	178.6	181.0	Pesos
Australia	160	162	31,673	34,655	23.3	24.1	29.5	30.6	Dollars
Austria	57	57	11,332	12,232	6.5	6.7	5.5	5.6	Euro
Bangladesh	1,129	1,130	223,222	242,392	3.8	4.1	317.5	341.4	Taka
Belgium	72	72	14,204	15,410	7.5	7.7	6.3	6.4	Euro
Brazil	1,375	1,387	271,844	297,346	28.5	28.4	92,214.9	91,855.6	Real
Canada	241	242	47,643	51,815	27.0	27.9	33.5	34.5	Dollars
Chile	133	134	26,357	28,797	4.7	4.8	2,820.7	2,914.2	Pesos*
China	9,511	9,479	1,880,201	2,032,647	238.6	253.7	1,548.3	1,646.3	RMB
Colombia	286	286	56,534	61,333	5.1	5.4	14.9	15.6	Pesos*
Czech Republic	69	68	13,551	14,617	3.5	3.7	74.0	77.8	Koruna
Denmark	36	36	7,129	7,692	5.0	5.1	31.1	32.0	Kroner
Egypt	608	623	120,274	133,609	5.9	6.0	103.1	106.1	Pounds
Finland	36	36	7,061	7,623	3.8	3.8	3.2	3.2	Euro
France	399	398	78,870	85,380	38.4	39.3	32.1	32.8	Euro
Germany	508	501	100,402	107,517	59.0	60.9	49.3	50.8	Euro
Greece	67	66	13,209	14,224	3.0	3.0	2.5	2.5	Euro
Hong Kong	41	41	8,102	8,748	4.4	4.6	34,294.9	35,601.8	Dollar
Hungary	60	59	11,914	12,758	2.1	2.2	541.8	569.1	Forint*
India	7,986	8,107	1,578,902	1,738,443	38.2	40.8	2,423.3	2,592.4	Rupees
Indonesia	1,986	2,011	392,618	431,334	18.9	20.1	254.1	269.8	Rupiah*

Computer Systems Designs Services Industry (NAICS 54151)

Country Estimates

Country	Establishments 2018	Establishments 2019	Employment 2018	Employment 2019	Sales ($B) 2018	Sales ($B) 2019	Local Sales (B) 2018	Local Sales (B) 2019	Currency
Iran	544	550	107,530	118,021	6.8	6.9	246.0	248.1	Rial*
Iraq	285	290	56,393	62,105	3.6	3.6	4.3	4.3	Dinar*
Ireland	40	41	7,912	8,691	8.8	10.2	7.3	8.5	Euro
Israel	57	57	11,212	12,329	5.6	5.8	19.1	19.9	Shekel
Italy	402	400	79,450	85,774	30.7	31.3	25.6	26.1	Euro
Japan	846	837	167,212	179,513	73.1	74.6	8,250.8	8,417.0	Yen*
Kazakhstan	138	138	27,243	29,690	3.6	3.8	1,195.3	1,242.3	Tenge
Kuwait	32	34	6,367	7,205	2.1	2.1	0.6	0.6	Dinar
Malaysia	264	268	52,123	57,492	6.7	7.2	27.0	28.8	Ringgit
Mexico	859	869	169,807	186,319	19.8	20.6	380.7	394.8	New pesos
Netherlands	107	107	21,241	22,908	12.6	13.0	10.5	10.9	Euro
New Zealand	29	29	5,712	6,233	2.8	3.0	4.0	4.1	Dollar
Nigeria	1,482	1,506	292,901	323,023	10.1	10.4	3,618,614.4	3,752,998.9	Naira
Norway	40	40	7,847	8,538	7.5	7.8	60.8	62.8	Krone
Pakistan	1,187	1,212	234,707	259,875	4.5	4.7	493.5	522.8	Rupees
Peru	235	235	46,460	50,455	3.6	3.7	11.6	12.0	Nuevo Sol
Phillipines	640	651	126,509	139,604	5.4	5.8	271.4	291.3	Pesos
Poland	219	217	43,338	46,493	8.9	9.3	31.0	32.4	Zloty
Portugal	69	69	13,702	14,743	3.3	3.4	2.8	2.8	Euro
Puerto Rico	30	30	5,928	6,329	2.0	2.0	2.0	2.0	Dollar
Qatar	30	34	5,969	7,374	3.4	3.5	12.3	12.6	Riyal
Romania	158	155	31,194	33,299	3.6	3.7	13.9	14.5	New Leu
Russia	980	969	193,757	207,731	23.4	23.5	1,197.5	1,199.8	Rubles
Saudi Arabia	275	284	54,356	60,834	14.4	14.8	0.1	0.1	Rials*
Singapore	44	45	8,676	9,636	5.5	5.8	7,371.4	7,665.1	Dollar
South Africa	271	274	53,585	58,851	5.0	5.2	62,395.0	64,101.0	Rand
South Korea	383	382	75,739	81,826	27.5	28.7	29,366.9	30,628.8	Won*
Spain	318	320	62,870	68,581	21.1	21.4	17,598.4	17,887.7	Euro
Sweden	65	65	12,884	13,954	9.0	9.5	74,124.0	77,676.6	Krona
Switzerland	60	60	11,787	12,817	12.4	12.7	12,075.7	12,446.7	Swiss franc
Taiwan	239	247	47,202	52,896	9.4	9.7	277,461.6	286,918.2	Dollar
Thailand	577	580	114,097	124,371	7.9	8.2	255,379.0	263,453.5	Baht
Turkey	437	435	86,457	93,337	15.1	15.9	56,710.9	59,464.7	Euro
Ukraine	319	314	63,069	67,378	1.2	1.1	33,044.2	30,104.0	Hryvna
UAE	149	166	29,393	35,697	8.2	8.4	30,145.5	30,987.1	Dirham
United Kingdom	416	414	82,176	88,880	49.0	50.9	36,084.2	37,503.0	Pounds
United States	2,018	2,019	398,953	432,951	296.9	308.3	296,914.1	308,339.9	Dollars
Venezuela	206	209	40,696	44,814	8.1	8.0	80,802.5	79,831.3	Bolivar
Vietnam	724	725	143,185	155,393	4.2	4.6	96,436.0	103,720.9	Dong*

Note: Due to rounding, establishments will vary by + or - one establishment. Therefore, zero establishments may also be one establishment.

* Local Sales are in trillions

© Barnes Reports: 2018 World Industry & Market Outlook

MANAGEMENT CONSULTING SERVICES INDUSTRY (NAICS 54161)

NAICS 54161: Management Consulting Services . This industry comprises establishments primarily engaged in providing advice and assistance to businesses and other organizations on management issues, such as strategic and organizational planning; financial planning and budgeting; marketing objectives and policies; human resource policies, practices, and planning; production scheduling; and control planning.

COUNTRY ESTIMATES

Country	Establishments		Employment		Sales ($B)		Local Sales (B)		
	2018	2019	2018	2019	2018	2019	2018	2019	Currency
Algeria	124	124	10,810	11,728	1.8	1.9	205.7	214.0	Dinar
Argentina	86	86	7,494	8,089	4.2	4.3	81.0	82.9	Pesos
Australia	53	54	4,663	5,075	10.5	11.0	13.4	14.0	Dollars
Austria	19	19	1,668	1,791	3.0	3.1	2.5	2.5	Euro
Bangladesh	376	377	32,866	35,498	1.7	1.9	144.0	156.3	Taka
Belgium	24	24	2,091	2,257	3.4	3.5	2.8	2.9	Euro
Brazil	458	462	40,025	43,545	12.9	13.0	41,815.5	42,059.5	Real
Canada	80	81	7,015	7,588	12.3	12.8	15.2	15.8	Dollars
Chile	44	45	3,881	4,217	2.1	2.2	1,279.1	1,334.4	Pesos*
China	3,170	3,160	276,832	297,675	108.2	116.1	702.1	753.8	RMB
Colombia	95	95	8,324	8,982	2.3	2.5	6.7	7.1	Pesos*
Czech Republic	23	23	1,995	2,141	1.6	1.7	33.5	35.6	Koruna
Denmark	12	12	1,050	1,126	2.3	2.4	14.1	14.6	Kroner
Egypt	203	208	17,709	19,567	2.7	2.8	46.7	48.6	Pounds
Finland	12	12	1,040	1,116	1.7	1.8	1.4	1.5	Euro
France	133	133	11,612	12,504	17.4	18.0	14.5	15.0	Euro
Germany	169	167	14,783	15,745	26.8	27.9	22.4	23.3	Euro
Greece	22	22	1,945	2,083	1.4	1.4	1.1	1.1	Euro
Hong Kong	14	14	1,193	1,281	2.0	2.1	15,551.3	16,301.6	Dollar
Hungary	20	20	1,754	1,868	1.0	1.0	245.7	260.6	Forint*
India	2,662	2,702	232,470	254,590	17.3	18.7	1,098.8	1,187.0	Rupees
Indonesia	662	670	57,807	63,167	8.6	9.2	115.2	123.5	Rupiah*

MANAGEMENT CONSULTING SERVICES INDUSTRY (NAICS 54161)

COUNTRY ESTIMATES

Country	Establishments 2018	Establishments 2019	Employment 2018	Employment 2019	Sales ($B) 2018	Sales ($B) 2019	Local Sales (B) 2018	Local Sales (B) 2019	Currency
Iran	181	183	15,832	17,284	3.1	3.1	111.5	113.6	Rial*
Iraq	95	97	8,303	9,095	1.6	1.7	1.9	2.0	Dinar*
Ireland	13	14	1,165	1,273	4.0	4.7	3.3	3.9	Euro
Israel	19	19	1,651	1,806	2.5	2.7	8.7	9.1	Shekel
Italy	134	133	11,698	12,561	13.9	14.3	11.6	12.0	Euro
Japan	282	279	24,619	26,289	33.1	34.1	3,741.4	3,854.0	Yen*
Kazakhstan	46	46	4,011	4,348	1.6	1.7	542.0	568.9	Tenge
Kuwait	11	11	937	1,055	1.0	1.0	0.3	0.3	Dinar
Malaysia	88	89	7,674	8,419	3.1	3.3	12.2	13.2	Ringgit
Mexico	286	290	25,002	27,286	9.0	9.4	172.6	180.8	New pesos
Netherlands	36	36	3,127	3,355	5.7	6.0	4.8	5.0	Euro
New Zealand	10	10	841	913	1.3	1.4	1.8	1.9	Dollar
Nigeria	494	502	43,125	47,306	4.6	4.8	1,640,886.0	1,718,449.6	Naira
Norway	13	13	1,155	1,250	3.4	3.6	27.6	28.8	Krone
Pakistan	396	404	34,557	38,058	2.0	2.2	223.8	239.4	Rupees
Peru	78	78	6,841	7,389	1.6	1.7	5.2	5.5	Nuevo Sol
Phillipines	213	217	18,627	20,445	2.5	2.7	123.1	133.4	Pesos
Poland	73	72	6,381	6,809	4.0	4.3	14.0	14.9	Zloty
Portugal	23	23	2,017	2,159	1.5	1.5	1.3	1.3	Euro
Puerto Rico	10	10	873	927	0.9	0.9	0.9	0.9	Dollar
Qatar	10	11	879	1,080	1.5	1.6	5.6	5.8	Riyal
Romania	53	52	4,593	4,877	1.6	1.7	6.3	6.6	New Leu
Russia	327	323	28,528	30,422	10.6	10.8	543.0	549.4	Rubles
Saudi Arabia	92	95	8,003	8,909	6.5	6.8	0.0	0.0	Rials*
Singapore	15	15	1,277	1,411	2.5	2.6	3,342.6	3,509.7	Dollar
South Africa	90	91	7,890	8,619	2.3	2.4	28,293.4	29,351.0	Rand
South Korea	128	127	11,151	11,983	12.5	13.1	13,316.6	14,024.5	Won*
Spain	106	107	9,257	10,044	9.6	9.8	7,980.1	8,190.5	Euro
Sweden	22	22	1,897	2,044	4.1	4.3	33,612.0	35,567.1	Krona
Switzerland	20	20	1,735	1,877	5.6	5.8	5,475.8	5,699.2	Swiss franc
Taiwan	80	82	6,950	7,746	4.3	4.5	125,816.9	131,376.1	Dollar
Thailand	192	193	16,799	18,214	3.6	3.7	115,803.4	120,632.0	Baht
Turkey	146	145	12,730	13,669	6.9	7.3	25,715.9	27,228.1	Euro
Ukraine	106	105	9,286	9,867	0.5	0.5	14,984.1	13,784.2	Hryvna
UAE	50	55	4,328	5,228	3.7	3.9	13,669.7	14,188.6	Dirham
United Kingdom	139	138	12,099	13,016	22.2	23.3	16,362.6	17,172.1	Pounds
United States	2,018	2,019	176,220	190,213	403.9	423.6	403,913.3	423,554.5	Dollars
Venezuela	69	70	5,992	6,563	3.7	3.7	36,640.5	36,553.7	Bolivar
Vietnam	241	242	21,082	22,757	1.9	2.1	43,729.6	47,492.4	Dong*

Note: Due to rounding, establishments will vary by + or - one establishment. Therefore, zero establishments may also be one establishment.

* Local Sales are in trillions

Advertising Agencies Industry
(NAICS 54181)

NAICS 54181: Advertising Agencies . This industry comprises establishments primarily engaged in designing and implementing public relations campaigns. These campaigns are designed to promote the interests and image of their clients. Establishments providing lobbying, political consulting, or public relations consulting are included in this industry.

Country Estimates

Country	Establishments 2018	Establishments 2019	Employment 2018	Employment 2019	Sales ($B) 2018	Sales ($B) 2019	Local Sales (B) 2018	Local Sales (B) 2019	Currency
Algeria	371	373	13,251	13,942	0.4	0.4	49.7	49.4	Dinar
Argentina	257	258	9,187	9,616	1.0	1.0	19.6	19.1	Pesos
Australia	160	162	5,717	6,033	2.5	2.6	3.2	3.2	Dollars
Austria	57	57	2,045	2,129	0.7	0.7	0.6	0.6	Euro
Bangladesh	1,129	1,130	40,290	42,198	0.4	0.4	34.8	36.1	Taka
Belgium	72	72	2,564	2,683	0.8	0.8	0.7	0.7	Euro
Brazil	1,375	1,387	49,066	51,765	3.1	3.0	10,095.8	9,718.5	Real
Canada	241	242	8,599	9,020	3.0	2.9	3.7	3.7	Dollars
Chile	133	134	4,757	5,013	0.5	0.5	308.8	308.3	Pesos*
China	9,511	9,479	339,361	353,861	26.1	26.8	169.5	174.2	RMB
Colombia	286	286	10,204	10,677	0.6	0.6	1.6	1.7	Pesos*
Czech Republic	69	68	2,446	2,545	0.4	0.4	8.1	8.2	Koruna
Denmark	36	36	1,287	1,339	0.5	0.5	3.4	3.4	Kroner
Egypt	608	623	21,709	23,260	0.6	0.6	11.3	11.2	Pounds
Finland	36	36	1,274	1,327	0.4	0.4	0.3	0.3	Euro
France	399	398	14,235	14,864	4.2	4.2	3.5	3.5	Euro
Germany	508	501	18,122	18,717	6.5	6.4	5.4	5.4	Euro
Greece	67	66	2,384	2,476	0.3	0.3	0.3	0.3	Euro
Hong Kong	41	41	1,462	1,523	0.5	0.5	3,754.6	3,766.7	Dollar
Hungary	60	59	2,150	2,221	0.2	0.2	59.3	60.2	Forint*
India	7,986	8,107	284,979	302,644	4.2	4.3	265.3	274.3	Rupees
Indonesia	1,986	2,011	70,864	75,090	2.1	2.1	27.8	28.5	Rupiah*

Advertising Agencies Industry
(NAICS 54181)

Country Estimates

Country	Establishments 2018	2019	Employment 2018	2019	Sales ($B) 2018	2019	Local Sales (B) 2018	2019	Currency
Iran	544	550	19,408	20,546	0.7	0.7	26.9	26.3	Rial*
Iraq	285	290	10,179	10,812	0.4	0.4	0.5	0.5	Dinar*
Ireland	40	41	1,428	1,513	1.0	1.1	0.8	0.9	Euro
Israel	57	57	2,024	2,146	0.6	0.6	2.1	2.1	Shekel
Italy	402	400	14,340	14,932	3.4	3.3	2.8	2.8	Euro
Japan	846	837	30,180	31,251	8.0	7.9	903.3	890.5	Yen*
Kazakhstan	138	138	4,917	5,169	0.4	0.4	130.9	131.4	Tenge
Kuwait	32	34	1,149	1,254	0.2	0.2	0.1	0.1	Dinar
Malaysia	264	268	9,408	10,009	0.7	0.8	3.0	3.0	Ringgit
Mexico	859	869	30,649	32,436	2.2	2.2	41.7	41.8	New pesos
Netherlands	107	107	3,834	3,988	1.4	1.4	1.2	1.1	Euro
New Zealand	29	29	1,031	1,085	0.3	0.3	0.4	0.4	Dollar
Nigeria	1,482	1,506	52,866	56,235	1.1	1.1	396,169.3	397,074.7	Naira
Norway	40	40	1,416	1,486	0.8	0.8	6.7	6.6	Krone
Pakistan	1,187	1,212	42,363	45,241	0.5	0.5	54.0	55.3	Rupees
Peru	235	235	8,386	8,784	0.4	0.4	1.3	1.3	Nuevo Sol
Phillipines	640	651	22,834	24,304	0.6	0.6	29.7	30.8	Pesos
Poland	219	217	7,822	8,094	1.0	1.0	3.4	3.4	Zloty
Portugal	69	69	2,473	2,567	0.4	0.4	0.3	0.3	Euro
Puerto Rico	30	30	1,070	1,102	0.2	0.2	0.2	0.2	Dollar
Qatar	30	34	1,077	1,284	0.4	0.4	1.3	1.3	Riyal
Romania	158	155	5,630	5,797	0.4	0.4	1.5	1.5	New Leu
Russia	980	969	34,972	36,164	2.6	2.5	131.1	126.9	Rubles
Saudi Arabia	275	284	9,811	10,591	1.6	1.6	0.0	0.0	Rials*
Singapore	44	45	1,566	1,677	0.6	0.6	807.0	811.0	Dollar
South Africa	271	274	9,672	10,245	0.6	0.5	6,831.1	6,782.0	Rand
South Korea	383	382	13,670	14,245	3.0	3.0	3,215.1	3,240.6	Won*
Spain	318	320	11,348	11,939	2.3	2.3	1,926.7	1,892.6	Euro
Sweden	65	65	2,325	2,429	1.0	1.0	8,115.2	8,218.3	Krona
Switzerland	60	60	2,127	2,231	1.4	1.3	1,322.1	1,316.9	Swiss franc
Taiwan	239	247	8,520	9,209	1.0	1.0	30,376.8	30,356.5	Dollar
Thailand	577	580	20,594	21,652	0.9	0.9	27,959.1	27,873.9	Baht
Turkey	437	435	15,605	16,249	1.7	1.7	6,208.8	6,291.5	Euro
Ukraine	319	314	11,383	11,730	0.1	0.1	3,617.7	3,185.1	Hryvna
UAE	149	166	5,305	6,215	0.9	0.9	3,300.4	3,278.5	Dirham
United Kingdom	416	414	14,832	15,473	5.4	5.4	3,950.5	3,967.9	Pounds
United States	2,018	2,019	72,008	75,372	32.5	32.6	32,506.4	32,623.0	Dollars
Venezuela	206	209	7,345	7,802	0.9	0.8	8,846.3	8,446.3	Bolivar
Vietnam	724	725	25,844	27,052	0.5	0.5	10,557.9	10,973.9	Dong*

Note: Due to rounding, establishments will vary by + or - one establishment. Therefore, zero establishments may also be one establishment.

* Local Sales are in trillions

Public Relations Agencies Industry (NAICS 54182)

NAICS 54182: Public Relations Agencies . This industry comprises establishments primarily engaged in designing and implementing public relations campaigns. These campaigns are designed to promote the interests and image of their clients. Establishments providing lobbying, political consulting, or public relations consulting are included in this industry.

COUNTRY ESTIMATES

Country	Establishments 2018	Establishments 2019	Employment 2018	Employment 2019	Sales ($B) 2018	Sales ($B) 2019	Local Sales (B) 2018	Local Sales (B) 2019	Currency
Algeria	371	373	2,547	2,771	0.3	0.3	34.4	34.9	Dinar
Argentina	257	258	1,766	1,911	0.7	0.7	13.6	13.5	Pesos
Australia	160	162	1,099	1,199	1.8	1.8	2.2	2.3	Dollars
Austria	57	57	393	423	0.5	0.5	0.4	0.4	Euro
Bangladesh	1,129	1,130	7,743	8,387	0.3	0.3	24.1	25.5	Taka
Belgium	72	72	493	533	0.6	0.6	0.5	0.5	Euro
Brazil	1,375	1,387	9,430	10,289	2.2	2.1	6,996.8	6,865.9	Real
Canada	241	242	1,653	1,793	2.1	2.1	2.5	2.6	Dollars
Chile	133	134	914	996	0.4	0.4	214.0	217.8	Pesos*
China	9,511	9,479	65,219	70,335	18.1	19.0	117.5	123.1	RMB
Colombia	286	286	1,961	2,122	0.4	0.4	1.1	1.2	Pesos*
Czech Republic	69	68	470	506	0.3	0.3	5.6	5.8	Koruna
Denmark	36	36	247	266	0.4	0.4	2.4	2.4	Kroner
Egypt	608	623	4,172	4,623	0.4	0.5	7.8	7.9	Pounds
Finland	36	36	245	264	0.3	0.3	0.2	0.2	Euro
France	399	398	2,736	2,954	2.9	2.9	2.4	2.5	Euro
Germany	508	501	3,483	3,720	4.5	4.5	3.7	3.8	Euro
Greece	67	66	458	492	0.2	0.2	0.2	0.2	Euro
Hong Kong	41	41	281	303	0.3	0.3	2,602.1	2,661.1	Dollar
Hungary	60	59	413	441	0.2	0.2	41.1	42.5	Forint*
India	7,986	8,107	54,768	60,154	2.9	3.1	183.9	193.8	Rupees
Indonesia	1,986	2,011	13,619	14,925	1.4	1.5	19.3	20.2	Rupiah*

PUBLIC RELATIONS AGENCIES INDUSTRY
(NAICS 54182)

COUNTRY ESTIMATES

Country	Establishments 2018	Establishments 2019	Employment 2018	Employment 2019	Sales ($B) 2018	Sales ($B) 2019	Local Sales (B) 2018	Local Sales (B) 2019	Currency
Iran	544	550	3,730	4,084	0.5	0.5	18.7	18.5	Rial*
Iraq	285	290	1,956	2,149	0.3	0.3	0.3	0.3	Dinar*
Ireland	40	41	274	301	0.7	0.8	0.6	0.6	Euro
Israel	57	57	389	427	0.4	0.4	1.4	1.5	Shekel
Italy	402	400	2,756	2,968	2.3	2.3	1.9	2.0	Euro
Japan	846	837	5,800	6,212	5.5	5.6	626.0	629.1	Yen*
Kazakhstan	138	138	945	1,027	0.3	0.3	90.7	92.9	Tenge
Kuwait	32	34	221	249	0.2	0.2	0.0	0.0	Dinar
Malaysia	264	268	1,808	1,989	0.5	0.5	2.0	2.2	Ringgit
Mexico	859	869	5,890	6,447	1.5	1.5	28.9	29.5	New pesos
Netherlands	107	107	737	793	1.0	1.0	0.8	0.8	Euro
New Zealand	29	29	198	216	0.2	0.2	0.3	0.3	Dollar
Nigeria	1,482	1,506	10,160	11,177	0.8	0.8	274,562.9	280,523.6	Naira
Norway	40	40	272	295	0.6	0.6	4.6	4.7	Krone
Pakistan	1,187	1,212	8,141	8,992	0.3	0.4	37.4	39.1	Rupees
Peru	235	235	1,612	1,746	0.3	0.3	0.9	0.9	Nuevo Sol
Phillipines	640	651	4,388	4,831	0.4	0.4	20.6	21.8	Pesos
Poland	219	217	1,503	1,609	0.7	0.7	2.3	2.4	Zloty
Portugal	69	69	475	510	0.3	0.3	0.2	0.2	Euro
Puerto Rico	30	30	206	219	0.2	0.1	0.2	0.1	Dollar
Qatar	30	34	207	255	0.3	0.3	0.9	0.9	Riyal
Romania	158	155	1,082	1,152	0.3	0.3	1.1	1.1	New Leu
Russia	980	969	6,721	7,188	1.8	1.8	90.9	89.7	Rubles
Saudi Arabia	275	284	1,885	2,105	1.1	1.1	0.0	0.0	Rials*
Singapore	44	45	301	333	0.4	0.4	559.3	572.9	Dollar
South Africa	271	274	1,859	2,036	0.4	0.4	4,734.2	4,791.3	Rand
South Korea	383	382	2,627	2,831	2.1	2.1	2,228.2	2,289.4	Won*
Spain	318	320	2,181	2,373	1.6	1.6	1,335.3	1,337.0	Euro
Sweden	65	65	447	483	0.7	0.7	5,624.2	5,806.1	Krona
Switzerland	60	60	409	444	0.9	1.0	916.2	930.3	Swiss franc
Taiwan	239	247	1,637	1,830	0.7	0.7	21,052.4	21,446.1	Dollar
Thailand	577	580	3,958	4,304	0.6	0.6	19,376.9	19,692.2	Baht
Turkey	437	435	2,999	3,230	1.1	1.2	4,302.9	4,444.8	Euro
Ukraine	319	314	2,188	2,331	0.1	0.1	2,507.2	2,250.2	Hryvna
UAE	149	166	1,020	1,235	0.6	0.6	2,287.3	2,316.2	Dirham
United Kingdom	416	414	2,850	3,075	3.7	3.8	2,737.9	2,803.2	Pounds
United States	2,018	2,019	13,839	14,981	22.5	23.0	22,528.4	23,047.3	Dollars
Venezuela	206	209	1,412	1,551	0.6	0.6	6,130.9	5,967.1	Bolivar
Vietnam	724	725	4,967	5,377	0.3	0.3	7,317.1	7,752.8	Dong*

Note: Due to rounding, establishments will vary by + or - one establishment. Therefore, zero establishments may also be one establishment.

* Local Sales are in trillions

DIRECT MAIL ADVERTISING INDUSTRY (NAICS 54186)

NAICS 54186: Direct Mail Advertising . This industry comprises establishments primarily engaged in (1) creating and designing advertising campaigns for the purpose of distributing advertising materials (e.g., coupons, flyers, samples) or specialties (e.g., key chains, magnets, pens with customized messages imprinted) by mail or other direct distribution; and/or (2) preparing advertising materials or specialties for mailing or other direct distribution. These establishments may also compile, maintain, sell, and rent mailing lists.

COUNTRY ESTIMATES

Country	Establishments		Employment		Sales ($B)		Local Sales (B)		
	2018	2019	2018	2019	2018	2019	2018	2019	Currency
Algeria	371	373	1,354	1,391	0.1	0.1	9.5	9.2	Dinar
Argentina	257	258	939	960	0.2	0.2	3.7	3.6	Pesos
Australia	160	162	584	602	0.5	0.5	0.6	0.6	Dollars
Austria	57	57	209	213	0.1	0.1	0.1	0.1	Euro
Bangladesh	1,129	1,130	4,117	4,212	0.1	0.1	6.6	6.7	Taka
Belgium	72	72	262	268	0.2	0.2	0.1	0.1	Euro
Brazil	1,375	1,387	5,014	5,166	0.6	0.6	1,926.5	1,812.2	Real
Canada	241	242	879	900	0.6	0.5	0.7	0.7	Dollars
Chile	133	134	486	500	0.1	0.1	58.9	57.5	Pesos*
China	9,511	9,479	34,679	35,317	5.0	5.0	32.3	32.5	RMB
Colombia	286	286	1,043	1,066	0.1	0.1	0.3	0.3	Pesos*
Czech Republic	69	68	250	254	0.1	0.1	1.5	1.5	Koruna
Denmark	36	36	131	134	0.1	0.1	0.6	0.6	Kroner
Egypt	608	623	2,218	2,321	0.1	0.1	2.2	2.1	Pounds
Finland	36	36	130	132	0.1	0.1	0.1	0.1	Euro
France	399	398	1,455	1,483	0.8	0.8	0.7	0.6	Euro
Germany	508	501	1,852	1,868	1.2	1.2	1.0	1.0	Euro
Greece	67	66	244	247	0.1	0.1	0.1	0.0	Euro
Hong Kong	41	41	149	152	0.1	0.1	716.5	702.4	Dollar
Hungary	60	59	220	222	0.0	0.0	11.3	11.2	Forint*
India	7,986	8,107	29,122	30,205	0.8	0.8	50.6	51.1	Rupees
Indonesia	1,986	2,011	7,242	7,494	0.4	0.4	5.3	5.3	Rupiah*

DIRECT MAIL ADVERTISING INDUSTRY
(NAICS 54186)

COUNTRY ESTIMATES

Country	Establishments 2018	Establishments 2019	Employment 2018	Employment 2019	Sales ($B) 2018	Sales ($B) 2019	Local Sales (B) 2018	Local Sales (B) 2019	Currency
Iran	544	550	1,983	2,051	0.1	0.1	5.1	4.9	Rial*
Iraq	285	290	1,040	1,079	0.1	0.1	0.1	0.1	Dinar*
Ireland	40	41	146	151	0.2	0.2	0.2	0.2	Euro
Israel	57	57	207	214	0.1	0.1	0.4	0.4	Shekel
Italy	402	400	1,465	1,490	0.6	0.6	0.5	0.5	Euro
Japan	846	837	3,084	3,119	1.5	1.5	172.4	166.1	Yen*
Kazakhstan	138	138	502	516	0.1	0.1	25.0	24.5	Tenge
Kuwait	32	34	117	125	0.0	0.0	0.0	0.0	Dinar
Malaysia	264	268	961	999	0.1	0.1	0.6	0.6	Ringgit
Mexico	859	869	3,132	3,237	0.4	0.4	8.0	7.8	New pesos
Netherlands	107	107	392	398	0.3	0.3	0.2	0.2	Euro
New Zealand	29	29	105	108	0.1	0.1	0.1	0.1	Dollar
Nigeria	1,482	1,506	5,402	5,612	0.2	0.2	75,598.3	74,042.4	Naira
Norway	40	40	145	148	0.2	0.2	1.3	1.2	Krone
Pakistan	1,187	1,212	4,329	4,515	0.1	0.1	10.3	10.3	Rupees
Peru	235	235	857	877	0.1	0.1	0.2	0.2	Nuevo Sol
Phillipines	640	651	2,333	2,426	0.1	0.1	5.7	5.7	Pesos
Poland	219	217	799	808	0.2	0.2	0.6	0.6	Zloty
Portugal	69	69	253	256	0.1	0.1	0.1	0.1	Euro
Puerto Rico	30	30	109	110	0.0	0.0	0.0	0.0	Dollar
Qatar	30	34	110	128	0.1	0.1	0.3	0.2	Riyal
Romania	158	155	575	579	0.1	0.1	0.3	0.3	New Leu
Russia	980	969	3,574	3,609	0.5	0.5	25.0	23.7	Rubles
Saudi Arabia	275	284	1,003	1,057	0.3	0.3	0.0	0.0	Rials*
Singapore	44	45	160	167	0.1	0.1	154.0	151.2	Dollar
South Africa	271	274	988	1,023	0.1	0.1	1,303.5	1,264.6	Rand
South Korea	383	382	1,397	1,422	0.6	0.6	613.5	604.3	Won*
Spain	318	320	1,160	1,192	0.4	0.4	367.7	352.9	Euro
Sweden	65	65	238	242	0.2	0.2	1,548.6	1,532.5	Krona
Switzerland	60	60	217	223	0.3	0.3	252.3	245.6	Swiss franc
Taiwan	239	247	871	919	0.2	0.2	5,796.6	5,660.6	Dollar
Thailand	577	580	2,104	2,161	0.2	0.2	5,335.3	5,197.6	Baht
Turkey	437	435	1,595	1,622	0.3	0.3	1,184.8	1,173.2	Euro
Ukraine	319	314	1,163	1,171	0.0	0.0	690.3	593.9	Hryvna
UAE	149	166	542	620	0.2	0.2	629.8	611.3	Dirham
United Kingdom	416	414	1,516	1,544	1.0	1.0	753.9	739.9	Pounds
United States	2,018	2,019	7,358	7,522	6.2	6.1	6,203.0	6,083.2	Dollars
Venezuela	206	209	751	779	0.2	0.2	1,688.1	1,575.0	Bolivar
Vietnam	724	725	2,641	2,700	0.1	0.1	2,014.7	2,046.3	Dong*

Note: Due to rounding, establishments will vary by + or - one establishment. Therefore, zero establishments may also be one establishment.

* Local Sales are in trillions

NAICS 54191: Marketing Research & Public Opinion Polling . This industry comprises establishments primarily engaged in systematically gathering, recording, tabulating, and presenting marketing and public opinion data.

COUNTRY ESTIMATES

Country	Establishments 2018	Establishments 2019	Employment 2018	Employment 2019	Sales ($B) 2018	Sales ($B) 2019	Local Sales (B) 2018	Local Sales (B) 2019	Currency
Algeria	371	373	3,512	3,673	0.3	0.3	37.1	36.9	Dinar
Argentina	257	258	2,435	2,533	0.8	0.7	14.6	14.3	Pesos
Australia	160	162	1,515	1,589	1.9	1.9	2.4	2.4	Dollars
Austria	57	57	542	561	0.5	0.5	0.4	0.4	Euro
Bangladesh	1,129	1,130	10,678	11,117	0.3	0.3	26.0	26.9	Taka
Belgium	72	72	679	707	0.6	0.6	0.5	0.5	Euro
Brazil	1,375	1,387	13,004	13,637	2.3	2.2	7,537.9	7,244.0	Real
Canada	241	242	2,279	2,376	2.2	2.2	2.7	2.7	Dollars
Chile	133	134	1,261	1,321	0.4	0.4	230.6	229.8	Pesos*
China	9,511	9,479	89,940	93,223	19.5	20.0	126.6	129.8	RMB
Colombia	286	286	2,704	2,813	0.4	0.4	1.2	1.2	Pesos*
Czech Republic	69	68	648	670	0.3	0.3	6.0	6.1	Koruna
Denmark	36	36	341	353	0.4	0.4	2.5	2.5	Kroner
Egypt	608	623	5,753	6,128	0.5	0.5	8.4	8.4	Pounds
Finland	36	36	338	350	0.3	0.3	0.3	0.3	Euro
France	399	398	3,773	3,916	3.1	3.1	2.6	2.6	Euro
Germany	508	501	4,803	4,931	4.8	4.8	4.0	4.0	Euro
Greece	67	66	632	652	0.2	0.2	0.2	0.2	Euro
Hong Kong	41	41	388	401	0.4	0.4	2,803.4	2,807.7	Dollar
Hungary	60	59	570	585	0.2	0.2	44.3	44.9	Forint*
India	7,986	8,107	75,527	79,730	3.1	3.2	198.1	204.4	Rupees
Indonesia	1,986	2,011	18,781	19,782	1.5	1.6	20.8	21.3	Rupiah*

MARKETING RESEARCH & PUBLIC OPINION POLLING (NAICS 54191)

COUNTRY ESTIMATES

Country	Establishments 2018	Establishments 2019	Employment 2018	Employment 2019	Sales ($B) 2018	Sales ($B) 2019	Local Sales (B) 2018	Local Sales (B) 2019	Currency
Iran	544	550	5,144	5,413	0.6	0.5	20.1	19.6	Rial*
Iraq	285	290	2,698	2,848	0.3	0.3	0.3	0.3	Dinar*
Ireland	40	41	378	399	0.7	0.8	0.6	0.7	Euro
Israel	57	57	536	565	0.5	0.5	1.6	1.6	Shekel
Italy	402	400	3,801	3,934	2.5	2.5	2.1	2.1	Euro
Japan	846	837	7,999	8,233	6.0	5.9	674.4	663.8	Yen*
Kazakhstan	138	138	1,303	1,362	0.3	0.3	97.7	98.0	Tenge
Kuwait	32	34	305	330	0.2	0.2	0.1	0.1	Dinar
Malaysia	264	268	2,493	2,637	0.6	0.6	2.2	2.3	Ringgit
Mexico	859	869	8,123	8,545	1.6	1.6	31.1	31.1	New pesos
Netherlands	107	107	1,016	1,051	1.0	1.0	0.9	0.9	Euro
New Zealand	29	29	273	286	0.2	0.2	0.3	0.3	Dollar
Nigeria	1,482	1,506	14,011	14,815	0.8	0.8	295,795.6	295,973.5	Naira
Norway	40	40	375	392	0.6	0.6	5.0	5.0	Krone
Pakistan	1,187	1,212	11,227	11,919	0.4	0.4	40.3	41.2	Rupees
Peru	235	235	2,222	2,314	0.3	0.3	0.9	0.9	Nuevo Sol
Phillipines	640	651	6,052	6,403	0.4	0.5	22.2	23.0	Pesos
Poland	219	217	2,073	2,132	0.7	0.7	2.5	2.6	Zloty
Portugal	69	69	655	676	0.3	0.3	0.2	0.2	Euro
Puerto Rico	30	30	284	290	0.2	0.2	0.2	0.2	Dollar
Qatar	30	34	286	338	0.3	0.3	1.0	1.0	Riyal
Romania	158	155	1,492	1,527	0.3	0.3	1.1	1.1	New Leu
Russia	980	969	9,268	9,527	1.9	1.9	97.9	94.6	Rubles
Saudi Arabia	275	284	2,600	2,790	1.2	1.2	0.0	0.0	Rials*
Singapore	44	45	415	442	0.5	0.5	602.6	604.5	Dollar
South Africa	271	274	2,563	2,699	0.4	0.4	5,100.3	5,055.2	Rand
South Korea	383	382	3,623	3,753	2.2	2.3	2,400.5	2,415.5	Won*
Spain	318	320	3,007	3,145	1.7	1.7	1,438.5	1,410.7	Euro
Sweden	65	65	616	640	0.7	0.7	6,059.1	6,125.8	Krona
Switzerland	60	60	564	588	1.0	1.0	987.1	981.6	Swiss franc
Taiwan	239	247	2,258	2,426	0.8	0.8	22,680.5	22,627.3	Dollar
Thailand	577	580	5,458	5,704	0.6	0.6	20,875.4	20,776.8	Baht
Turkey	437	435	4,136	4,281	1.2	1.3	4,635.7	4,689.6	Euro
Ukraine	319	314	3,017	3,090	0.1	0.1	2,701.1	2,374.1	Hryvna
UAE	149	166	1,406	1,637	0.7	0.7	2,464.2	2,443.7	Dirham
United Kingdom	416	414	3,931	4,076	4.0	4.0	2,949.6	2,957.6	Pounds
United States	2,018	2,019	19,084	19,856	24.3	24.3	24,270.6	24,316.7	Dollars
Venezuela	206	209	1,947	2,055	0.7	0.6	6,605.0	6,295.8	Bolivar
Vietnam	724	725	6,849	7,127	0.3	0.4	7,883.0	8,179.8	Dong*

Note: Due to rounding, establishments will vary by + or - one establishment. Therefore, zero establishments may also be one establishment.

* Local Sales are in trillions

TELEMARKETING SERVICES INDUSTRY (NAICS 561422)

NAICS 561422: Telemarketing Services. This industry comprises establishments primarily engaged in providing telemarketing services on a contract or fee basis for others, such as: (1) promoting clients' products or services by telephone, (2) taking orders for clients by telephone, and (3) soliciting contributions or providing information for clients by telephone. These establishments never own the product or provide the services they are representing and generally can originate and/or receive calls for others.

COUNTRY ESTIMATES

Country	Establishments 2018	2019	Employment 2018	2019	Sales ($B) 2018	2019	Local Sales (B) 2018	2019	Currency
Algeria	371	373	6,467	6,909	0.2	0.2	20.1	20.4	Dinar
Argentina	257	258	4,484	4,765	0.4	0.4	7.9	7.9	Pesos
Australia	160	162	2,790	2,990	1.0	1.1	1.3	1.3	Dollars
Austria	57	57	998	1,055	0.3	0.3	0.2	0.2	Euro
Bangladesh	1,129	1,130	19,664	20,911	0.2	0.2	14.1	14.9	Taka
Belgium	72	72	1,251	1,329	0.3	0.3	0.3	0.3	Euro
Brazil	1,375	1,387	23,947	25,651	1.3	1.2	4,085.9	4,007.2	Real
Canada	241	242	4,197	4,470	1.2	1.2	1.5	1.5	Dollars
Chile	133	134	2,322	2,484	0.2	0.2	125.0	127.1	Pesos*
China	9,511	9,479	165,626	175,352	10.6	11.1	68.6	71.8	RMB
Colombia	286	286	4,980	5,291	0.2	0.2	0.7	0.7	Pesos*
Czech Republic	69	68	1,194	1,261	0.2	0.2	3.3	3.4	Koruna
Denmark	36	36	628	664	0.2	0.2	1.4	1.4	Kroner
Egypt	608	623	10,595	11,526	0.3	0.3	4.6	4.6	Pounds
Finland	36	36	622	658	0.2	0.2	0.1	0.1	Euro
France	399	398	6,948	7,366	1.7	1.7	1.4	1.4	Euro
Germany	508	501	8,844	9,275	2.6	2.7	2.2	2.2	Euro
Greece	67	66	1,164	1,227	0.1	0.1	0.1	0.1	Euro
Hong Kong	41	41	714	755	0.2	0.2	1,519.6	1,553.1	Dollar
Hungary	60	59	1,050	1,101	0.1	0.1	24.0	24.8	Forint*
India	8,785	8,918	152,994	164,969	1.9	2.0	118.1	124.4	Rupees
Indonesia	1,986	2,011	34,586	37,210	0.8	0.9	11.3	11.8	Rupiah*

Telemarketing Services Industry (NAICS 561422)

Country Estimates

Country	Establishments 2018	Establishments 2019	Employment 2018	Employment 2019	Sales ($B) 2018	Sales ($B) 2019	Local Sales (B) 2018	Local Sales (B) 2019	Currency
Iran	544	550	9,472	10,181	0.3	0.3	10.9	10.8	Rial*
Iraq	285	290	4,968	5,358	0.2	0.2	0.2	0.2	Dinar*
Ireland	40	41	697	750	0.4	0.4	0.3	0.4	Euro
Israel	57	57	988	1,064	0.2	0.3	0.8	0.9	Shekel
Italy	402	400	6,999	7,400	1.4	1.4	1.1	1.1	Euro
Japan	846	837	14,730	15,486	3.2	3.3	365.6	367.2	Yen*
Kazakhstan	138	138	2,400	2,561	0.2	0.2	53.0	54.2	Tenge
Kuwait	32	34	561	622	0.1	0.1	0.0	0.0	Dinar
Malaysia	264	268	4,591	4,960	0.3	0.3	1.2	1.3	Ringgit
Mexico	859	869	14,958	16,073	0.9	0.9	16.9	17.2	New pesos
Netherlands	107	107	1,871	1,976	0.6	0.6	0.5	0.5	Euro
New Zealand	29	29	503	538	0.1	0.1	0.2	0.2	Dollar
Nigeria	1,482	1,506	25,802	27,867	0.4	0.5	160,336.7	163,724.3	Naira
Norway	40	40	691	737	0.3	0.3	2.7	2.7	Krone
Pakistan	1,187	1,212	20,675	22,419	0.2	0.2	21.9	22.8	Rupees
Peru	235	235	4,093	4,353	0.2	0.2	0.5	0.5	Nuevo Sol
Phillipines	640	651	11,144	12,043	0.2	0.3	12.0	12.7	Pesos
Poland	219	217	3,818	4,011	0.4	0.4	1.4	1.4	Zloty
Portugal	69	69	1,207	1,272	0.1	0.1	0.1	0.1	Euro
Puerto Rico	30	30	522	546	0.1	0.1	0.1	0.1	Dollar
Qatar	30	34	526	636	0.1	0.2	0.5	0.6	Riyal
Romania	158	155	2,748	2,873	0.2	0.2	0.6	0.6	New Leu
Russia	980	969	17,068	17,921	1.0	1.0	53.1	52.3	Rubles
Saudi Arabia	275	284	4,788	5,248	0.6	0.6	0.0	0.0	Rials*
Singapore	44	45	764	831	0.2	0.3	326.6	334.4	Dollar
South Africa	271	274	4,720	5,077	0.2	0.2	2,764.7	2,796.4	Rand
South Korea	383	382	6,672	7,059	1.2	1.3	1,301.2	1,336.2	Won*
Spain	318	320	5,538	5,916	0.9	0.9	779.8	780.3	Euro
Sweden	65	65	1,135	1,204	0.4	0.4	3,284.3	3,388.6	Krona
Switzerland	60	60	1,038	1,106	0.5	0.6	535.1	543.0	Swiss franc
Taiwan	239	247	4,158	4,563	0.4	0.4	12,294.0	12,516.8	Dollar
Thailand	577	580	10,051	10,729	0.4	0.4	11,315.6	11,493.1	Baht
Turkey	437	435	7,616	8,052	0.7	0.7	2,512.8	2,594.1	Euro
Ukraine	319	314	5,556	5,813	0.1	0.0	1,464.1	1,313.3	Hryvna
UAE	149	166	2,589	3,080	0.4	0.4	1,335.7	1,351.8	Dirham
United Kingdom	416	414	7,239	7,668	2.2	2.2	1,598.8	1,636.1	Pounds
United States	2,018	2,019	35,144	37,350	13.2	13.5	13,155.9	13,451.3	Dollars
Venezuela	206	209	3,585	3,866	0.4	0.3	3,580.3	3,482.6	Bolivar
Vietnam	724	725	12,613	13,405	0.2	0.2	4,273.0	4,524.8	Dong*

Note: Due to rounding, establishments will vary by + or - one establishment. Therefore, zero establishments may also be one establishment.

* Local Sales are in trillions

SECURITY GUARDS & PATROL SERVICES INDUSTRY (NAICS 561612)

NAICS 561612: Security Guards & Patrol Services. This industry comprises establishments primarily engaged in providing detective, guard, and armored car services. Establishments primarily engaged in monitoring and maintaining security systems devices, such as burglar and fire alarms, are classified in 7382.

COUNTRY ESTIMATES

Country	Establishments 2018	Establishments 2019	Employment 2018	Employment 2019	Sales ($B) 2018	Sales ($B) 2019	Local Sales (B) 2018	Local Sales (B) 2019	Currency
Algeria	371	373	9,182	9,743	0.5	0.6	62.5	65.1	Dinar
Argentina	257	258	6,366	6,719	1.3	1.3	24.6	25.2	Pesos
Australia	160	162	3,961	4,216	3.2	3.4	4.1	4.3	Dollars
Austria	57	57	1,417	1,488	0.9	0.9	0.8	0.8	Euro
Bangladesh	1,129	1,130	27,919	29,488	0.5	0.6	43.7	47.5	Taka
Belgium	72	72	1,777	1,875	1.0	1.1	0.9	0.9	Euro
Brazil	1,375	1,387	34,000	36,173	3.9	4.0	12,701.4	12,792.7	Real
Canada	241	242	5,959	6,303	3.7	3.9	4.6	4.8	Dollars
Chile	133	134	3,297	3,503	0.6	0.7	388.5	405.9	Pesos*
China	9,511	9,479	235,160	247,276	32.9	35.3	213.3	229.3	RMB
Colombia	286	286	7,071	7,461	0.7	0.7	2.0	2.2	Pesos*
Czech Republic	69	68	1,695	1,778	0.5	0.5	10.2	10.8	Koruna
Denmark	36	36	892	936	0.7	0.7	4.3	4.5	Kroner
Egypt	608	623	15,043	16,254	0.8	0.8	14.2	14.8	Pounds
Finland	36	36	883	927	0.5	0.5	0.4	0.4	Euro
France	399	398	9,864	10,387	5.3	5.5	4.4	4.6	Euro
Germany	508	501	12,557	13,080	8.1	8.5	6.8	7.1	Euro
Greece	67	66	1,652	1,730	0.4	0.4	0.3	0.3	Euro
Hong Kong	41	41	1,013	1,064	0.6	0.6	4,723.7	4,958.2	Dollar
Hungary	60	59	1,490	1,552	0.3	0.3	74.6	79.3	Forint*
India	7,986	8,107	197,476	211,486	5.3	5.7	333.8	361.0	Rupees
Indonesia	1,986	2,011	49,105	52,473	2.6	2.8	35.0	37.6	Rupiah*

SECURITY GUARDS & PATROL SERVICES INDUSTRY (NAICS 561612)

COUNTRY ESTIMATES

Country	Establishments 2018	2019	Employment 2018	2019	Sales ($B) 2018	2019	Local Sales (B) 2018	2019	Currency
Iran	544	550	13,449	14,357	0.9	1.0	33.9	34.6	Rial*
Iraq	285	290	7,053	7,555	0.5	0.5	0.6	0.6	Dinar*
Ireland	40	41	990	1,057	1.2	1.4	1.0	1.2	Euro
Israel	57	57	1,402	1,500	0.8	0.8	2.6	2.8	Shekel
Italy	402	400	9,937	10,435	4.2	4.4	3.5	3.6	Euro
Japan	846	837	20,913	21,838	10.1	10.4	1,136.4	1,172.2	Yen*
Kazakhstan	138	138	3,407	3,612	0.5	0.5	164.6	173.0	Tenge
Kuwait	32	34	796	876	0.3	0.3	0.1	0.1	Dinar
Malaysia	264	268	6,519	6,994	0.9	1.0	3.7	4.0	Ringgit
Mexico	859	869	21,238	22,666	2.7	2.9	52.4	55.0	New pesos
Netherlands	107	107	2,657	2,787	1.7	1.8	1.5	1.5	Euro
New Zealand	29	29	714	758	0.4	0.4	0.5	0.6	Dollar
Nigeria	1,482	1,506	36,634	39,296	1.4	1.5	498,416.4	522,676.9	Naira
Norway	40	40	981	1,039	1.0	1.1	8.4	8.7	Krone
Pakistan	1,187	1,212	29,355	31,614	0.6	0.7	68.0	72.8	Rupees
Peru	235	235	5,811	6,138	0.5	0.5	1.6	1.7	Nuevo Sol
Phillipines	640	651	15,823	16,983	0.7	0.8	37.4	40.6	Pesos
Poland	219	217	5,420	5,656	1.2	1.3	4.3	4.5	Zloty
Portugal	69	69	1,714	1,794	0.5	0.5	0.4	0.4	Euro
Puerto Rico	30	30	741	770	0.3	0.3	0.3	0.3	Dollar
Qatar	30	34	747	897	0.5	0.5	1.7	1.8	Riyal
Romania	158	155	3,901	4,051	0.5	0.5	1.9	2.0	New Leu
Russia	980	969	24,234	25,271	3.2	3.3	164.9	167.1	Rubles
Saudi Arabia	275	284	6,798	7,401	2.0	2.1	0.0	0.0	Rials*
Singapore	44	45	1,085	1,172	0.8	0.8	1,015.3	1,067.5	Dollar
South Africa	271	274	6,702	7,159	0.7	0.7	8,594.1	8,927.3	Rand
South Korea	383	382	9,473	9,954	3.8	4.0	4,044.9	4,265.6	Won*
Spain	318	320	7,863	8,343	2.9	3.0	2,423.9	2,491.2	Euro
Sweden	65	65	1,611	1,698	1.2	1.3	10,209.6	10,818.0	Krona
Switzerland	60	60	1,474	1,559	1.7	1.8	1,663.3	1,733.4	Swiss franc
Taiwan	239	247	5,904	6,435	1.3	1.4	38,216.7	39,958.9	Dollar
Thailand	577	580	14,270	15,130	1.1	1.1	35,175.1	36,690.9	Baht
Turkey	437	435	10,813	11,355	2.1	2.2	7,811.2	8,281.6	Euro
Ukraine	319	314	7,888	8,197	0.2	0.1	4,551.4	4,192.6	Hryvna
UAE	149	166	3,676	4,343	1.1	1.2	4,152.1	4,315.5	Dirham
United Kingdom	416	414	10,278	10,813	6.7	7.1	4,970.1	5,223.0	Pounds
United States	2,018	2,019	49,898	52,669	40.9	42.9	40,896.0	42,942.2	Dollars
Venezuela	206	209	5,090	5,452	1.1	1.1	11,129.5	11,118.0	Bolivar
Vietnam	724	725	17,908	18,904	0.6	0.6	13,282.8	14,445.1	Dong*

Note: Due to rounding, establishments will vary by + or - one establishment. Therefore, zero establishments may also be one establishment.

* Local Sales are in trillions

COLLEGES & UNIVERSITIES INDUSTRY (NAICS 61131)

NAICS 61131: Colleges & Universities. This industry comprises establishments primarily furnishing academic courses and granting academic degrees. The requirement for admission is at least a high school diploma or equivalent general academic training.

COUNTRY ESTIMATES

Country	Establishments		Employment		Sales ($B)		Local Sales (B)		Currency
	2018	2019	2018	2019	2018	2019	2018	2019	
Algeria	371	373	44,208	46,821	0.3	0.4	40.1	41.1	Dinar
Argentina	257	258	30,649	32,292	0.8	0.8	15.8	15.9	Pesos
Australia	160	162	19,072	20,260	2.1	2.1	2.6	2.7	Dollars
Austria	57	57	6,823	7,151	0.6	0.6	0.5	0.5	Euro
Bangladesh	1,129	1,130	134,413	141,711	0.3	0.4	28.0	30.0	Taka
Belgium	72	72	8,553	9,009	0.7	0.7	0.6	0.6	Euro
Brazil	1,375	1,387	163,690	173,839	2.5	2.5	8,146.2	8,075.5	Real
Canada	241	242	28,688	30,293	2.4	2.4	3.0	3.0	Dollars
Chile	133	134	15,871	16,836	0.4	0.4	249.2	256.2	Pesos*
China	9,511	9,479	1,132,159	1,188,357	21.1	22.3	136.8	144.7	RMB
Colombia	286	286	34,042	35,857	0.5	0.5	1.3	1.4	Pesos*
Czech Republic	69	68	8,160	8,545	0.3	0.3	6.5	6.8	Koruna
Denmark	36	36	4,293	4,497	0.4	0.5	2.7	2.8	Kroner
Egypt	608	623	72,423	78,112	0.5	0.5	9.1	9.3	Pounds
Finland	36	36	4,252	4,457	0.3	0.3	0.3	0.3	Euro
France	399	398	47,491	49,916	3.4	3.5	2.8	2.9	Euro
Germany	508	501	60,457	62,858	5.2	5.3	4.4	4.5	Euro
Greece	67	66	7,954	8,316	0.3	0.3	0.2	0.2	Euro
Hong Kong	41	41	4,878	5,114	0.4	0.4	3,029.6	3,129.9	Dollar
Hungary	60	59	7,174	7,459	0.2	0.2	47.9	50.0	Forint*
India	7,986	8,107	950,733	1,016,355	3.4	3.6	214.1	227.9	Rupees
Indonesia	1,986	2,011	236,414	252,173	1.7	1.8	22.4	23.7	Rupiah*

COLLEGES & UNIVERSITIES INDUSTRY
(NAICS 61131)

COUNTRY ESTIMATES

Country	Establishments 2018	2019	Employment 2018	2019	Sales ($B) 2018	2019	Local Sales (B) 2018	2019	Currency
Iran	544	550	64,749	68,999	0.6	0.6	21.7	21.8	Rial*
Iraq	285	290	33,957	36,309	0.3	0.3	0.4	0.4	Dinar*
Ireland	40	41	4,764	5,081	0.8	0.9	0.6	0.7	Euro
Israel	57	57	6,751	7,208	0.5	0.5	1.7	1.8	Shekel
Italy	402	400	47,841	50,147	2.7	2.7	2.3	2.3	Euro
Japan	846	837	100,686	104,950	6.5	6.6	728.9	740.0	Yen*
Kazakhstan	138	138	16,404	17,358	0.3	0.3	105.6	109.2	Tenge
Kuwait	32	34	3,834	4,212	0.2	0.2	0.1	0.1	Dinar
Malaysia	264	268	31,386	33,612	0.6	0.6	2.4	2.5	Ringgit
Mexico	859	869	102,249	108,929	1.8	1.8	33.6	34.7	New pesos
Netherlands	107	107	12,790	13,393	1.1	1.1	0.9	1.0	Euro
New Zealand	29	29	3,439	3,644	0.3	0.3	0.3	0.4	Dollar
Nigeria	1,482	1,506	176,370	188,850	0.9	0.9	319,667.8	329,943.6	Naira
Norway	40	40	4,725	4,992	0.7	0.7	5.4	5.5	Krone
Pakistan	1,187	1,212	141,328	151,932	0.4	0.4	43.6	46.0	Rupees
Peru	235	235	27,976	29,498	0.3	0.3	1.0	1.1	Nuevo Sol
Phillipines	640	651	76,177	81,617	0.5	0.5	24.0	25.6	Pesos
Poland	219	217	26,096	27,181	0.8	0.8	2.7	2.9	Zloty
Portugal	69	69	8,251	8,620	0.3	0.3	0.2	0.2	Euro
Puerto Rico	30	30	3,570	3,700	0.2	0.2	0.2	0.2	Dollar
Qatar	30	34	3,594	4,311	0.3	0.3	1.1	1.1	Riyal
Romania	158	155	18,783	19,468	0.3	0.3	1.2	1.3	New Leu
Russia	980	969	116,670	121,447	2.1	2.1	105.8	105.5	Rubles
Saudi Arabia	275	284	32,731	35,566	1.3	1.3	0.0	0.0	Rials*
Singapore	44	45	5,224	5,633	0.5	0.5	651.2	673.9	Dollar
South Africa	271	274	32,266	34,406	0.4	0.5	5,512.0	5,635.4	Rand
South Korea	383	382	45,606	47,838	2.4	2.5	2,594.3	2,692.7	Won*
Spain	318	320	37,857	40,095	1.9	1.9	1,554.6	1,572.6	Euro
Sweden	65	65	7,758	8,158	0.8	0.8	6,548.1	6,828.9	Krona
Switzerland	60	60	7,098	7,494	1.1	1.1	1,066.8	1,094.2	Swiss franc
Taiwan	239	247	28,423	30,925	0.8	0.9	24,510.9	25,224.3	Dollar
Thailand	577	580	68,703	72,712	0.7	0.7	22,560.1	23,161.4	Baht
Turkey	437	435	52,060	54,568	1.3	1.4	5,009.8	5,227.8	Euro
Ukraine	319	314	37,977	39,392	0.1	0.1	2,919.1	2,646.6	Hryvna
UAE	149	166	17,699	20,870	0.7	0.7	2,663.0	2,724.2	Dirham
United Kingdom	416	414	49,482	51,963	4.3	4.5	3,187.7	3,297.1	Pounds
United States	2,018	2,019	240,229	253,118	26.2	27.1	26,229.3	27,107.6	Dollars
Venezuela	206	209	24,505	26,200	0.7	0.7	7,138.1	7,018.3	Bolivar
Vietnam	724	725	86,219	90,848	0.4	0.4	8,519.1	9,118.6	Dong*

Note: Due to rounding, establishments will vary by + or - one establishment. Therefore, zero establishments may also be one establishment.

* Local Sales are in trillions

EXAM PREPARATION & TUTORING INDUSTRY (NAICS 611691)

NAICS 6111691: Exam Preparation & Tutoring. This industry comprises establishments primarily engaged in offering educational courses and services, not elsewhere classified. Includes music schools, drama schools, language schools, short-term examination preparatory schools, student exchange programs, curriculum development, and vocational counseling, except rehabilitation counseling. Dance schools are classified in 7911, and rehabilitation counseling is classified in 8331.

COUNTRY ESTIMATES

Country	Establishments 2018	2019	Employment 2018	2019	Sales ($B) 2018	2019	Local Sales (B) 2018	2019	Currency
Algeria	371	373	1,625	1,788	0.7	0.8	84.4	87.5	Dinar
Argentina	257	258	1,127	1,233	1.7	1.8	33.2	33.9	Pesos
Australia	160	162	701	774	4.3	4.5	5.5	5.7	Dollars
Austria	57	57	251	273	1.2	1.2	1.0	1.0	Euro
Bangladesh	1,129	1,130	4,942	5,411	0.7	0.8	59.0	63.9	Taka
Belgium	72	72	314	344	1.4	1.4	1.2	1.2	Euro
Brazil	1,375	1,387	6,018	6,638	5.3	5.3	17,147.3	17,196.5	Real
Canada	241	242	1,055	1,157	5.0	5.2	6.2	6.5	Dollars
Chile	133	134	583	643	0.9	0.9	524.5	545.6	Pesos*
China	9,511	9,479	41,623	45,374	44.4	47.5	287.9	308.2	RMB
Colombia	286	286	1,252	1,369	1.0	1.0	2.8	2.9	Pesos*
Czech Republic	69	68	300	326	0.6	0.7	13.8	14.6	Koruna
Denmark	36	36	158	172	0.9	1.0	5.8	6.0	Kroner
Egypt	608	623	2,663	2,982	1.1	1.1	19.2	19.9	Pounds
Finland	36	36	156	170	0.7	0.7	0.6	0.6	Euro
France	399	398	1,746	1,906	7.1	7.4	6.0	6.1	Euro
Germany	508	501	2,223	2,400	11.0	11.4	9.2	9.5	Euro
Greece	67	66	292	318	0.6	0.6	0.5	0.5	Euro
Hong Kong	41	41	179	195	0.8	0.9	6,377.1	6,665.1	Dollar
Hungary	60	59	264	285	0.4	0.4	100.8	106.5	Forint*
India	7,986	8,107	34,953	38,806	7.1	7.6	450.6	485.3	Rupees
Indonesia	1,986	2,011	8,692	9,628	3.5	3.8	47.3	50.5	Rupiah*

Exam Preparation & Tutoring Industry (NAICS 611691)

COUNTRY ESTIMATES

Country	Establishments 2018	Establishments 2019	Employment 2018	Employment 2019	Sales ($B) 2018	Sales ($B) 2019	Local Sales (B) 2018	Local Sales (B) 2019	Currency
Iran	544	550	2,380	2,635	1.3	1.3	45.7	46.5	Rial*
Iraq	285	290	1,248	1,386	0.7	0.7	0.8	0.8	Dinar*
Ireland	40	41	175	194	1.6	1.9	1.4	1.6	Euro
Israel	57	57	248	275	1.0	1.1	3.6	3.7	Shekel
Italy	402	400	1,759	1,915	5.7	5.9	4.8	4.9	Euro
Japan	846	837	3,702	4,007	13.6	14.0	1,534.2	1,575.8	Yen*
Kazakhstan	138	138	603	663	0.7	0.7	222.3	232.6	Tenge
Kuwait	32	34	141	161	0.4	0.4	0.1	0.1	Dinar
Malaysia	264	268	1,154	1,283	1.3	1.3	5.0	5.4	Ringgit
Mexico	859	869	3,759	4,159	3.7	3.8	70.8	73.9	New pesos
Netherlands	107	107	470	511	2.3	2.4	2.0	2.0	Euro
New Zealand	29	29	126	139	0.5	0.6	0.7	0.8	Dollar
Nigeria	1,482	1,506	6,484	7,211	1.9	2.0	672,879.6	702,607.9	Naira
Norway	40	40	174	191	1.4	1.5	11.3	11.8	Krone
Pakistan	1,187	1,212	5,196	5,801	0.8	0.9	91.8	97.9	Rupees
Peru	235	235	1,029	1,126	0.7	0.7	2.2	2.3	Nuevo Sol
Phillipines	640	651	2,801	3,116	1.0	1.1	50.5	54.5	Pesos
Poland	219	217	959	1,038	1.7	1.7	5.8	6.1	Zloty
Portugal	69	69	303	329	0.6	0.6	0.5	0.5	Euro
Puerto Rico	30	30	131	141	0.4	0.4	0.4	0.4	Dollar
Qatar	30	34	132	165	0.6	0.6	2.3	2.4	Riyal
Romania	158	155	691	743	0.7	0.7	2.6	2.7	New Leu
Russia	980	969	4,289	4,637	4.4	4.4	222.7	224.6	Rubles
Saudi Arabia	275	284	1,203	1,358	2.7	2.8	0.0	0.0	Rials*
Singapore	44	45	192	215	1.0	1.1	1,370.7	1,435.0	Dollar
South Africa	271	274	1,186	1,314	0.9	1.0	11,602.3	12,000.5	Rand
South Korea	383	382	1,677	1,827	5.1	5.4	5,460.8	5,734.1	Won*
Spain	318	320	1,392	1,531	3.9	4.0	3,272.4	3,348.8	Euro
Sweden	65	65	285	311	1.7	1.8	13,783.3	14,542.0	Krona
Switzerland	60	60	261	286	2.3	2.4	2,245.5	2,330.2	Swiss franc
Taiwan	239	247	1,045	1,181	1.7	1.8	51,593.8	53,714.6	Dollar
Thailand	577	580	2,526	2,776	1.5	1.5	47,487.6	49,321.8	Baht
Turkey	437	435	1,914	2,084	2.8	3.0	10,545.4	11,132.5	Euro
Ukraine	319	314	1,396	1,504	0.2	0.2	6,144.5	5,635.8	Hryvna
UAE	149	166	651	797	1.5	1.6	5,605.5	5,801.2	Dirham
United Kingdom	416	414	1,819	1,984	9.1	9.5	6,709.8	7,021.0	Pounds
United States	2,018	2,019	8,832	9,665	55.2	57.7	55,211.0	57,725.0	Dollars
Venezuela	206	209	901	1,000	1.5	1.5	15,025.2	14,945.4	Bolivar
Vietnam	724	725	3,170	3,469	0.8	0.9	17,932.2	19,417.8	Dong*

Note: Due to rounding, establishments will vary by + or - one establishment. Therefore, zero establishments may also be one establishment.

* Local Sales are in trillions

Educational Support Services Industry (NAICS 61171)

NAICS 61171: Educational Support Services. This industry comprises establishments primarily engaged in offering educational courses and services, not elsewhere classified. Includes music schools, drama schools, language schools, short-term examination preparatory schools, student exchange programs, curriculum development, and vocational counseling, except rehabilitation counseling. Dance schools are classified in 7911, and rehabilitation counseling is classified in 8331.

COUNTRY ESTIMATES

Country	Establishments 2018	2019	Employment 2018	2019	Sales ($B) 2018	2019	Local Sales (B) 2018	2019	Currency
Algeria	371	373	2,808	2,981	0.6	0.6	66.7	68.1	Dinar
Argentina	257	258	1,947	2,056	1.4	1.4	26.3	26.4	Pesos
Australia	160	162	1,211	1,290	3.4	3.5	4.3	4.5	Dollars
Austria	57	57	433	455	1.0	1.0	0.8	0.8	Euro
Bangladesh	1,129	1,130	8,537	9,021	0.6	0.6	46.7	49.8	Taka
Belgium	72	72	543	574	1.1	1.1	0.9	0.9	Euro
Brazil	1,375	1,387	10,397	11,067	4.2	4.1	13,555.2	13,391.4	Real
Canada	241	242	1,822	1,928	4.0	4.1	4.9	5.0	Dollars
Chile	133	134	1,008	1,072	0.7	0.7	414.6	424.9	Pesos*
China	9,511	9,479	71,910	75,651	35.1	37.0	227.6	240.0	RMB
Colombia	286	286	2,162	2,283	0.8	0.8	2.2	2.3	Pesos*
Czech Republic	69	68	518	544	0.5	0.5	10.9	11.3	Koruna
Denmark	36	36	273	286	0.7	0.7	4.6	4.7	Kroner
Egypt	608	623	4,600	4,973	0.9	0.9	15.2	15.5	Pounds
Finland	36	36	270	284	0.6	0.6	0.5	0.5	Euro
France	399	398	3,016	3,178	5.6	5.7	4.7	4.8	Euro
Germany	508	501	3,840	4,002	8.7	8.9	7.2	7.4	Euro
Greece	67	66	505	529	0.4	0.4	0.4	0.4	Euro
Hong Kong	41	41	310	326	0.6	0.7	5,041.2	5,190.3	Dollar
Hungary	60	59	456	475	0.3	0.3	79.6	83.0	Forint*
India	7,986	8,107	60,386	64,701	5.6	6.0	356.2	377.9	Rupees
Indonesia	1,986	2,011	15,016	16,053	2.8	2.9	37.4	39.3	Rupiah*

Educational Support Services Industry (NAICS 61171)

Country Estimates

Country	Establishments 2018	2019	Employment 2018	2019	Sales ($B) 2018	2019	Local Sales (B) 2018	2019	Currency
Iran	544	550	4,113	4,392	1.0	1.0	36.2	36.2	Rial*
Iraq	285	290	2,157	2,311	0.5	0.5	0.6	0.6	Dinar*
Ireland	40	41	303	323	1.3	1.5	1.1	1.2	Euro
Israel	57	57	429	459	0.8	0.8	2.8	2.9	Shekel
Italy	402	400	3,039	3,192	4.5	4.6	3.8	3.8	Euro
Japan	846	837	6,395	6,681	10.7	10.9	1,212.8	1,227.1	Yen*
Kazakhstan	138	138	1,042	1,105	0.5	0.5	175.7	181.1	Tenge
Kuwait	32	34	244	268	0.3	0.3	0.1	0.1	Dinar
Malaysia	264	268	1,993	2,140	1.0	1.0	4.0	4.2	Ringgit
Mexico	859	869	6,494	6,934	2.9	3.0	56.0	57.6	New pesos
Netherlands	107	107	812	853	1.9	1.9	1.5	1.6	Euro
New Zealand	29	29	218	232	0.4	0.4	0.6	0.6	Dollar
Nigeria	1,482	1,506	11,202	12,022	1.5	1.5	531,922.8	547,140.4	Naira
Norway	40	40	300	318	1.1	1.1	8.9	9.2	Krone
Pakistan	1,187	1,212	8,977	9,672	0.7	0.7	72.5	76.2	Rupees
Peru	235	235	1,777	1,878	0.5	0.5	1.7	1.8	Nuevo Sol
Phillipines	640	651	4,838	5,196	0.8	0.8	39.9	42.5	Pesos
Poland	219	217	1,657	1,730	1.3	1.4	4.6	4.7	Zloty
Portugal	69	69	524	549	0.5	0.5	0.4	0.4	Euro
Puerto Rico	30	30	227	236	0.3	0.3	0.3	0.3	Dollar
Qatar	30	34	228	274	0.5	0.5	1.8	1.8	Riyal
Romania	158	155	1,193	1,239	0.5	0.5	2.0	2.1	New Leu
Russia	980	969	7,410	7,731	3.4	3.4	176.0	174.9	Rubles
Saudi Arabia	275	284	2,079	2,264	2.1	2.2	0.0	0.0	Rials*
Singapore	44	45	332	359	0.8	0.8	1,083.6	1,117.5	Dollar
South Africa	271	274	2,049	2,190	0.7	0.8	9,171.8	9,345.1	Rand
South Korea	383	382	2,897	3,045	4.0	4.2	4,316.8	4,465.3	Won*
Spain	318	320	2,405	2,552	3.1	3.1	2,586.9	2,607.8	Euro
Sweden	65	65	493	519	1.3	1.4	10,895.9	11,324.3	Krona
Switzerland	60	60	451	477	1.8	1.9	1,775.1	1,814.6	Swiss franc
Taiwan	239	247	1,805	1,969	1.4	1.4	40,785.8	41,829.1	Dollar
Thailand	577	580	4,364	4,629	1.2	1.2	37,539.8	38,408.2	Baht
Turkey	437	435	3,307	3,474	2.2	2.3	8,336.3	8,669.2	Euro
Ukraine	319	314	2,412	2,508	0.2	0.2	4,857.4	4,388.8	Hryvna
UAE	149	166	1,124	1,329	1.2	1.2	4,431.3	4,517.5	Dirham
United Kingdom	416	414	3,143	3,308	7.2	7.4	5,304.2	5,467.5	Pounds
United States	2,018	2,019	15,258	16,114	43.6	45.0	43,645.3	44,952.1	Dollars
Venezuela	206	209	1,556	1,668	1.2	1.2	11,877.7	11,638.4	Bolivar
Vietnam	724	725	5,476	5,783	0.6	0.7	14,175.7	15,121.2	Dong*

Note: Due to rounding, establishments will vary by + or - one establishment. Therefore, zero establishments may also be one establishment.

* Local Sales are in trillions

Offices of Physicians Industry (NAICS 62111)

NAICS 62111: Offices of Physicians. This industry comprises establishments primarily of licensed practitioners having the degree of M.D. and engaged in the practice of general or specialized medicine and surgery. Establishments operating as clinics of physicians are included in this business. Osteopathic physicians are classified in 8031.

COUNTRY ESTIMATES

Country	Establishments 2018	Establishments 2019	Employment 2018	Employment 2019	Sales ($B) 2018	Sales ($B) 2019	Local Sales (B) 2018	Local Sales (B) 2019	Currency
Algeria	371	373	70,422	75,068	3.7	3.8	430.0	432.3	Dinar
Argentina	257	258	48,822	51,774	8.9	8.8	169.3	167.4	Pesos
Australia	160	162	30,380	32,483	22.0	22.3	28.0	28.3	Dollars
Austria	43	43	8,172	8,621	4.7	4.6	3.9	3.9	Euro
Bangladesh	565	565	107,057	113,602	1.8	1.9	150.4	157.9	Taka
Belgium	54	54	10,244	10,860	5.3	5.3	4.5	4.5	Euro
Brazil	1,375	1,387	260,752	278,715	27.1	26.3	87,388.6	84,954.1	Real
Canada	181	182	34,360	36,518	19.3	19.4	23.9	24.0	Dollars
Chile	133	134	25,282	26,992	4.4	4.4	2,673.1	2,695.3	Pesos*
China	9,511	9,479	1,803,485	1,905,282	226.1	234.6	1,467.3	1,522.6	RMB
Colombia	286	286	54,228	57,490	4.9	5.0	14.1	14.4	Pesos*
Czech Republic	69	68	12,998	13,701	3.3	3.4	70.1	72.0	Koruna
Denmark	27	27	5,141	5,421	3.6	3.6	22.1	22.2	Kroner
Egypt	608	623	115,367	125,237	5.6	5.6	97.7	98.1	Pounds
Finland	27	27	5,092	5,373	2.7	2.7	2.3	2.2	Euro
France	300	299	56,881	60,173	27.4	27.3	22.9	22.8	Euro
Germany	382	377	72,410	75,774	42.1	42.3	35.1	35.3	Euro
Greece	50	50	9,527	10,024	2.1	2.1	1.8	1.7	Euro
Hong Kong	41	41	7,771	8,200	4.2	4.2	32,500.0	32,926.9	Dollar
Hungary	60	59	11,428	11,959	2.0	2.0	513.5	526.3	Forint*
India	7,986	8,107	1,514,479	1,629,514	36.2	37.8	2,296.4	2,397.7	Rupees
Indonesia	1,986	2,011	376,599	404,307	17.9	18.6	240.8	249.5	Rupiah*

Offices of Physicians Industry
(NAICS 62111)

Country Estimates

Country	Establishments 2018	2019	Employment 2018	2019	Sales ($B) 2018	2019	Local Sales (B) 2018	2019	Currency
Iran	544	550	103,143	110,626	6.5	6.4	233.1	229.5	Rial*
Iraq	143	145	27,046	29,107	1.7	1.7	2.0	2.0	Dinar*
Ireland	30	30	5,706	6,125	6.2	7.1	5.2	5.9	Euro
Israel	57	57	10,755	11,557	5.3	5.4	18.1	18.4	Shekel
Italy	302	301	57,300	60,451	21.9	21.7	18.3	18.2	Euro
Japan	846	837	160,389	168,265	69.3	69.0	7,818.9	7,784.6	Yen*
Kazakhstan	138	138	26,132	27,829	3.4	3.5	1,132.8	1,149.0	Tenge
Kuwait	32	34	6,107	6,753	2.0	2.0	0.6	0.6	Dinar
Malaysia	264	268	49,996	53,889	6.4	6.6	25.6	26.6	Ringgit
Mexico	859	869	162,878	174,644	18.8	19.0	360.8	365.1	New pesos
Netherlands	81	80	15,319	16,145	9.0	9.1	7.5	7.6	Euro
New Zealand	29	29	5,479	5,842	2.7	2.8	3.8	3.8	Dollar
Nigeria	741	753	140,475	151,391	4.8	4.8	1,714,612.5	1,735,510.6	Naira
Norway	30	30	5,659	6,017	5.4	5.4	43.4	43.7	Krone
Pakistan	1,187	1,212	225,130	243,591	4.2	4.4	467.7	483.5	Rupees
Peru	235	235	44,564	47,293	3.4	3.5	11.0	11.1	Nuevo Sol
Phillipines	640	651	121,347	130,856	5.1	5.4	257.2	269.4	Pesos
Poland	219	217	41,569	43,580	8.4	8.6	29.3	30.0	Zloty
Portugal	52	52	9,882	10,391	2.4	2.3	2.0	1.9	Euro
Puerto Rico	30	30	5,686	5,932	1.9	1.8	1.9	1.8	Dollar
Qatar	30	34	5,725	6,912	3.2	3.2	11.6	11.7	Riyal
Romania	158	155	29,921	31,213	3.4	3.5	13.1	13.4	New Leu
Russia	980	969	185,851	194,715	22.2	21.7	1,134.8	1,109.7	Rubles
Saudi Arabia	275	284	52,139	57,022	13.6	13.7	0.1	0.1	Rials*
Singapore	44	45	8,322	9,032	5.3	5.3	6,985.6	7,089.2	Dollar
South Africa	271	274	51,398	55,163	4.8	4.8	59,129.4	59,284.9	Rand
South Korea	383	382	72,649	76,699	26.1	26.5	27,829.9	28,327.5	Won*
Spain	239	240	45,342	48,334	15.0	14.9	12,539.3	12,438.9	Euro
Sweden	49	49	9,292	9,834	6.4	6.6	52,815.4	54,015.4	Krona
Switzerland	45	45	8,501	9,033	8.8	8.9	8,604.3	8,655.3	Swiss franc
Taiwan	239	247	45,276	49,582	8.9	9.0	262,939.9	265,360.9	Dollar
Thailand	577	580	109,441	116,578	7.5	7.6	242,013.1	243,659.2	Baht
Turkey	437	435	82,929	87,488	14.3	14.7	53,742.8	54,996.9	Euro
Ukraine	240	236	45,485	47,486	0.8	0.7	23,544.9	20,933.9	Hryvna
UAE	74	83	14,097	16,730	3.9	3.9	14,283.9	14,329.4	Dirham
United Kingdom	313	312	59,266	62,640	34.9	35.4	25,711.0	26,079.1	Pounds
United States	2,018	2,019	382,675	405,822	281.4	285.2	281,374.3	285,173.1	Dollars
Venezuela	206	209	39,035	42,006	7.7	7.4	76,573.5	73,833.2	Bolivar
Vietnam	724	725	137,343	145,656	4.0	4.2	91,388.8	95,927.9	Dong*

Note: Due to rounding, establishments will vary by + or - one establishment. Therefore, zero establishments may also be one establishment.

* Local Sales are in trillions

NAICS 62121: Offices of Dentists. This industry comprises establishments primarily of licensed practitioners having the degree of D.M.D. or D.D.S. (or D.D.Sc.) and engaged in the practice of general or specialized dentistry, including dental surgery. Establishments operating as clinics of dentists are included in this business.

COUNTRY ESTIMATES

Country	Establishments 2018	Establishments 2019	Employment 2018	Employment 2019	Sales ($B) 2018	Sales ($B) 2019	Local Sales (B) 2018	Local Sales (B) 2019	Currency
Algeria	371	373	21,460	23,003	2.1	2.1	240.0	242.9	Dinar
Argentina	257	258	14,878	15,865	5.0	4.9	94.5	94.0	Pesos
Australia	160	162	9,258	9,954	12.3	12.5	15.6	15.9	Dollars
Austria	43	43	2,490	2,642	2.6	2.6	2.2	2.2	Euro
Bangladesh	565	565	32,624	34,811	1.0	1.1	84.0	88.7	Taka
Belgium	54	54	3,122	3,328	3.0	3.0	2.5	2.5	Euro
Brazil	1,375	1,387	79,459	85,406	15.1	14.8	48,784.0	47,732.8	Real
Canada	181	182	10,471	11,190	10.8	10.9	13.3	13.5	Dollars
Chile	133	134	7,704	8,271	2.5	2.5	1,492.2	1,514.4	Pesos*
China	9,511	9,479	549,576	583,831	126.2	131.8	819.1	855.5	RMB
Colombia	286	286	16,525	17,616	2.7	2.8	7.9	8.1	Pesos*
Czech Republic	69	68	3,961	4,198	1.8	1.9	39.1	40.4	Koruna
Denmark	27	27	1,567	1,661	2.0	2.0	12.4	12.5	Kroner
Egypt	608	623	35,156	38,376	3.1	3.1	54.5	55.1	Pounds
Finland	27	27	1,552	1,646	1.5	1.5	1.3	1.3	Euro
France	300	299	17,333	18,439	15.3	15.3	12.8	12.8	Euro
Germany	382	377	22,065	23,219	23.5	23.8	19.6	19.9	Euro
Greece	50	50	2,903	3,072	1.2	1.2	1.0	1.0	Euro
Hong Kong	41	41	2,368	2,513	2.3	2.4	18,142.9	18,500.5	Dollar
Hungary	60	59	3,482	3,665	1.1	1.1	286.6	295.7	Forint*
India	7,986	8,107	461,507	499,328	20.2	21.2	1,282.0	1,347.2	Rupees
Indonesia	1,986	2,011	114,761	123,891	10.0	10.4	134.4	140.2	Rupiah*

Offices of Dentists Industry (NAICS 62121)

Country Estimates

Country	Establishments 2018	2019	Employment 2018	2019	Sales ($B) 2018	2019	Local Sales (B) 2018	2019	Currency
Iran	544	550	31,431	33,899	3.6	3.6	130.1	128.9	Rial*
Iraq	143	145	8,242	8,919	0.9	0.9	1.1	1.1	Dinar*
Ireland	30	30	1,739	1,877	3.5	4.0	2.9	3.3	Euro
Israel	57	57	3,277	3,541	2.9	3.0	10.1	10.4	Shekel
Italy	302	301	17,461	18,524	12.2	12.2	10.2	10.2	Euro
Japan	846	837	48,875	51,561	38.7	38.7	4,364.9	4,373.9	Yen*
Kazakhstan	138	138	7,963	8,528	1.9	2.0	632.4	645.6	Tenge
Kuwait	32	34	1,861	2,069	1.1	1.1	0.3	0.3	Dinar
Malaysia	264	268	15,235	16,513	3.6	3.7	14.3	15.0	Ringgit
Mexico	859	869	49,634	53,516	10.5	10.7	201.4	205.1	New pesos
Netherlands	81	80	4,668	4,947	5.0	5.1	4.2	4.2	Euro
New Zealand	29	29	1,670	1,790	1.5	1.5	2.1	2.2	Dollar
Nigeria	741	753	42,807	46,390	2.7	2.7	957,169.6	975,123.0	Naira
Norway	30	30	1,725	1,844	3.0	3.0	24.2	24.5	Krone
Pakistan	1,187	1,212	68,604	74,643	2.4	2.5	261.1	271.7	Rupees
Peru	235	235	13,580	14,492	1.9	1.9	6.1	6.3	Nuevo Sol
Phillipines	640	651	36,978	40,098	2.9	3.0	143.6	151.4	Pesos
Poland	219	217	12,667	13,354	4.7	4.8	16.4	16.9	Zloty
Portugal	52	52	3,011	3,184	1.3	1.3	1.1	1.1	Euro
Puerto Rico	30	30	1,733	1,818	1.1	1.0	1.1	1.0	Dollar
Qatar	30	34	1,745	2,118	1.8	1.8	6.5	6.6	Riyal
Romania	158	155	9,118	9,564	1.9	1.9	7.3	7.5	New Leu
Russia	980	969	56,634	59,666	12.4	12.2	633.5	623.5	Rubles
Saudi Arabia	275	284	15,888	17,473	7.6	7.7	0.0	0.0	Rials*
Singapore	44	45	2,536	2,768	2.9	3.0	3,899.7	3,983.2	Dollar
South Africa	271	274	15,663	16,904	2.7	2.7	33,008.5	33,310.1	Rand
South Korea	383	382	22,138	23,503	14.6	14.9	15,535.8	15,916.2	Won*
Spain	239	240	13,817	14,811	8.4	8.4	7,000.0	6,989.0	Euro
Sweden	49	49	2,832	3,014	3.6	3.7	29,483.8	30,349.4	Krona
Switzerland	45	45	2,590	2,768	4.9	5.0	4,803.3	4,863.1	Swiss franc
Taiwan	239	247	13,797	15,193	5.0	5.1	146,784.2	149,097.1	Dollar
Thailand	577	580	33,350	35,723	4.2	4.3	135,102.0	136,903.6	Baht
Turkey	437	435	25,271	26,809	8.0	8.2	30,001.5	30,900.8	Euro
Ukraine	240	236	13,861	14,551	0.5	0.4	13,143.8	11,762.0	Hryvna
UAE	74	83	4,296	5,127	2.2	2.2	7,973.9	8,051.2	Dirham
United Kingdom	313	312	18,060	19,195	19.5	19.9	14,353.0	14,653.0	Pounds
United States	2,018	2,019	116,613	124,355	157.1	160.2	157,075.1	160,228.8	Dollars
Venezuela	206	209	11,895	12,872	4.3	4.2	42,746.6	41,484.3	Bolivar
Vietnam	724	725	41,853	44,633	2.2	2.4	51,017.1	53,898.6	Dong*

Note: Due to rounding, establishments will vary by + or - one establishment. Therefore, zero establishments may also be one establishment.

* Local Sales are in trillions

MEDICAL LABORATORIES INDUSTRY
(NAICS 621511)

NAICS 621511: Medical Laboratories. This industry comprises establishments primarily engaged in providing professional analytic or diagnostic services to the medical profession, or to the patient on prescription of a physician.

COUNTRY ESTIMATES

Country	Establishments 2018	Establishments 2019	Employment 2018	Employment 2019	Sales ($B) 2018	Sales ($B) 2019	Local Sales (B) 2018	Local Sales (B) 2019	Currency
Algeria	371	373	5,861	6,359	0.2	0.2	25.9	26.8	Dinar
Argentina	257	258	4,064	4,386	0.5	0.5	10.2	10.4	Pesos
Australia	160	162	2,529	2,752	1.3	1.4	1.7	1.8	Dollars
Austria	43	43	680	730	0.3	0.3	0.2	0.2	Euro
Bangladesh	565	565	8,911	9,623	0.1	0.1	9.1	9.8	Taka
Belgium	54	54	853	920	0.3	0.3	0.3	0.3	Euro
Brazil	1,375	1,387	21,703	23,610	1.6	1.6	5,267.2	5,258.9	Real
Canada	181	182	2,860	3,093	1.2	1.2	1.4	1.5	Dollars
Chile	133	134	2,104	2,287	0.3	0.3	161.1	166.8	Pesos*
China	9,511	9,479	150,107	161,396	13.6	14.5	88.4	94.3	RMB
Colombia	286	286	4,513	4,870	0.3	0.3	0.8	0.9	Pesos*
Czech Republic	69	68	1,082	1,161	0.2	0.2	4.2	4.5	Koruna
Denmark	27	27	428	459	0.2	0.2	1.3	1.4	Kroner
Egypt	608	623	9,602	10,609	0.3	0.3	5.9	6.1	Pounds
Finland	27	27	424	455	0.2	0.2	0.1	0.1	Euro
France	300	299	4,734	5,097	1.6	1.7	1.4	1.4	Euro
Germany	382	377	6,027	6,419	2.5	2.6	2.1	2.2	Euro
Greece	50	50	793	849	0.1	0.1	0.1	0.1	Euro
Hong Kong	41	41	647	695	0.3	0.3	1,958.9	2,038.3	Dollar
Hungary	60	59	951	1,013	0.1	0.1	30.9	32.6	Forint*
India	7,986	8,107	126,053	138,036	2.2	2.3	138.4	148.4	Rupees
Indonesia	1,986	2,011	31,345	34,249	1.1	1.2	14.5	15.4	Rupiah*

MEDICAL LABORATORIES INDUSTRY
(NAICS 621511)

COUNTRY ESTIMATES

Country	Establishments 2018	Establishments 2019	Employment 2018	Employment 2019	Sales ($B) 2018	Sales ($B) 2019	Local Sales (B) 2018	Local Sales (B) 2019	Currency
Iran	544	550	8,585	9,371	0.4	0.4	14.0	14.2	Rial*
Iraq	143	145	2,251	2,466	0.1	0.1	0.1	0.1	Dinar*
Ireland	30	30	475	519	0.4	0.4	0.3	0.4	Euro
Israel	57	57	895	979	0.3	0.3	1.1	1.1	Shekel
Italy	302	301	4,769	5,121	1.3	1.3	1.1	1.1	Euro
Japan	846	837	13,349	14,254	4.2	4.3	471.3	481.9	Yen*
Kazakhstan	138	138	2,175	2,357	0.2	0.2	68.3	71.1	Tenge
Kuwait	32	34	508	572	0.1	0.1	0.0	0.0	Dinar
Malaysia	264	268	4,161	4,565	0.4	0.4	1.5	1.6	Ringgit
Mexico	859	869	13,557	14,794	1.1	1.2	21.7	22.6	New pesos
Netherlands	81	80	1,275	1,368	0.5	0.6	0.5	0.5	Euro
New Zealand	29	29	456	495	0.2	0.2	0.2	0.2	Dollar
Nigeria	741	753	11,692	12,824	0.3	0.3	103,345.0	107,434.0	Naira
Norway	30	30	471	510	0.3	0.3	2.6	2.7	Krone
Pakistan	1,187	1,212	18,738	20,635	0.3	0.3	28.2	29.9	Rupees
Peru	235	235	3,709	4,006	0.2	0.2	0.7	0.7	Nuevo Sol
Phillipines	640	651	10,100	11,085	0.3	0.3	15.5	16.7	Pesos
Poland	219	217	3,460	3,692	0.5	0.5	1.8	1.9	Zloty
Portugal	52	52	822	880	0.1	0.1	0.1	0.1	Euro
Puerto Rico	30	30	473	503	0.1	0.1	0.1	0.1	Dollar
Qatar	30	34	477	585	0.2	0.2	0.7	0.7	Riyal
Romania	158	155	2,490	2,644	0.2	0.2	0.8	0.8	New Leu
Russia	980	969	15,469	16,494	1.3	1.3	68.4	68.7	Rubles
Saudi Arabia	275	284	4,340	4,830	0.8	0.8	0.0	0.0	Rials*
Singapore	44	45	693	765	0.3	0.3	421.0	438.8	Dollar
South Africa	271	274	4,278	4,673	0.3	0.3	3,563.9	3,669.9	Rand
South Korea	383	382	6,047	6,497	1.6	1.6	1,677.4	1,753.6	Won*
Spain	239	240	3,774	4,094	0.9	0.9	755.8	770.0	Euro
Sweden	49	49	773	833	0.4	0.4	3,183.3	3,343.7	Krona
Switzerland	45	45	708	765	0.5	0.5	518.6	535.8	Swiss franc
Taiwan	239	247	3,768	4,200	0.5	0.6	15,848.2	16,426.7	Dollar
Thailand	577	580	9,109	9,875	0.5	0.5	14,586.9	15,083.3	Baht
Turkey	437	435	6,902	7,411	0.9	0.9	3,239.2	3,404.5	Euro
Ukraine	240	236	3,786	4,023	0.1	0.0	1,419.1	1,295.9	Hryvna
UAE	74	83	1,173	1,417	0.2	0.2	860.9	887.0	Dirham
United Kingdom	313	312	4,933	5,306	2.1	2.2	1,549.7	1,614.4	Pounds
United States	2,018	2,019	31,851	34,377	17.0	17.7	16,959.3	17,653.2	Dollars
Venezuela	206	209	3,249	3,558	0.5	0.5	4,615.3	4,570.5	Bolivar
Vietnam	724	725	11,431	12,338	0.2	0.3	5,508.3	5,938.3	Dong*

Note: Due to rounding, establishments will vary by + or - one establishment. Therefore, zero establishments may also be one establishment.

* Local Sales are in trillions

Home Health Care Services Industry (NAICS 62161)

NAICS 62161: Home Health Care Services. This industry comprises establishments primarily engaged in providing skilled nursing or medical care in the home, under supervision of a physician. Registered or practical nurses engaged in the independent practice of their profession are classified in 8049, and nurses' registries are classified in 7361. Selling health care products for personal or household consumption is classified in retail trade and renting or leasing products for health care is classified in 7352.

COUNTRY ESTIMATES

Country	Establishments 2018	Establishments 2019	Employment 2018	Employment 2019	Sales ($B) 2018	Sales ($B) 2019	Local Sales (B) 2018	Local Sales (B) 2019	Currency
Algeria	371	373	22,343	24,124	2.7	2.8	311.2	319.7	Dinar
Argentina	257	258	15,490	16,638	6.4	6.5	122.5	123.8	Pesos
Australia	160	162	9,639	10,439	15.9	16.5	20.3	21.0	Dollars
Austria	43	43	2,593	2,770	3.4	3.4	2.8	2.9	Euro
Bangladesh	565	565	33,967	36,507	1.3	1.4	108.9	116.8	Taka
Belgium	54	54	3,250	3,490	3.9	4.0	3.2	3.3	Euro
Brazil	1,375	1,387	82,731	89,568	19.6	19.5	63,240.4	62,837.7	Real
Canada	181	182	10,902	11,735	13.9	14.3	17.3	17.8	Dollars
Chile	133	134	8,021	8,674	3.2	3.3	1,934.5	1,993.6	Pesos*
China	9,511	9,479	572,206	612,286	163.6	173.5	1,061.8	1,126.2	RMB
Colombia	286	286	17,205	18,475	3.5	3.7	10.2	10.7	Pesos*
Czech Republic	69	68	4,124	4,403	2.4	2.5	50.7	53.2	Koruna
Denmark	27	27	1,631	1,742	2.6	2.6	16.0	16.4	Kroner
Egypt	608	623	36,603	40,246	4.0	4.1	70.7	72.6	Pounds
Finland	27	27	1,616	1,727	2.0	2.0	1.6	1.7	Euro
France	300	299	18,047	19,337	19.8	20.2	16.5	16.9	Euro
Germany	382	377	22,974	24,351	30.4	31.3	25.4	26.1	Euro
Greece	50	50	3,023	3,221	1.5	1.5	1.3	1.3	Euro
Hong Kong	41	41	2,466	2,635	3.0	3.1	23,519.3	24,354.9	Dollar
Hungary	60	59	3,626	3,843	1.4	1.5	371.6	389.3	Forint*
India	7,986	8,107	480,511	523,664	26.2	27.9	1,661.9	1,773.5	Rupees
Indonesia	1,986	2,011	119,487	129,929	13.0	13.7	174.3	184.6	Rupiah*

HOME HEALTH CARE SERVICES INDUSTRY
(NAICS 62161)

COUNTRY ESTIMATES

Country	Establishments 2018	Establishments 2019	Employment 2018	Employment 2019	Sales ($B) 2018	Sales ($B) 2019	Local Sales (B) 2018	Local Sales (B) 2019	Currency
Iran	544	550	32,725	35,551	4.7	4.7	168.7	169.7	Rial*
Iraq	143	145	8,581	9,354	1.2	1.2	1.5	1.5	Dinar*
Ireland	30	30	1,811	1,968	4.5	5.2	3.8	4.4	Euro
Israel	57	57	3,412	3,714	3.8	4.0	13.1	13.6	Shekel
Italy	302	301	18,180	19,427	15.8	16.1	13.2	13.4	Euro
Japan	846	837	50,888	54,074	50.1	51.0	5,658.3	5,758.0	Yen*
Kazakhstan	138	138	8,291	8,943	2.5	2.6	819.8	849.9	Tenge
Kuwait	32	34	1,938	2,170	1.5	1.5	0.4	0.4	Dinar
Malaysia	264	268	15,863	17,318	4.6	4.9	18.5	19.7	Ringgit
Mexico	859	869	51,678	56,124	13.6	14.1	261.1	270.1	New pesos
Netherlands	81	80	4,860	5,188	6.5	6.7	5.4	5.6	Euro
New Zealand	29	29	1,738	1,877	2.0	2.0	2.7	2.8	Dollar
Nigeria	741	753	44,570	48,651	3.4	3.6	1,240,812.8	1,283,698.7	Naira
Norway	30	30	1,796	1,934	3.9	4.0	31.4	32.3	Krone
Pakistan	1,187	1,212	71,429	78,281	3.1	3.2	338.5	357.6	Rupees
Peru	235	235	14,139	15,198	2.5	2.6	7.9	8.2	Nuevo Sol
Phillipines	640	651	38,501	42,052	3.7	4.0	186.1	199.3	Pesos
Poland	219	217	13,189	14,005	6.1	6.4	21.2	22.2	Zloty
Portugal	52	52	3,135	3,339	1.7	1.7	1.4	1.4	Euro
Puerto Rico	30	30	1,804	1,906	1.4	1.4	1.4	1.4	Dollar
Qatar	30	34	1,816	2,221	2.3	2.4	8.4	8.6	Riyal
Romania	158	155	9,493	10,031	2.5	2.6	9.5	9.9	New Leu
Russia	980	969	58,967	62,574	16.1	16.1	821.2	820.8	Rubles
Saudi Arabia	275	284	16,542	18,325	9.8	10.1	0.0	0.0	Rials*
Singapore	44	45	2,640	2,903	3.8	3.9	5,055.3	5,243.6	Dollar
South Africa	271	274	16,308	17,727	3.5	3.5	42,790.1	43,851.0	Rand
South Korea	383	382	23,050	24,648	18.9	19.6	20,139.7	20,952.9	Won*
Spain	239	240	14,386	15,533	10.9	11.0	9,074.3	9,200.6	Euro
Sweden	49	49	2,948	3,160	4.7	4.9	38,220.9	39,953.4	Krona
Switzerland	45	45	2,697	2,903	6.4	6.6	6,226.7	6,402.0	Swiss franc
Taiwan	239	247	14,365	15,934	6.5	6.7	190,281.6	196,278.5	Dollar
Thailand	577	580	34,723	37,464	5.4	5.6	175,137.5	180,226.5	Baht
Turkey	437	435	26,312	28,115	10.4	10.8	38,892.0	40,679.3	Euro
Ukraine	240	236	14,432	15,260	0.6	0.5	17,038.7	15,484.1	Hryvna
UAE	74	83	4,473	5,376	2.8	2.9	10,336.8	10,599.0	Dirham
United Kingdom	313	312	18,804	20,130	25.2	26.2	18,606.3	19,289.9	Pounds
United States	2,018	2,019	121,414	130,416	203.6	210.9	203,622.0	210,932.9	Dollars
Venezuela	206	209	12,385	13,499	5.6	5.5	55,413.9	54,612.0	Bolivar
Vietnam	724	725	43,576	46,808	2.9	3.1	66,135.3	70,954.6	Dong*

Note: Due to rounding, establishments will vary by + or - one establishment. Therefore, zero establishments may also be one establishment.

* Local Sales are in trillions

MEDICAL & SURGICAL HOSPITALS INDUSTRY (NAICS 62211)

NAICS 62211: Medical & Surgical Hospital. This industry comprises establishments primarily engaged in providing general medical and surgical services and other hospital services. Specialty hospitals are classified in 8063 and 8069.

COUNTRY ESTIMATES

Country	Establishments 2018	Establishments 2019	Employment 2018	Employment 2019	Sales ($B) 2018	Sales ($B) 2019	Local Sales (B) 2018	Local Sales (B) 2019	Currency
Algeria	371	373	187,767	202,615	0.1	0.1	8.7	8.7	Dinar
Argentina	257	258	130,175	139,741	0.2	0.2	3.4	3.4	Pesos
Australia	160	162	81,003	87,675	0.4	0.4	0.6	0.6	Dollars
Austria	43	43	21,790	23,267	0.1	0.1	0.1	0.1	Euro
Bangladesh	565	565	285,447	306,621	0.0	0.0	3.0	3.2	Taka
Belgium	54	54	27,314	29,313	0.1	0.1	0.1	0.1	Euro
Brazil	1,375	1,387	695,243	752,273	0.5	0.5	1,759.2	1,704.9	Real
Canada	181	182	91,615	98,564	0.4	0.4	0.5	0.5	Dollars
Chile	133	134	67,409	72,855	0.1	0.1	53.8	54.1	Pesos*
China	9,511	9,479	4,808,633	5,142,503	4.6	4.7	29.5	30.6	RMB
Colombia	286	286	144,587	155,169	0.1	0.1	0.3	0.3	Pesos*
Czech Republic	69	68	34,656	36,979	0.1	0.1	1.4	1.4	Koruna
Denmark	27	27	13,708	14,631	0.1	0.1	0.4	0.4	Kroner
Egypt	608	623	307,602	338,024	0.1	0.1	2.0	2.0	Pounds
Finland	27	27	13,578	14,501	0.1	0.1	0.0	0.0	Euro
France	300	299	151,662	162,411	0.6	0.5	0.5	0.5	Euro
Germany	382	377	193,067	204,520	0.8	0.8	0.7	0.7	Euro
Greece	50	50	25,401	27,057	0.0	0.0	0.0	0.0	Euro
Hong Kong	41	41	20,720	22,132	0.1	0.1	654.3	660.8	Dollar
Hungary	60	59	30,470	32,278	0.0	0.0	10.3	10.6	Forint*
India	7,986	8,107	4,038,057	4,398,182	0.7	0.8	46.2	48.1	Rupees
Indonesia	1,986	2,011	1,004,125	1,091,254	0.4	0.4	4.8	5.0	Rupiah*

COUNTRY ESTIMATES

Country	Establishments 2018	Establishments 2019	Employment 2018	Employment 2019	Sales ($B) 2018	Sales ($B) 2019	Local Sales (B) 2018	Local Sales (B) 2019	Currency
Iran	544	550	275,010	298,587	0.1	0.1	4.7	4.6	Rial*
Iraq	143	145	72,113	78,561	0.0	0.0	0.0	0.0	Dinar*
Ireland	30	30	15,215	16,532	0.1	0.1	0.1	0.1	Euro
Israel	57	57	28,675	31,193	0.1	0.1	0.4	0.4	Shekel
Italy	302	301	152,778	163,161	0.4	0.4	0.4	0.4	Euro
Japan	846	837	427,646	454,159	1.4	1.4	157.4	156.2	Yen*
Kazakhstan	138	138	69,675	75,114	0.1	0.1	22.8	23.1	Tenge
Kuwait	32	34	16,284	18,227	0.0	0.0	0.0	0.0	Dinar
Malaysia	264	268	133,305	145,451	0.1	0.1	0.5	0.5	Ringgit
Mexico	859	869	434,282	471,378	0.4	0.4	7.3	7.3	New pesos
Netherlands	81	80	40,845	43,575	0.2	0.2	0.2	0.2	Euro
New Zealand	29	29	14,608	15,769	0.1	0.1	0.1	0.1	Dollar
Nigeria	741	753	374,548	408,616	0.1	0.1	34,516.8	34,829.2	Naira
Norway	30	30	15,089	16,241	0.1	0.1	0.9	0.9	Krone
Pakistan	1,187	1,212	600,265	657,472	0.1	0.1	9.4	9.7	Rupees
Peru	235	235	118,822	127,648	0.1	0.1	0.2	0.2	Nuevo Sol
Phillipines	640	651	323,548	353,192	0.1	0.1	5.2	5.4	Pesos
Poland	219	217	110,836	117,625	0.2	0.2	0.6	0.6	Zloty
Portugal	52	52	26,348	28,045	0.0	0.0	0.0	0.0	Euro
Puerto Rico	30	30	15,161	16,011	0.0	0.0	0.0	0.0	Dollar
Qatar	30	34	15,265	18,655	0.1	0.1	0.2	0.2	Riyal
Romania	158	155	79,778	84,246	0.1	0.1	0.3	0.3	New Leu
Russia	980	969	495,535	525,551	0.4	0.4	22.8	22.3	Rubles
Saudi Arabia	275	284	139,017	153,908	0.3	0.3	0.0	0.0	Rials*
Singapore	44	45	22,189	24,378	0.1	0.1	140.6	142.3	Dollar
South Africa	271	274	137,044	148,890	0.1	0.1	1,190.3	1,189.8	Rand
South Korea	383	382	193,704	207,016	0.5	0.5	560.2	568.5	Won*
Spain	239	240	120,895	130,457	0.3	0.3	252.4	249.6	Euro
Sweden	49	49	24,775	26,544	0.1	0.1	1,063.2	1,084.0	Krona
Switzerland	45	45	22,666	24,382	0.2	0.2	173.2	173.7	Swiss franc
Taiwan	239	247	120,719	133,825	0.2	0.2	5,293.2	5,325.4	Dollar
Thailand	577	580	291,804	314,652	0.2	0.2	4,872.0	4,889.9	Baht
Turkey	437	435	221,114	236,138	0.3	0.3	1,081.9	1,103.7	Euro
Ukraine	240	236	121,278	128,168	0.0	0.0	474.0	420.1	Hryvna
UAE	74	83	37,587	45,156	0.1	0.1	287.5	287.6	Dirham
United Kingdom	313	312	158,020	169,070	0.7	0.7	517.6	523.4	Pounds
United States	2,018	2,019	1,020,327	1,095,345	5.7	5.7	5,664.3	5,723.0	Dollars
Venezuela	206	209	104,080	113,377	0.2	0.1	1,541.5	1,481.7	Bolivar
Vietnam	724	725	366,197	393,137	0.1	0.1	1,839.7	1,925.1	Dong*

Note: Due to rounding, establishments will vary by + or - one establishment. Therefore, zero establishments may also be one establishment.

* Local Sales are in trillions

NURSING CARE FACILITIES INDUSTRY
(NAICS 62311)

NAICS 62311: Nursing Care Facilities. This industry comprises establishments primarily engaged in providing inpatient nursing and rehabilitative services, but not on a continuous basis. Staffing must include 24-hour per day personnel with a licensed nurse on duty full-time during each day shift. At least once a week, consultation from a registered nurse on the delivery of care is required. Included are facilities certified to deliver intermediate care under the Medicaid program.

COUNTRY ESTIMATES

Country	Establishments 2018	2019	Employment 2018	2019	Sales ($B) 2018	2019	Local Sales (B) 2018	2019	Currency
Algeria	371	373	27,763	29,666	0.3	0.3	34.9	35.0	Dinar
Argentina	257	258	19,248	20,460	0.7	0.7	13.7	13.6	Pesos
Australia	160	162	11,977	12,837	1.8	1.8	2.3	2.3	Dollars
Austria	43	43	3,222	3,407	0.4	0.4	0.3	0.3	Euro
Bangladesh	565	565	42,206	44,894	0.1	0.2	12.2	12.8	Taka
Belgium	54	54	4,039	4,292	0.4	0.4	0.4	0.4	Euro
Brazil	1,375	1,387	102,798	110,144	2.2	2.1	7,092.9	6,880.1	Real
Canada	181	182	13,546	14,431	1.6	1.6	1.9	1.9	Dollars
Chile	133	134	9,967	10,667	0.4	0.4	217.0	218.3	Pesos*
China	9,511	9,479	711,002	752,941	18.4	19.0	119.1	123.3	RMB
Colombia	286	286	21,379	22,719	0.4	0.4	1.1	1.2	Pesos*
Czech Republic	69	68	5,124	5,414	0.3	0.3	5.7	5.8	Koruna
Denmark	27	27	2,027	2,142	0.3	0.3	1.8	1.8	Kroner
Egypt	608	623	45,482	49,492	0.5	0.5	7.9	7.9	Pounds
Finland	27	27	2,008	2,123	0.2	0.2	0.2	0.2	Euro
France	300	299	22,425	23,779	2.2	2.2	1.9	1.8	Euro
Germany	382	377	28,547	29,945	3.4	3.4	2.9	2.9	Euro
Greece	50	50	3,756	3,962	0.2	0.2	0.1	0.1	Euro
Hong Kong	41	41	3,064	3,241	0.3	0.3	2,637.9	2,666.6	Dollar
Hungary	60	59	4,505	4,726	0.2	0.2	41.7	42.6	Forint*
India	7,986	8,107	597,065	643,961	2.9	3.1	186.4	194.2	Rupees
Indonesia	1,986	2,011	148,469	159,776	1.5	1.5	19.5	20.2	Rupiah*

NURSING CARE FACILITIES INDUSTRY
(NAICS 62311)

COUNTRY ESTIMATES

Country	Establishments 2018	2019	Employment 2018	2019	Sales ($B) 2018	2019	Local Sales (B) 2018	2019	Currency
Iran	544	550	40,663	43,718	0.5	0.5	18.9	18.6	Rial*
Iraq	143	145	10,663	11,503	0.1	0.1	0.2	0.2	Dinar*
Ireland	30	30	2,250	2,420	0.5	0.6	0.4	0.5	Euro
Israel	57	57	4,240	4,567	0.4	0.4	1.5	1.5	Shekel
Italy	302	301	22,590	23,889	1.8	1.8	1.5	1.5	Euro
Japan	846	837	63,232	66,496	5.6	5.6	634.6	630.4	Yen*
Kazakhstan	138	138	10,302	10,998	0.3	0.3	91.9	93.1	Tenge
Kuwait	32	34	2,408	2,669	0.2	0.2	0.0	0.0	Dinar
Malaysia	264	268	19,710	21,296	0.5	0.5	2.1	2.2	Ringgit
Mexico	859	869	64,213	69,017	1.5	1.5	29.3	29.6	New pesos
Netherlands	81	80	6,039	6,380	0.7	0.7	0.6	0.6	Euro
New Zealand	29	29	2,160	2,309	0.2	0.2	0.3	0.3	Dollar
Nigeria	741	753	55,381	59,828	0.4	0.4	139,167.5	140,552.9	Naira
Norway	30	30	2,231	2,378	0.4	0.4	3.5	3.5	Krone
Pakistan	1,187	1,212	88,755	96,264	0.3	0.4	38.0	39.2	Rupees
Peru	235	235	17,569	18,690	0.3	0.3	0.9	0.9	Nuevo Sol
Phillipines	640	651	47,840	51,713	0.4	0.4	20.9	21.8	Pesos
Poland	219	217	16,388	17,222	0.7	0.7	2.4	2.4	Zloty
Portugal	52	52	3,896	4,106	0.2	0.2	0.2	0.2	Euro
Puerto Rico	30	30	2,242	2,344	0.2	0.1	0.2	0.1	Dollar
Qatar	30	34	2,257	2,731	0.3	0.3	0.9	0.9	Riyal
Romania	158	155	11,796	12,335	0.3	0.3	1.1	1.1	New Leu
Russia	980	969	73,270	76,949	1.8	1.8	92.1	89.9	Rubles
Saudi Arabia	275	284	20,555	22,534	1.1	1.1	0.0	0.0	Rials*
Singapore	44	45	3,281	3,569	0.4	0.4	567.0	574.1	Dollar
South Africa	271	274	20,263	21,800	0.4	0.4	4,799.3	4,801.3	Rand
South Korea	383	382	28,641	30,310	2.1	2.2	2,258.8	2,294.1	Won*
Spain	239	240	17,876	19,101	1.2	1.2	1,017.8	1,007.4	Euro
Sweden	49	49	3,663	3,886	0.5	0.5	4,286.8	4,374.5	Krona
Switzerland	45	45	3,351	3,570	0.7	0.7	698.4	701.0	Swiss franc
Taiwan	239	247	17,850	19,594	0.7	0.7	21,341.7	21,490.7	Dollar
Thailand	577	580	43,146	46,070	0.6	0.6	19,643.1	19,733.1	Baht
Turkey	437	435	32,694	34,574	1.2	1.2	4,362.1	4,454.0	Euro
Ukraine	240	236	17,932	18,766	0.1	0.1	1,911.0	1,695.4	Hryvna
UAE	74	83	5,558	6,612	0.3	0.3	1,159.4	1,160.5	Dirham
United Kingdom	313	312	23,365	24,754	2.8	2.9	2,086.8	2,112.1	Pounds
United States	2,018	2,019	150,865	160,375	22.8	23.1	22,837.9	23,095.2	Dollars
Venezuela	206	209	15,389	16,600	0.6	0.6	6,215.1	5,979.5	Bolivar
Vietnam	724	725	54,146	57,561	0.3	0.3	7,417.6	7,768.9	Dong*

Note: Due to rounding, establishments will vary by + or - one establishment. Therefore, zero establishments may also be one establishment.

* Local Sales are in trillions

COMMUNITY CARE FACILITIES FOR THE ELDERLY (NAICS 62331)

NAICS 62331: Community Care Facilities for the Elderly. This industry comprises establishments primarily engaged in the provision of residential social and personal care for children, the aged, and special categories of persons with some limits on ability for self-care, but where medical care is not a major element. Included are establishments providing 24-hour year-round care for children. Boarding schools providing elementary and secondary education are classified in 8211.

COUNTRY ESTIMATES

Country	Establishments 2018	Establishments 2019	Employment 2018	Employment 2019	Sales ($B) 2018	Sales ($B) 2019	Local Sales (B) 2018	Local Sales (B) 2019	Currency
Algeria	371	373	15,540	16,877	0.5	0.5	53.0	54.3	Dinar
Argentina	257	258	10,774	11,640	1.1	1.1	20.9	21.0	Pesos
Australia	160	162	6,704	7,303	2.7	2.8	3.5	3.6	Dollars
Austria	43	43	1,803	1,938	0.6	0.6	0.5	0.5	Euro
Bangladesh	565	565	23,625	25,541	0.2	0.2	18.5	19.8	Taka
Belgium	54	54	2,261	2,442	0.7	0.7	0.5	0.6	Euro
Brazil	1,375	1,387	57,541	62,663	3.3	3.3	10,772.5	10,671.4	Real
Canada	181	182	7,582	8,210	2.4	2.4	2.9	3.0	Dollars
Chile	133	134	5,579	6,069	0.5	0.6	329.5	338.6	Pesos*
China	9,511	9,479	397,983	428,360	27.9	29.5	180.9	191.3	RMB
Colombia	286	286	11,967	12,925	0.6	0.6	1.7	1.8	Pesos*
Czech Republic	69	68	2,868	3,080	0.4	0.4	8.6	9.0	Koruna
Denmark	27	27	1,135	1,219	0.4	0.4	2.7	2.8	Kroner
Egypt	608	623	25,458	28,157	0.7	0.7	12.0	12.3	Pounds
Finland	27	27	1,124	1,208	0.3	0.3	0.3	0.3	Euro
France	300	299	12,552	13,529	3.4	3.4	2.8	2.9	Euro
Germany	382	377	15,979	17,036	5.2	5.3	4.3	4.4	Euro
Greece	50	50	2,102	2,254	0.3	0.3	0.2	0.2	Euro
Hong Kong	41	41	1,715	1,844	0.5	0.5	4,006.3	4,136.1	Dollar
Hungary	60	59	2,522	2,689	0.2	0.3	63.3	66.1	Forint*
India	7,986	8,107	334,207	366,359	4.5	4.7	283.1	301.2	Rupees
Indonesia	1,986	2,011	83,106	90,899	2.2	2.3	29.7	31.3	Rupiah*

COMMUNITY CARE FACILITIES FOR THE ELDERLY (NAICS 62331)

COUNTRY ESTIMATES

Country	Establishments 2018	Establishments 2019	Employment 2018	Employment 2019	Sales ($B) 2018	Sales ($B) 2019	Local Sales (B) 2018	Local Sales (B) 2019	Currency
Iran	544	550	22,761	24,872	0.8	0.8	28.7	28.8	Rial*
Iraq	143	145	5,968	6,544	0.2	0.2	0.2	0.3	Dinar*
Ireland	30	30	1,259	1,377	0.8	0.9	0.6	0.7	Euro
Israel	57	57	2,373	2,598	0.6	0.7	2.2	2.3	Shekel
Italy	302	301	12,645	13,591	2.7	2.7	2.3	2.3	Euro
Japan	846	837	35,394	37,831	8.5	8.7	963.8	977.8	Yen*
Kazakhstan	138	138	5,767	6,257	0.4	0.4	139.6	144.3	Tenge
Kuwait	32	34	1,348	1,518	0.2	0.2	0.1	0.1	Dinar
Malaysia	264	268	11,033	12,116	0.8	0.8	3.1	3.3	Ringgit
Mexico	859	869	35,943	39,265	2.3	2.4	44.5	45.9	New pesos
Netherlands	81	80	3,381	3,630	1.1	1.1	0.9	0.9	Euro
New Zealand	29	29	1,209	1,313	0.3	0.3	0.5	0.5	Dollar
Nigeria	741	753	30,999	34,037	0.6	0.6	211,362.2	218,004.4	Naira
Norway	30	30	1,249	1,353	0.7	0.7	5.3	5.5	Krone
Pakistan	1,187	1,212	49,680	54,766	0.5	0.5	57.7	60.7	Rupees
Peru	235	235	9,834	10,633	0.4	0.4	1.4	1.4	Nuevo Sol
Phillipines	640	651	26,778	29,420	0.6	0.7	31.7	33.8	Pesos
Poland	219	217	9,173	9,798	1.0	1.1	3.6	3.8	Zloty
Portugal	52	52	2,181	2,336	0.3	0.3	0.2	0.2	Euro
Puerto Rico	30	30	1,255	1,334	0.2	0.2	0.2	0.2	Dollar
Qatar	30	34	1,263	1,554	0.4	0.4	1.4	1.5	Riyal
Romania	158	155	6,603	7,017	0.4	0.4	1.6	1.7	New Leu
Russia	980	969	41,013	43,777	2.7	2.7	139.9	139.4	Rubles
Saudi Arabia	275	284	11,506	12,820	1.7	1.7	0.0	0.0	Rials*
Singapore	44	45	1,836	2,031	0.6	0.7	861.1	890.5	Dollar
South Africa	271	274	11,342	12,402	0.6	0.6	7,288.9	7,447.0	Rand
South Korea	383	382	16,032	17,244	3.2	3.3	3,430.6	3,558.3	Won*
Spain	239	240	10,006	10,867	1.9	1.9	1,545.7	1,562.5	Euro
Sweden	49	49	2,051	2,211	0.8	0.8	6,510.6	6,785.1	Krona
Switzerland	45	45	1,876	2,031	1.1	1.1	1,060.7	1,087.2	Swiss franc
Taiwan	239	247	9,991	11,147	1.1	1.1	32,412.9	33,333.0	Dollar
Thailand	577	580	24,151	26,210	0.9	1.0	29,833.2	30,607.0	Baht
Turkey	437	435	18,300	19,670	1.8	1.8	6,624.9	6,908.4	Euro
Ukraine	240	236	10,037	10,676	0.1	0.1	2,902.4	2,629.6	Hryvna
UAE	74	83	3,111	3,761	0.5	0.5	1,760.8	1,800.0	Dirham
United Kingdom	313	312	13,078	14,083	4.3	4.4	3,169.4	3,275.9	Pounds
United States	2,018	2,019	84,447	91,240	34.7	35.8	34,685.3	35,821.7	Dollars
Venezuela	206	209	8,614	9,444	0.9	0.9	9,439.3	9,274.5	Bolivar
Vietnam	724	725	30,308	32,747	0.5	0.5	11,265.6	12,049.9	Dong*

Note: Due to rounding, establishments will vary by + or - one establishment. Therefore, zero establishments may also be one establishment.

* Local Sales are in trillions

MUSICAL GROUPS & ARTISTS INDUSTRY (NAICS 71113)

NAICS 71113: Musical Groups and Artists . This industry comprises (1) groups primarily engaged in producing live musical entertainment (except theatrical musical or opera productions) and (2) independent (i.e., freelance) artists primarily engaged in providing live musical entertainment. Musical groups and artists may perform in front of a live audience or in a studio, and may or may not operate their own facilities for staging their shows.

COUNTRY ESTIMATES

Country	Establishments 2018	2019	Employment 2018	2019	Sales ($B) 2018	2019	Local Sales (B) 2018	2019	Currency
Algeria	371	373	1,102	1,171	0.4	0.4	44.7	44.4	Dinar
Argentina	257	258	764	808	0.9	0.9	17.6	17.2	Pesos
Australia	160	162	475	507	2.3	2.3	2.9	2.9	Dollars
Austria	57	57	170	179	0.6	0.6	0.5	0.5	Euro
Bangladesh	1,129	1,130	3,349	3,544	0.4	0.4	31.3	32.5	Taka
Belgium	72	72	213	225	0.7	0.7	0.6	0.6	Euro
Brazil	1,375	1,387	4,079	4,347	2.8	2.7	9,093.6	8,731.6	Real
Canada	241	242	715	758	2.7	2.6	3.3	3.3	Dollars
Chile	133	134	395	421	0.5	0.5	278.2	277.0	Pesos*
China	9,511	9,479	28,210	29,719	23.5	24.1	152.7	156.5	RMB
Colombia	286	286	848	897	0.5	0.5	1.5	1.5	Pesos*
Czech Republic	69	68	203	214	0.3	0.3	7.3	7.4	Koruna
Denmark	36	36	107	112	0.5	0.5	3.1	3.0	Kroner
Egypt	608	623	1,805	1,953	0.6	0.6	10.2	10.1	Pounds
Finland	36	36	106	111	0.4	0.4	0.3	0.3	Euro
France	399	398	1,183	1,248	3.8	3.7	3.2	3.1	Euro
Germany	508	501	1,506	1,572	5.8	5.8	4.9	4.8	Euro
Greece	67	66	198	208	0.3	0.3	0.2	0.2	Euro
Hong Kong	41	41	122	128	0.4	0.4	3,381.9	3,384.2	Dollar
Hungary	60	59	179	187	0.2	0.2	53.4	54.1	Forint*
India	7,986	8,107	23,690	25,418	3.8	3.9	239.0	246.4	Rupees
Indonesia	1,986	2,011	5,891	6,307	1.9	1.9	25.1	25.6	Rupiah*

MUSICAL GROUPS & ARTISTS INDUSTRY
(NAICS 71113)

COUNTRY ESTIMATES

Country	Establishments 2018	Establishments 2019	Employment 2018	Employment 2019	Sales ($B) 2018	Sales ($B) 2019	Local Sales (B) 2018	Local Sales (B) 2019	Currency
Iran	544	550	1,613	1,726	0.7	0.7	24.3	23.6	Rial*
Iraq	285	290	846	908	0.4	0.3	0.4	0.4	Dinar*
Ireland	40	41	119	127	0.9	1.0	0.7	0.8	Euro
Israel	57	57	168	180	0.5	0.6	1.9	1.9	Shekel
Italy	402	400	1,192	1,254	3.0	3.0	2.5	2.5	Euro
Japan	846	837	2,509	2,625	7.2	7.1	813.6	800.1	Yen*
Kazakhstan	138	138	409	434	0.4	0.4	117.9	118.1	Tenge
Kuwait	32	34	96	105	0.2	0.2	0.1	0.1	Dinar
Malaysia	264	268	782	841	0.7	0.7	2.7	2.7	Ringgit
Mexico	859	869	2,548	2,724	2.0	2.0	37.5	37.5	New pesos
Netherlands	107	107	319	335	1.2	1.2	1.0	1.0	Euro
New Zealand	29	29	86	91	0.3	0.3	0.4	0.4	Dollar
Nigeria	1,482	1,506	4,395	4,723	1.0	1.0	356,844.7	356,752.4	Naira
Norway	40	40	118	125	0.7	0.7	6.0	6.0	Krone
Pakistan	1,187	1,212	3,521	3,800	0.4	0.4	48.7	49.7	Rupees
Peru	235	235	697	738	0.4	0.4	1.1	1.1	Nuevo Sol
Phillipines	640	651	1,898	2,041	0.5	0.6	26.8	27.7	Pesos
Poland	219	217	650	680	0.9	0.9	3.1	3.1	Zloty
Portugal	69	69	206	216	0.3	0.3	0.3	0.3	Euro
Puerto Rico	30	30	89	93	0.2	0.2	0.2	0.2	Dollar
Qatar	30	34	90	108	0.3	0.3	1.2	1.2	Riyal
Romania	158	155	468	487	0.4	0.4	1.4	1.4	New Leu
Russia	980	969	2,907	3,037	2.3	2.2	118.1	114.1	Rubles
Saudi Arabia	275	284	816	889	1.4	1.4	0.0	0.0	Rials*
Singapore	44	45	130	141	0.5	0.5	726.9	728.6	Dollar
South Africa	271	274	804	860	0.5	0.5	6,153.0	6,093.3	Rand
South Korea	383	382	1,136	1,196	2.7	2.7	2,896.0	2,911.5	Won*
Spain	318	320	943	1,003	2.1	2.0	1,735.4	1,700.4	Euro
Sweden	65	65	193	204	0.9	0.9	7,309.6	7,383.8	Krona
Switzerland	60	60	177	187	1.2	1.2	1,190.8	1,183.2	Swiss franc
Taiwan	239	247	708	773	0.9	0.9	27,361.5	27,273.9	Dollar
Thailand	577	580	1,712	1,818	0.8	0.8	25,183.8	25,043.4	Baht
Turkey	437	435	1,297	1,365	1.5	1.5	5,592.5	5,652.6	Euro
Ukraine	319	314	946	985	0.1	0.1	3,258.6	2,861.6	Hryvna
UAE	149	166	441	522	0.8	0.8	2,972.8	2,945.6	Dirham
United Kingdom	416	414	1,233	1,300	4.8	4.8	3,558.4	3,565.0	Pounds
United States	2,018	2,019	5,986	6,330	29.3	29.3	29,279.8	29,310.2	Dollars
Venezuela	206	209	611	655	0.8	0.8	7,968.2	7,588.6	Bolivar
Vietnam	724	725	2,148	2,272	0.4	0.4	9,509.9	9,859.5	Dong*

Note: Due to rounding, establishments will vary by + or - one establishment. Therefore, zero establishments may also be one establishment.

* Local Sales are in trillions

NAICS 71121: Spectator Sports . This industry comprises (1) sports teams or clubs primarily participating in live sporting events before a paying audience; (2) establishments primarily engaged in operating racetracks; (3) independent athletes engaged in participating in live sporting or racing events before a paying audience; (4) owners of racing participants, such as cars, dogs, and horses, primarily engaged in entering them in racing events or other spectator sports events; and (5) establishments, such as sports trainers, primarily engaged in providing specialized services to support participants in sports events or competitions.

COUNTRY ESTIMATES

Country	Establishments 2018	2019	Employment 2018	2019	Sales ($B) 2018	2019	Local Sales (B) 2018	2019	Currency
Algeria	371	373	7,104	7,609	1.6	1.5	179.9	177.5	Dinar
Argentina	257	258	4,925	5,248	3.7	3.6	70.8	68.7	Pesos
Australia	160	162	3,065	3,292	9.2	9.2	11.7	11.6	Dollars
Austria	57	57	1,097	1,162	2.6	2.5	2.2	2.1	Euro
Bangladesh	1,129	1,130	21,601	23,029	1.5	1.6	125.9	129.6	Taka
Belgium	72	72	1,375	1,464	3.0	2.9	2.5	2.4	Euro
Brazil	1,375	1,387	26,306	28,250	11.3	10.8	36,570.8	34,874.9	Real
Canada	241	242	4,610	4,923	10.7	10.6	13.3	13.1	Dollars
Chile	133	134	2,551	2,736	1.8	1.8	1,118.7	1,106.5	Pesos*
China	9,511	9,479	181,942	193,117	94.6	96.3	614.0	625.0	RMB
Colombia	286	286	5,471	5,827	2.0	2.0	5.9	5.9	Pesos*
Czech Republic	69	68	1,311	1,389	1.4	1.4	29.3	29.5	Koruna
Denmark	36	36	690	731	2.0	2.0	12.3	12.1	Kroner
Egypt	608	623	11,639	12,694	2.3	2.3	40.9	40.3	Pounds
Finland	36	36	683	724	1.5	1.5	1.3	1.2	Euro
France	399	398	7,632	8,112	15.2	14.9	12.7	12.5	Euro
Germany	508	501	9,716	10,215	23.4	23.1	19.6	19.3	Euro
Greece	67	66	1,278	1,351	1.2	1.1	1.0	0.9	Euro
Hong Kong	41	41	784	831	1.7	1.7	13,600.8	13,517.0	Dollar
Hungary	60	59	1,153	1,212	0.8	0.8	214.9	216.1	Forint*
India	7,986	8,107	152,786	165,165	15.1	15.5	961.0	984.3	Rupees
Indonesia	1,986	2,011	37,993	40,980	7.5	7.6	100.8	102.4	Rupiah*

SPECTATOR SPORTS INDUSTRY
(NAICS 71121)

COUNTRY ESTIMATES

Country	Establishments 2018	Establishments 2019	Employment 2018	Employment 2019	Sales ($B) 2018	Sales ($B) 2019	Local Sales (B) 2018	Local Sales (B) 2019	Currency
Iran	544	550	10,405	11,213	2.7	2.6	97.5	94.2	Rial*
Iraq	285	290	5,457	5,900	1.4	1.4	1.7	1.6	Dinar*
Ireland	40	41	766	826	3.5	3.9	2.9	3.2	Euro
Israel	57	57	1,085	1,171	2.2	2.2	7.6	7.6	Shekel
Italy	402	400	7,688	8,149	12.2	11.9	10.2	9.9	Euro
Japan	846	837	16,181	17,055	29.0	28.3	3,272.1	3,195.7	Yen*
Kazakhstan	138	138	2,636	2,821	1.4	1.4	474.1	471.7	Tenge
Kuwait	32	34	616	684	0.8	0.8	0.3	0.2	Dinar
Malaysia	264	268	5,044	5,462	2.7	2.7	10.7	10.9	Ringgit
Mexico	859	869	16,432	17,702	7.9	7.8	151.0	149.9	New pesos
Netherlands	107	107	2,055	2,176	5.0	4.9	4.2	4.1	Euro
New Zealand	29	29	553	592	1.1	1.1	1.6	1.6	Dollar
Nigeria	1,482	1,506	28,343	30,690	4.0	4.0	1,435,081.0	1,424,906.1	Naira
Norway	40	40	759	811	3.0	3.0	24.1	23.8	Krone
Pakistan	1,187	1,212	22,712	24,690	1.8	1.8	195.7	198.5	Rupees
Peru	235	235	4,496	4,794	1.4	1.4	4.6	4.6	Nuevo Sol
Phillipines	640	651	12,242	13,263	2.1	2.2	107.6	110.6	Pesos
Poland	219	217	4,194	4,417	3.5	3.5	12.3	12.3	Zloty
Portugal	69	69	1,326	1,401	1.3	1.3	1.1	1.1	Euro
Puerto Rico	30	30	574	601	0.8	0.8	0.8	0.8	Dollar
Qatar	30	34	578	701	1.3	1.3	4.9	4.8	Riyal
Romania	158	155	3,019	3,164	1.4	1.4	5.5	5.5	New Leu
Russia	980	969	18,749	19,736	9.3	8.9	474.9	455.5	Rubles
Saudi Arabia	275	284	5,260	5,780	5.7	5.6	0.0	0.0	Rials*
Singapore	44	45	840	915	2.2	2.2	2,923.4	2,910.2	Dollar
South Africa	271	274	5,185	5,591	2.0	2.0	24,744.8	24,337.3	Rand
South Korea	383	382	7,329	7,774	10.9	10.9	11,646.4	11,628.9	Won*
Spain	318	320	6,084	6,516	8.4	8.1	6,979.2	6,791.4	Euro
Sweden	65	65	1,247	1,326	3.6	3.6	29,396.3	29,491.6	Krona
Switzerland	60	60	1,141	1,218	4.9	4.8	4,789.0	4,725.6	Swiss franc
Taiwan	239	247	4,568	5,026	3.7	3.7	110,036.5	108,934.6	Dollar
Thailand	577	580	11,041	11,816	3.1	3.1	101,279.0	100,025.7	Baht
Turkey	437	435	8,366	8,868	6.0	6.0	22,490.6	22,577.0	Euro
Ukraine	319	314	6,103	6,401	0.5	0.4	13,104.8	11,429.6	Hryvna
UAE	149	166	2,844	3,392	3.3	3.2	11,955.2	11,764.9	Dirham
United Kingdom	416	414	7,952	8,444	19.4	19.3	14,310.4	14,238.8	Pounds
United States	2,018	2,019	38,606	41,134	117.8	117.1	117,751.1	117,067.8	Dollars
Venezuela	206	209	3,938	4,258	3.2	3.0	32,044.9	30,309.6	Bolivar
Vietnam	724	725	13,856	14,763	1.7	1.7	38,244.9	39,379.8	Dong*

Note: Due to rounding, establishments will vary by + or - one establishment. Therefore, zero establishments may also be one establishment.

* Local Sales are in trillions

GOLF COURSES & COUNTRY CLUBS INDUSTRY (NAICS 71391)

NAICS 71391: Golf Courses and Country Clubs . This industry comprises (1) establishments primarily engaged in operating golf courses (except miniature) and (2) establishments primarily engaged in operating golf courses, along with dining facilities and other recreational facilities that are known as country clubs. These establishments often provide food and beverage services, equipment rental services, and golf instruction services.

COUNTRY ESTIMATES

Country	Establishments 2018	2019	Employment 2018	2019	Sales ($B) 2018	2019	Local Sales (B) 2018	2019	Currency
Algeria	124	124	1,558	1,629	0.1	0.1	11.7	11.6	Dinar
Argentina	86	86	1,080	1,124	0.2	0.2	4.6	4.5	Pesos
Australia	53	54	672	705	0.6	0.6	0.8	0.8	Dollars
Austria	19	19	240	249	0.2	0.2	0.1	0.1	Euro
Bangladesh	376	377	4,737	4,931	0.1	0.1	8.2	8.5	Taka
Belgium	24	24	301	313	0.2	0.2	0.2	0.2	Euro
Brazil	458	462	5,769	6,048	0.7	0.7	2,381.3	2,276.6	Real
Canada	80	81	1,011	1,054	0.7	0.7	0.9	0.9	Dollars
Chile	44	45	559	586	0.1	0.1	72.8	72.2	Pesos*
China	3,170	3,160	39,898	41,347	6.2	6.3	40.0	40.8	RMB
Colombia	95	95	1,200	1,248	0.1	0.1	0.4	0.4	Pesos*
Czech Republic	23	23	288	297	0.1	0.1	1.9	1.9	Koruna
Denmark	12	12	151	156	0.1	0.1	0.8	0.8	Kroner
Egypt	203	208	2,552	2,718	0.2	0.1	2.7	2.6	Pounds
Finland	12	12	150	155	0.1	0.1	0.1	0.1	Euro
France	133	133	1,674	1,737	1.0	1.0	0.8	0.8	Euro
Germany	169	167	2,131	2,187	1.5	1.5	1.3	1.3	Euro
Greece	22	22	280	289	0.1	0.1	0.1	0.1	Euro
Hong Kong	14	14	172	178	0.1	0.1	885.6	882.4	Dollar
Hungary	20	20	253	260	0.1	0.1	14.0	14.1	Forint*
India	2,662	2,702	33,504	35,362	1.0	1.0	62.6	64.3	Rupees
Indonesia	662	670	8,331	8,774	0.5	0.5	6.6	6.7	Rupiah*

Golf Courses & Country Clubs Industry (NAICS 71391)

Country Estimates

Country	Establishments 2018	2019	Employment 2018	2019	Sales ($B) 2018	2019	Local Sales (B) 2018	2019	Currency
Iran	181	183	2,282	2,401	0.2	0.2	6.4	6.1	Rial*
Iraq	95	97	1,197	1,263	0.1	0.1	0.1	0.1	Dinar*
Ireland	13	14	168	177	0.2	0.3	0.2	0.2	Euro
Israel	19	19	238	251	0.1	0.1	0.5	0.5	Shekel
Italy	134	133	1,686	1,745	0.8	0.8	0.7	0.6	Euro
Japan	282	279	3,548	3,652	1.9	1.8	213.1	208.6	Yen*
Kazakhstan	46	46	578	604	0.1	0.1	30.9	30.8	Tenge
Kuwait	11	11	135	147	0.1	0.1	0.0	0.0	Dinar
Malaysia	88	89	1,106	1,169	0.2	0.2	0.7	0.7	Ringgit
Mexico	286	290	3,603	3,790	0.5	0.5	9.8	9.8	New pesos
Netherlands	36	36	451	466	0.3	0.3	0.3	0.3	Euro
New Zealand	10	10	121	127	0.1	0.1	0.1	0.1	Dollar
Nigeria	494	502	6,215	6,571	0.3	0.3	93,444.3	93,017.2	Naira
Norway	13	13	167	174	0.2	0.2	1.6	1.6	Krone
Pakistan	396	404	4,980	5,286	0.1	0.1	12.7	13.0	Rupees
Peru	78	78	986	1,026	0.1	0.1	0.3	0.3	Nuevo Sol
Phillipines	213	217	2,685	2,840	0.1	0.1	7.0	7.2	Pesos
Poland	73	72	920	946	0.2	0.2	0.8	0.8	Zloty
Portugal	23	23	291	300	0.1	0.1	0.1	0.1	Euro
Puerto Rico	10	10	126	129	0.1	0.0	0.1	0.0	Dollar
Qatar	10	11	127	150	0.1	0.1	0.3	0.3	Riyal
Romania	53	52	662	677	0.1	0.1	0.4	0.4	New Leu
Russia	327	323	4,112	4,226	0.6	0.6	30.9	29.7	Rubles
Saudi Arabia	92	95	1,153	1,237	0.4	0.4	0.0	0.0	Rials*
Singapore	15	15	184	196	0.1	0.1	190.4	190.0	Dollar
South Africa	90	91	1,137	1,197	0.1	0.1	1,611.2	1,588.7	Rand
South Korea	128	127	1,607	1,664	0.7	0.7	758.3	759.1	Won*
Spain	106	107	1,334	1,395	0.5	0.5	454.4	443.3	Euro
Sweden	22	22	273	284	0.2	0.2	1,914.1	1,925.2	Krona
Switzerland	20	20	250	261	0.3	0.3	311.8	308.5	Swiss franc
Taiwan	80	82	1,002	1,076	0.2	0.2	7,165.0	7,111.2	Dollar
Thailand	192	193	2,421	2,530	0.2	0.2	6,594.7	6,529.6	Baht
Turkey	146	145	1,835	1,899	0.4	0.4	1,464.5	1,473.8	Euro
Ukraine	319	314	4,015	4,112	0.1	0.1	2,559.9	2,238.4	Hryvna
UAE	149	166	1,871	2,178	0.6	0.6	2,335.4	2,304.0	Dirham
United Kingdom	416	414	5,231	5,424	3.8	3.8	2,795.4	2,788.5	Pounds
United States	2,018	2,019	25,397	26,420	23.0	22.9	23,001.8	22,926.4	Dollars
Venezuela	69	70	864	912	0.2	0.2	2,086.6	1,978.6	Bolivar
Vietnam	241	242	3,038	3,161	0.1	0.1	2,490.3	2,570.7	Dong*

Note: Due to rounding, establishments will vary by + or - one establishment. Therefore, zero establishments may also be one establishment.

* Local Sales are in trillions

FITNESS & RECREATIONAL SPORTS CENTERS (NAICS 71394)

NAICS 71394: Fitness and Recreational Sports Centers . This industry comprises establishments primarily engaged in operating fitness and recreational sports facilities featuring exercise and other active physical fitness conditioning or recreational sports activities, such as swimming, skating, or racquet sports.

COUNTRY ESTIMATES

Country	Establishments 2018	Establishments 2019	Employment 2018	Employment 2019	Sales ($B) 2018	Sales ($B) 2019	Local Sales (B) 2018	Local Sales (B) 2019	Currency
Algeria	186	187	3,057	3,316	0.5	0.5	56.9	59.2	Dinar
Argentina	129	129	2,119	2,287	1.2	1.2	22.4	22.9	Pesos
Australia	80	81	1,319	1,435	2.9	3.1	3.7	3.9	Dollars
Austria	29	29	472	507	0.8	0.8	0.7	0.7	Euro
Bangladesh	565	565	9,295	10,037	0.5	0.5	39.8	43.2	Taka
Belgium	36	36	591	638	0.9	1.0	0.8	0.8	Euro
Brazil	688	693	11,320	12,313	3.6	3.6	11,569.0	11,626.0	Real
Canada	120	121	1,984	2,146	3.4	3.5	4.2	4.4	Dollars
Chile	67	67	1,098	1,192	0.6	0.6	353.9	368.9	Pesos*
China	4,755	4,739	78,293	84,172	29.9	32.1	194.2	208.4	RMB
Colombia	143	143	2,354	2,540	0.6	0.7	1.9	2.0	Pesos*
Czech Republic	34	34	564	605	0.4	0.5	9.3	9.9	Koruna
Denmark	18	18	297	319	0.6	0.7	3.9	4.0	Kroner
Egypt	304	312	5,008	5,533	0.7	0.8	12.9	13.4	Pounds
Finland	18	18	294	316	0.5	0.5	0.4	0.4	Euro
France	199	199	3,284	3,536	4.8	5.0	4.0	4.2	Euro
Germany	254	251	4,181	4,452	7.4	7.7	6.2	6.4	Euro
Greece	33	33	550	589	0.4	0.4	0.3	0.3	Euro
Hong Kong	20	20	337	362	0.6	0.6	4,302.5	4,506.1	Dollar
Hungary	30	30	496	528	0.3	0.3	68.0	72.0	Forint*
India	3,993	4,053	65,747	71,989	4.8	5.2	304.0	328.1	Rupees
Indonesia	993	1,006	16,349	17,862	2.4	2.5	31.9	34.1	Rupiah*

FITNESS & RECREATIONAL SPORTS CENTERS
(NAICS 71394)

COUNTRY ESTIMATES

Country	Establishments 2018	Establishments 2019	Employment 2018	Employment 2019	Sales ($B) 2018	Sales ($B) 2019	Local Sales (B) 2018	Local Sales (B) 2019	Currency
Iran	272	275	4,478	4,887	0.9	0.9	30.9	31.4	Rial*
Iraq	143	145	2,348	2,572	0.4	0.5	0.5	0.5	Dinar*
Ireland	20	20	329	360	1.1	1.3	0.9	1.1	Euro
Israel	28	29	467	511	0.7	0.7	2.4	2.5	Shekel
Italy	201	200	3,308	3,552	3.9	4.0	3.2	3.3	Euro
Japan	423	419	6,963	7,434	9.2	9.4	1,035.1	1,065.3	Yen*
Kazakhstan	69	69	1,134	1,229	0.5	0.5	150.0	157.2	Tenge
Kuwait	16	17	265	298	0.3	0.3	0.1	0.1	Dinar
Malaysia	132	134	2,170	2,381	0.8	0.9	3.4	3.6	Ringgit
Mexico	429	434	7,071	7,715	2.5	2.6	47.8	50.0	New pesos
Netherlands	54	53	884	949	1.6	1.6	1.3	1.4	Euro
New Zealand	14	15	238	258	0.4	0.4	0.5	0.5	Dollar
Nigeria	741	753	12,197	13,376	1.3	1.3	453,981.3	475,011.8	Naira
Norway	20	20	327	354	0.9	1.0	7.6	7.9	Krone
Pakistan	594	606	9,773	10,761	0.6	0.6	61.9	66.2	Rupees
Peru	118	118	1,935	2,089	0.5	0.5	1.5	1.5	Nuevo Sol
Phillipines	320	326	5,268	5,781	0.7	0.7	34.1	36.9	Pesos
Poland	110	108	1,805	1,925	1.1	1.2	3.9	4.1	Zloty
Portugal	35	34	571	611	0.4	0.4	0.3	0.4	Euro
Puerto Rico	15	15	247	262	0.3	0.3	0.3	0.3	Dollar
Qatar	15	17	249	305	0.4	0.4	1.5	1.6	Riyal
Romania	79	78	1,299	1,379	0.4	0.5	1.7	1.8	New Leu
Russia	490	484	8,068	8,602	2.9	3.0	150.2	151.9	Rubles
Saudi Arabia	137	142	2,263	2,519	1.8	1.9	0.0	0.0	Rials*
Singapore	22	22	361	399	0.7	0.7	924.8	970.2	Dollar
South Africa	136	137	2,231	2,437	0.6	0.7	7,827.9	8,113.2	Rand
South Korea	192	191	3,154	3,388	3.5	3.6	3,684.3	3,876.6	Won*
Spain	159	160	2,618	2,840	2.6	2.7	2,207.8	2,264.0	Euro
Sweden	33	33	537	578	1.1	1.2	9,299.4	9,831.4	Krona
Switzerland	30	30	491	531	1.6	1.6	1,515.0	1,575.4	Swiss franc
Taiwan	119	123	1,966	2,190	1.2	1.2	34,809.6	36,314.8	Dollar
Thailand	289	290	4,751	5,150	1.0	1.0	32,039.1	33,344.9	Baht
Turkey	219	218	3,600	3,865	1.9	2.0	7,114.8	7,526.4	Euro
Ukraine	160	157	2,626	2,790	0.1	0.1	4,145.6	3,810.2	Hryvna
UAE	74	83	1,224	1,478	1.0	1.1	3,782.0	3,922.0	Dirham
United Kingdom	208	207	3,422	3,681	6.1	6.4	4,527.0	4,746.7	Pounds
United States	2,018	2,019	33,226	35,857	74.5	78.1	74,500.0	78,052.3	Dollars
Venezuela	103	104	1,695	1,856	1.0	1.0	10,137.3	10,104.1	Bolivar
Vietnam	362	362	5,962	6,435	0.5	0.6	12,098.6	13,127.8	Dong*

Note: Due to rounding, establishments will vary by + or - one establishment. Therefore, zero establishments may also be one establishment.

* Local Sales are in trillions

HOTELS & MOTELS INDUSTRY
(NAICS 72111)

NAICS 72111: Hotels (except Casino Hotels) and Motels . This industry comprises establishments primarily engaged in providing short-term lodging in facilities known as hotels, motor hotels, resort hotels, and motels. The establishments in this industry may offer services, such as food and beverage services, recreational services, conference rooms and convention services, laundry services, parking, and other services.

COUNTRY ESTIMATES

Country	Establishments 2018	2019	Employment 2018	2019	Sales ($B) 2018	2019	Local Sales (B) 2018	2019	Currency
Algeria	371	373	30,196	31,606	0.8	0.8	91.2	90.2	Dinar
Argentina	257	258	20,935	21,799	1.9	1.8	35.9	34.9	Pesos
Australia	160	162	13,027	13,677	4.7	4.7	5.9	5.9	Dollars
Austria	57	57	4,661	4,827	1.3	1.3	1.1	1.1	Euro
Bangladesh	1,129	1,130	91,810	95,661	0.8	0.8	63.8	65.9	Taka
Belgium	72	72	5,842	6,082	1.5	1.5	1.3	1.2	Euro
Brazil	1,375	1,387	111,808	117,349	5.7	5.5	18,536.9	17,729.9	Real
Canada	241	242	19,595	20,449	5.4	5.4	6.7	6.7	Dollars
Chile	133	134	10,841	11,365	0.9	0.9	567.0	562.5	Pesos*
China	9,511	9,479	773,316	802,194	48.0	49.0	311.2	317.8	RMB
Colombia	286	286	23,252	24,205	1.0	1.0	3.0	3.0	Pesos*
Czech Republic	69	68	5,573	5,769	0.7	0.7	14.9	15.0	Koruna
Denmark	36	36	2,932	3,035	1.0	1.0	6.2	6.2	Kroner
Egypt	608	623	49,468	52,729	1.2	1.2	20.7	20.5	Pounds
Finland	36	36	2,904	3,009	0.8	0.7	0.6	0.6	Euro
France	399	398	32,439	33,696	7.7	7.6	6.4	6.3	Euro
Germany	508	501	41,295	42,432	11.9	11.7	9.9	9.8	Euro
Greece	67	66	5,433	5,613	0.6	0.6	0.5	0.5	Euro
Hong Kong	41	41	3,332	3,453	0.9	0.9	6,893.9	6,871.8	Dollar
Hungary	60	59	4,900	5,035	0.4	0.4	108.9	109.8	Forint*
India	7,986	8,107	649,394	686,085	7.7	7.9	487.1	500.4	Rupees
Indonesia	1,986	2,011	161,482	170,228	3.8	3.9	51.1	52.1	Rupiah*

HOTELS & MOTELS INDUSTRY
(NAICS 72111)

COUNTRY ESTIMATES

Country	Establishments 2018	Establishments 2019	Employment 2018	Employment 2019	Sales ($B) 2018	Sales ($B) 2019	Local Sales (B) 2018	Local Sales (B) 2019	Currency
Iran	544	550	44,227	46,577	1.4	1.3	49.4	47.9	Rial*
Iraq	285	290	23,194	24,510	0.7	0.7	0.9	0.8	Dinar*
Ireland	40	41	3,254	3,430	1.8	2.0	1.5	1.6	Euro
Israel	57	57	4,611	4,866	1.1	1.1	3.8	3.9	Shekel
Italy	402	400	32,677	33,851	6.2	6.0	5.2	5.0	Euro
Japan	846	837	68,773	70,846	14.7	14.4	1,658.6	1,624.6	Yen*
Kazakhstan	138	138	11,205	11,717	0.7	0.7	240.3	239.8	Tenge
Kuwait	32	34	2,619	2,843	0.4	0.4	0.1	0.1	Dinar
Malaysia	264	268	21,438	22,689	1.4	1.4	5.4	5.6	Ringgit
Mexico	859	869	69,841	73,532	4.0	4.0	76.5	76.2	New pesos
Netherlands	107	107	8,736	9,041	2.5	2.5	2.1	2.1	Euro
New Zealand	29	29	2,349	2,460	0.6	0.6	0.8	0.8	Dollar
Nigeria	1,482	1,506	120,468	127,483	2.0	2.0	727,407.5	724,403.0	Naira
Norway	40	40	3,227	3,370	1.5	1.5	12.2	12.1	Krone
Pakistan	1,187	1,212	96,534	102,561	0.9	0.9	99.2	100.9	Rupees
Peru	235	235	19,109	19,912	0.7	0.7	2.3	2.3	Nuevo Sol
Phillipines	640	651	52,032	55,095	1.1	1.1	54.6	56.2	Pesos
Poland	219	217	17,824	18,349	1.8	1.8	6.2	6.3	Zloty
Portugal	69	69	5,636	5,819	0.7	0.6	0.6	0.5	Euro
Puerto Rico	30	30	2,438	2,498	0.4	0.4	0.4	0.4	Dollar
Qatar	30	34	2,455	2,910	0.7	0.7	2.5	2.4	Riyal
Romania	158	155	12,830	13,142	0.7	0.7	2.8	2.8	New Leu
Russia	980	969	79,691	81,982	4.7	4.5	240.7	231.6	Rubles
Saudi Arabia	275	284	22,356	24,009	2.9	2.9	0.0	0.0	Rials*
Singapore	44	45	3,568	3,803	1.1	1.1	1,481.8	1,479.5	Dollar
South Africa	271	274	22,039	23,226	1.0	1.0	12,542.5	12,372.8	Rand
South Korea	383	382	31,151	32,293	5.5	5.5	5,903.3	5,912.0	Won*
Spain	318	320	25,858	27,066	4.2	4.1	3,537.6	3,452.7	Euro
Sweden	65	65	5,299	5,507	1.8	1.8	14,900.3	14,993.1	Krona
Switzerland	60	60	4,848	5,058	2.5	2.5	2,427.4	2,402.5	Swiss franc
Taiwan	239	247	19,414	20,876	1.9	1.9	55,774.8	55,380.9	Dollar
Thailand	577	580	46,927	49,084	1.6	1.6	51,335.8	50,851.7	Baht
Turkey	437	435	35,559	36,836	3.0	3.1	11,399.9	11,477.9	Euro
Ukraine	319	314	25,940	26,591	0.2	0.2	6,642.5	5,810.7	Hryvna
UAE	149	166	12,089	14,088	1.7	1.6	6,059.8	5,981.1	Dirham
United Kingdom	416	414	33,799	35,077	9.8	9.8	7,253.6	7,238.8	Pounds
United States	2,018	2,019	164,087	170,866	59.7	59.5	59,685.1	59,515.7	Dollars
Venezuela	206	209	16,738	17,686	1.6	1.5	16,242.8	15,409.0	Bolivar
Vietnam	724	725	58,891	61,327	0.9	0.9	19,385.4	20,020.2	Dong*

Note: Due to rounding, establishments will vary by + or - one establishment. Therefore, zero establishments may also be one establishment.

* Local Sales are in trillions

FULL-SERVICE RESTAURANTS INDUSTRY (NAICS 722511)

NAICS 722511: Full-Service Restaurants -- This industry comprises establishments primarily engaged in providing food services to patrons who order and are served while seated (i.e. waiter/waitress service) and pay after eating. These establishments may provide this type of food services to patrons in combination with selling alcoholic beverages, providing takeout services, or presenting live nontheatrical entertainment.

COUNTRY ESTIMATES

Country	Establishments 2018	2019	Employment 2018	2019	Sales ($B) 2018	2019	Local Sales (B) 2018	2019	Currency
Algeria	371	373	50,953	53,977	3.6	3.6	413.4	418.9	Dinar
Argentina	257	258	35,325	37,227	8.5	8.5	162.8	162.2	Pesos
Australia	160	162	21,981	23,357	21.2	21.6	26.9	27.5	Dollars
Austria	57	57	7,864	8,244	5.9	6.0	5.0	5.0	Euro
Bangladesh	1,129	1,130	154,919	163,369	3.5	3.7	289.3	306.0	Taka
Belgium	72	72	9,858	10,386	6.8	6.9	5.7	5.8	Euro
Brazil	1,375	1,387	188,663	200,407	26.0	25.5	84,012.8	82,321.9	Real
Canada	241	242	33,065	34,923	24.6	25.0	30.6	31.0	Dollars
Chile	133	134	18,292	19,409	4.2	4.3	2,569.9	2,611.8	Pesos*
China	9,511	9,479	1,304,881	1,369,972	217.4	227.3	1,410.6	1,475.4	RMB
Colombia	286	286	39,236	41,337	4.7	4.8	13.5	14.0	Pesos*
Czech Republic	69	68	9,404	9,851	3.2	3.3	67.4	69.8	Koruna
Denmark	36	36	4,947	5,184	4.6	4.6	28.3	28.6	Kroner
Egypt	608	623	83,472	90,050	5.3	5.4	93.9	95.0	Pounds
Finland	36	36	4,900	5,138	3.5	3.4	2.9	2.9	Euro
France	399	398	54,737	57,545	35.0	35.2	29.2	29.4	Euro
Germany	508	501	69,680	72,464	53.8	54.5	44.9	45.5	Euro
Greece	67	66	9,167	9,587	2.7	2.7	2.3	2.2	Euro
Hong Kong	41	41	5,623	5,896	4.0	4.1	31,244.6	31,906.7	Dollar
Hungary	60	59	8,269	8,599	1.9	2.0	493.6	510.0	Forint*
India	7,986	8,107	1,095,776	1,171,683	34.8	36.6	2,207.7	2,323.4	Rupees
Indonesia	1,986	2,011	272,482	290,712	17.2	18.0	231.5	241.8	Rupiah*

FULL-SERVICE RESTAURANTS INDUSTRY
(NAICS 722511)

COUNTRY ESTIMATES

Country	Establishments 2018	Establishments 2019	Employment 2018	Employment 2019	Sales ($B) 2018	Sales ($B) 2019	Local Sales (B) 2018	Local Sales (B) 2019	Currency
Iran	544	550	74,627	79,544	6.2	6.2	224.1	222.4	Rial*
Iraq	285	290	39,138	41,858	3.3	3.3	3.9	3.9	Dinar*
Ireland	40	41	5,491	5,857	8.0	9.1	6.7	7.6	Euro
Israel	57	57	7,781	8,310	5.1	5.2	17.4	17.9	Shekel
Italy	402	400	55,139	57,810	28.0	28.0	23.4	23.4	Euro
Japan	846	837	116,047	120,989	66.6	66.8	7,516.9	7,543.4	Yen*
Kazakhstan	138	138	18,907	20,010	3.3	3.4	1,089.0	1,113.4	Tenge
Kuwait	32	34	4,419	4,856	1.9	1.9	0.6	0.6	Dinar
Malaysia	264	268	36,174	38,749	6.1	6.4	24.6	25.8	Ringgit
Mexico	859	869	117,848	125,576	18.1	18.4	346.8	353.8	New pesos
Netherlands	107	107	14,742	15,439	11.5	11.7	9.6	9.7	Euro
New Zealand	29	29	3,964	4,201	2.6	2.7	3.6	3.7	Dollar
Nigeria	1,482	1,506	203,276	217,712	9.2	9.3	3,296,756.3	3,363,476.3	Naira
Norway	40	40	5,446	5,755	6.9	7.0	55.4	56.3	Krone
Pakistan	1,187	1,212	162,889	175,152	4.1	4.2	449.6	468.5	Rupees
Peru	235	235	32,244	34,006	3.3	3.4	10.5	10.8	Nuevo Sol
Phillipines	640	651	87,799	94,091	4.9	5.2	247.3	261.1	Pesos
Poland	219	217	30,077	31,335	8.1	8.4	28.2	29.1	Zloty
Portugal	69	69	9,509	9,937	3.0	3.0	2.5	2.5	Euro
Puerto Rico	30	30	4,114	4,265	1.8	1.8	1.8	1.8	Dollar
Qatar	30	34	4,142	4,970	3.1	3.1	11.2	11.3	Riyal
Romania	158	155	21,649	22,443	3.3	3.4	12.6	13.0	New Leu
Russia	980	969	134,469	140,008	21.3	21.0	1,090.9	1,075.3	Rubles
Saudi Arabia	275	284	37,724	41,001	13.1	13.3	0.0	0.0	Rials*
Singapore	44	45	6,021	6,494	5.0	5.2	6,715.7	6,869.5	Dollar
South Africa	271	274	37,188	39,664	4.6	4.6	56,845.3	57,448.0	Rand
South Korea	383	382	52,564	55,149	25.1	25.7	26,754.9	27,449.8	Won*
Spain	318	320	43,633	46,223	19.2	19.2	16,033.1	16,031.1	Euro
Sweden	65	65	8,942	9,405	8.2	8.5	67,531.0	69,614.6	Krona
Switzerland	60	60	8,180	8,639	11.3	11.4	11,001.6	11,154.8	Swiss franc
Taiwan	239	247	32,759	35,651	8.6	8.7	252,782.7	257,139.1	Dollar
Thailand	577	580	79,184	83,824	7.2	7.3	232,664.2	236,109.8	Baht
Turkey	437	435	60,002	62,908	13.8	14.2	51,666.7	53,292.9	Euro
Ukraine	319	314	43,771	45,412	1.1	1.0	30,105.0	26,979.5	Hryvna
UAE	149	166	20,399	24,059	7.5	7.6	27,464.2	27,770.9	Dirham
United Kingdom	416	414	57,031	59,904	44.6	45.6	32,874.7	33,610.6	Pounds
United States	2,018	2,019	276,878	291,802	270.5	276.3	270,505.0	276,337.4	Dollars
Venezuela	206	209	28,243	30,204	7.4	7.2	73,615.6	71,545.6	Bolivar
Vietnam	724	725	99,372	104,732	3.9	4.1	87,858.5	92,955.7	Dong*

Note: Due to rounding, establishments will vary by + or - one establishment. Therefore, zero establishments may also be one establishment.

* Local Sales are in trillions

Fast Food Restaurants Industry
(NAICS 722513)

NAICS 722513: Fast Food Restaurants. This industry comprises establishments primarily engaged in the retail sale of prepared food and drinks for on-premise or immediate consumption. Caterers and industrial and institutional food service establishments are also included in this business.

COUNTRY ESTIMATES

Country	Establishments 2018	2019	Employment 2018	2019	Sales ($B) 2018	2019	Local Sales (B) 2018	2019	Currency
Algeria	371	373	43,145	45,764	3.4	3.4	389.5	395.0	Dinar
Argentina	257	258	29,912	31,563	8.0	8.0	153.4	153.0	Pesos
Australia	160	162	18,613	19,803	20.0	20.4	25.4	25.9	Dollars
Austria	57	57	6,659	6,990	5.6	5.6	4.7	4.7	Euro
Bangladesh	1,129	1,130	131,180	138,511	3.3	3.5	272.6	288.6	Taka
Belgium	72	72	8,347	8,806	6.4	6.5	5.4	5.4	Euro
Brazil	1,375	1,387	159,754	169,914	24.5	24.0	79,171.5	77,638.7	Real
Canada	241	242	27,998	29,609	23.2	23.5	28.8	29.2	Dollars
Chile	133	134	15,489	16,455	4.0	4.1	2,421.8	2,463.2	Pesos*
China	9,511	9,479	1,104,932	1,161,522	204.8	214.4	1,329.3	1,391.5	RMB
Colombia	286	286	33,223	35,048	4.4	4.5	12.8	13.2	Pesos*
Czech Republic	69	68	7,963	8,352	3.0	3.1	63.5	65.8	Koruna
Denmark	36	36	4,189	4,395	4.3	4.3	26.7	27.0	Kroner
Egypt	608	623	70,681	76,348	5.0	5.1	88.5	89.6	Pounds
Finland	36	36	4,150	4,356	3.3	3.3	2.7	2.7	Euro
France	399	398	46,349	48,789	33.0	33.2	27.5	27.7	Euro
Germany	508	501	59,003	61,439	50.7	51.4	42.3	42.9	Euro
Greece	67	66	7,763	8,128	2.6	2.5	2.1	2.1	Euro
Hong Kong	41	41	4,761	4,999	3.8	3.8	29,444.1	30,091.5	Dollar
Hungary	60	59	7,002	7,291	1.8	1.9	465.2	481.0	Forint*
India	7,986	8,107	927,869	993,405	32.8	34.5	2,080.5	2,191.2	Rupees
Indonesia	1,986	2,011	230,729	246,478	16.2	17.0	218.2	228.0	Rupiah*

Fast Food Restaurants Industry
(NAICS 722513)

Country Estimates

Country	Establishments 2018	Establishments 2019	Employment 2018	Employment 2019	Sales ($B) 2018	Sales ($B) 2019	Local Sales (B) 2018	Local Sales (B) 2019	Currency
Iran	544	550	63,192	67,441	5.9	5.8	211.2	209.7	Rial*
Iraq	285	290	33,140	35,489	3.1	3.1	3.7	3.7	Dinar*
Ireland	40	41	4,650	4,966	7.5	8.6	6.3	7.2	Euro
Israel	57	57	6,589	7,045	4.8	4.9	16.4	16.9	Shekel
Italy	402	400	46,690	49,014	26.4	26.4	22.0	22.1	Euro
Japan	846	837	98,265	102,580	62.7	63.0	7,083.7	7,114.2	Yen*
Kazakhstan	138	138	16,010	16,966	3.1	3.2	1,026.3	1,050.1	Tenge
Kuwait	32	34	3,742	4,117	1.8	1.8	0.6	0.5	Dinar
Malaysia	264	268	30,631	32,853	5.8	6.1	23.1	24.3	Ringgit
Mexico	859	869	99,790	106,469	17.0	17.4	326.9	333.7	New pesos
Netherlands	107	107	12,483	13,090	10.8	11.0	9.1	9.2	Euro
New Zealand	29	29	3,357	3,562	2.4	2.5	3.4	3.5	Dollar
Nigeria	1,482	1,506	172,128	184,586	8.6	8.8	3,106,777.6	3,172,130.1	Naira
Norway	40	40	4,611	4,879	6.5	6.6	52.2	53.1	Krone
Pakistan	1,187	1,212	137,929	148,501	3.8	4.0	423.7	441.9	Rupees
Peru	235	235	27,303	28,832	3.1	3.2	9.9	10.2	Nuevo Sol
Phillipines	640	651	74,345	79,774	4.7	4.9	233.0	246.2	Pesos
Poland	219	217	25,468	26,568	7.6	7.9	26.6	27.4	Zloty
Portugal	69	69	8,052	8,425	2.9	2.8	2.4	2.4	Euro
Puerto Rico	30	30	3,484	3,616	1.7	1.7	1.7	1.7	Dollar
Qatar	30	34	3,508	4,214	2.9	2.9	10.5	10.7	Riyal
Romania	158	155	18,331	19,028	3.1	3.2	11.9	12.3	New Leu
Russia	980	969	113,865	118,705	20.1	19.8	1,028.1	1,014.1	Rubles
Saudi Arabia	275	284	31,943	34,763	12.3	12.5	0.0	0.0	Rials*
Singapore	44	45	5,099	5,506	4.8	4.9	6,328.7	6,478.7	Dollar
South Africa	271	274	31,490	33,629	4.3	4.4	53,569.5	54,179.8	Rand
South Korea	383	382	44,509	46,758	23.6	24.3	25,213.1	25,888.2	Won*
Spain	318	320	36,947	39,190	18.1	18.1	15,109.2	15,119.1	Euro
Sweden	65	65	7,572	7,974	7.8	8.0	63,639.5	65,654.3	Krona
Switzerland	60	60	6,927	7,324	10.6	10.8	10,367.7	10,520.2	Swiss franc
Taiwan	239	247	27,739	30,227	8.1	8.2	238,215.9	242,510.6	Dollar
Thailand	577	580	67,051	71,070	6.8	6.9	219,256.8	222,677.6	Baht
Turkey	437	435	50,808	53,336	13.0	13.4	48,689.4	50,261.1	Euro
Ukraine	319	314	37,064	38,502	1.0	0.9	28,370.2	25,444.6	Hryvna
UAE	149	166	17,273	20,399	7.1	7.1	25,881.5	26,191.1	Dirham
United Kingdom	416	414	48,292	50,789	42.0	43.0	30,980.2	31,698.5	Pounds
United States	2,018	2,019	234,452	247,402	254.9	260.6	254,916.9	260,616.7	Dollars
Venezuela	206	209	23,916	25,608	7.0	6.8	69,373.4	67,475.4	Bolivar
Vietnam	724	725	84,145	88,797	3.6	3.9	82,795.6	87,667.5	Dong*

Note: Due to rounding, establishments will vary by + or - one establishment. Therefore, zero establishments may also be one establishment.

* Local Sales are in trillions

DRINKING PLACES & BARS INDUSTRY (NAICS 72241)

NAICS 72241: Drinking Places (Alcoholic Beverages) . This industry comprises establishments known as bars, taverns, nightclubs or drinking places primarily engaged in preparing and serving alcoholic beverages for immediate consumption. These establishments may also provide limited food services.

COUNTRY ESTIMATES

Country	Establishments 2018	Establishments 2019	Employment 2018	Employment 2019	Sales ($B) 2018	Sales ($B) 2019	Local Sales (B) 2018	Local Sales (B) 2019	Currency
Algeria	-	-	-	-	-	-	0.0	0.0	Dinar
Argentina	129	129	1,401	1,422	0.7	0.7	13.5	12.8	Pesos
Australia	80	81	872	892	1.8	1.7	2.2	2.2	Dollars
Austria	29	29	312	315	0.5	0.5	0.4	0.4	Euro
Bangladesh	565	565	6,145	6,242	0.3	0.3	23.9	24.2	Taka
Belgium	36	36	391	397	0.6	0.5	0.5	0.5	Euro
Brazil	688	693	7,484	7,657	2.2	2.0	6,946.6	6,498.6	Real
Canada	120	121	1,312	1,334	2.0	2.0	2.5	2.4	Dollars
Chile	67	67	726	742	0.4	0.3	212.5	206.2	Pesos*
China	4,755	4,739	51,762	52,344	18.0	17.9	116.6	116.5	RMB
Colombia	143	143	1,556	1,579	0.4	0.4	1.1	1.1	Pesos*
Czech Republic	34	34	373	376	0.3	0.3	5.6	5.5	Koruna
Denmark	18	18	196	198	0.4	0.4	2.3	2.3	Kroner
Egypt	-	-	-	-	-	-	0.0	0.0	Pounds
Finland	18	18	194	196	0.3	0.3	0.2	0.2	Euro
France	199	199	2,171	2,199	2.9	2.8	2.4	2.3	Euro
Germany	254	251	2,764	2,769	4.4	4.3	3.7	3.6	Euro
Greece	33	33	364	366	0.2	0.2	0.2	0.2	Euro
Hong Kong	20	20	223	225	0.3	0.3	2,583.4	2,518.8	Dollar
Hungary	30	30	328	329	0.2	0.2	40.8	40.3	Forint*
India	3,993	4,053	43,467	44,768	2.9	2.9	182.5	183.4	Rupees
Indonesia	-	-	-	-	-	-	0.0	0.0	Rupiah*

Drinking Places & Bars Industry
(NAICS 72241)

Country Estimates

Country	Establishments 2018	2019	Employment 2018	2019	Sales ($B) 2018	2019	Local Sales (B) 2018	2019	Currency
Iran	-	-	-	-	-	-	0.0	0.0	Rial*
Iraq	-	-	-	-	-	-	0.0	0.0	Dinar*
Ireland	20	20	218	224	0.7	0.7	0.6	0.6	Euro
Israel	28	29	309	318	0.4	0.4	1.4	1.4	Shekel
Italy	201	200	2,187	2,209	2.3	2.2	1.9	1.8	Euro
Japan	423	419	4,603	4,623	5.5	5.3	621.5	595.5	Yen*
Kazakhstan	69	69	750	765	0.3	0.3	90.0	87.9	Tenge
Kuwait	-	-	-	-	-	-	0.0	0.0	Dinar
Malaysia	-	-	-	-	-	-	0.0	0.0	Ringgit
Mexico	429	434	4,675	4,798	1.5	1.5	28.7	27.9	New pesos
Netherlands	54	53	585	590	1.0	0.9	0.8	0.8	Euro
New Zealand	14	15	157	161	0.2	0.2	0.3	0.3	Dollar
Nigeria	741	753	8,064	8,318	0.8	0.7	272,591.1	265,517.5	Naira
Norway	20	20	216	220	0.6	0.5	4.6	4.4	Krone
Pakistan	-	-	-	-	-	-	0.0	0.0	Rupees
Peru	118	118	1,279	1,299	0.3	0.3	0.9	0.9	Nuevo Sol
Phillipines	320	326	3,483	3,595	0.4	0.4	20.4	20.6	Pesos
Poland	110	108	1,193	1,197	0.7	0.7	2.3	2.3	Zloty
Portugal	35	34	377	380	0.3	0.2	0.2	0.2	Euro
Puerto Rico	15	15	163	163	0.2	0.1	0.2	0.1	Dollar
Qatar	-	-	-	-	-	-	0.0	0.0	Riyal
Romania	15	17	164	190	0.3	0.2	1.0	1.0	New Leu
Russia	490	484	5,334	5,349	1.8	1.7	90.2	84.9	Rubles
Saudi Arabia	-	-	-	-	-	-	0.0	0.0	Rials*
Singapore	22	22	239	248	0.4	0.4	555.3	542.3	Dollar
South Africa	136	137	1,475	1,515	0.4	0.4	4,700.2	4,535.0	Rand
South Korea	192	191	2,085	2,107	2.1	2.0	2,212.2	2,166.9	Won*
Spain	159	160	1,731	1,766	1.6	1.5	1,325.7	1,265.5	Euro
Sweden	33	33	355	359	0.7	0.7	5,583.8	5,495.5	Krona
Switzerland	30	30	324	330	0.9	0.9	909.7	880.6	Swiss franc
Taiwan	119	123	1,299	1,362	0.7	0.7	20,901.2	20,298.9	Dollar
Thailand	289	290	3,141	3,203	0.6	0.6	19,237.8	18,638.8	Baht
Turkey	-	-	-	-	-	-	0.0	0.0	Euro
Ukraine	160	157	1,736	1,735	0.1	0.1	2,489.2	2,129.8	Hryvna
UAE	-	-	-	-	-	-	0.0	0.0	Dirham
United Kingdom	208	207	2,262	2,289	3.7	3.6	2,718.2	2,653.3	Pounds
United States	2,018	2,019	21,966	22,298	44.7	43.6	44,733.2	43,628.9	Dollars
Venezuela	103	104	1,120	1,154	0.6	0.6	6,086.9	5,647.9	Bolivar
Vietnam	362	362	3,942	4,002	0.3	0.3	7,264.6	7,338.1	Dong*

Note: Due to rounding, establishments will vary by + or - one establishment. Therefore, zero establishments may also be one establishment.

* Local Sales are in trillions

Methodology

Barnes Reports' Global reports provide estimates of the size and characteristics of the largest industries in the world's largest countries. These estimates are produced by a proprietary economic model that is based on a number of sources and factors:

-The size and characteristics of the largest U.S. industries (based on the U.S. Bureau of the Census statistics, as well as other trade association and private research sources, inflation rates and industry trends).
-The relative revenue size and characteristics of other countries (based on GDP and proportion of economies based on manufacturing, services, agricultural and resource industries).
-The employment and establishment characteristics of each industry (based population estimates from the CIA World Factbook and Heritage Foundation's Index of Economic Freedom)
-Secondary sources from foreign countries are used to validate estimates published in our Global reports and adjust factors and weights in the Barnes Reports proprietary economic model.
-Local currency estimates are based on U.S. sales estimates and the most current currency exchange rates.

NAICS codes (North American Classification System codes) are used in each industry definition in order to aid report users in clarifying and standardizing the definitions of each industry.

Number of Establishments

General Definition

An establishment is a single physical location at which business is conducted and/or services are provided. It is not necessarily identical with a company or enterprise, which may consist of one establishment or more. Economic census figures represent a summary of reports for individual establishments rather than companies. For cases where a census report was received, separate information was obtained for each location where business was conducted. When aEuroinistrative records of other Federal agencies were used instead of a census report, no information was available on the number of locations operated. Each economic census establishment was tabulated according to the physical location at which the business was conducted.

When two activities or more were carried on at a single location under a single ownership, all activities generally were grouped together as a single establishment. The entire establishment was classified on the basis of its major activity and all data for it were included in that classification. However, when distinct and separate economic activities (for which different industry classification codes were appropriate) were conducted at a single location under a single ownership, separate establishment reports for each of the different activities were obtained in the census.

Sector-Specific Information

Construction sector. Establishments are defined as a relatively permanent office or other place of business where the usual business activities related to construction are conducted. Establishments do not represent each project or construction site. Includes all establishments that were in business at any time during the year. It covers all full-year and part-year operations. Construction establishments which were inactive or idle for the entire year were not included. Establishments are based on a survey which included all large employers and a sample of the smaller ones.

Information; Professional, Scientific, and Technical Services; AEuroinistrative and Support and Waste Management and Remediation Services; Educational Services; Health Care and Social Assistance; Arts, Entertainment, and Recreation; and Other Services (Except Public AEuroinistration) sectors. An establishment is included in the census if it is an employer, the establishment has $1,000 in payroll, and was in operation at any time during 1997. Leased service departments (separately owned businesses operated as departments or concessions of other service establishments or of retail businesses, such as a separately owned shoeshine parlor in a barber shop, or a beauty shop in a department store) are treated as separate service establishments for census purposes. Leased retail departments located in service establishments (e.g., a gift shop located in a hotel) are considered separate retail establishments. Manufacturing sector. Includes all manufacturing establishments (plants) with one employee or more and establishments in operation at any time during the year.

Mining sector. Includes all mineral establishments with one employee or more and establishments in operation at any time during the year. Establishments in the crude petroleum and natural gas and support activities for mining represent statewide operations rather than those at a single physical location.

Real Estate and Rental and Leasing sector. Data for individual properties leased or managed by property lessors or property managers are not normally considered separate establishments, but rather the permanent offices from which the properties are leased or managed are considered establishments. Data for separate automotive rental offices or concessions (e.g., airport locations) in the same metropolitan area for which a common fleet of cars is maintained are merged together and not considered as separate establishments.

Retail Trade sector. Leased departments are treated as separate establishments and are classified according to the kind of business they conduct. For example, a leased department selling shoes within a department store would be considered a separate retail establishment under the "shoe stores" classification.

Accommodation and Foodservices sector. Leased departments are treated as separate establishments and are classified according to the kind of business they conduct. For example, a leased department selling gifts/souvenirs within a hotel would be considered a separate retail establishment under the "gift, novelty, and souvenir stores" classification.

Auxiliaries sector. In the Standard Industrial Classification (SIC) system, auxiliary establishments (i.e., those establishments primarily serving other establishments of the same enterprise) were classified in the industry of the establishments served. In the North American Industry Classification System (NAICS), auxiliary establishments are classified according to the services performed rather than the industry served.

Sales, Shipments, Receipts, Revenue, or Business Done

General Definition

Includes the total sales, shipments, receipts, revenue, or business done by establishments within the scope of the economic census. The definition of each of these items is included in the information provided below.

Sector-Specific Information

Construction sector - Includes the value of construction work and other business receipts for work done by establishments during the year. Included is new construction, additions and alterations or reconstruction, and maintenance and repair construction work. Also included is the value of any construction work done by the reporting establishments for themselves.

Speculative builders were instructed to include the value of buildings and other structures built or being built for sale in the current year but not sold. They were to include the costs of such construction plus normal profit. Also included is the cost of construction work done on buildings for rent or lease.

Establishments engaged in the sale and installation of such construction components as plumbing, heating, and central air-conditioning supplies and equipment; lumber and building materials; paint, glass, and wallpaper; electrical and wiring supplies; and elevators or escalators were instructed to include both the value for the installation and the receipts covering the price of the items installed.

Excluded was the cost of industrial and other specialized machinery and equipment, which are not an integral part of a structure.

Finance and Insurance sector - Includes revenue from all business activities whether or not payment was received in the census year, including commissions and fees from all sources, rents, net investment income, interest, dividends, royalties, and net insurance premiums earned. Revenue from leasing property marketed under operating leases is included, as well as interest earned from property marketed in the census year under capital, finance, or full payout leases. Revenue also includes the total value of service contracts and amounts received for work subcontracted to others.

Revenue does not include sales and other taxes collected from customers and remitted directly by the firm to a local, state, or Federal tax agency.

Information sector - Includes receipts from customers or clients for services rendered, from the use of facilities, and from merchandise sold, whether or not payment was received. Receipts include royalties, license fees, and other payments from the marketing of intangible products (e.g., licensing the use of or granting reproduction rights for software, musical

compositions, and other intellectual property). Receipts also include the rental and leasing of vehicles, equipment, instruments, tools, etc.; total value of service contracts; market value of compensation received in lieu of cash; amounts received for work subcontracted to others; dues and assessments for members and affiliates; this establishment's share of receipts from departments, concessions, and vending and amusement machines operated by others. Receipts from services provided to foreign customers from U.S. locations, including services preformed for foreign parent firms, subsidiaries, and branches are included. For public broadcast stations and libraries, include receipts from contributions, gifts, grants, and income from interest, rental of real estate, and dividends.

Receipts DO NOT include sales and other taxes collected directly from customers or clients and paid directly to a local, state, or Federal tax agency. Also excluded are gross receipts collected on behalf of others; gross receipts or departments or concessions operated by others; sales of used equipment previously rented or leased to customers; proceeds from the sale of real estate (land and buildings), investments, or other assets (except inventory held for resale); contributions, gifts, grants, and income from interest, rental of real estate, and dividends EXCEPT for public broadcast stations and libraries; domestic intracompany transfers; receipts of foreign subsidiaries; and other nonoperating income.

Management of Companies and Enterprises sector- For holding companies, revenue includes revenue of only the holding company establishment, including net investment income, interest, and dividends.

Manufacturing sector - Covers the received or receivable net selling values, f.o.b. plant (exclusive of freight and taxes), of all products shipped, both primary and secondary, as well as all miscellaneous receipts, such as receipts for contract work performed for others, installation and repair, sales of scrap, and sales of products bought and resold without further processing. Included are all items made by or for the establishments from materials owned by it, whether sold, transferred to other plants of the same company, or shipped on consignment. The net selling value of products made in one plant on a contract basis from materials owned by another was reported by the plant providing the materials.

In the case of multiunit companies, the manufacturer was requested to report the value of products transferred to other establishments of the same company at full economic or commercial value, including not only the direct cost of production but also a reasonable proportion of "all other costs" (including company overhead) and profit.

Mining sector - Includes the net selling values, f.o.b. mine or plant after discounts and allowances, excluding freight charges and excise taxes. Shipments includes all products physically shipped from the establishment during the year, including material withdrawn from stockpiles and products shipped on consignment, whether or not sold in the current year. Prepared material or concentrates includes preparation from ores mined at the same establishment, purchased, received from other operations of the same company, or received for milling on a custom or toll basis. For products transferred to other establishments of the same company or prepared on a custom basis, companies were requested to report the estimated value, not merely the cost of producing the items. Multiestablishment companies were asked to report value information for each establishment as if it were a separate economic unit. They were instructed to report the value of all products transferred to other plants of the company at their full economic value; to include, in addition to direct cost of production, a reasonable proportion of company overhead and profits. For all establishments classified in an industry, value of shipments and receipts includes (1) the value of all primary products of the industry; (2) the value of secondary products which are primary to other industries; (3) the receipts for contract work done for others, except custom milling; and (4) the value of products purchased and resold without further processing. Receipts for custom milling are not included to avoid duplication with the value of custom milled ores included in an industry's primary and secondary products. Some duplication exists in industry and industry group totals because of the inclusion of materials transferred from one establishment to another for mineral preparation or resale.

Professional, Scientific, and Technical Services; AEuroinistrative and Support and Waste Management and Remediation Services; Educational Services; Health Care and Social Assistance; Arts, Entertainment, and Recreation; and Other Services (Except Public AEuroinistration) sectors - TAXABLE ESTABLISHMENTS: Includes receipts from customers or clients for services rendered, from the use of facilities, and from merchandise sold whether or not payment was received. For advertising agencies, travel industries, and other service establishments operating on a commission basis, receipts include commissions, fees, and other operating income, NOT gross billings and sales. Excise taxes on gasoline, liquor, tobacco, etc., which are paid by the manufacturer or wholesaler and passed on in the cost of goods purchased by the service establishment are also included. The establishments share of receipts from departments, concessions, and vending and amusement machines operated by others are included as part of receipts. Receipts also include the total value of service contracts, market value of compensation received in lieu of cash, amounts received for work subcontracted to others, and dues and assessments from members and affiliates. Receipts from services provided to foreign customers from U.S. locations, including services preformed for foreign parent firms, subsidiaries, and branches are included.

Receipts are net after deductions for refunds and allowances for merchandise returned by customers. Receipts DO NOT include sales, occupancy, aEuroissions, or other taxes collected from customers and remitted directly by the firm to a local, state, or Federal tax agency, nor do they include income from such sources as contributions, gifts, and grants; dividends, interest, and investments; or sale or rental of real estate. Also excluded are receipts (gross) of departments and concessions which are operated by others; sales of used equipment rented or leased to customers; domestic intracompany transfers; receipts of foreign subsidiaries; and other nonoperating income, such as royalties, franchise fees, etc. Receipts DO NOT include service receipts of manufacturers, wholesalers, retail establishments, or other businesses whose primary activity is other than service. They do, however, include receipts other than from services rendered (e.g., sale of merchandise to individuals or other businesses) by establishments primarily engaged in performing services and classified in the service industries.

TAX EXEMPT ESTABLISHMENTS: Includes revenue from customers or clients for services rendered and merchandise, whether or not payment was received, and gross sales of merchandise, minus returns and allowances. Also included are income from interest, dividends, gross rents (including display space rentals and share of receipts from departments operated by other companies), gross contributions, gifts, grants (whether or not restricted for use in operations), royalties, dues and assessments from members and affiliates, commissions earned from the sale of merchandise owned by others (including commissions from vending machine operators), and gross receipts from fundraising activities. Receipts from taxable business activities of firms exempt from Federal income tax (unrelated business income) are also included in revenue. Revenue DOES NOT include sales, aEuroissions, or other taxes collected by the organization from customers or clients and paid directly to a local, state, or Federal tax agency; income from the sale of real estate, investments, or other assets (except inventory held for resale); gross receipts of departments, concessions, etc., that are operated by others; and amounts transferred to operating funds from capital or reserve funds.

Real Estate and Rental and Leasing sector - Includes revenue from all business activities whether or not payment was received in the census year, including commissions and fees from all sources, rents, net investment income, interest, dividends, and royalties. Revenue from leasing property marketed under operating leases is included. Revenue also includes the total value of service contracts, amounts received for work subcontracted to others, and rents from real property sublet to others.

Revenue does not include sales and other taxes collected from customers and remitted directly by the firm to a local, state, or Federal tax agency.

Retail Trade sector - Includes merchandise sold for cash or credit at retail and wholesale by establishments primarily engaged in retail trade; amounts received from customers for layaway purchases; receipts from rental of vehicles, equipment, instruments, tools, etc.; receipts for delivery, installation, maintenance, repair, alteration, storage, and other services; the total value of service contracts; and gasoline, liquor, tobacco, and other excise taxes which are paid by the manufacturer or wholesaler and passed on to the retailer. Sales are net after deductions for refunds and allowances for merchandise returned by customers. Trade-in allowances are not deducted from sales. Sales do not include carrying or other credit charges; sales (or other) taxes collected from customers and forwarded to taxing authorities; gross sales and receipts of departments or concessions operated by other companies; and commissions or receipts from the sale of government lottery tickets.

Sales do not include retail sales made by manufacturers, wholesalers, service establishments, or other businesses whose primary activity is other than retail trade. They do include receipts other than from the sale of merchandise at retail, e.g., service receipts, sales to industrial users, and sales to other retailers, by establishments primarily engaged in retail trade.

Transportation and Warehousing sector - Includes revenue from all business activities whether or not payment was received in the census year, including commissions and fees for arranging the transportation of freight. Revenue does not include sales and other taxes collected from customers and remitted directly by the firm to a local, state, or Federal tax agency.

Utilities sector - Includes revenue from all business activities whether or not payment was received in the census year.

Revenue does not include sales and other taxes collected from customers and remitted directly by the firm to a local, state, or Federal tax agency.

Accommodation and Foodservices sector - Includes sales from customers for services rendered, from the use of facilities, and from merchandise sold. Also includes dues and assessments from members and affiliates.

Sales do not include carrying or other credit charges; sales (or other) taxes collected from customers and forwarded to taxing authorities; gross sales and receipts of departments or concessions operated by other companies; and commissions or receipts from the sale of government lottery tickets.

Excludes sales from civic and social organizations, amusement and recreation parks, theaters, and other recreation or entertainment facilities providing food and beverage services.

Number of Employees

General Definition

Paid employees consists of full-time and part-time employees, including salaried officers and executives of corporations. Included are employees on paid sick leave, paid holidays, and paid vacations; not included are proprietors and partners of unincorporated businesses. The definition of paid employees is the same as that used on IRS Form 941.

Sector-Specific Information

Construction and Manufacturing sectors. Comprises all full-time and part-time employees on the payrolls of establishments who worked or received pay for any part of the pay period including the 12th of March, May, August, and November, divided by 4.

Finance and Insurance sector. Includes all employees who were on the payroll during the pay period including March 12. Excludes independent (nonemployee) agents.

Information; Professional, Scientific, and Technical Services; AEuroinistrative and Support and Waste Management and Remediation Services; Educational Services; Health Care and Social Assistance; Arts, Entertainment, and Recreation; and Other Services (Except Public AEuroinistration) sectors - Includes all employees who were on the payroll during the pay period including March 12. Includes members of a professional service organization or association which operates under state professional corporation statutes and files a corporate Federal income tax return. Excludes employees of departments or concessions operated by other companies at the establishment.

Management of Companies and Enterprises sector. Includes all employees who were on the payroll during the pay period including March 12.

Mining sector. Also included are employees working for miners paid on a per ton, car, or yard basis. Excluded are employees at the mine but on the payroll of another employer (such as employees of contractors) and employees at company stores, boardinghouses, bunkhouses, and recreational centers. Also excluded are members of the Armed Forces and pensioners carried on the active rolls but not working during the period. Includes all employees who were on the payroll during the pay period including March 12.

Real Estate and Rental and Leasing sector. Includes all employees who were on the payroll during the pay period including March 12. Excludes independent (nonemployee) agents.

Retail Trade and Accommodation and Foodservices sectors. Includes all employees on the payroll during the pay period including March 12. Excludes employees of departments or concessions operated by other companies at the establishment.

Transportation and Warehousing sector. Includes all employees who were on the payroll during the pay period including March 12.

Utilities sector. Includes all employees who were on the payroll during the pay period including March 12.

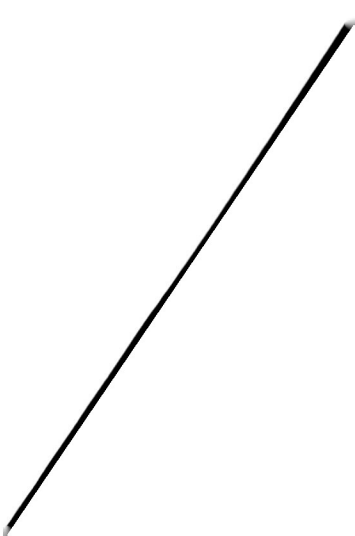